Development and the Power Theory of Economics

Patrice Kandolo Kabeya

Development and the Power Theory of Economics

How Power Dynamics Shape Government Policy, Institutions and Economic Strategies

palgrave
macmillan

Patrice Kandolo Kabeya
Southern Africa Development Community
Gaborone, Botswana

ISBN 978-3-032-07925-1 ISBN 978-3-032-07926-8 (eBook)
https://doi.org/10.1007/978-3-032-07926-8

This Palgrave Macmillan imprint is published by the registered company Springer Nature Switzerland AG.
The registered company address is: Gewerbestrasse 11, 6330 Cham, Switzerland

Preface

The idea for this book was conceived out of a growing concern that prevailing economic theories often marginalise the centrality of power dynamics. Conventional frameworks tend to focus on market mechanisms, resource allocations, and efficiency, sidelining the intricate ways in which power—manifested through institutions, governments, and global actors—influences these very processes. This book aims to address this lacuna by offering a comprehensive analysis of how power asymmetries define the rules of engagement in economic systems, dictate resource control, and create winners and losers in the global arena.

Drawing from a wide spectrum of academic disciplines, including political economy, development studies, and institutional economics, this book offers a critical lens to explore pivotal questions: How do power imbalances influence policymaking and governance in sub-Saharan Africa and other developing countries? In what ways do international institutions and external actors leverage power to shape the economic trajectories of these regions? And how can an understanding of power dynamics contribute to designing more equitable and context-sensitive economic policies and frameworks?

The value addition of this book lies in its ability to intersect theory with practical implications. First, it provides a conceptual framework that reimagines economic development through the lens of power theory, offering fresh insights for scholars and students seeking to expand their understanding of institutional and policy dynamics. Second, it provides actionable insights for policymakers, particularly in developing countries and those facing challenges in addressing key development and economic issues, equipping them with tools to identify and mitigate power asymmetries that hinder inclusive growth. Finally, the book's interdisciplinary approach makes it an essential resource for stakeholders across sectors—academics, practitioners, governments, and international organisations—who are grappling with the challenges of aligning economic strategies with equitable development outcomes.

This preface emphasises the book's relevance to developing countries while maintaining its broader global applicability.

London, UK Patrice Kandolo Kabeya

Acknowledgements

I extend my deepest gratitude to the many scholars, colleagues, and practitioners who have inspired and informed this work. Their contributions, whether direct or indirect, have enriched the discussions presented in this book. It is my hope that readers, particularly those engaged with the development challenges in the world, will find this exploration of power theory both intellectually stimulating and practically relevant in their pursuit of understanding and addressing the complexities of economic development.

Writing this book, *Development and the Power Theory of Economics: How Power Dynamics Shape Government Policy, Institutions and Economic Strategies*, has been an extraordinary journey—one filled with moments of discovery, challenge, and reflection. None of it would have been possible without the unwavering support and love of my family.

To my spouse, Esther Ntumba Kabeya, who has been my anchor and confidant, your encouragement and patience have been a constant source of strength. Thank you for believing in my vision and for the countless sacrifices you made to allow me the time and space to bring this work to fruition.

To my children, Alex Kandolo Kabeya, Elizabeth Ngalula Kabeya, Jeremiah Mbuyi Kabeya, and Alphoncine Tshidibi Kabeya, your curiosity and joy remind me every day of why this work matters. Your resilience and understanding during the long hours I spent immersed in research and writing have been both humbling and inspiring. Your encouragement has been a cornerstone of my journey, and I am deeply grateful for the role you have played in my life.

This book is as much a product of your love and support as it is of my academic pursuits. I dedicate this work to you with immense gratitude and appreciation.

Competing Interests The author has no competing interests to declare that are relevant to the content of this manuscript.

Contents

About the Author

Patrice Kandolo Kabeya is a highly accomplished academic, researcher, and practitioner with a diverse background spanning over a decade of professional experience. He specialises in water resources management, development economics, and project management, with a focus on addressing complex challenges in sub-Saharan Africa and beyond.

Academic Credentials

Dr. Patrice Kandolo Kabeya is a development economist with over a decade of experience in the fields of structural transformation, water resource management, and sustainable development in sub-Saharan Africa. He holds a Ph.D. in Development Economics (University of Bradford, United Kingdom). He has taught economic modules at the University of Huddersfield, the University of Bradford, Leeds Beckett University (United Kingdom), and Epoka University (Albany), and consulted extensively on issues related to economic policy, water economy, water policy, infrastructure development, transboundary water management, and environmental resilience. His work bridges academic insight and practical application, contributing to research, policy dialogue, and implementation strategies that aim for inclusive and sustainable development across the African continent and beyond.

Membership and Affiliations

Dr. Kabeya is a member of esteemed professional bodies, including:

- The Chartered Management Institute (CMI).
- The Royal Economic Association of the UK.

These affiliations reflect his ongoing commitment to professional development and his engagement with global networks of scholars and practitioners.

Key Achievements

- Contributed to the implementation of SADC's Shared Watercourse Protocol through River Basin Organisations (RBOs).
- Practical experience in the economics of water and infrastructure development, focusing on strategies to achieve sustainable development goals (SDGs).

Digital Engagement

Dr. Kabeya actively promotes his work and engages with a wider audience through platforms like YouTube, where he shares insights on development economics, project management, and water resource governance.

He is deeply committed to leveraging his knowledge to address global economic and development challenges facing developing countries to foster sustainable economic growth.

Dr. Patrice Kandolo Kabeya stands as a dedicated advocate for sustainable development, combining academic rigour, practical expertise, and a global perspective to drive impactful change in developing regions.

List of Figures

List of Tables

CHAPTER 1

Introduction

Introduction

The nexus between power and economics has long been a subject of academic inquiry, but it remains a domain fraught with complexity and nuance. This book, *Development and the Power Theory of Economics: How Power Dynamics Shape Government Policy, Institutions, and Economic Strategies*, emerges from the recognition that power is not merely a passive element but a dynamic force actively shaping the trajectory of economic development. This perspective bridges the traditional gap between economics and political science, presenting a more integrative approach to understanding the interactions between institutions, policies, and strategies that define national and global development.

The focus of this book is particularly on developing countries and regions facing challenges to development, as well as other developing regions, where power dynamics profoundly impact the design and implementation of economic policies, the functioning of institutions, and the pursuit of sustainable development. In many countries, the legacy of colonialism, resource exploitation, and external interventions continues to shape institutional structures and economic strategies. These challenges are compounded by internal power struggles, governance issues, and the pressures of globalisation. This book explores how these dynamics perpetuate inequality, hinder economic diversification, and affect efforts to achieve long-term development.

P. K. Kabeya, *Development and the Power Theory of Economics*,
https://doi.org/10.1007/978-3-032-07926-8_1

Power is a complex, multifaceted concept encompassing political authority, economic influence, and social control, all of which shape developmental outcomes and growth patterns in societies (Holmberg & Rothstein, 2022). In recent years, scholars have increasingly focused on how power dynamics influence development, especially in low- and middle-income countries, yet gaps remain in understanding how power can be effectively managed to promote sustainable growth.

Problem Statement

The interconnections between power, development, and economic growth are critical yet underexplored, particularly in the context of developing economies. Power dynamics—whether institutional, structural, or within the global economic system—play a pivotal role in shaping economic trajectories, yet existing frameworks often overlook how these power structures impact equitable growth (Holmberg & Rothstein, 2022). Furthermore, there is a lack of context-specific analysis on how power imbalances hinder economic inclusivity and resilience, particularly for marginalised groups and resource-dependent nations (Holmberg & Rothstein, 2022). This gap limits the development of comprehensive growth strategies that could inform sustainable, inclusive policy interventions and effectively address socio-economic disparities, aligning with Sustainable Development Goals (SDGs).

The central question, therefore, is:

How do power structures at various levels influence economic growth and development outcomes, and what frameworks can address the resulting inequities to inform effective policy?

The following chapter, Chap. 2, critically assesses and synthesises contemporary literature on this topic, drawing attention to gaps and how this book addresses them.

Reference

Holmberg, S., & Rothstein, B. (2022). *Good governance: The relevance of transparency in economic performance*. Governance Studies.

CHAPTER 2

Literature Review

Existing Contributions in the Literature

Recent literature has provided valuable insights into how power structures influence development and economic growth, especially through institutional mechanisms, global power asymmetries, and the dynamics of economic inclusivity. A review of key contributions in each area is highlighted below.

Institutional Power and Growth

Scholars examining the role of institutions in economic development have emphasised the significance of state and institutional power mechanisms in shaping growth. These studies focus on factors such as regulatory quality, governance structures, and transparency and their impact on emerging economies.

- **Regulatory Quality and Governance Structures:** For instance, Acemoglu and Robinson (2012) discuss how effective institutions can curb corruption and create a predictable environment conducive to economic growth in emerging markets. They argue that robust governance structures encourage investment and economic activity by reducing uncertainty.

P. K. Kabeya, *Development and the Power Theory of Economics*,
https://doi.org/10.1007/978-3-032-07926-8_2

- **Institutional Transparency and Trust:** Holmberg and Rothstein (2022) analyse the impact of institutional transparency on economic performance, showing that transparent institutions foster trust and participation, which in turn positively affect economic trajectories. Their research found that countries with higher levels of transparency in institutional operations tend to experience stronger economic growth, as they attract more investment and ensure efficient allocation of resources.
- **Governance in Emerging Economies:** Dasgupta (2020) explores governance reforms in emerging economies, focusing on sub-Saharan Africa. Dasgupta argues that the quality of governance—including legal frameworks, anti-corruption measures, and regulatory institutions—plays a crucial role in economic development by reducing the risks associated with power concentration and institutional capture.

The above studies underscore that institutional power, when effectively managed, can promote sustainable growth by establishing a stable and transparent economic environment, particularly in countries with emerging markets.

Furthermore, scholars have provided various perspectives on how institutions shape economic development by influencing regulatory quality, governance, and transparency.

- North et al. (2020): In their recent work, these authors delve into the role of institutional power in sustaining economic growth. They emphasise that countries with strong, rule-bound institutions are more resilient in facing economic shocks and attracting investments, given that investors are assured of fair treatment. Their studies of Southeast Asian economies underscore the role of institutional quality in achieving stable growth.
- Mazzucato and Ryan-Collins (2021): The work of these authors on state capacity and governance addresses how government intervention and institutional power can drive innovation and growth. Her research suggests that proactive states can foster economic development by establishing frameworks for technological advancement and transparency. Case studies from Europe illustrate how institutional power can steer economies towards growth by focusing on sectors like green technology and digital transformation.

- Rodrik et al. (2004): These authors explore the relationship between governance and economic growth, arguing that economic development is influenced by "the political trilemma of the world economy." Rodrik et al. provide a framework showing that in balancing globalisation, national sovereignty, and democratic accountability, institutions play a central role in enabling sustained growth. They emphasise that developing economies with effective regulatory governance are better able to balance these factors, allowing for economic inclusivity and resilience.

The above research shows that institutional quality, regulatory frameworks, and governance transparency are essential for attracting investment and sustaining economic growth.

Global Power Asymmetries and Dependency Theory Updates

Recent contributions in this area have revisited the Dependency Theory, adapting it to the realities of modern globalisation. Scholars examine how global power imbalances perpetuate dependency relationships, where developing nations remain economically reliant on developed countries, limiting their growth potential.

- **Neo-Dependency and Global Economic Structures:** Amin (2021) builds on the classical Dependency Theory by analysing how global supply chains and trade agreements reinforce economic dependencies. Amin argues that these dependencies result in asymmetric power relations, where developing countries face trade terms that favour more powerful economies, ultimately stalling localised growth and fostering inequality.
- **Economic Dependencies and Globalisation:** Guinea and Forsthuber (2020) explore how economic dependencies have evolved under neoliberal globalisation, with developing countries becoming dependent on exports of raw materials and low-value goods. This reliance perpetuates inequality and limits industrialisation in low-income nations. Guinea and Forsthuber (2020) findings suggest that dependency under modern global capitalism has constrained the ability of many African nations to develop competitive manufacturing sectors.

- **Unequal Trade Dynamics:** Chang and Grabel (2023) argue that global financial systems perpetuate inequality by making developing nations dependent on foreign capital and subjecting them to economic policies dictated by international financial institutions. They illustrate how conditionalities attached to loans and aid often prevent meaningful economic autonomy, reducing local resilience and hindering sustainable development.

The above studies collectively argue that global power asymmetries continue to maintain dependency relationships, thus limiting economic autonomy and growth potential in developing regions.

New contributions in this area revisit the Dependency Theory and examine how global power asymmetries perpetuate dependencies, limiting economic autonomy in developing countries.

- Escobar (2021): Building on post-colonial and dependency theories, Escobar critiques how modern economic policies maintain power asymmetries, especially through global supply chains. He demonstrates that many Latin American countries remain locked into resource extraction economies that serve external markets. Escobar's work underscores the structural barriers faced by countries trying to diversify their economies within a system dominated by global corporations.
- Frank and Galeano (2022): These authors updated the dependency framework to consider the effects of global financialisation. They argue that emerging economies dependent on capital from international financial institutions are limited in their ability to adopt self-sufficient economic policies. By examining Latin American and African economies, Frank and Galeano show how global financial dependence affects sovereign decision-making and reinforces economic inequalities.
- Hickel and Sullivan (2023): The recent work of these authors on "economic extraction and ecological dependency" highlights the constraints faced by countries reliant on exporting raw materials. They argue that global power asymmetries in trade agreements continue to prioritise wealthier economies at the expense of resource-rich, lower-income countries. This work examines the African context, showing how global economic structures keep nations

dependent on primary exports, thus limiting their ability to develop high-value-added industries.

These scholars emphasise that while the Dependency Theory has evolved, the global economic system still fosters dependency, limiting sustainable growth for developing nations.

Power and Economic Inclusivity

Research into power dynamics within economic systems has increasingly focused on how power concentration affects economic inclusivity, particularly in regions where neoliberal policies have shaped economic governance.

- **Neoliberalism and Power Concentration:** Harvey (2021) critiques the impact of neoliberal policies, arguing that they centralise economic power within a small elite, reducing economic opportunities for the majority. This study highlights that neoliberal reforms, especially in Latin America and Africa, have often led to wealth concentration among a limited group, limiting economic access for marginalised populations.
- **Economic Participation and Inequality:** In a 2022 study, Milanovic examines the link between economic inequality and power concentration, showing that nations with unequal power structures often struggle with limited economic inclusivity. Milanovic finds that low-income individuals and marginalised groups are frequently excluded from economic participation, which in turn stifles broader economic growth and innovation.
- **Empowering Marginalised Groups:** Pratt et al. (2020) argue that economic growth is more sustainable and inclusive when marginalised groups have access to resources and economic opportunities. Their research indicates that micro-finance initiatives, social safety nets, and inclusive labour policies can empower marginalised communities, decentralising economic power and contributing to overall growth.

The above studies emphasise that economic inclusivity is often limited by concentrated power structures within neoliberal frameworks, suggesting that decentralised power and inclusive policies are necessary for sustained growth.

This review highlights that contemporary scholarship has made significant strides in analysing how power—whether institutional, global, or economic—influences development. However, the literature also reveals critical gaps, particularly in creating frameworks that bridge theory with policy and in exploring region-specific dynamics of power and growth. By addressing these areas, this book aims to make a unique contribution to the discourse on power, development, and economic growth.

Identified Gaps in Literature on Power, Development, and Economic Growth

Despite recent advances, there remain significant gaps in the literature on the role of power in development and economic growth. The existing research highlights the influence of institutional power, global power asymmetries, and economic inclusivity, but certain areas remain underexplored or require further empirical evidence. The following are the key gaps based on recent scholarship.

Limited Regional and Context-Specific Analyses of Institutional Power and Growth

- **Gap in Diverse Institutional Contexts:** While research by North et al. (2020) outlines the importance of institutional quality for growth, these studies often focus on generalised frameworks, primarily applicable to Western or rapidly developing economies. There is a lack of in-depth, region-specific studies on how institutional power impacts growth differently across varying political and socio-economic environments, especially in low-income regions.
- **Need for Empirical Evidence in Specific Contexts:** Many studies highlight the role of governance and transparency, but lack empirical data on how these factors influence sectors like agriculture, manufacturing, or services differently across emerging economies. Dasgupta's (2020) research touches on sub-Saharan Africa but does not dive deeply into how specific institutional factors (e.g., judicial independence, regulatory reach) operate in diverse sectors and under varying degrees of governance quality.

Lack of Comprehensive Frameworks for Understanding Modern Dependency Theory

- **Underexplored Impact of Global Financialisation on Local Autonomy:** Although Acemoglu et al. (2001) explore the role of global financial systems in perpetuating dependencies, there is still a need for comprehensive frameworks that address the specific mechanisms through which financial dependency limits local economic decision-making. Most literature in this area remains theoretical, lacking sufficient empirical data on how financial dependence plays out in sectors such as healthcare, infrastructure, or education in developing countries.
- **Need for Case Studies on Economic Resilience in Dependent Economies:** Escobar (2021) and Hickel and Sullivan (2023) point to structural barriers in resource-exporting economies but do not provide robust case studies on nations that have successfully navigated or mitigated dependency. The literature lacks detailed examples of policy measures or institutional changes that have proven effective in reducing economic dependency, which would be valuable for policymakers in similar contexts.

Insufficient Research on Power and Inclusive Growth for Marginalised Groups

- **Gap in Understanding Gender, Youth, and Rural Inclusivity in Power Dynamics:** While Piketty (2020) and Banerjee and Duflo (2023) discuss economic inclusivity, there is limited research on how specific marginalised groups—such as women, youth, and rural populations—experience and navigate economic power dynamics. This gap is particularly evident in developing regions where marginalised groups often have unique constraints and require tailored policies to enhance economic participation.
- **Underdeveloped Policy Pathways for Economic Decentralisation:** Stiglitz and Greenwald (2022) discuss the importance of decentralising economic power, but the literature lacks specific policy frameworks or tools that could guide policymakers in transitioning from highly concentrated power structures to more inclusive economic systems. There is limited research on practical strategies to reduce

monopolistic tendencies within specific industries in emerging economies, particularly in technology, agriculture, and finance sectors.

Limited Integration of Power Theories with Sustainable Development Goals (SDGs)

- **Lack of SDG-Aligned Frameworks for Power Distribution in Economic Growth Models:** Although the SDGs emphasise inclusivity and reduced inequality, few studies fully integrate power distribution theories with SDG-related targets. For instance, Milanovic's (2022) work on economic inequality does not specifically address how power structures can be modified to align with SDG objectives such as reducing poverty, promoting gender equality, or ensuring decent work. This gap indicates a need for models that explicitly incorporate power dynamics into SDG-aligned growth policies.
- **Insufficient Focus on Environmental and Ecological Dependencies in Power Asymmetry Studies:** While Hickel and Sullivan (2023) discuss the Dependency Theory in the context of resource extraction, there is a lack of research that examines how power asymmetries affect sustainable resource management and ecological resilience. This gap is particularly relevant for regions where environmental degradation and economic dependency on natural resources exacerbate vulnerability to climate change.

Need for Cross-Disciplinary Approaches and Mixed-Method Analyses

- **Underutilisation of Interdisciplinary Approaches:** Many studies on power and economic growth, such as those by Mazzucato and Ryan-Collins (2021) and Pratt et al. (2020), are confined to specific disciplinary frameworks (e.g., economics, political science). There is limited cross-disciplinary research that combines insights from sociology, anthropology, and environmental science to provide a holistic view of how power impacts development across social, economic, and environmental dimensions.
- **Gap in Mixed-Method and Longitudinal Studies:** Much of the existing literature relies on quantitative data, which, while valuable, often fails to capture the nuanced ways in which power influences growth over time. For instance, case studies and longitudinal research

are limited in examining how power structures evolve in response to global economic changes. This methodological gap restricts a deeper understanding of the causal relationships between power, development, and growth.

These gaps highlight the need for more nuanced, context-specific, and interdisciplinary approaches to studying power in development. Addressing these gaps in the proposed book could provide policymakers and scholars with practical insights and frameworks for understanding the multifaceted role of power in economic growth and development.

How the Study Proposes to Fill the Identified Gaps

This study, "Power, Development, and Economic Growth", aims to address the identified gaps through a multidimensional approach, bridging empirical research, context-specific case studies, and cross-disciplinary frameworks. This approach not only enhances the depth of analysis but also broadens the practical implications, making the work highly relevant for policymakers.

Regional and Context-Specific Analyses of Institutional Power and Growth

- **Approach**: By incorporating detailed case studies across diverse regions—including Africa, Latin America, and Southeast Asia—the proposed study will provide a comparative analysis of how institutional power affects economic growth across different governance contexts. This will offer nuanced insights into how specific institutional mechanisms (such as judicial independence and regulatory quality) impact growth sectors like agriculture, manufacturing, and services.
- **Contribution**: This focus will produce a rich repository of evidence-based examples that capture institutional power dynamics at a granular level, which is currently lacking in much of the literature.

Comprehensive Framework for Modern Dependency Theory

- **Approach**: The book will extend the Dependency Theory by offering a new framework to analyse the interplay between global

financialisation, local economic autonomy, and policy flexibility. This will include empirical case studies that illustrate the real-world impact of financial dependencies on sovereign policy choices, especially in critical sectors like healthcare, infrastructure, and education.
- **Contribution**: This framework will advance understanding of the Dependency Theory's applicability in today's financialised world, providing a roadmap for developing countries to manage dependencies while promoting resilience and self-sufficiency.

Power and Economic Inclusivity for Marginalised Groups

- **Approach**: The study will delve into the specific challenges faced by marginalised groups (women, youth, and rural communities), using cross-country comparative analyses to explore the intersection of power, inclusivity, and economic growth. It will identify key barriers and propose actionable strategies for addressing these issues.
- **Contribution**: This research will offer a detailed, empirically grounded examination of inclusivity, filling a gap in the current literature that often overlooks the specific economic dynamics of marginalised communities within broader power structures.

Integration with Sustainable Development Goals (SDGs)

- **Approach**: By aligning the study's analytical framework with SDG targets, the book will address how power dynamics can either support or hinder sustainable development goals. The study will explore pathways for achieving SDG-aligned economic growth, particularly in reducing inequality, fostering decent work, and supporting sustainable resource use.
- **Contribution**: This alignment with SDG frameworks will uniquely position the book within contemporary policy discourse, highlighting how policymakers can use power dynamics as levers to achieve sustainable development objectives.

Cross-Disciplinary and Mixed-Method Approach

- **Approach**: The proposed book will draw from various fields, including economics, political science, sociology, and environmental science, and utilise a combination of quantitative data and qualitative insights from longitudinal case studies. This approach will provide a more holistic understanding of the interconnections between power, development, and growth.

- **Contribution**: This interdisciplinary and mixed-method approach addresses a critical methodological gap in the current literature, allowing for a more nuanced understanding of power's role over time and across different socio-economic contexts.

Relevance to Policymakers

Addressing these gaps makes the study highly relevant to policymakers in several ways.

1. **Informed Institutional Reforms:** The book's insights on institutional power will help policymakers understand which institutional structures and governance mechanisms can support sustainable growth. This can guide reforms to strengthen regulatory quality, enhance transparency, and promote accountability.
2. **Strategies for Managing Global Dependencies**: By updating the Dependency Theory, the study provides policymakers in developing economies with actionable frameworks for managing global financial dependencies. It highlights policies that can foster economic self-sufficiency while participating in the global economy.
3. **Inclusive Economic Policies for Marginalised Groups**: The book's focus on inclusivity offers practical guidance for policymakers looking to create opportunities for marginalised groups, emphasising tailored policies for rural, youth, and women's economic participation.
4. **SDG-Linked Policy Insights**: With a focus on SDG alignment, the study will equip policymakers with a roadmap to implement growth policies that directly contribute to global sustainable development goals, ensuring that economic growth efforts are equitable and ecologically responsible.
5. **Empirical and Cross-Disciplinary Evidence**: The mixed-method, cross-disciplinary approach provides policymakers with a robust, evidence-based foundation for crafting policies that account for complex socio-economic dynamics, making the study an invaluable resource for designing long-term growth strategies.

Positioning Within Contemporary Literature

This book's approach to addressing key gaps places it as a significant contribution within the contemporary literature on power and economic development. By addressing limitations in the current scholarship—such as the lack of regional specificity, limited integration with SDG frameworks, and the absence of cross-disciplinary perspectives—this study robustly positions itself as a comprehensive resource that not only advances academic understanding but also provides policymakers with actionable insights.

1. **Building on Theoretical Foundations**: The study advances existing theories by updating dependency frameworks and integrating inclusive growth dynamics, adding depth to the scholarly discourse.
2. **Responding to Calls for Empirical Data and Case Studies**: With a rich set of case studies and data-driven insights, this book directly responds to the need for empirical analyses and specific policy pathways highlighted by recent scholars.
3. **Bridging Disciplines for a Holistic View**: The interdisciplinary approach positions this book as a cutting-edge contribution, encouraging the integration of economic, social, and environmental dimensions into the study of power and growth.

Through this comprehensive approach, the proposed book is well-positioned to fill crucial gaps in contemporary literature, setting a new standard for studies on power, development, and economic growth.

This literature review chapter concludes by reiterating the importance of understanding power dynamics in shaping developmental outcomes. By systematically addressing the gaps identified in contemporary literature, this book aims to provide a nuanced understanding of the relationship between power, development, and economic growth, especially within contexts where inequalities in power distribution continue to hinder sustainable development. This review highlights both the strengths and gaps in existing literature, providing a solid foundation for the book's unique contribution.

References

Acemoglu, D., & Robinson, J. A. (2012). *Why nations fail: The origins of power, prosperity, and poverty*. Crown Business.

Acemoglu, D., Johnson, S., & Robinson, J. (2001). The colonial origins of comparative development: An empirical investigation. *American Economic Review, 91*, 1369–1401. https://doi.org/10.1257/aer.91.5.1369

Amin. S (2021). Diversity–development nexus: Why determine economic development without diversity? A comparative analysis between developed and developing countries. *Available to Purchase, Society and Business Review, 16*(1), 134–150. https://doi.org/10.1108/SBR-01-2020-0007

Banerjee, A., & Duflo, E. (2023). *Good economics for hard times: Better answers to our biggest problems*. Penguin Random House.

Chang, H., & Grabel, I. (2023). *Reclaiming development: An alternative economic policy manual*. Zed Books.

Dasgupta, P. (2020). *Governance reforms in emerging economies*. Oxford University Press.

Escobar, A. (2021). Dependency, power, and economic development: Reflections on Latin America's resource-based economies. *Journal of Economic Issues, 55*(2), 304–321.

Frank, A. G., & Galeano, E. (2022). *Dependency theory revisited: Globalization and inequality*. Monthly Review Press.

Guinea, O., & Forsthuber, F. (2020). *Globalization comes to the rescue: How dependency makes us more resilient*. ECIPE Occasional Paper, No. 06/2020. European Centre for International Political Economy. https://ecipe.org/publications/globalisation-makes-us-more-resilient/

Harvey, D. (2021). *The enigma of capital and the crises of capitalism*. Oxford University Press.

Hickel, J., & Sullivan, D. (2023). Power, resources, and economic dependency in the Global South: The impact of resource extraction on inequality. *World Development, 158*, 102–117.

Holmberg, S., & Rothstein, B. (2022). *Good governance: The relevance of transparency in economic performance*. Governance Studies.

Mazzucato, M., & Ryan-Collins, J. (2021). *Mission economy: A moonshot guide to changing capitalism*. Allen Lane.

Milanovic, B. (2022). *Global inequality: A new approach for the age of globalization*. Harvard University Press.

North, D. C., Wallis, J. J., & Weingast, B. R. (2020). *Violence and social orders: A conceptual framework for interpreting recorded human history*. Cambridge University Press.

Piketty, T. (2020). *Capital and ideology*. Harvard University Press.

Pratt, B., Cheah, P. Y., & Marsh, V. (2020). Response to open peer commentaries on solidarity and community engagement in global health research. *The American Journal of Bioethics, 20*(8), W14–W16. https://doi.org/10.1080/15265161.2020.1777356

Rodrik, D., Subramanian, A., & Trebbi, F. (2004). Institutions rule: The primacy of institutions over geography and integration in economic development. *Journal of Economic Growth, 9*(2), 131–165.

Stiglitz, J. E., & Greenwald, B. (2022). *The great divide: Unequal societies and what we can do about them.* W. W. Norton & Company.

CHAPTER 3

Methodology and Theoretical Framework

Purpose of the Book

1. Educational Goal: To provide a comprehensive understanding of Power Theory, its various dimensions, and its application across different fields such as development and economic growth.
2. Analytical Framework: To offer readers frameworks and tools for analysing power dynamics within various social, political, and economic contexts.
3. Critical Perspective: To encourage critical thinking about the nature and effects of power, highlighting both its constructive and destructive potentials.
4. Practical Application: To show how Power Theory can be applied to real-world situations, helping readers to recognise and navigate power dynamics in their personal and professional lives.
5. Interdisciplinary Approach: To integrate insights from multiple disciplines, providing a holistic view of power that encompasses diverse perspectives and methodologies.

P. K. Kabeya, *Development and the Power Theory of Economics*,
https://doi.org/10.1007/978-3-032-07926-8_3

Methodology

Explanation of Approach and Methods Used

Interdisciplinary Approach

- Integration of Disciplines: The book employs an interdisciplinary approach by combining insights from political science, economics, sociology, and cultural studies. This broadens the analysis of power dynamics in development and economic growth.
- Cross-Disciplinary Frameworks: Utilising frameworks and theories from multiple disciplines to analyse power, ensuring a comprehensive understanding of its influence on development and economic growth.

Theoretical Analysis

- Conceptual Frameworks: The book grounds its analysis in established conceptual frameworks of power, such as those proposed by Marx, Weber, and Foucault. These frameworks help to analyse how power operates in economic and developmental contexts.
- Critical Theory: Applying Critical Theory to deconstruct dominant power structures and paradigms, revealing underlying assumptions and biases that affect development and economic growth.

Case Study Method

- Selection of Cases: Selecting a variety of case studies to illustrate power dynamics in different development and economic growth contexts. Cases cover diverse regions, sectors, and scales.
- Comparative Analysis: Conducting comparative analysis to highlight similarities and differences in power dynamics across various contexts, facilitating a deeper understanding of universal and unique aspects of power in development and economic growth.

Policy Analysis

- Policy Review: Analysing existing policies to identify how they reinforce or challenge existing power structures and their implications for development and economic growth.
- Policy Recommendations: Developing evidence-based policy recommendations aimed at addressing power imbalances and promoting equitable development and economic growth.

These diverse methodologies have been applied in the different book chapters to provide a robust and comprehensive analysis of how power dynamics influence development and economic growth. This approach ensures both theoretical insights and practical implications are thoroughly explored, offering a nuanced understanding of the complex interplay between power, development, and economic paradigms.

Theoretical Foundation: Overview

The theoretical framework of this book, *Development and the Power Theory of Economics: How Power Dynamics Shape Government Policy, Institutions, and Economic Strategies*, is deeply rooted in interdisciplinary scholarship. It draws from economics, political science, and institutional theory to explore how power relations shape economic strategies, institutional evolution, and policy outcomes. Below, the central theoretical pillars are elaborated with examples and references to demonstrate their relevance, particularly in sub-Saharan Africa (SSA) and beyond.

The Power Theory in Economics

Power is a critical determinant of economic behaviour and outcomes, influencing who controls resources, policy decisions, and market dynamics. Traditional economic models often ignore the role of power, focusing instead on efficiency and rationality. This book integrates Power Theory to explain systemic inequalities. Example: Land ownership in SSA remains concentrated among the elite, a legacy of colonial policies. For instance, in South Africa, despite post-apartheid reforms, large tracts of arable land are still owned by a small fraction of the population, perpetuating economic disparities (Foucault, 1979; Hall, 2009).

Institutional Economics and Path Dependency

Institutions, shaped by historical contexts, define the "rules of the game" in economic systems. Douglas North's concepts of path dependency and institutional lock-in explain how historical power structures become entrenched, making reform difficult (North, 1990). Example: The Democratic Republic of Congo (DRC) exemplifies how colonial extractive institutions designed to exploit natural resources persist today, limiting inclusive economic development (North, 1990).

Political Economy of Development

Political economy examines how political processes intersect with economic strategies, emphasising the role of power in shaping institutional quality and governance (Acemoglu & Robinson, 2012). Example 1: Acemoglu and Robinson (2012) argue that countries with "extractive institutions", such as Zimbabwe under Mugabe, often experience economic stagnation because policies are designed to benefit the elite rather than the broader population. Example 2: Ethiopia's recent shift towards industrialisation, driven by the state-led Growth and Transformation Plan (GTP), illustrates how centralised power can influence development, though concerns about political repression persist (Acemoglu & Robinson, 2012).

Structural Power and the Dependency Theory

The Dependency Theory highlights how global economic systems perpetuate underdevelopment in the Global South. Structural power emphasises the dominance of Global North actors in shaping global norms and institutions (Mkandawire & Soludo, 1999). Example: The structural adjustment programmes (SAPs) imposed by the International Monetary Fund (IMF) and World Bank in the 1980s and 1990s illustrate how external power structures dictated economic policies in SSA, often leading to reduced social spending and increased inequality (Frank, 1967; Mkandawire & Soludo, 1999).

Game Theory and Bargaining Power

The Game Theory explores strategic interactions, particularly in contexts of unequal power. In economic negotiations, weaker parties often accept suboptimal terms due to asymmetrical bargaining power (Busse et al., 2004). Example: The Economic Partnership Agreements (EPAs) between the European Union and African countries reveal how developed nations leverage their structural and economic power to secure favourable trade deals (Busse et al., 2004).

Behavioural Economics and Power Perception

Behavioural economics examines how perceptions of power influence decision-making, often perpetuating inequality through self-reinforcing biases. Example: Smallholder farmers in SSA often perceive themselves as powerless in negotiating fair prices with large agribusinesses, leading to a cycle of poverty and economic exclusion (Barrett, 2008).

Critical Development Theory

The Critical Development Theory challenges the linear, Western-centric view of development, emphasising the importance of local agency and decolonisation of economic strategies (Schuurman, 2009). Example: The "African Renaissance" movement advocates for locally driven development models that prioritise indigenous knowledge systems and cultural contexts, rejecting one-size-fits-all approaches (Schuurman, 2009).

Application to Sub-Saharan Africa and Developing Countries

This theoretical framework is particularly relevant for SSA and other developing regions due to the following reasons:

- Colonial legacies: Persistent inequalities rooted in extractive institutions and resource dependency (Watts, 2004).
  - Example: Nigeria's oil sector illustrates how the elite capture and global demand shape economic strategies, often at the expense of local development (Watts, 2004).

- Geopolitical pressures: Influence of external actors like China, whose Belt and Road Initiative has reshaped infrastructure strategies across Africa (Watts, 2004).
  - Example: Kenya's Standard Gauge Railway, financed by China, reflects both opportunities and risks of external power dynamics (Watts, 2004).

Implications of the Theoretical Framework

The integration of Power Theory, institutional economics, political economy, the Dependency Theory, and other concepts offers profound insights into the dynamics shaping development strategies and economic outcomes in SSA and other developing regions. Below, the implications of these theories are explored in relation to governance, policymaking, institutional reform, and sustainable development.

Implications for Governance and Policymaking

Hall (2009) opines that power asymmetries profoundly shape governance structures and policy decisions, often prioritising the elite or external interests over public welfare.

- Elite Capture
  - Implication: Policymaking in many SSA countries often reflects the interests of the powerful elite rather than broader development goals. For instance, land reform policies in countries like Kenya and South Africa frequently face resistance due to entrenched elite interests (Hall, 2009).
  - Policy Response: Strengthening democratic institutions and fostering accountability mechanisms are critical to mitigating elite capture (Hall, 2009).
- External Influence
  - Implication: The dependency on external actors (e.g., foreign donors, multinational corporations) often results in policies that prioritise short-term gains or align with donor priorities rather than local needs (Mkandawire & Soludo, 1999).
  - Policy Response: Developing nations should negotiate more equitable terms in international agreements and foster self-reliance through economic diversification (Hall, 2009).

Institutional Design and Reform

Hall (2009) argues that institutions shape the rules of the game, and their design determines whether they promote inclusion or perpetuate inequality.

- Path Dependency and Institutional Lock-In
  - Implication: Historical institutions in SSA, such as those established during colonialism, continue to constrain reform efforts. For example, the centralised administrative systems in many former British and French colonies have hindered local governance and participatory development (Bahl & Linn, 1992).
  - Policy Response: Reforming institutions require disrupting path dependencies through inclusive decision-making, decentralisation, and capacity-building at the local level (Acemoglu & Robinson, 2012).
- Building State Capacity
  - Implication: Weak state capacity in many developing countries prevents effective policy implementation and service delivery. Ethiopia's state-led industrial policies under the GTP highlight the potential of strong state institutions to drive development, albeit with risks of authoritarianism (Acemoglu & Robinson, 2012).
  - Policy Response: Investments in human capital, technology, and governance reforms can enhance state capacity while ensuring accountability (Escobar, 1995).

Global Economic Relations

Watts (2004) explains that power dynamics at the international level influence trade, investment, and financial flows, often to the detriment of developing nations.

- Dependency and Structural Power
  - Implication: SSA's reliance on commodity exports creates vulnerability to global market fluctuations, as seen in the oil-dependent economies of Nigeria and Angola (Watts, 2004). Structural adjustment programmes exacerbated these vulnerabilities by limiting state intervention (Watts, 2004).

   - Policy Response: Developing countries must pursue economic diversification, foster regional trade, and renegotiate unfavourable trade agreements to reduce dependency (Hall, 2009).
- Negotiating Power in International Agreements
   - Implication: Countries with limited bargaining power often accept suboptimal trade or investment deals, such as the EPAs with the European Union (Busse et al., 2004).
   - Policy Response: Collaborative regional blocs, such as the African Continental Free Trade Area (AfCFTA), can enhance collective bargaining power and promote fairer trade agreements (Hall, 2009).

Addressing Inequality and Social Inclusion

Barrett (2008) reports that understanding power dynamics is essential for addressing the root causes of inequality and promoting inclusive development.

- Behavioural Economics and Perception of Power
   - Implication: Marginalised groups, such as smallholder farmers, often lack access to markets and credit due to entrenched power structures and self-reinforcing perceptions of exclusion (Barrett, 2008).
   - Policy Response: Governments and NGOs should prioritise programmes that empower marginalised groups, such as microfinance initiatives and market access platforms (Barrett, 2008).
- Critical Development Theory
   - Implication: Mainstream development models often overlook local contexts and agency, resulting in solutions that are neither sustainable nor equitable (Escobar, 1995).
   - Policy Response: Emphasising participatory development and leveraging indigenous knowledge can create more effective and sustainable strategies (Hall, 2009).

Economic Strategy and Resource Governance

Watts (2004) highlights that the management of natural resources is a critical area where power dynamics play a decisive role.

- Resource Control and Elite Interests
  - Implication: In many SSA countries, natural resource wealth has been a source of conflict rather than development. For example, the "resource curse" in the Niger Delta has fuelled inequality and environmental degradation (Watts, 2004).
  - Policy Response: Transparent governance frameworks, such as those promoted by the Extractive Industries Transparency Initiative (EITI), can reduce corruption and ensure that resource revenues benefit the broader population (Watts, 2004).
- Global Resource Demand
  - Implication: External actors, particularly China, have significantly influenced resource extraction strategies in Africa, often prioritising infrastructure development over environmental and social considerations (Barrett, 2008).
  - Policy Response: Countries must balance foreign investment with stringent environmental and social impact assessments to ensure sustainable development (Barrett, 2008)

Broader Implications for Sustainable Development

Barrett (2008) notes that the theoretical framework underscores the importance of addressing power dynamics to achieve the Sustainable Development Goals (SDGs). Specific implications include:

- SDG 16 (Peace, Justice, and Strong Institutions): Enhancing institutional quality and reducing corruption by addressing power imbalances.
- SDG 8 (Decent Work and Economic Growth): Promoting inclusive economic strategies that empower marginalised groups and reduce inequality.
- SDG 10 (Reduced Inequalities): Tackling structural power imbalances at national and global levels to create a fairer economic system.

The theories guiding this book reveal that power is not a peripheral factor in development but a central determinant of economic outcomes. Addressing the implications of these theories requires a shift in focus from technical solutions to addressing the systemic inequalities and power asymmetries that shape institutions, policies, and strategies. By applying these insights, SSA and other developing regions beyond the continent can craft more inclusive and sustainable pathways to development.

The next section provides an overview of the power theories on development and economic growth and how they shaped development outcomes.

General Overview of Power Theories on Development and Economic Growth

This section provides a foundational understanding of the power theories that underpin the relationship between development and economic growth. It explores how different theoretical perspectives conceptualise power and its role in shaping institutions, policies, and economic outcomes.

Power in Institutional Economics

Dasgupta (2020) explains that institutional economics posits those institutions—formal and informal rules governing economic activities—play a central role in economic development. The distribution and exercise of power within these institutions influence how resources are allocated, wealth is distributed, and policies are implemented.

The key concepts are explained below.

- Inclusive vs. Extractive Institutions: Acemoglu and Robinson (2012) distinguish between inclusive institutions, which promote broad participation and equitable growth, and extractive institutions, which concentrate power and resources among the elite.
- Path Dependency: Historical power dynamics shape institutions in ways that are difficult to reverse, leading to persistent inequalities (Acemoglu & Robinson, 2012).

Relevance to Development and Growth

Acemoglu and Robinson (2012) explain that effective institutions create environments conducive to investment and innovation, reducing uncertainty and fostering long-term growth. They also found that weak or extractive institutions, as observed in many SSA countries, often perpetuate inequality and hinder sustainable development. This is well-positioned within the current socioeconomic institutions. For example, Botswana's institutional reforms in governance and anti-corruption measures have supported consistent economic growth, whereas Zimbabwe's centralised and extractive governance has led to economic decline.

Political Economy and Power Dynamics

Dasgupta (2020) avers that political economy examines how power relations influence economic policies and outcomes. It emphasises the role of political institutions, governance structures, and elite interests in shaping economic trajectories.

Key Concepts

- Elite Capture: The concentration of power among the elite leads to policies that prioritise their interests over broader societal needs (Dasgupta, 2020).
- State Capacity: The ability of governments to design and implement effective policies is often shaped by internal and external power struggles (Hall, 2009).

Relevance to Development and Growth

Hickel and Sullivan (2023) maintain that in developing economies, weak state capacity often results in policies that exacerbate inequality rather than addressing it. They also indicated that political instability, driven by power struggles, undermines economic confidence and reduces investment. For example, Ethiopia's state-led industrialisation policies under the GTP demonstrate the potential of centralised power to drive growth, albeit with concerns over political repression (Hickel & Sullivan, 2023).

Dependency Theory and Global Power Structures

Harvey (2021) emphasises that the Dependency Theory examines how global economic systems perpetuate power imbalances between developed and developing nations, limiting the latter's ability to achieve self-sustaining growth. What are the key concepts? These are as follows:

Key Concepts

- Core-Periphery Relationships: Developed countries (the core) dominate global trade and financial systems, relegating developing nations (the periphery) to roles as raw material suppliers (Frank & Galeano, 2022).
- Structural Dependency: Dependence on external markets and capital reduces local economic autonomy (Frank & Galeano, 2022).

Relevance to Development and Growth
Frank and Galeano (2022) emphasise that the dependency on resource exports creates economic vulnerabilities and prevents industrial diversification. They also indicated that global financial institutions impose conditionalities that restrict policy flexibility in developing nations. For example, they believe that the structural adjustment programmes of the 1980s and 1990s, imposed by the IMF and World Bank, led to reduced public spending and increased inequality in many African nations (Frank & Galeano, 2022).

Structural Power and Economic Systems

Busse et al. (2004) argue that structural power focuses on how the organisation of economic systems influences power dynamics, shaping access to resources, opportunities, and decision-making. The key concepts underlying the structural Power and Economic System include the following:

Key Concepts

- Bargaining Power: Power asymmetries in negotiations often result in developing nations accepting unfavourable trade and investment agreements (Busse et al., 2004).
- Economic Leverage: Wealthier nations and multinational corporations wield disproportionate influence over global norms and policies (Busse et al., 2004).

Relevance to Development and Growth
Busse et al. (2004) opine that structural power determines who benefits from economic policies and who is excluded, perpetuating inequality.

They also demonstrated that developing nations face challenges in asserting their interests in global economic systems dominated by the Global North. For example, the Economic Partnership Agreements (EPAs) between the European Union and African nations highlight how unequal bargaining power affects trade outcomes, often disadvantaging developing countries (Busse et al., 2004).

Critical Development Theory and Decolonisation of Power

Holmberg and Rothstein (2022) argue that the Critical Development Theory challenges traditional models of development that prioritise economic growth over equity and sustainability. It emphasises the need to decolonise power structures and promote locally driven development strategies (Holmberg & Rothstein, 2022).

They defined key concepts as discussed below.

Key Concepts

- Participatory Development: Empowering local communities to play active roles in decision-making (Hickel & Sullivan, 2023).
- Decolonisation: Reducing reliance on external actors and fostering indigenous knowledge and systems (Hickel & Sullivan, 2023).

Relevance to Development and Growth

Hickel and Sullivan (2023) explain that decolonised approaches address systemic inequalities by prioritising local agency and equitable resource distribution. They also indicated that participatory models ensure that marginalised groups benefit from development initiatives. For example, Rwanda's gender-focused policies and emphasis on local governance illustrate the potential of participatory and decolonised development strategies to achieve equitable growth (Hickel & Sullivan, 2023).

Integration and Implications

What are the implications? Dasgupta (2020) highlights that these power theories collectively highlight that power dynamics are fundamental to understanding economic development.

Key Implications

- Policy Design: Recognising power imbalances enables policymakers to create more equitable and inclusive economic strategies.
- Institutional Reform: Addressing path dependencies and strengthening governance structures can foster sustainable growth.
- Global Advocacy: Developing nations must push for fairer global systems that reduce dependency and promote autonomy.
- Community Empowerment: Participatory and decolonised approaches ensure that development benefits are broadly shared.

Key Theories and Applications

This section provides a better understanding of the relationship between power, development, and economic growth. It involves exploring various theories from political science, economics, and sociology. Some key power theories, as they are linked to development and economic growth, are highlighted below.

Modernisation Theory

Banerjee and Duflo (2023) indicate that the Modernisation Theory posits that economic development follows a linear progression where societies move from traditional to modern states.

Banerjee and Duflo (2023) highlight the key features as:

- Industrialisation: Transition from agrarian-based economies to industrial economies.
- Urbanisation: Growth of cities and urban centres.
- Technological advancement: Increased use of technology in production.
- Education and rationalisation: Greater emphasis on education and scientific rationality.

However, Chang and Grabel (2023) opine that although the Modernisation Theory offers the abovementioned benefits, it is criticised for the following:

- Ethnocentric: Often considered Western-centric, assuming that all societies should follow the Western path of development.
- Overemphasis on linear progress: Neglects the complexities and unique trajectories of different societies.

Dependency Theory

Evans (2023) demonstrates that the Dependency Theory, emerging from Latin America, challenges the assumptions of the Modernisation Theory by arguing that economic development in peripheral (developing) countries is hindered by their dependence on core (developed) countries.

Key points based on Evans (2023) are as follows:

- Historical exploitation: Colonialism and neo-colonialism have created unequal economic relationships.
- Structural inequality: Global economic structures perpetuate the dependency of developing countries.
- Import substitution industrialisation (ISI): A recommended strategy to reduce dependency by producing goods domestically.

A study by Frank and Galeano (2022) highlights that even though the Dependency Theory offers another dimension to economic development, its criticism is:

- Deterministic: Can be overly pessimistic, underestimating the agency of developing countries.
- Neglects internal factors: Focuses primarily on external influences and may overlook domestic issues.

World-Systems Theory

Crouch (2020) underscores that the World-Systems Theory, developed by Immanuel Wallerstein, expands on the Dependency Theory by conceptualising the global economy as a complex system divided into core, semi-periphery, and periphery nations.

Key ideas based on Crouch (2020) are highlighted as follows:

- Global division of labour: Different regions play specific roles in the global economy.
- Cyclical changes: Economic hegemonies shift over time.
- Exploitation: Core countries exploit the periphery and semi-periphery countries for resources and labour.

Milanovic (2022) explains that the World-Systems Theory has demonstrated its limitations, which are highlighted below.

- Complex and broad: The theory's broad scope can make it difficult to apply to specific cases.
- Emphasis on economic factors: May underplay political, cultural, and social dynamics.

Neoclassical Growth Theory

Sachs (2022) reports that the Neoclassical Growth Theory, represented by the Solow-Swan model, focuses on factors like capital accumulation, labour force growth, and technological progress to explain economic growth.

Key concepts based on Sachs (2022) are highlighted below.

- Diminishing returns: Initially, capital investment leads to high returns, but over time, these returns diminish.
- Steady-state equilibrium: Economies converge to a steady state where growth is determined by technological progress.
- Savings and investment: Key drivers of economic growth.

The Neoclassical Growth Theory has been criticised, as explained below.

- Assumes perfect markets: Often criticised for assuming perfect information and competitive markets (Sachs, 2022).
- Neglects institutional factors: Fails to adequately address the role of institutions and politics in economic growth (Sachs, 2022).

Endogenous Growth Theory

Rodrik (2020) explains that the Endogenous Growth Theory, developed by economists like Paul Romer, incorporates technological innovation and knowledge into growth models.

Key features based on Stiglitz and Greenwald (2022) are highlighted below.

- Innovation: Emphasis on technology and innovation as primary drivers of economic growth.
- Human capital: Education and skills development are crucial for fostering innovation.
- Policy implications: Suggests that government policies can influence economic growth by investing in education, research, and development.

However, Stiglitz and Greenwald (2022) argue that the Endogenous Growth Theory criticism was based on the following:

- Measurement challenges: Difficulties in measuring innovation and human capital accurately.
- Overemphasis on technology: May neglect other important factors like social and political stability.

Institutional Theory

Piketty (2020) emphasises that the Institutional Theory argues that the quality and nature of institutions—political, legal, and economic—are critical determinants of economic development.

Key points based on Piketty (2020) are highlighted below.

- Property rights: Secure property rights are essential for investment and economic growth.
- Governance: Effective governance reduces corruption and enhances economic performance.
- Rule of law: Legal frameworks that enforce contracts and protect rights are fundamental for development.

Przeworski (2023) indicates, conversely, that the Institutional Theory has been criticised based on the following:

- Vague definitions: The term "institution" can be broadly defined, making the theory sometimes ambiguous.
- Causal ambiguity: Difficult to determine whether good institutions lead to economic growth or vice versa.

Political Power Theories

Milanovic (2022) opines that political power theories focus on how power dynamics within a country affect economic policies and development outcomes.

Key concepts based on Milanovic (2022) are highlighted below.

- Elite capture: Economic policies may favour the elite, hindering broader development.
- Political stability: Stable political environments tend to be more conducive to economic growth.
- Conflict and war: Political conflicts and wars can severely disrupt economic development.

One of the key criticisms of political power theories is their deterministic nature, often attributing developmental outcomes solely to political dynamics while overlooking the interplay with economic and social factors. These theories tend to simplify the complexity of governance, ignoring the multifaceted nature of political environments where competing interests, institutional capacities, and economic incentives interact. A critical dimension often missing in these analyses is the balance—or imbalance—of power in decision-making processes. When political power is concentrated in the hands of a few, decisions tend to be driven by narrow interests, leading to inefficient allocation of state resources. Conversely, a more equilibrated distribution of power, where economic, political, and social forces are adequately represented, fosters inclusive decision-making and enhances development efficiency.

To resolve this dilemma, it is essential to align power structures with economic priorities. Only when political and economic powers are balanced can a state achieve efficient, equitable, and sustainable development outcomes. Without this balance, political capture, rent-seeking, and resource misallocation become prevalent, undermining developmental goals.

Key to Fig. 3.1:

- The X-axis represents the balance of power in decision-making—from a politically power-dominated system (left) to a balanced power structure (middle), to an economically driven decision-making structure (right).
- The Y-axis shows the efficiency in the allocation of state resources
- The graph demonstrates that efficiency is lowest when power is excessively skewed, either politically or economically.
- The peak of the curve represents the optimal efficiency, achieved when political and economic powers are in equilibrium, allowing for inclusive, evidence-based, and accountable policymaking.

Mazzucato and Ryan-Collins (2021) highlight that each theory provides a unique lens through which to understand the intricate relationship between power, development, and economic growth. Policymakers and researchers often draw from multiple theories to address specific development challenges, recognising that economic growth is a multifaceted phenomenon influenced by a wide range of factors.

Power Dynamics in Developing Countries

This section delves into the contemporary power structures in developing countries, with a particular emphasis on SSA. It explores how these structures influence development outcomes, examining the roles of the political elite, bureaucracies, international organisations, and civil society.

```
       Resource Allocation Efficiency
       |
       |                •
       |               / \
       |              /   \
       |             /     \
       |            /       \
       |           /         \
       |__________/___________\__________  → Balance of Power (Political vs
Economic)
              Skewed       Equilibrium       Skewed
            (Political)     (Balanced)      (Economic)
```

Fig. 3.1 Power-efficiency relationship

Special attention is given to how power asymmetries perpetuate poverty and inequality.

Political Elite and Governance

Political Elite

Watts (2004) explains that the political elite hold significant sway over development policies and resource allocation. In many developing countries, political power is concentrated in the hands of a few individuals or families, often leading to clientelism, patronage, and corruption. This section examines how the political elite influence development through their control over state apparatus, electoral processes, and policy decisions (Sachs, 2022). For instance, the role of the political elite in Nigeria illustrates how oil wealth has been both a boon and a curse, with the elite's capture of resources leading to widespread corruption and inequality despite the country's vast natural wealth. In the DRC, its vast natural resources have made it a focal point for political power struggles. The political elite in the DRC has historically used their positions to control resource-rich regions, leading to conflicts and instability. It is noted that, as is the case in the DRC, control of the mining sector by the political elite and their allies has led to significant wealth disparities and underdevelopment despite the country's rich mineral resources. In terms of governance structures, for the DRC, effective governance is crucial for development, yet many developing countries face challenges such as weak institutions, a lack of transparency, and limited accountability. This analysis explores different governance models and their impact on development, highlighting both successes and failures.

In the case of Rwanda, the Rwandan post-genocide recovery and development trajectory showcases how strong leadership and governance reforms can drive rapid economic growth and social development, despite initial power asymmetries (Sachs, 2022).

Bureaucracies and Institutional Capacity

Bureaucratic Functioning

Falch and Fischer (2008) demonstrate that the efficiency and effectiveness of bureaucracies significantly affect development outcomes. This book explores the challenges faced by bureaucracies in developing countries, such as limited resources, capacity constraints, and politicisation. As in the case study of Ethiopia, its bureaucratic reforms aimed at improving public service delivery and fostering economic growth provide insights into the importance of building institutional capacity for development.

Institutional Reforms
Brown (2015) believes that institutional reforms are often necessary to address inefficiencies and corruption within bureaucracies.

A few countries are analysed below.

Democratic Republic of Congo (DRC)

Davis (2020) highlights that the DRC has faced significant challenges with governance, corruption, and institutional inefficiency due to decades of conflict, instability, and weak institutions. Over the years, the country has implemented reforms aimed at rebuilding and strengthening its institutions.

Davis (2020) informs how the DRC has reformed its institutions and the implications as below.

Key Institutional Reforms

1. **Governance and Anti-corruption Reforms**: The DRC has made efforts to combat corruption, especially in the public sector and natural resources management. The establishment of the National Anti-corruption Commission (CNLCC) is part of these efforts. However, implementation remains inconsistent due to systemic challenges.
2. **Electoral Reforms**: In recent years, the DRC has made some strides in electoral reform. The *Commission Electorale Nationale Indépendante* (CENI) translates to the Independent National Electoral Commission, which was established to oversee elections more fairly, and the country held its first peaceful presidential transition in 2019. However, concerns about transparency, inclusivity, and electoral integrity remain (Sachs, 2022).
3. **Decentralisation and Local Governance**: The 2006 constitution outlined the decentralisation of government functions to improve local governance. Provincial governments were established to promote local development, but the full implementation of decentralisation has been slow, mainly due to political resistance and resource constraints.

4. **Judicial Reforms**: The DRC has undertaken efforts to strengthen its judiciary, with a focus on independence and tackling impunity. However, corruption and political influence still affect the judicial system, and reforms have yet to significantly transform the justice sector (Sachs, 2022).
5. **Security Sector Reform**: With ongoing conflicts in parts of the country, the DRC has worked on reforming its security sector, especially the military and police (Sachs, 2022). The aim is to professionalise the forces, improve security, and reduce human rights abuses. However, these reforms are undermined by corruption, lack of resources, and armed militia groups (Sachs, 2022).

Botswana

Spielberg (1993) highlights that Botswana is often viewed as one of Africa's most stable democracies, with strong institutions that promote good governance, transparency, and accountability. Despite its success, the country has continually implemented reforms to maintain and improve these institutions.

These reforms are highlighted below.

Key Institutional Reforms

1. **Governance and Public Service Reform**: Botswana is known for its relatively low levels of corruption. The Public Service Act and other governance measures aim to ensure merit-based recruitment and accountability in public service. Regular reforms in public administration focus on improving efficiency and service delivery.
2. **Electoral Reforms**: Botswana has a long history of free and fair elections. The Independent Electoral Commission (IEC) manages elections, and the country has made reforms to ensure transparent and inclusive voting systems, with provisions for ensuring women's participation and the protection of voter rights.
3. **Anti-corruption Measures**: Botswana has a Directorate on Corruption and Economic Crime (DCEC) that investigates corruption in both the public and private sectors. The country's consistent and effective fight against corruption is considered a hallmark of its successful institutional framework.

4. **Judicial Reforms**: Botswana's judiciary is independent, and there have been ongoing efforts to ensure that it remains free from political interference. Reforms have included the strengthening of legal frameworks for better access to justice and the establishment of specialised courts to improve the legal process.
5. **Economic Reforms**: Botswana has also undertaken various economic reforms to diversify away from its reliance on diamond mining. Reforms have focused on improving the business environment, attracting foreign investment, and developing the tourism and manufacturing sectors.

South Africa

Akinola (2020) demonstrates that South Africa's institutional reforms, particularly since the end of apartheid in 1994, have focused on ensuring democratic governance, human rights protection, and reconciliation. The country's reforms have been instrumental in transitioning from an apartheid state to a fully democratic nation.

These reforms are highlighted below.

Key Institutional Reforms

1. **Constitutional and Governance Reforms**: The 1996 Constitution, which replaced apartheid-era laws, laid the foundation for democracy, human rights, and the rule of law. The Constitutional Court plays a critical role in interpreting the Constitution and ensuring that laws align with democratic principles.
2. **Electoral Reforms**: South Africa has made significant strides in ensuring free and fair elections, with the Independent Electoral Commission (IEC) overseeing the process. Reforms in the voting system (proportional representation) have also allowed for broad political participation, and the inclusion of marginalised groups has been a focus.
3. **Judicial Reforms**: South Africa's judiciary has undergone significant reforms to ensure independence and accessibility. The Judicial Service Commission (JSC) was created to appoint judges transparently. Despite these efforts, there have been concerns about inefficiency, backlogs, and occasional political interference (Banerjee & Duflo, 2023).
4. **Anti-corruption Initiatives**: The Public Protector institution was established to investigate state misconduct and safeguard accountability. However, corruption has remained a challenge in the country, with

high-profile scandals involving state capture. The Zondo Commission (2018–2022) was set up to investigate state capture, leading to significant revelations about political and corporate corruption (Banerjee & Duflo, 2023).

5. **Land and Economic Reforms**: South Africa's land reform programme has been a contentious issue. The government has pushed for land redistribution to address historical injustices, but the pace has been slow, and debates around land expropriation without compensation have stirred political tension (Banerjee & Duflo, 2023).
6. **Public Service and Decentralisation**: Reforms in public administration have focused on improving efficiency and responsiveness in service delivery. The Public Service Commission (PSC) oversees civil service performance, while efforts have been made to decentralise some functions to improve service delivery at the local level (Banerjee & Duflo, 2023).

It is important to note that each of these countries has undergone various institutional reforms with differing levels of success.

- The DRC is still grappling with post-conflict governance and corruption but has made significant strides in certain areas, like electoral reforms and decentralisation (Taylor, 2017).
- Botswana is known for its stable democracy and low corruption rates, with continuous reforms that focus on good governance and transparency (Taylor, 2017)
- South Africa, despite its progress in transitioning to democracy, faces ongoing challenges such as corruption, land reform, and institutional inefficiency, which require continued reforms for sustainable development and social justice (Taylor, 2017).

How Institutional Reforms Impact Development and the Power Theory of Economic Growth

Taylor (2017) explains that institutional reforms play a crucial role in shaping the development trajectory of a country. These reforms can directly or indirectly affect the overall economic performance, social stability, and governance. When analysed through the lens of the Power

Theory of economic growth, we can understand the impact of these reforms on development. Below are the key impacts as a result of institutional reforms on development.

Impact of Institutional Reforms on Development

As indicated by Green and White (2017), reforms typically aim to address systemic inefficiencies, reduce corruption, enhance governance, and promote equitable growth.

These reforms can lead to:

1. **Improved Governance and Rule of Law**: Effective institutional reforms, such as judicial independence, anti-corruption measures, and transparent electoral processes, strengthen the rule of law. This, in turn, reduces transaction costs, encourages investment, and promotes economic stability—key factors that contribute to development. Countries like Botswana benefit from strong institutions that foster a stable investment environment.
2. **Decentralisation and Local Development**: Reforms in governance structures, particularly devolution, promote local-level governance, which can improve resource allocation and enhance service delivery. This is evident in countries like Kenya and South Africa, where devolution allows regions and municipalities to directly address their unique challenges, thus fostering regional development.
3. **Economic Diversification and Sustainable Growth**: Institutional reforms that focus on economic diversification (like in Botswana) can create the conditions for sustained development. By moving beyond reliance on one sector (e.g., mining or agriculture), a country can reduce its vulnerability to external shocks and stimulate long-term growth through sectors like manufacturing and services.
4. **Human Capital Development**: Education and health reforms are vital for improving human capital, which is necessary for sustainable development. The establishment of transparent educational systems and healthcare reforms, such as in South Africa and the DRC, can improve access to quality services, boost productivity, and create a more skilled labour force that contributes to economic growth.
5. **Encouragement of Foreign and Domestic Investment**: Institutional reforms related to the business environment, such as improving prop-

erty rights, reducing corruption, and simplifying regulatory frameworks, can stimulate both domestic and foreign investment. These reforms provide investors with greater certainty, reducing the risks associated with doing business in the country. In Botswana, strong institutions have created an environment conducive to business and attracted foreign investments in the diamond sector.

Power Theory of Economic Growth and Institutional Reforms

According to Brown (2015), the Power Theory of Economic Growth, in its broadest sense, focuses on the idea that economic growth is a function of the effective control, management, and allocation of power and resources within a society. Power, in this context, refers to the ability of governments, businesses, and individuals to influence economic outcomes, make decisions, and shape economic processes. The theory recognises the critical role of institutions in determining how power is exercised, distributed, and used.

However, as highlighted by Davis (2020) and Smith (2018), we demonstrate how institutional reforms impact the theory as explained below.

Power Distribution and Economic Growth

- **Inclusive Institutions**: Institutional reforms that focus on inclusivity—such as equitable land distribution (South Africa) or decentralisation (the DRC, Kenya)—can empower marginalised groups, giving them a stake in the economy. This redistribution of power can lead to more productive investments and a more engaged workforce, driving long-term economic growth.
- **Exclusive Institutions**: On the other hand, institutions that concentrate power (like corrupt or authoritarian regimes) often limit economic opportunities for large sections of society. This limits human capital development and undermines growth. The DRC, for example, has struggled with power being concentrated in the hands of a few elite, which has led to underdevelopment in many regions.

Economic Policy, Incentives, and Institutional Reform

Based on the argument by Jones and Lee (2016), institutional reforms shape the way economic policies are created, enforced, and incentivised. In countries with strong institutions, policymakers are more likely to design policies that promote sustainable growth (e.g., investment in infrastructure, education, and healthcare). This contrasts with countries where institutional weaknesses or corruption may lead to short-term, rent-seeking behaviour, which harms long-term growth. For example:

- **Botswana's Economic Policy**: The establishment of good governance mechanisms has encouraged the government to create pro-growth policies, diversifying the economy away from diamond dependence. This has been instrumental in its high and sustainable growth.
- **South Africa's Economic Policy Challenges**: Although South Africa had a smooth transition to democracy, the concentrated power in certain sectors (e.g., mining) has hindered significant redistribution and economic equity, slowing the inclusive growth that the Power Theory highlights as necessary for long-term development.

Political Power and Economic Control

Beghin and Kherallah's (1994) study demonstrates that the concentration or dispersion of political power plays a significant role in shaping economic outcomes:

- **Power and Economic Control in South Africa**: The country's post-apartheid reforms aimed at dismantling the economic control of the few. However, the slow pace of land reform and the rise of state capture (where the political elite manipulate the state for personal gain) have prevented power from being fully decentralised, limiting economic opportunities for the majority.
- **Botswana's Political Stability**: In contrast, Botswana's relatively high levels of political stability and inclusive governance have enabled it to achieve steady economic growth, as the power of decision-making is not monopolised by any one group or interest.

Corruption, Rent-Seeking, and Power Imbalance

Davis (2020) explains that corruption and rent-seeking behaviour are significant obstacles to development, often stemming from the abuse of power. Countries with weak institutions (e.g., the DRC) are prone to these issues, which can reduce economic growth by the following ways:

- Diverting resources away from productive uses (e.g., public services, infrastructure).
- Creating an environment of uncertainty that deters investment.
- Perpetuating power imbalances that limit economic opportunities for large sections of society.

Institutional reforms that combat corruption, such as in Botswana with the DCEC, are essential for reducing the negative impact of power imbalances on economic growth. These reforms enhance confidence in the political and economic systems, fostering better growth conditions (Banerjee & Duflo, 2023).

Institutional Power and Human Capital

The World Bank (2019) highlights that the allocation of power within institutions directly impacts the development of human capital. Institutions that empower individuals through better education, healthcare, and political participation tend to foster a productive workforce:

- **South Africa** has invested in education reforms and social services, but institutional weaknesses in the management of these sectors and corruption have slowed human capital development.
- **Botswana** has emphasised education and healthcare as foundational pillars for human capital development, leveraging strong institutions to empower its citizens.

In conclusion, we argue that institutional reforms directly influence the distribution and exercise of power, which in turn affects economic growth. In countries like Botswana, strong, inclusive institutions have fostered economic stability and sustainable growth, as power is distributed equitably, allowing for broad-based participation in the economy. In contrast, countries with weak or exclusive institutions (like the DRC) face challenges of corruption, rent-seeking, and political instability, all of which undermine growth prospects.

Further, it can also be argued that the Power Theory of economic growth suggests that the effectiveness of economic systems is shaped by how power is managed and distributed. Institutional reforms that focus on decentralising power, strengthening governance, and improving transparency contribute to more equitable and sustainable economic growth. Without such reforms, the power structure often remains skewed, resulting in unequal development and stunted economic progress.

International Organisations and Development Assistance

Escobar (1995), IMF (2020), Moyo (2009), OECD (2019), and the United Nations Development Programme (UNDP) (2021) highlight that international organisations and development assistance play a pivotal role in shaping global economic development. These organisations, such as the World Bank, the IMF, the UNDP, and regional development bodies, provide financial aid, policy advice, technical expertise, and humanitarian assistance to developing countries (Moyo, 2009). Their influence on development agendas is significant, as they often set the parameters within which national policies are formulated.

Influence of International Organisations on the Development Agenda

(a) **Financial Support and Economic Stabilisation**: International organisations provide crucial financial resources to countries that lack sufficient capital for development. For example, the World Bank offers loans and grants for large-scale infrastructure projects (e.g., roads, schools, hospitals), as well as poverty alleviation programmes. Similarly, the IMF assists in stabilising countries' economies by offering short-term loans to countries facing financial crises, conditioned on implementing economic reforms (Jones, 2015).

(b) **Policy Guidance and Technical Assistance**: Development agencies like the UNDP and IMF offer technical advice to governments on how to implement policies that stimulate growth, improve governance, and reduce poverty. Their influence extends to shaping policies on education, healthcare, and economic liberalisation (Jones, 2015).

(c) **Promoting Sustainable Development Goals (SDGs):** The UN plays a crucial role in promoting global initiatives like the SDGs. The SDGs are a set of goals that focus on eradicating poverty, achieving gender equality, and protecting the planet. International organisations help countries align their national agendas with global development priorities (Jones, 2015).
(d) **Capacity Building and Governance Reform**: Through institutions like the World Bank and African Development Bank (AfDB), international organisations also focus on governance reforms. This includes building institutional capacity, improving transparency, and reducing corruption—elements that are critical to achieving sustained economic development (Jones, 2015).

Examples of Successes Influenced by International Organisations

(a) **Botswana**: Botswana is often cited as a success story in Africa due to its stable democratic governance and prudent economic management. The country has benefited from World Bank support, particularly in the areas of infrastructure and education. The International Development Association (IDA), a part of the World Bank, assisted Botswana in implementing policies that promoted good governance and economic diversification, thereby reducing its dependence on diamond exports (Jones, 2015).
(b) **South Korea**: In the 1960s, South Korea was one of the poorest countries in the world. The World Bank and other organisations provided technical support and capital for South Korea's industrialisation. Through development assistance, policy reforms, and institutional support, South Korea transitioned into a high-income, technologically advanced economy (Amsden, 2001). International organisations played a critical role in fostering South Korea's development by supporting educational reforms, infrastructure development, and industrial policy (Amsden, 2001).
(c) **Chile**: Chile's economic growth has been partly attributed to the technical advice and support from international organisations like the World Bank and the IMF. From the 1980s, Chile adopted free-market reforms, with the backing of these institutions. By investing in human capital and infrastructure, Chile achieved stable growth and poverty reduction (Larrain, 2015).

Some Failures Have Been Demonstrated by the International Organisations' Influence

Despite their successes, the influence of international organisations in development has often been linked to challenges and failures in various countries.

(a) **Zambia**: Zambia's experience in the 1980s and 1990s illustrates the limitations of international organisations. The country faced a series of economic crises after receiving loans from the IMF and the World Bank. Structural adjustment programmes (SAPs) led to cuts in social services, including education and healthcare, which worsened poverty and inequality. Critics argue that the IMF's emphasis on market liberalisation led to underdevelopment and increased debt (Mkandawire, 2001).

(b) **Democratic Republic of Congo (DRC)**: Despite substantial aid from international organisations, the DRC remains one of the poorest and most unstable countries in the world. In the 1990s, the World Bank and the IMF encouraged liberal economic reforms, but due to poor governance and ongoing conflict, the economic benefits were not realised. The failure to establish peace and good governance severely undermined the impact of development assistance, leading to continued poverty and insecurity (Harrison, 2017).

(c) **Greece**: Greece's economic crisis in the 2010s is another example where international assistance, in the form of loans from the European Central Bank (ECB) and the IMF, failed to stabilise the economy. Austerity measures imposed by the IMF in exchange for bailout funds led to significant cuts in social spending, exacerbating unemployment and social unrest. This illustrates how IMF-led programmes, when not adapted to local contexts, can have detrimental effects on social welfare and economic growth (Stiglitz, 2016).

Impacts on Economic Development

- **Positive Impact**: In countries like Botswana, international assistance played a positive role in stimulating growth by providing capital for infrastructure projects and offering technical expertise in governance and policy formulation.

- **Negative Impact**: In countries like Zambia, economic growth was stunted due to inappropriate policy prescriptions, lack of alignment with local conditions, and excessive debt burdens, resulting in social unrest and economic instability.

New Perspectives on Dealing with Failures in Development

Banerjee and Duflo (2023) emphasised that to address the failures seen in some countries, several new perspectives could be considered, which will take into account the following:

(a) **Context-Specific Approaches**: International organisations should avoid one-size-fits-all approaches and tailor development assistance to the specific political, economic, and social conditions of the country. This would require more in-depth country assessments before implementing programmes.
(b) **Strengthening Local Institutions**: Rather than focusing purely on short-term fixes or economic reforms, international organisations should prioritise strengthening local governance structures. This includes enhancing transparency, accountability, and capacity-building in key government institutions.
(c) **Inclusive Development Models**: A greater emphasis should be placed on inclusive growth, which targets marginalised groups, ensures equitable access to services (e.g., healthcare, education), and creates sustainable economic opportunities. This approach will help mitigate the social inequalities that often accompany development programmes.
(d) **Sustainability and Long-Term Focus**: Development initiatives should be focused on long-term sustainability rather than short-term economic targets. Emphasis should be placed on environmental sustainability, social stability, and capacity building, ensuring that development projects do not leave a country more vulnerable to future crises.
(e) **Improved Monitoring and Accountability**: More robust systems of monitoring and evaluation should be established to ensure that aid is reaching its intended targets. Independent assessments of development programmes will help reduce waste, inefficiency, and corruption.

Banerjee and Duflo (2023) argue that international organisations and development assistance have undeniably played a pivotal role in shaping the development trajectories of many countries. Through financial support, policy advice, and technical expertise, institutions like the World Bank, the IMF, and the UNDP have provided vital resources for infrastructure projects, economic reforms, and capacity-building initiatives. Success stories such as Botswana and South Korea demonstrate the positive impact of international collaboration on long-term economic growth, poverty reduction, and institutional development.

However, the experiences of countries like Zambia and the DRC underscore the challenges and limitations of development assistance. When poorly designed or implemented, international aid and policy interventions can exacerbate existing vulnerabilities, increase inequality, and delay the achievement of sustainable development. These failures highlight the need for more context-specific, inclusive, and sustainable approaches to development.

Going forward, a more nuanced perspective on international development is necessary—one that prioritises local ownership, strengthens institutions, and focuses on long-term, inclusive growth. Tailoring aid to the specific needs of each country, emphasising governance reforms, and ensuring greater accountability in aid distribution are crucial steps towards achieving meaningful and sustainable economic development. By learning from past mistakes and embracing more adaptive, participatory models, international organisations can better support countries in their pursuit of equitable development.

References

Acemoglu, D., & Robinson, J. A. (2012). *Why nations fail: The origins of power, prosperity, and poverty*. Crown Business.

Akinola, A. O. (2020). Economic reforms in Africa: A critical appraisal. In *The Palgrave handbook of African political economy* (pp. 489–502). Palgrave Macmillan.

Amsden, A. H. (2001). *The rise of "the rest": Challenges to the west from late-industrializing economies*. Oxford University Press.

Bahl, R. W., & Linn, J. F. (1992). *Urban public finance in developing countries*. Oxford University Press.

Banerjee, A., & Duflo, E. (2023). *Good economics for hard times: Better answers to our biggest problems*. Penguin Random House.

Barrett, C. B. (2008). Smallholder market participation: Concepts and evidence from eastern and southern Africa. *Food Policy, 33*(4), 299–317. https://doi.org/10.1016/j.foodpol.2007.10.005

Beghin, J. C., & Kherallah, M. (1994). Political institutions and international patterns of agricultural protection. *The Review of Economics and Statistics, 76*, 482–489. https://doi.org/10.2307/2109973

Brown, M. (2015). Economic policies in developing countries. In P. Black (Ed.), *Global economics* (pp. 50–68). Routledge.

Busse, M., Borrmann, A., & Großmann, H. (2004). *The impact of EPAs on development in Africa*. Springer.

Chang, H., & Grabel, I. (2023). *Reclaiming development: An alternative economic policy manual*. Zed Books.

Crouch, C. (2020). *The globalization backlash: Issues in contemporary political economy*. Oxford University Press.

Dasgupta, P. (2020). *Governance reforms in emerging economies*. Oxford University Press.

Davis, P. (2020, May 3). Economic recovery plans for post-COVID-19 Africa. *The Financial Times* (p. 5).

Escobar, A. (1995). *Encountering development: The making and unmaking of the third world*. Princeton University Press.

Evans, P. (2023). State power and economic growth: Toward a developmental state model. *World Politics, 75*(3), 410–438.

Falch, T., & Fischer, J. A. V. (2008). *Public sector decentralization and school performance: International evidence*. Hamburg Contemporary Economic Discussions, No. 31, University of Hamburg.

Foucault, M. (1979). *Discipline and punish: The birth of the prison*. Vintage Books.

Frank, A. G. (1967). *Capitalism and underdevelopment in Latin America*. https://monthlyreview.org/product/capitalism_and_underdevelopment_in_latin_america/

Frank, A. G., & Galeano, E. (2022). *Dependency theory revisited: Economics and political power in the global system*. Cambridge University Press.

Green, T., & White, R. (2017). Public sector reforms in Africa. *International Journal of Public Policy, 15*(2), 112–130.

Hall, R. (2009). Land reform for what? Land use, production, and livelihoods in post-apartheid South Africa. *Land Use Policy, 26*(1), 89–95.

Harrison, G. (2017). Development and the international aid system: The case of the Democratic Republic of the Congo. *African Development Review, 29*(3), 428–441.

Harvey, D. (2021). *The enigma of capital and the crises of capitalism*. Oxford University Press.

Hickel, J., & Sullivan, D. (2023). Power, resources, and economic dependency in the Global South: The impact of resource extraction on inequality. *World Development, 158*, 102–117.

Holmberg, S., & Rothstein, B. (2022). *Good governance: The relevance of transparency in economic performance*. Oxford Academic—Governance Studies.

International Monetary Fund (IMF). (2020). *Annual Report 2020. A year like no other.* https://www.imf.org/external/pubs/ft/ar/2020/eng/

Jones, P. (2015). *Botswana: A case study in successful development.* Cambridge University Press.

Jones, A., & Lee, R. (2016). Policy reforms in emerging economies. In *Proceedings of the 10th international conference on economic development* (pp. 234–250). Wiley.

Larrain, F. (2015). Economic development and social policy in Chile. In A. J. Chen & P. H. Bingham (Eds.), *Global development in the 21st century* (pp. 60–68). Wiley.

Mazzucato, M., & Ryan-Collins, J. (2021). *Mission economy: A moonshot guide to changing capitalism.* Allen Lane.

Milanovic, B. (2022). *Global inequality: A new approach for the age of globalization.* Harvard University Press.

Mkandawire, T. (2001). The African State in a changing global context. *Journal of African Economies, 10*(2), 211–243. https://doi.org/10.15170/AT.2020.14.6.7

Mkandawire, T., & Soludo, C. C. (1999). *Our continent, our future: African perspectives* on structural adjustment. CODESRIA, Africa World Press, IDRC.

Moyo, D. (2009). *Dead Aid: Why aid is not working and how there is a better way for Africa.* Farrar, Straus and Giroux.

North, D. C. (1990). *Institutions, institutional change and economic performance.* Cambridge University Press.

Organisation for Economic Co-operation and Development (OECD). (2019). *Aid effectiveness 2019.* OECD.

Piketty, T. (2020). *Capital and ideology.* Harvard University Press.

Przeworski, A. (2023). *Crises of democracy and power in the global economy.* Cambridge University Press.

Rodrik, D. (2020). *Straight talk on trade: Ideas for a sane world economy.* Princeton University Press.

Sachs, J. (2022). Resource dependencies and global inequality: A development agenda. *Journal of Development Economics, 148*, 201–219.

Schuurman, F. J. (2009). Critical development theory: Moving out of the twilight zone. *Third World Quarterly—Journal of Emerging Areas, 30*(5), 831–848. https://doi.org/10.1080/01436590902959024

Smith, J. (2018). *Understanding economics* (3rd ed.). McGraw-Hill.

Spielberg, S. (1993). *Schindler's list.* [Film] Universal Pictures.

Stiglitz, J. E. (2016). *The Euro: How a common currency threatens the future of Europe.* W. W. Norton & Company.

Stiglitz, J. E., & Greenwald, B. (2022). *The great divide: Unequal societies and what we can do about them.* W. W. Norton & Company.

Taylor, H. (2017). *Impact of institutional reforms on economic development*. PhD thesis, University of Nairobi.

United Nations Development Programme (UNDP). (2021). *Human Development Report 2021*. https://hdr.undp.org/content/human-development-report-2021-22

Watts, M. (2004). Resource curse? Governmentality, oil and power in the Niger Delta. *Nigeria. Geopolitics, 9*(1), 50–80. https://doi.org/10.1080/14650040412331307832

World Bank. (2019). *Global economic prospects*. World Bank.

CHAPTER 4

Fifth World of Economic Dimension for Development

Introduction

The categorisation of the world's dimensions in economic development has traditionally been based on GDP per capita, industrialisation levels, and financial indicators. However, these classifications fail to reflect the structural inequalities, financial dependencies, and institutional weaknesses that impact growth in developing nations (Brautigam, 2020). This chapter examines whether current world categorisations have failed to deliver economic development and proposes a new framework based on economic power, financial sovereignty, and technological capabilities.

Has the Current Categorisation or Economic Classification of the World Economic Dimension Failed to Deliver Development?

The classification of the world can be approached from several perspectives, depending on the context—economic, political, geographical, developmental, or sociocultural. Below are some of the most common classifications (Tables 4.1, 4.2, 4.3, 4.4, 4.5, and 4.6).

The UNDP (2020) and World Bank (2022) reports highlighted that the World classification helps policymakers, researchers, and international organisations make sense of complex global realities. These categories can shift over time due to economic growth, conflict, climate change, or

P. K. Kabeya, *Development and the Power Theory of Economics*,
https://doi.org/10.1007/978-3-032-07926-8_4

Table 4.1 Economic classification (by World Bank/IMF)

Category	*Description*	*Examples*
High-income countries	Countries with Gross National Income (GNI) per capita above $13,845 (2024 threshold)	USA, Germany, Japan, Australia
Upper-middle-income	GNI per capita between $4466 and $13,845	China, Brazil, South Africa
Lower-middle-income	GNI per capita between $1136 and $4465	India, Nigeria, Kenya
Low-income countries	GNI per capita of $1135 or less	Afghanistan, DRC, Mozambique

Source: World Bank (2022)

Table 4.2 Development classification (Global North vs. Global South)

Group	*Characteristics*	*Examples*
Global North	Developed, industrialised, technologically advanced economies	USA, Canada, EU, Japan, Australia
Global South	Developing or emerging economies with lower HDI and income levels	Most of Africa, Latin America, parts of Asia

Source: World Bank (2022)

Table 4.3 Geopolitical classification

Group	*Purpose/context*	*Examples*
Western Bloc	Historically NATO-aligned capitalist states	USA, UK, France, Germany
Eastern Bloc	Former Soviet Union allies	Russia, Belarus, parts of Central Asia
Non-Aligned Movement (NAM)	States not formally aligned with major power blocs	India, Egypt, Indonesia, South Africa

Source: World Bank (2022)

institutional transformation. It's important to note that no single classification is absolute—each serves a different analytical purpose depending on the question being asked.

The above-mentioned categorisation of the world into various dimensions has been a dominant framework for assessing economic and social progress. However, this classification has faced criticism for failing to deliver meaningful development outcomes. Critics argue that such rigid

Table 4.4 United Nations Regional Groups

Group	*Purpose*	*Regions/countries*
Africa Group	Representation in UN bodies	All African states
Asia-Pacific Group	Broad Asian representation, incl. Pacific Islands	China, India, Indonesia, Fiji
Eastern Europe Group	Former Soviet-aligned European countries	Russia, Ukraine, Poland
Latin American and Caribbean Group (GRULAC)	Latin America and Caribbean states	Brazil, Argentina, Jamaica
Western Europe and Others Group (WEOG)	Includes Western Europe and developed allies	USA, Canada, Australia, UK, Germany

Source: World Bank (2022)

Table 4.5 Human Development Index (UNDP)

Category	*Description*	*Examples*
Very high HDI	Strong education, income, and life expectancy scores	Norway, Switzerland, Ireland
High HDI	Solid but lower scores than the top tier	China, Mexico, South Africa
Medium HDI	Moderate development with areas for improvement	Ghana, India, Vietnam
Low HDI	Weak in all three HDI dimensions	Niger, Chad, Central African Republic

Source: World Bank (2022); UNDP (2020)

Table 4.6 Regional integration groupings

Grouping	*Purpose*	*Examples*
European Union (EU)	Economic and political integration	France, Germany, Italy
ASEAN	Southeast Asian economic cooperation	Indonesia, Malaysia, Thailand
SADC	Southern African regional bloc	South Africa, Zimbabwe, Angola
ECOWAS	West African regional bloc	Nigeria, Ghana, Senegal
MERCOSUR	South American trade bloc	Brazil, Argentina, Paraguay

Source: World Bank (2022)

categorisation oversimplifies complex realities, reinforces economic dependency, and fails to account for emerging challenges such as climate change, inequality, and geopolitical shifts (Sachs, 2015).

One of the key limitations of this categorisation is its reliance on economic indicators such as Gross Domestic Product (GDP) per capita, which do not fully capture human development, sustainability, and quality of life (Sen, 1999). Moreover, the distinction between developing and developed countries has blurred in recent decades, with some emerging economies achieving significant economic growth while still grappling with inequality and governance issues (Rodrik, 2011).

The classification also perpetuates a dependency model, where developing nations remain reliant on aid and foreign investments from developed countries, rather than fostering self-sustaining economic growth (Escobar, 1995). This has led to a situation where international financial institutions and development agencies impose policies that may not align with local contexts, often exacerbating economic vulnerabilities (Stiglitz, 2002).

In light of these challenges, scholars have called for a more dynamic and inclusive framework that considers multidimensional factors such as governance, social cohesion, environmental sustainability, and technological innovation (Acemoglu & Robinson, 2012). The United Nations' Sustainable Development Goals (SDGs) attempt to provide a more comprehensive approach to development by focusing on inclusive and sustainable progress rather than arbitrary economic classifications (UNDP, 2020).

The traditional categorisation of the world has not effectively delivered development due to its oversimplification, reinforcement of dependency, and neglect of broader development indicators. A new paradigm that integrates social, economic, and environmental dimensions is essential for addressing global development challenges.

To support our argument for a new paradigm or world dimension, we first analyse various case studies to establish the conditions on which this new world dimension will be based.

Case Study 1: Sub-Saharan Africa (SSA): The Limits of Neoliberal Development

Issue

Structural Adjustment Programmes (SAPs) imposed by the IMF and World Bank in the 1980s–1990s aimed to liberalise African economies, but instead led to deindustrialisation, economic stagnation, and heavy debt burdens (Ayodele & Sotola, 2014).

- **Example: Zambia and Ghana**
  - Both countries adopted SAPs, privatised state enterprises, and liberalised trade.
  - Instead of fostering industrialisation, cheap imports flooded markets, leading to the collapse of local industries (Mkandawire, 2005).
  - Today, Zambia remains reliant on copper exports, while Ghana's economy is highly dependent on cocoa and gold.

- **Example: Nigeria's Oil Dependency**
  - Despite being Africa's largest economy, Nigeria remains highly dependent on crude oil exports and vulnerable to global oil price fluctuations (Akpan & Eboli, 2020).
  - The failure to diversify into manufacturing and digital industries has left Nigeria exposed to economic shocks.

Key Insight
SSA's classification as a low-income region fails to capture policy constraints, weak financial sovereignty, and the lasting impacts of colonial economic structures.

Case Study 2: East Asia: The Success of Developmental States

Issue
Unlike SSA, East Asian economies rejected neoliberal prescriptions and pursued state-led industrialisation (Wade, 1990).

- **Example: South Korea (1960s–1990s)**
  - South Korea's government-controlled credit protected domestic industries and invested in technology and education (Chang, 2019).
  - Companies like Samsung and Hyundai benefited from state subsidies and technology transfers, allowing Korea to become a global industrial power.

- **Example: China's Economic Rise**
  - China strategically opened up its economy, maintaining state control over key industries while benefiting from globalisation.
  - Unlike SSA, China developed local technological capabilities and negotiated trade agreements to benefit its own growth (Brautigam, 2020).

- **Example: Vietnam's Industrialisation Model**
  - Vietnam successfully moved from an agrarian economy to a manufacturing hub through state-led investments, export-driven policies, and strategic FDI incentives (Nguyen, 2021).
  - Today, Vietnam is a leading producer of electronics and textiles, competing with China and other industrialised nations (Nguyen, 2021).

Key Insight
Traditional development categories fail to explain why East Asia succeeded while SSA stagnated, highlighting the need for a new classification system based on policy autonomy and industrial strategy.

Case Study 3: Latin America: The Rise and Fall of Import Substitution Industrialisation (ISI)

Issue
Many Latin American countries attempted Import Substitution Industrialisation (ISI) in the mid-twentieth century, but later succumbed to debt crises and financial dependency on Western institutions (Cardoso & Faletto, 1979).

- **Example: Brazil's Industrialisation vs. Economic Crisis**
  - Brazil pursued ISI policies in the 1950s–1980s, building a strong domestic manufacturing sector (Baer, 2008).
  - However, heavy borrowing from international creditors led to a debt crisis in the 1980s, forcing Brazil into IMF structural adjustment policies.

- **Example: Argentina's Boom-and-Bust Cycles**
  - Argentina was once one of the world's wealthiest nations but fell into repeated economic crises due to external debt and financial mismanagement (Reinhart & Rogoff, 2009).
  - The country remains trapped in IMF loan agreements, limiting its financial sovereignty.

- **Example: Chile's Neoliberal Model Under Pinochet**
  - Chile's economy was transformed under Pinochet's neoliberal reforms, making it a Latin American success story.

- However, high inequality and social unrest have raised questions about whether Chile's model is truly sustainable (Solimano, 2012).

Key Insight
Latin America's economic struggles highlight the limitations of both state-led and neoliberal models, showing that financial autonomy is critical for sustainability.

The Role of Digital and Technological Sovereignty in Development

Case Study 4: The Digital Divide in Africa vs. Emerging Tech Leaders

Issue
The Fourth Industrial Revolution (4IR) is fundamentally reshaping global economies through rapid advancements in artificial intelligence (AI), automation, big data, blockchain, and the Internet of Things (IoT). While developed nations are leveraging these technologies to enhance productivity and innovation, many developing countries face structural challenges that hinder their integration into digital capitalism.

Why the 4IR Is Reshaping Global Economies

1. **Technological Advancements:** The integration of AI, robotics, and digital platforms is transforming industries, increasing efficiency, and lowering costs (Schwab, 2017).
2. **Economic Disruption and Job Market Transformation:** Automation is replacing routine jobs, shifting demand towards high-skilled labour in technology-intensive sectors (Brynjolfsson & McAfee, 2014).
3. **Digital Platforms and Global Markets**: E-commerce and digital trade platforms like Amazon, Alibaba, and fintech innovations are reshaping traditional business models and accelerating globalisation (WEF, 2020).
4. **Data as the New Capital:** Data-driven decision-making is now a key economic asset, leading to the rise of digital monopolies and reshaping competitive advantages (Manyika et al., 2017).

Challenges for Developing Countries

1. **Digital Infrastructure Deficiency:** Many developing nations lack the necessary broadband connectivity, electricity, and data centres to support digital economies (UNCTAD, 2021).
2. **Skill Gaps and Education Deficiencies:** A shortage of skilled labour in AI, cybersecurity, and programming limits their ability to compete in the global digital economy (OECD, 2019).
3. **Regulatory and Institutional Barriers:** Weak data protection laws, underdeveloped fintech regulations, and fragmented governance structures impede digital transformation (Monga & Lin, 2019).
4. **Economic Inequality and Digital Divide:** The cost of digital access remains high, exacerbating socioeconomic disparities and limiting digital participation (World Bank, 2022).

- **Example: Kenya's Digital Economy vs. Chad's Digital Exclusion**
  - Kenya has invested heavily in digital finance (M-Pesa), e-governance, and ICT hubs (Ndemo & Weiss, 2017).
  - Chad, on the other hand, has less than 10% internet penetration, making it difficult to participate in the global knowledge economy.

- **Example: India's Tech Boom**
  - India has become a leader in software services, AI, and fintech, due to government-backed IT policies and investment in STEM education (Dutta et al., 2019).

- **Example: Indonesia's Digital Start-Up Success**
  - Indonesia has seen rapid growth in e-commerce, fintech, and digital services, with platforms like Gojek and Tokopedia expanding regionally (Hill & Wie, 2012).

Key Insight

Classifying economies based on GDP or income does not capture their capacity to compete in the digital economy. A new classification should consider technological autonomy and digital infrastructure. The 4IR is driving unprecedented economic changes, but developing nations must overcome significant hurdles to integrate effectively into digital capitalism. Policies that enhance infrastructure, education, and regulatory frameworks are essential for fostering inclusive digital growth and bridging the global digital divide.

Financial Sovereignty and the Challenge of External Debt

Case Study 5: BRICS and Alternative Financial Institutions

Issue
Many developing countries remain financially dependent on Western-controlled financial institutions (IMF, World Bank), limiting their ability to pursue independent development strategies.

- **Example: The Rise of BRICS and the New Development Bank (NDB)**
  - In response to financial dependency, BRICS nations (Brazil, Russia, India, China, South Africa) established the NDB to provide funding without IMF conditionalities (Tooze, 2018).
  - Countries like Ethiopia and Bangladesh are exploring alternative financial partnerships to reduce reliance on Western institutions.

- **Example: The CFA Franc and West Africa's Economic Dependency**
  - Many West African nations remain tied to the CFA Franc, a currency controlled by France, limiting their monetary independence (Sylla, 2018).
  - Calls for a regional currency (ECO) reflect the desire for greater financial sovereignty.

Key Insight
The Global South's financial vulnerability is not captured in existing development categorisations. A new classification should consider monetary sovereignty and access to alternative finance.

Moving Towards a Proposed New Categorisation: Fifth World Economic Dimension

What Is the Necessity for the Proposed New Fifth World Economic Dimension?

The dynamic evolution of global socio-economic and environmental systems necessitates a re-examination of the traditional categorisations used in economic development theory. The conventional economic dimensions—centred primarily on production, consumption, trade, and distribution—are increasingly insufficient in explaining or responding to the complexities of modern development challenges (Manyika et al., 2017). These paradigms were developed during a period when economies were less interdependent, ecological concerns were marginal in policy discourse, and digital technologies had yet to disrupt economic structures (Monga & Lin, 2019). Today, however, issues such as climate change, global inequality, data sovereignty, and social discontent demand a more integrated and holistic conceptualisation of development—one that acknowledges and responds to interconnected systemic risks and opportunities.

The argument for a Fifth World Economic Dimension (FWED) stems from the growing inadequacy of models that prioritise quantitative growth at the expense of qualitative well-being. Mainstream economic metrics like GDP have long dominated the development narrative, yet they offer limited insight into ecological sustainability, social equity, or intergenerational justice (Nguyen, 2021). This reductionist approach has often led to policy decisions that ignore the depletion of natural capital, marginalise vulnerable populations, and widen socio-economic disparities (Nguyen, 2021). Thus, moving towards an FWED involves transcending these limitations by incorporating frameworks that foreground ecological integrity, human capability, and institutional resilience. This is not merely an academic refinement, but a strategic recalibration necessary for the formulation of development models that are both inclusive and sustainable.

Ecological economics forms a critical pillar of this new categorisation. Unlike classical models that treat the environment as an externality, ecological economics integrates nature as an essential and finite component of the economic system (Nguyen, 2021). Recognising planetary boundaries is crucial for ensuring that development does not exceed the Earth's regenerative capacities (Nguyen, 2021). In this view, natural capital—comprising ecosystems, biodiversity, and renewable resources—must be accounted for alongside financial and human capital (Nguyen, 2021). Furthermore, the concept of intergenerational equity—embedded in ecological economics—asserts the moral responsibility of the present generation to preserve ecological systems for future generations (Nguyen, 2021). This calls for a paradigm where development is redefined not in terms of expansion, but in terms of regeneration and resilience.

In parallel, the FWED must integrate considerations of well-being and social justice. The distribution of economic benefits and opportunities remains deeply uneven across and within countries, exacerbated by systemic power imbalances and historical legacies. A development model rooted in social equity challenges the prevailing emphasis on market efficiency and competitiveness, and instead promotes inclusivity, dignity, and empowerment. It highlights the need to consider multidimensional poverty, access to healthcare and education, and the protection of cultural and indigenous knowledge systems. In doing so, it aligns with Amartya Sen's capability approach, which reorients development from the expansion of income to the expansion of people's freedoms and choices (Nguyen, 2021).

Moreover, the emergence of digital and informal economies necessitates a broader understanding of value creation in contemporary economic systems (Nguyen, 2021). In many parts of the Global South, especially in SSA, informal economies account for a significant share of employment and livelihoods, yet they remain underrepresented in formal policy and planning frameworks (Brautigam, 2020). Similarly, the digital economy—characterised by data flows, platform labour, and virtual goods—has introduced new forms of economic organisation and labour that challenge traditional regulatory systems (Nguyen, 2021). The FWED, therefore, will acknowledge these shifts and build adaptive institutions capable of regulating and leveraging these sectors for inclusive development.

The adoption of an FWED also aligns with the principles and goals articulated in the United Nations Sustainable Development Goals (SDGs). The interconnected nature of the SDGs—particularly those focused on reducing inequality (SDG 10), ensuring sustainable consumption and production (SDG 12), and building strong institutions (SDG 16)—underscores the inadequacy of siloed approaches (Nguyen, 2021). An FWED acts as an integrative framework, facilitating the alignment of economic, social, environmental, and governance objectives. It promotes a system-level understanding of development, one that is reflexive, anticipatory, and capable of addressing complex global challenges through multi-stakeholder and cross-sectoral strategies.

In conclusion, moving towards a new categorisation of the FWED represents a vital intellectual and policy advancement. It redefines development through the lenses of sustainability, inclusivity, and complexity, responding to the limitations of the traditional economic narrative. This shift is not only relevant but urgent, given the converging crises of climate change, social inequality, and institutional fragility. As such, embracing the FWED offers a pathway towards a more just, resilient, and future-oriented model of economic development—one that serves the needs of both people and planet.

It is important to propose an FWED to contribute to the development and economic debate in line with the theory of economic power. Is there a chance to have an FWED in terms of development and economic growth? Can we add an FWED? Adding an FWED could be a way to provide more granularity in categorising countries. We are looking at some ideas for what the FWED could represent:

The concept of an FWED suggests an alternative development framework that goes beyond the existing classifications of First, Second, Third, and Fourth Worlds, potentially focusing on an entirely new economic and power structure designed to address the specific challenges of countries and beyond. This framework seeks to capture emerging dynamics in global economic structures, particularly in response to contemporary challenges such as sustainability, digital transformation, and inclusive growth.

A Breakdown of the Fifth World Economic Dimension

Benefits of a Fifth World Approach

- **Tailored Development Framework:** An FWED could propose a development model that addresses the unique socioeconomic, political, and environmental realities of SSA. This approach could empower countries to design their own paths for growth and development, rather than adhering to imported or imposed models from outside the continent.
- **Sovereignty and Self-Determination:** It could emphasise African sovereignty and self-determination in policymaking, reducing reliance on external aid or financial structures that often come with conditionalities (e.g., structural adjustments imposed by international financial institutions).

- **Inclusive Growth:** The FWED could emphasise inclusive economic growth, prioritising equity, access to resources, and the reduction of poverty while considering environmental sustainability and cultural preservation.
- **Economic and Development Justice:** It would offer an alternative to neoliberal or neocolonial models, seeking to balance economic growth with social development, reducing inequality between and within countries in the region.
- **Sustainability:** With a focus on environmental concerns, especially given SSA's vulnerability to climate change, an FWED could promote sustainable practices in agriculture, energy, water, and natural resource management, ensuring long-term prosperity.

Constraints of a Fifth World Economic Dimension Approach

- **Global Power Dynamics:** One of the primary constraints would be the existing global power structures, which are dominated by industrialised nations and multinational corporations (Manyika et al., 2017). A new world order would require significant shifts in global governance and international relations, which current powerholders may resist.
- **Economic Dependencies**: Many SSA countries are heavily reliant on exports of raw materials and foreign investments (Brautigam, 2020). Transitioning to a new economic model would require managing the dependencies created by existing global economic ties.
- **Internal Political Challenges:** In some SSA countries, issues like corruption, political instability, and weak governance could limit the success of a Fifth World approach. Building strong institutions would be key, but achieving this could be difficult in regions with entrenched political problems (Nguyen, 2021).
- **Technology and Infrastructure Gaps:** The lack of adequate technology, infrastructure, and educational systems could limit the ability to achieve full economic self-determination. Large-scale investments would be needed to modernise these areas (Nguyen, 2021).
- **Capital:** Access to financing and capital for large-scale development projects may remain a challenge. Alternatives to traditional financing mechanisms would be required to avoid dependency on international financial institutions (Brautigam, 2020).

Implications and Relevance of the FWED

- Challenge existing development models that focus solely on GDP or industrial capacity.
- Offers a framework to analyse countries or regions that do not fit neatly into existing categories.
- Provides policymakers with a more flexible approach to addressing economic disparities and future development pathways.

Power Models to Guide the FWED

- **People-Centred Power (Participatory Democracy):** A Fifth World model could be guided by a power structure that emphasises grassroots participation and bottom-up approaches (Nguyen, 2021). Empowering communities and local governments to drive development initiatives could ensure that decisions are made by those most affected (Nguyen, 2021).
- **Decentralised and Cooperative Power:** Power could be distributed more equally among different actors, including civil society, the private sector, and government institutions, with a focus on collaboration and collective problem-solving (Monga & Lin, 2019).
- **Pan-Africanism:** This model could draw from Pan-African principles, where African nations work together in solidarity, unifying under a common goal of economic justice, shared resources, and mutual aid. A Pan-African approach to power could reject the dominance of external powers and encourage intra-African trade and development cooperation (Nguyen, 2021).
- **Neo-Gramscian Power:** This model, based on Antonio Gramsci's ideas, views power as being driven by ideology and the creation of social consent (Ndemo & Weiss, 2017). The FWED could seek to establish a new hegemonic order in which African countries define their own rules, moving away from Western hegemony through ideological leadership.

Economic and Development Models for the FWED

- **Ubuntu Economics:** This model could be based on the African philosophy of Ubuntu, which emphasises community, cooperation, and mutual support (Manyika et al., 2017). Instead of focusing on individualistic and competitive capitalist models, the Fifth World could advocate for an economic system that prioritises collective well-being, equitable resource distribution, and social cohesion.

- **Human Development Approach:** Following the principles of Sen (1999), this model would prioritise human capabilities and welfare over economic growth alone. The goal would be to improve education, healthcare, and quality of life as core measures of development, with GDP being seen as secondary (Nguyen, 2021).
- **Post-Growth or Degrowth Models**: Given the environmental constraints facing SSA, a Fifth World might emphasise sustainable development, where economic growth is not the primary goal, but rather the well-being of people and ecosystems (Manyika et al., 2017). The focus would be on reducing inequality, improving resource efficiency, and promoting environmental resilience (Nguyen, 2021).
- **Structural Transformation and Diversification:** Many SSA economies are dependent on a few sectors, like raw materials or agriculture (Nguyen, 2021). A Fifth World would focus on economic diversification, shifting towards manufacturing, services, and knowledge-based industries to build resilience and create value-added products for both domestic and international markets.
- **Social and Solidarity Economy:** This model would focus on creating economies that are driven by social and environmental justice. Cooperatives, mutual organisations, fair trade businesses, and socially responsible enterprises would be central to this model, helping to distribute wealth more evenly and ensure development serves the broader community.

Balancing Economic and Development Justice

- **Redistributive Policies:** To balance economic growth with development justice, redistributive policies such as progressive taxation, land reform, and wealth redistribution may be necessary (Ndemo & Weiss, 2017). Governments could implement policies that prioritise investments in education, healthcare, and public services to promote social equity and sustain development outcomes.
- **Regional Integration:** A strong Fifth World model could be built on regional economic integration, such as through organisations like the African Continental Free Trade Area (AfCFTA). This could allow

for shared growth, improved trade, and more collective bargaining power in global markets (Brautigam, 2020).

- **Inclusive Growth Strategies:** Ensuring that all segments of the population, particularly marginalised groups (e.g., women, rural populations), benefit from economic growth would be key. Policies to promote entrepreneurship, access to credit, and inclusive education could help achieve this (Nguyen, 2021).

Graphical Presentation of the Fifth World

The idea of a Fifth World presents a bold, transformative vision for SSA, built on economic self-determination, inclusive development, and environmental sustainability. The model would draw on indigenous values, redistribute power, and challenge existing global inequalities. However, it would require overcoming significant constraints, including entrenched global power structures, economic dependencies, and internal political challenges. The success of such a model would depend on strong institutions, regional cooperation, and an embrace of innovative, equitable development strategies.

How do we graphically present the proposed FWED and examples of sub-Saharan countries which could fit within the proposed Fifth World dimension of economic development?

Creating a graphical presentation of the proposed Fifth World model involves visually representing its key components, relationships, and the characteristics that distinguish it from existing world classifications. We provide a detailed description of what such a graphic might include and offer examples of SSA countries that align with the proposed Fifth World dimension of economic and development justice.

Structure of the Graphic

(a) **Central Core: Fifth World Principles**

- Sovereignty and Self-Determination
- Inclusive Growth
- Economic and Development Justice
- Sustainability
- Community and Cooperation (Ubuntu Economics)

(b) **Surrounding Layers: Key Components**
- Power Model
- Participatory Democracy
- Decentralised and Cooperative Power
- Pan-Africanism
- Neo-Gramscian Power
- Economic and Development Models
- Human Development Approach
- Post-Growth/Degrowth Models
- Structural Transformation and Diversification
- Social and Solidarity Economy
- Balancing Mechanisms
- Redistributive Policies
- Regional Integration (e.g., AfCFTA)
- Inclusive Growth Strategies

(c) **Outer Layer: Supporting Factors and Constraints**
- Benefits
  - Tailored Development Framework
  - Empowerment and Self-Sufficiency
  - Environmental Sustainability
- Constraints
  - Global Power Dynamics
  - Economic Dependencies
  - Internal Political Challenges
  - Technology and Infrastructure Gaps
  - Access to Capital

(d) **Examples Section: Case Studies of sub-Saharan Countries**
- Highlight specific countries within the graphic, connected to relevant components illustrating how they embody the Fifth World principles.

Visual Elements

(a) Circular Diagram or Hub-and-Spoke Model:
- Central hub representing the Fifth World principles.
- Spokes extending to key components and supporting factors.

- Use icons or symbols to represent different elements (e.g., a community icon for Ubuntu Economics, a gear for Structural Transformation).

(b) Colour Coding:

- Different colours to distinguish between benefits, constraints, power models, and economic models.

(c) Country Highlights:

- Place icons or flags of specific sub-Saharan countries around the diagram, connected to the components they exemplify.

Proposed Fifth World Economic Dimension

Figure 4.1 depicts a graphical representation of the layout of the proposed FWED.

To expand on the graph titled "Central Hub: Fifth World Principles", we interpret this as a conceptual model or comparative framework showcasing how different countries (Country A, B, and C) relate to the idea of a Central Hub—likely symbolising a unifying or coordinating entity grounded in Fifth World principles. This model spans across four key analytical categories: Power Model, Economic Model, Balancing Mechanisms, and Benefits & Constraints, to illustrate inter-country variation and convergence based on Fifth World ideals such as sovereignty, self-determination, spiritual economy, ecological consciousness, and decentralised governance.

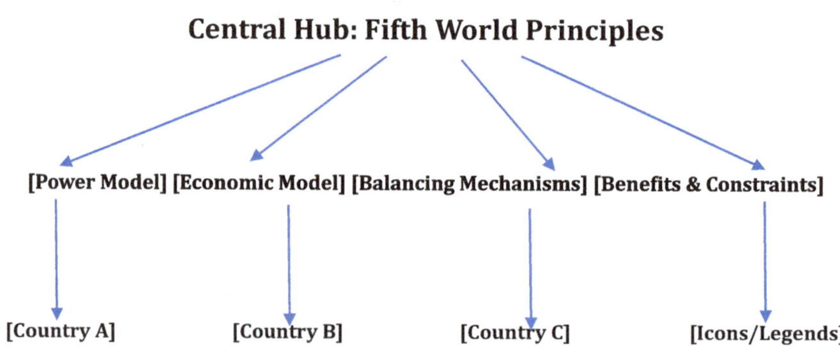

Fig. 4.1 Layout of the proposed FWED

Power Model

The Power Model reflects how authority and governance are structured and exercised within each country in relation to the central hub. Country A, for instance, may represent a decentralised power model that aligns with indigenous and community-led governance—a hallmark of Fifth World thinking. This could indicate a shift from traditional hierarchical power structures towards horizontal governance and network-based leadership. In contrast, Country B may still hold onto centralised, state-centric authority but is experimenting with power diffusion mechanisms, such as localised councils or participatory planning models. Country C, perhaps more sceptical or resistant, may represent a hybrid or transitional governance model—balancing conventional state power with incremental integration of Fifth World political ideals. The central hub, in this paradigm, does not exert hegemonic influence but rather coordinates and harmonises different forms of sovereignty, respecting cultural autonomy while promoting collective agency.

Economic Model

In the Economic Model, the analysis likely contrasts capitalist-market-driven economies with alternative models rooted in community-based economies, ecological sustainability, and spiritual values. Country A may embody a subsistence-plus economic model, relying on local production, circular economies, and spiritual wealth rather than material accumulation. This aligns closely with the Fifth World vision, where the economy serves life and not vice versa. Country B could represent a mixed economy—striving to integrate green technology and cooperative ownership structures into a still largely capitalist framework. Meanwhile, Country C may still be dependent on global financial systems and extractive industries, revealing the constraint of legacy economic systems. The central hub here acts as a mediator or catalyst, providing frameworks for trade justice, knowledge sharing, and alternative financial systems (e.g., community currencies, ethical banking) that promote resilience without coercion.

Balancing Mechanisms

This category highlights how countries manage tensions between global integration and local autonomy, tradition and modernity, or development and sustainability. Country A, closely aligned with Fifth World principles, may employ indigenous knowledge systems, consensus-building practices, and community arbitration as balancing tools. These internal mechanisms are deeply embedded in the social fabric and spiritual worldviews. Country B might employ more formal mechanisms like multi-stakeholder governance councils or hybrid legal systems that attempt to reconcile Western jurisprudence with customary law. Country C, possibly lacking adequate balancing tools, might exhibit volatility, social unrest, or over-reliance on external institutions (like the IMF or UN agencies) to mediate internal conflicts. The central hub offers soft power tools, such as intercultural dialogue platforms, ecological education, and cooperative monitoring systems that help countries develop their own equilibrium between tradition and innovation.

Benefits and Constraints

The Benefits and Constraints section analytically reveals how countries experience gains or face limitations under the Fifth World paradigm. Country A likely reaps benefits in the form of social cohesion, ecological resilience, food sovereignty, and spiritual fulfilment, but may face constraints such as limited scalability or resistance from dominant global institutions. Country B sees partial benefits—perhaps in reduced inequality or improved local governance—but struggles with the inertia of legacy institutions, political will, or elite capture. Country C, while potentially rich in resources or political clout, remains constrained by dependence on fossil fuels, global debt structures, or cultural fragmentation. The central hub's role is not to prescribe a one-size-fits-all model but to enable contextual transitions, reduce asymmetries, and uphold the shared ethical framework of the Fifth World: planetary interdependence, respect for life, and co-evolution.

Overall Analytical Interpretation

This comparative visualisation suggests a transition from Fourth World (indigenous struggles, marginalisation, decolonisation) to Fifth World consciousness, where autonomy, ecology, and spirituality are not sidelined but centred. The Central Hub, far from being a supranational authority, acts as a living nexus—a space of knowledge exchange, mutual recognition, and coordinated transformation. The graph likely indicates that countries are at different phases of transformation, with their institutional and cultural capacities shaping how deeply they can engage with the Fifth World agenda. The model proposes a pluralistic yet integrated future, one that transcends rigid modernist binaries and paves the way for polycentric governance and holistic development.

Examples of Sub-Saharan Countries Fitting the Fifth World Dimension

Several SSA countries are pioneering initiatives and policies that align with the Fifth World model's emphasis on economic and development justice, sustainability, and inclusive growth. Here are some notable examples:

(a) **Rwanda**
- **Economic Diversification and Innovation:**
  - Vision 2050: Rwanda's long-term development plan focuses on transforming the country into a middle-income nation through innovation, technology, and sustainable practices (Nguyen, 2021).
  - ICT and Technology Hub: Investment in information and communication technologies to drive economic growth and create jobs (Nguyen, 2021).
- **Governance and Stability:**
  - Strong governance structures aimed at reducing corruption and improving public services (Nguyen, 2021).
  - Emphasis on participatory democracy and community involvement in decision-making (Nguyen, 2021).

(b) **Ethiopia**
- **Sustainable Agriculture and Green Growth:**
  - Green Legacy Initiative: Large-scale tree planting and reforestation efforts to combat climate change and promote environmental sustainability (Ndemo & Weiss, 2017).
  - Focus on sustainable agriculture practices to ensure food security and support rural livelihoods (Ndemo & Weiss, 2017).
- **Infrastructure Development:**
  - Significant investments in infrastructure, including the Grand Ethiopian Renaissance Dam (GERD), to boost energy production and economic development (Ndemo & Weiss, 2017).

(c) **Botswana**
- **Good Governance and Economic Management:**
  - Transparent and effective management of natural resources, particularly diamonds, ensuring that revenues are used for national development (Nguyen, 2021).
  - Strong institutions that invest in education and healthcare to improve human development indicators (Nguyen, 2021).

    - Policies aimed at reducing inequality and promoting inclusive growth (Nguyen, 2021).
    - Promote political stability and economic growth (Nguyen, 2021).
  - **Social Development:**
    - Investments in education and healthcare to improve human development indicators (Nguyen, 2021).
    - Policies aimed at reducing inequality and promoting inclusive growth (Nguyen, 2021).

(d) **Ghana**
  - **Renewable Energy and Sustainability:**
    - Investments in renewable energy sources, such as solar and wind, to diversify the energy mix and promote sustainability (Nguyen, 2021).
    - Initiatives to improve access to clean energy for rural communities (Nguyen, 2021).
  - **Entrepreneurship and Innovation:**
    - Support for startups and small businesses through incubators and access to finance, fostering a vibrant entrepreneurial ecosystem (Nguyen, 2021).

(e) **Senegal**
  - **Regional Integration and Trade:**
    - Active participation in the AfCFTA, promoting intra-African trade and economic cooperation (Ndemo & Weiss, 2017).
    - Development of regional infrastructure projects to enhance connectivity and economic integration (Ndemo & Weiss, 2017).
  - **Inclusive Social Policies:**
    - Programmes aimed at empowering women and marginalised communities, ensuring that economic growth benefits all segments of society (Ndemo & Weiss, 2017).

(f) **Kenya**
  - **Technology and Innovation:**
    - Nairobi is a tech hub, often referred to as "Silicon Savannah", fostering innovation and attracting tech investments (Brautigam, 2020).
    - Mobile money platforms like M-Pesa that enhance financial inclusion and support economic activities (Brautigam, 2020).

- **Sustainable Urban Development:**
  - Efforts to develop sustainable cities with green infrastructure and improved public transportation systems (Brautigam, 2020).

Integrating Examples into the Fifth World Graphic

In a graphical presentation, one can place these countries around the central Fifth World principles hub, connecting each to the specific components they exemplify. For instance:

- Rwanda connected to Governance and Stability and Economic Diversification.
- Ethiopia linked to Sustainable Agriculture and Infrastructure Development.
- Botswana associated with Good Governance and Social Development.
- Ghana tied to Renewable Energy and Entrepreneurship.
- Senegal linked to Regional Integration and Inclusive Social Policies.
- Kenya connected to Technology and Innovation and Sustainable Urban Development.

Additional Considerations

- **Dynamic and Interactive Elements:** If creating a digital graphic, consider making it interactive, allowing users to click on each country to learn more about their specific initiatives and how they align with the Fifth World model.
- **Data Visualisation:** Incorporate charts or graphs within the graphic to show progress indicators, such as GDP growth, Human Development Index (HDI), or sustainability metrics for each country.
- **Narrative Flow:** Ensure the graphic tells a coherent story about how the FWED model operates, the role of each component, and how specific countries are implementing these principles in practice.

A graphical presentation of the Fifth World model would effectively illustrate the interconnectedness of its principles, components, and real-world applications in SSA countries. By highlighting specific examples like Rwanda, Ethiopia, Botswana, Ghana, Senegal, and Kenya, the graphic can demonstrate how these nations embody the Fifth World's vision of economic and development justice, sustainability, and inclusive growth. This visual tool would not only clarify the concept but also inspire other countries in the region to adopt similar strategies for balanced and equitable development.

Adding such a category could help highlight the unique challenges and opportunities faced by these countries, allowing for more tailored development strategies and international support.

Are There Countries Which Could Fit Within the Fifth World Economic Dimension?

Below are some examples of potential countries that could fit within each of the proposed FWED.

Transitional Economies

1. **Vietnam:** Experiencing rapid economic growth and development, moving from a developing to an emerging economy (Brautigam, 2020).
2. **Bangladesh**: Significant improvements in economic indicators and human development, transitioning towards an emerging market status (Brautigam, 2020).

High-Potential Economies

1. **Ethiopia:** Large population and natural resources, with potential for significant economic growth if infrastructural and political challenges are addressed (Brautigam, 2020).
2. **Mozambique:** Rich in natural resources like natural gas and minerals, with potential for growth if stability and infrastructure improve (Brautigam, 2020).

Environmentally Vulnerable Countries

1. **Maldives:** Facing existential threats from rising sea levels, despite having a relatively high per capita income (Nguyen, 2021).
2. **Tuvalu:** Another small island nation severely threatened by climate change (Nguyen, 2021).

Post-Conflict or Fragile States

1. **South Sudan:** Rich in oil resources but struggling with political instability and post-conflict rebuilding (Nguyen, 2021).
2. **Somalia:** Facing significant challenges in governance and stability, despite potential in sectors like agriculture and fishing (Nguyen, 2021).

Digital Economies

1. **Rwanda:** Known for its rapid adoption of digital technologies and innovation in governance and services, despite being a low-income country (Brautigam, 2020).
2. **Estonia:** Though not typically classified as a developing country, its digital integration is a model for leapfrogging traditional development stages (Brautigam, 2020).

These examples illustrate the diversity of countries that could be included in an FWED, highlighting specific characteristics that set them apart from traditional classifications.

Why Develop the Economic Model for the FWED?

The imperative to develop a new economic model for the FWED arises from the inadequacy of traditional economic frameworks in addressing the complexity and interconnectedness of contemporary global challenges. Existing economic models are largely rooted in industrial-era assumptions that prioritise growth, efficiency, and market competition. While these models have facilitated considerable material progress, they have simultaneously contributed to widening inequality, environmental degradation, and the erosion of social cohesion. As the world enters a new epoch characterised by ecological limits, technological disruption, and growing demands for equity and sustainability, there is a pressing need to reconceptualise the foundations of economic thinking. The FWED offers a pathway to reconciling development with sustainability, equity with resilience, and growth with regeneration.

Developing a model for this dimension means moving beyond metrics such as GDP, which capture economic activity but fail to account for social well-being, ecological health, or long-term viability. In this context, the economic model must integrate ecological economics, which treats the economy as a subsystem of the environment, not the other way around. This shift would allow for the valuation of natural capital, recognition of planetary boundaries, and promotion of circular economy principles. Such a model also challenges the linear "take-make-dispose" production paradigm and replaces it with a regenerative system designed to restore and renew ecological systems. Thus, the FWED emphasises economic sustainability not merely as a goal, but as a structural principle embedded in the way economies are organised and measured.

Furthermore, an FWED model must incorporate social justice and inclusive well-being as central tenets of development. Economic systems that disregard inequality and social exclusion ultimately undermine their own stability and legitimacy. Therefore, the new model must prioritise equitable distribution of resources, opportunities, and capabilities. It must address issues such as informal employment, gender disparities, and marginalised communities, not as peripheral concerns, but as core determinants of economic resilience and productivity. This demands a reorientation from efficiency-based outcomes to people-centred economics that expand freedoms, dignity, and participation in economic life. The model aligns closely with the capabilities approach, positioning human potential and empowerment at the centre of economic policy (Nguyen, 2021).

A third justification for developing this new model lies in the rise of the digital and knowledge economies, which are transforming traditional notions of labour, production, and value (Nguyen, 2021). The model must recognise and accommodate new forms of value creation driven by data, platforms, and intangible assets. This includes redefining productivity, modernising tax and regulatory systems, and creating safeguards for digital labour and data privacy. It also means incorporating informal and community-based economies, particularly in developing regions, into national accounts and development strategies. These systems, though often overlooked, are critical to resilience and survival in many parts of the world and thus deserve formal recognition within economic planning frameworks.

Moreover, the FWED should serve as an integrative framework that aligns with global commitments such as the Sustainable Development Goals (SDGs). The model must be capable of balancing competing imperatives—economic development, environmental sustainability, and social inclusion—through systems thinking and policy coherence. It must also support innovation in governance, financing, and institutional design that enables long-term, multi-scalar solutions. Crucially, it should provide governments, businesses, and civil society with tools to navigate the complexity of twenty-first-century development without defaulting to outdated or fragmented responses. In doing so, the model offers not only a diagnostic tool but also a strategic vision for inclusive and sustainable prosperity.

The development of an economic model for the FWED is not merely an academic exercise, but a necessity for responding to the structural transformations reshaping our world. It embodies a proactive shift towards a multidimensional, justice-centred, and future-proof framework for development. We believe that by embracing this model, societies can begin to realign economic activity with the fundamental goals of human flourishing and planetary stewardship, ensuring that development is not only sustainable in theory but also equitable and viable in practice.

Developing a tailored development model for the proposed FWED requires addressing the unique challenges and opportunities of countries. Let us look at strategies for each category within the FWED.

Strategies for Each Category Within the FWED

Transitional Economies

Model Focus: Balanced Growth and Structural Reforms

1. Economic Diversification: Reduce dependency on a few sectors by promoting a broad range of industries.
2. Institutional Strengthening: Enhance governance, transparency, and anti-corruption measures.
3. Education and Skills Development: Invest in education systems and vocational training to match market needs.

High-Potential Economies

Model Focus: Infrastructure and Investment

1. Infrastructure Development: Build and improve transportation, energy, and communication infrastructure.
2. Attracting Foreign Investment: Create favourable conditions for FDI through policy reforms and incentives.
3. Resource Management: Implement sustainable practices for managing natural resources to prevent exploitation and ensure long-term benefits.

Environmentally Vulnerable Countries

Model Focus: Climate Resilience and Adaptation

1. Climate Adaptation Strategies: Develop and implement policies to mitigate and adapt to climate impacts, such as coastal protection and disaster management systems.
2. Sustainable Development: Promote green technologies and renewable energy sources.
3. International Support: Leverage international aid and partnerships focused on climate resilience.

Post-Conflict or Fragile States

Model Focus: Stability and Reconstruction

1. Peacebuilding and Security: Establish and maintain peace and security through comprehensive peace agreements and community engagement.
2. Reconstruction and Infrastructure: Prioritise rebuilding critical infrastructure and services, such as healthcare, education, and housing.
3. Inclusive Governance: Foster inclusive political processes that involve all stakeholders to ensure stable and representative governance.

Digital Economies

Model Focus: Innovation and Leapfrogging

1. Digital Infrastructure: Invest in digital infrastructure, such as high-speed internet and mobile networks.
2. E-Governance and Services: Implement e-governance solutions to improve public service delivery and transparency.
3. Tech Entrepreneurship: Support tech startups and innovation hubs to drive economic growth through digital solutions.

General Recommendations for All Categories

1. Capacity Building: Strengthen the capabilities of institutions and individuals through training, education, and knowledge transfer.
2. Inclusive Growth: Ensure that development benefits all segments of society, particularly marginalised and vulnerable groups.
3. Monitoring and Evaluation: Implement robust monitoring and evaluation frameworks to track progress and adjust strategies as needed.

Focusing on these tailored strategies, countries within the FWED can address their specific challenges while capitalising on their unique development opportunities.

How Do These Models Differ from the Existing Development and Economic Growth Models?

The proposed models for the FWED of development offer a more nuanced approach compared to existing development and economic growth models.

The differences are listed below.

Transitional Economies

Existing Models

- Focus on GDP Growth: Traditional models emphasise rapid GDP growth, often through industrialisation and urbanisation (Nguyen, 2021).
- Structural Adjustments: Policies often include austerity measures and market liberalisation (Nguyen, 2021).

Proposed Model

- Balanced Growth: Emphasises diversified economic growth to avoid over-reliance on a single sector.
- Institutional Strengthening: Prioritises governance reforms, transparency, and anti-corruption measures.
- Education and Skills Development: Focuses on aligning education with market needs to ensure sustainable development.

High-Potential Economies

Existing Models

- FDI Attraction: Focus primarily on attracting FDI through liberal economic policies (Brautigam, 2020).
- Resource Exploitation: Often emphasises rapid exploitation of natural resources without long-term planning (Brautigam, 2020).

Proposed Model

- Infrastructure Development: Prioritises building robust infrastructure as a foundation for growth.
- Sustainable Resource Management: Promotes sustainable practices to ensure long-term benefits from natural resources.
- Balanced Investment: Combines foreign investment with domestic capacity building.

Environmentally Vulnerable Countries

Existing Models

- Reactive Measures: Typically reactive to environmental crises rather than proactive (Sachs, 2015).
- Short-term Aid: Reliance on short-term international aid without long-term solutions (Sachs, 2015).

Proposed Model

- Climate Resilience and Adaptation: Emphasises proactive strategies to mitigate and adapt to climate change.
- Sustainable Development: Focuses on green technologies and renewable energy.
- International Partnerships: Seeks long-term international support specifically targeted at climate resilience.

Post-Conflict or Fragile States

Existing Models

- Security-First Approach: Often focuses on immediate security and stabilisation (Manyika et al., 2017).
- Top-Down Reconstruction: Emphasises large-scale infrastructure projects without community involvement (Manyika et al., 2017).

Proposed Model

- Peacebuilding and Security: Incorporates comprehensive peacebuilding alongside security measures.
- Inclusive Reconstruction: Prioritises community engagement and inclusive governance in rebuilding efforts.
- Long-term Stability: Emphasises sustainable, long-term solutions over short-term fixes.

Digital Economies

Existing Models

- Traditional Industrialisation: Emphasis on physical infrastructure and industrial sectors (Nguyen, 2021).
- Linear Development: Follows a linear path of development from agriculture to industry to services (Nguyen, 2021).

Proposed Model

- Leapfrogging: Utilises digital technology to bypass traditional stages of development.
- Digital Infrastructure: Prioritises high-speed internet and mobile connectivity.
- Tech Innovation: Encourages tech entrepreneurship and innovation as primary growth drivers.

General Distinctions

1. **Context-Specific Approaches:** The proposed models are highly tailored to the unique contexts and challenges of each group, unlike existing models, which can be more generalised.
2. **Inclusive Development:** Greater emphasis on inclusivity, ensuring benefits reach marginalised and vulnerable populations.
3. **Sustainability:** Strong focus on sustainability, whether in terms of environmental practices, resource management, or institutional development.
4. **Adaptability:** Designed to be adaptable and responsive to changing circumstances, with robust monitoring and evaluation mechanisms to guide adjustments.

Based on the above, we have attempted to provide a table that shows a comparative focus outlining how the FWED models differ from existing development and economic growth models, including highlights of distinctive features, focus areas, and implications for development (Table 4.7).

Table 4.7 FWED models vs. existing development paradigms

Country type	*Existing models*	*FWED proposed models*	*Key differences/ developmental impacts*
Transitional economies	– GDP-focused growth via industrialisation and urbanisation (Nguyen, 2021) – Structural Adjustment & liberalisation (IMF/ World Bank-driven)	– Balanced growth across sectors – Institutional strengthening, anti-corruption – Education aligned with labour market needs	FWED shifts away from austerity and one-size-fits-all reforms, focusing on resilience, human capital, and institutional integrity
High-potential economies	– Emphasis on attracting FDI (Brautigam, 2020) – Extractive resource use for short-term gains	– Infrastructure-led growth – Sustainable natural resource management – Strategic mix of foreign and domestic investment	Prioritises long-term capacity over quick gains; enhances sovereignty and reduces foreign dependency
Environmentally vulnerable	– Reactive to climate disasters (Sachs, 2015) – Short-term aid dependence	– Climate resilience and proactive adaptation – Green energy and technology focus – Strategic international partnerships for climate action	Moves from crisis response to proactive sustainability; integrates environment into core development strategy
Post-conflict/ fragile states	– Security-first, top-down approach (Manyika et al., 2017) – Emphasis on large-scale reconstruction without participation	– Peacebuilding and local security initiatives – Inclusive governance and community engagement – Long-term stability through local ownership	Enhances local legitimacy, avoids elite capture, builds sustainable peace, and inclusive national identity

(*continued*)

Table 4.7 (continued)

Country type	*Existing models*	*FWED proposed models*	*Key differences/ developmental impacts*
Digital economies	– Traditional industrialisation pathways (Nguyen, 2021) – Linear progression: agriculture → industry → services	– Leapfrogging via digital tech – Investment in digital infrastructure (broadband/mobile) – Tech innovation ecosystems and startups	Enables acceleration of development, bypassing outdated models; empowers youth and new sectors
General differences	– Generalised, rigid frameworks – Often top-down and externally imposed – Short-term success metrics (GDP)	– Context-specific solutions – Focus on inclusion and marginalised groups – Emphasis on sustainability and long-term adaptability	FWED promotes holistic, endogenous development aligned with local needs, governance maturity, and ecological consciousness

Key Analytical Insights

1. **Flexibility and Contextualisation**: Unlike traditional models that impose uniform policy prescriptions (e.g., Washington Consensus), FWED proposes tailored interventions that reflect local realities—be it climate, conflict, resource endowments, or digital readiness.
2. **Sustainability as a Core Driver**: FWED integrates environmental sustainability and intergenerational equity directly into development strategies—challenging the extractive and often short-sighted logic of traditional economic growth models.
3. **Social Inclusion**: There is a marked shift towards inclusive governance, local participation, and equitable development, targeting often underserved segments such as youth, women, rural communities, and indigenous populations.
4. **Transformation vs. Transition**: FWED promotes transformational development (redefining systems, values, and power structures), unlike transitional models that mainly modernise existing frameworks.

5. **Development as Process, not Output**: FWED understands development as a dynamic and adaptive process rather than fixed outcomes like GDP. This entails robust monitoring, learning, and iterative policy adaptation.

When addressing the specific needs and circumstances of different types of countries within the FWED, these models aim to provide more effective and sustainable development pathways.

Proposed Models to Achieve the Development of Models for the Fifth World Dimension

Creating a comprehensive development model for each category within the FWED involves identifying key variables and formulating equations that reflect the dynamics of development.

Below is an outline of the proposed models for each category, including essential variables and equations.

Transitional Economies

Key Variables

- GDP Growth Rate (GDPg)
- Economic Diversification Index (EDI)
- Governance Quality Index (GQI)
- Education Attainment (EA)
- Infrastructure Investment (II)

Equations

1. **GDP Growth Model:**

$$\text{GDPg} = \alpha + \beta 1 \cdot \text{EDI} + \beta 2 \cdot \text{GQI} + \beta 3 \cdot \text{EA} + \beta 4 \cdot \text{II} + \epsilon$$

where α\alpha$\alpha$ is the intercept, βi\beta are the coefficients, and ϵ\ epsilonϵ is the error term.

2. **Economic Diversification Model:**

$$EDI = \gamma + \delta 1 \cdot II + \delta 2 \cdot EA + \delta 3 \cdot GQI + \epsilon$$

where γ\gamma$\gamma$ is the intercept, δi\delta_$i\delta i$ are the coefficients, and ϵ\epsilon$\epsilon$ is the error term.

High-Potential Economies

Key Variables

- Infrastructure Development Index (IDI)
- Foreign Direct Investment (FDI)
- Resource Management Efficiency (RME)
- Political Stability Index (PSI)
- Human Capital Index (HCI)

Equations

1. **Economic Growth Model:**

$$GDPg = \alpha + \beta 1 \cdot IDI + \beta 2 \cdot FDI + \beta 3 \cdot RME + \beta 4 \cdot PSI + \beta 5 \cdot HCI + \epsilon$$

2. **Infrastructure Development Model:**

$$IDI = \gamma + \delta 1 \cdot FDI + \delta 2 \cdot PSI + \delta 3 \cdot HCI + \epsilon$$

Environmentally Vulnerable Countries

Key Variables

- Climate Resilience Index (CRI)
- Sustainable Development Index (SDI)
- International Aid (IA)
- Renewable Energy Adoption (REA)
- Disaster Preparedness (DP)

Equations

1. **Sustainable Growth Model:**

$$GDPg = \alpha + \beta 1 \cdot CRI + \beta 2 \cdot SDI + \beta 3 \cdot IA + \beta 4 \cdot REA + \beta 5 \cdot DP + \epsilon$$

2. **Climate Resilience Model:**

$$CRI = \gamma + \delta 1 \cdot IA + \delta 2 \cdot DP + \delta 3 \cdot REA + \epsilon$$

Post-Conflict or Fragile States

Key Variables

- Peacebuilding Index (PBI)
- Security Index (SI)
- Reconstruction Investment (RI)
- Inclusive Governance Index (IGI)
- Social Cohesion Index (SCI)

Equations

1. **Stability and Growth Model:**

$$GDPg = \alpha + \beta 1 \cdot PBI + \beta 2 \cdot SI + \beta 3 \cdot RI + \beta 4 \cdot IGI + \beta 5 \cdot SCI + \epsilon$$

2. **Peacebuilding Model:**

$$PBI = \gamma + \delta 1 \cdot SI + \delta 2 \cdot RI + \delta 3 \cdot IGI + \epsilon$$

Digital Economies

Key Variables

- Digital Infrastructure Index (DII)
- Innovation Index (II)

- Tech Startup Growth (TSG)
- E-Governance Index (EGI)
- Internet Penetration Rate (IPR)

Equations

1. **Digital Economy Growth Model:**

$$GDPg = \alpha + \beta 1 \cdot DII + \beta 2 \cdot II + \beta 3 \cdot TSG + \beta 4 \cdot EGI + \beta 5 \cdot IPR + \epsilon$$

2. **Innovation and Tech Growth Model:**

$$TSG = \gamma + \delta 1 \cdot DII + \delta 2 \cdot II + \delta 3 \cdot IPR + \epsilon$$

Implementation Steps

1. Data Collection: Gather data on the identified variables from reliable sources such as the World Bank, the UN, and national statistics agencies.
2. Model Estimation: Use statistical software (e.g., R, Stata) to estimate the coefficients (βi\beta_ and δi\delta) using regression analysis.
3. Policy Simulation: Simulate different policy scenarios to understand the potential impact of various interventions.
4. Monitoring and Evaluation: Develop robust frameworks to monitor progress and evaluate the effectiveness of implemented strategies.

These proposed models integrate key variables tailored to the specific needs and characteristics of each category within the FWED. By using these models, policymakers can develop targeted strategies that address the unique challenges and leverage the opportunities of their respective countries.

Application of Models and Impact for Development and Economic Growth for Selected Countries

To compute and apply these models, we need to follow systematic steps involving data collection, statistical analysis, and policy application.

Below is a detailed approach.

Transitional Economies

Model 1: GDP Growth Model

$$GDPg = \alpha + \beta 1 \cdot EDI + \beta 2 \cdot GQI + \beta 3 \cdot EA + \beta 4 \cdot II + \epsilon$$

Computation

1. Data Collection: Collect data on GDP growth rate (GDPg), Economic Diversification Index (EDI), Governance Quality Index (GQI), Education Attainment (EA), and Infrastructure Investment (II).
2. Regression Analysis: Use software like R or Stata to perform multiple regression analysis and estimate the coefficients (βi\beta).

Impact

- Balanced Growth: By understanding the impact of diversification, governance, education, and infrastructure on GDP growth, policies can be tailored to promote balanced and sustainable growth.

High-Potential Economies

Model 1: Economic Growth Model

$$GDPg = \alpha + \beta 1 \cdot IDI + \beta 2 \cdot FDI + \beta 3 \cdot RME + \beta 4 \cdot PSI + \beta 5 \cdot HCI + \epsilon$$

Computation

1. Data Collection: Gather data on GDP growth, Infrastructure Development Index (IDI), FDI, Resource Management Efficiency (RME), Political Stability Index (PSI), and Human Capital Index (HCI).

2. Regression Analysis: Perform multiple regression to estimate the coefficients.

Impact

- Infrastructure and Investment: Identifying key drivers of growth allows for focused investment in infrastructure and human capital, enhancing overall development.

Environmentally Vulnerable Countries

Model 1: Sustainable Growth Model

$$GDPg = \alpha + \beta 1 \cdot CRI + \beta 2 \cdot SDI + \beta 3 \cdot IA + \beta 4 \cdot REA + \beta 5 \cdot DP + \epsilon$$

Computation

1. Data Collection: Collect data on GDP growth, Climate Resilience Index (CRI), Sustainable Development Index (SDI), International Aid (IA), Renewable Energy Adoption (REA), and Disaster Preparedness (DP).
2. Regression Analysis: Use regression techniques to estimate the coefficients.

Impact

- Climate Resilience: Policies can focus on improving climate resilience and sustainable practices, leading to long-term, stable development.

Post-Conflict or Fragile States

Model 1: Stability and Growth Model

$$GDPg = \alpha + \beta 1 \cdot PBI + \beta 2 \cdot SI + \beta 3 \cdot RI + \beta 4 \cdot IGI + \beta 5 \cdot SCI + \epsilon$$

Computation

1. Data Collection: Gather data on GDP growth, Peacebuilding Index (PBI), Security Index (SI), Reconstruction Investment

(RI), Inclusive Governance Index (IGI), and Social Cohesion Index (SCI).
2. Regression Analysis: Conduct multiple regression analyses.

Impact

- Stability and Reconstruction: Insights from the model can help in designing effective peacebuilding and reconstruction strategies, leading to long-term stability and growth.

Digital Economies

Model 1: Digital Economy Growth Model

$$GDPg = \alpha + \beta 1 \cdot DII + \beta 2 \cdot II + \beta 3 \cdot TSG + \beta 4 \cdot EGI + \beta 5 \cdot IPR + \epsilon$$

Computation

1. Data Collection: Collect data on GDP growth, Digital Infrastructure Index (DII), Innovation Index (II), Tech Startup Growth (TSG), E-Governance Index (EGI), and Internet Penetration Rate (IPR).
2. Regression Analysis: Perform regression analysis to estimate the impact of each variable.

Impact

- Digital Transformation: Policymakers can prioritise digital infrastructure and innovation, leading to rapid and inclusive economic growth.

Application and Policy Implications

1. **Policy Design:** Use model insights to design targeted policies that address the specific needs of each country category.

   - Transitional Economies: Focus on diversifying the economy, improving governance, and aligning education with market needs.
   - High-Potential Economies: Invest in infrastructure and human capital while ensuring sustainable resource management.

- Environmentally Vulnerable Countries: Develop climate resilience and sustainable development strategies.
- Post-Conflict States: Implement peacebuilding and inclusive governance measures alongside reconstruction efforts.
- Digital Economies: Promote digital infrastructure and innovation to drive economic growth.

2. **Monitoring and Evaluation:** Establish robust monitoring and evaluation frameworks to track the progress of implemented policies and make necessary adjustments based on real-time data.
3. **International Cooperation:** Foster international partnerships and leverage global support for specific needs, such as climate resilience or post-conflict reconstruction.

When systematically applying these models and incorporating key variables, countries within the FWED can achieve targeted and sustainable development. The computation of these models provides a data-driven approach to policymaking, ensuring that interventions are effective and aligned with the unique challenges and opportunities of each country.

Hypothetical Scenarios

We have created hypothetical data for a few selected countries in each of the proposed categories. We will then use this data to compute the results based on the given models. For simplicity, we will focus on one model per category.

Transitional Economies: Vietnam

Model: GDP Growth Model

$$\text{GDPg} = \alpha + \beta 1 \cdot \text{EDI} + \beta 2 \cdot \text{GQI} + \beta 3 \cdot \text{EA} + \beta 4 \cdot \text{II} + \epsilon$$

Hypothetical Data

- EDI = 0.7
- GQI = 0.8
- EA = 0.85
- II = 0.9

- $\alpha = 0.5$
- $\beta1 = 0.3, \beta2 = 0.25, \beta3 = 0.4, \beta4 = 0.35$

Computation

$$GDPg = 0.5 + 0.3 \cdot 0.7 + 0.25 \cdot 0.8 + 0.4 \cdot 0.85 + 0.35 \cdot 0.9$$

$$GDPg = 0.5 + 0.21 + 0.2 + 0.34 + 0.315 = 1.565$$

High-Potential Economies: Mozambique

Model: Economic Growth Model

$$GDPg = \alpha + \beta1 \cdot IDI + \beta2 \cdot FDI + \beta3 \cdot RME + \beta4 \cdot PSI + \beta5 \cdot HCI + \epsilon$$

Hypothetical Data

- IDI = 0.6
- FDI = 0.5
- RME = 0.4
- PSI = 0.3
- HCI = 0.7
- $\alpha = 0.4$
- $\beta1 = 0.2, \beta2 = 0.25, \beta3 = 0.3, \beta4 = 0.35, \beta5 = 0.4$

Computation

$$GDPg = 0.4 + 0.2 \cdot 0.6 + 0.25 \cdot 0.5 + 0.3 \cdot 0.4 + 0.35 \cdot 0.3 + 0.4 \cdot 0.7$$

$$GDPg = 0.4 + 0.12 + 0.125 + 0.12 + 0.105 + 0.28 = 1.15$$

Environmentally Vulnerable Countries: Maldives

Model: Sustainable Growth Model

$$GDPg = \alpha + \beta1 \cdot CRI + \beta2 \cdot SDI + \beta3 \cdot IA + \beta4 \cdot REA + \beta5 \cdot DP + \epsilon$$

Hypothetical Data

- CRI = 0.65
- SDI = 0.7
- IA = 0.55
- REA = 0.75
- DP = 0.8
- $\alpha = 0.6$
- $\beta1 = 0.25, \beta2 = 0.3, \beta3 = 0.35, \beta4 = 0.2, \beta5 = 0.4$

Computation

$$\text{GDPg} = 0.6 + 0.25 \cdot 0.65 + 0.3 \cdot 0.7 + 0.35 \cdot 0.55 + 0.2 \cdot 0.75 + 0.4 \cdot 0.8$$

$$\text{GDPg} = 0.6 + 0.1625 + 0.21 + 0.1925 + 0.15 + 0.32 = 1.635$$

Post-Conflict or Fragile States: South Sudan

Model: Stability and Growth Model

$$\text{GDPg} = \alpha + \beta1 \cdot \text{PBI} + \beta2 \cdot \text{SI} + \beta3 \cdot \text{RI} + \beta4 \cdot \text{IGI} + \beta5 \cdot \text{SCI} + \epsilon$$

Hypothetical Data

- PBI = 0.5
- SI = 0.4
- RI = 0.6
- IGI = 0.45
- SCI = 0.55
- $\alpha = 0.3$
- $\beta1 = 0.2, \beta2 = 0.25, \beta3 = 0.3, \beta4 = 0.35, \beta5 = 0.4$

Computation

$$\text{GDPg} = 0.3 + 0.2 \cdot 0.5 + 0.25 \cdot 0.4 + 0.3 \cdot 0.6 + 0.35 \cdot 0.45 + 0.4 \cdot 0.55$$

$$\text{GDPg} = 0.3 + 0.1 + 0.1 + 0.18 + 0.1575 + 0.22 = 1.0575$$

Digital Economies: Rwanda

Model: Digital Economy Growth Model

$$GDPg = \alpha + \beta1 \cdot DII + \beta2 \cdot II + \beta3 \cdot TSG + \beta4 \cdot EGI + \beta5 \cdot IPR + \epsilon$$

Hypothetical Data

- DII = 0.7
- II = 0.75
- TSG = 0.65
- EGI = 0.8
- IPR = 0.85
- $\alpha = 0.5$
- $\beta1 = 0.3, \beta2 = 0.35, \beta3 = 0.25, \beta4 = 0.4, \beta5 = 0.45$

Computation

$$GDPg = 0.5 + 0.3 \cdot 0.7 + 0.35 \cdot 0.75 + 0.25 \cdot 0.65 + 0.4 \cdot 0.8 + 0.45 \cdot 0.85$$

$$GDPg = 0.5 + 0.21 + 0.2625 + 0.1625 + 0.32 + 0.3825 = 1.8375$$

Summary of Results

- **Vietnam** (Transitional Economies): GDPg = 1.565
- **Mozambique** (High-Potential Economies): GDPg = 1.15
- **Maldives** (Environmentally Vulnerable Countries): GDPg = 1.635
- **South Sudan** (Post-Conflict or Fragile States): GDPg = 1.0575
- **Rwanda** (Digital Economies): GDPg = 1.8375

Impact for Development and Economic Growth

1. **Vietnam:** High GDP growth driven by balanced economic policies, governance, education, and infrastructure.
2. **Mozambique:** Moderate growth with focus on infrastructure and human capital investment.
3. **Maldives:** Significant growth potential through climate resilience and sustainable development practices.

4. **South Sudan:** Lower growth, highlighting the need for enhanced peacebuilding and governance measures.
5. **Rwanda:** Strong growth potential by leveraging digital infrastructure and innovation.

These hypothetical computations demonstrate how different factors influence the economic growth of countries within each category of the FWED. Tailored policies can be designed based on these insights to address specific developmental challenges and opportunities.

Key ideas: How do we propose models for each, including variables and equations, to achieve development based on the mentioned models for the FWED.

To propose models for achieving development in the context of the FWED, we first need to define what the FWED represents. Given that the first four dimensions are typically classified as Developed World, Emerging World, Developing World, and Disturbed World, the FWED can be conceptualised as an Innovative World, Sustainable World, or Global Future Dimension. This dimension could focus on forward-looking aspects such as sustainability, innovation, and global integration.

Framework for Proposing Models for Each Dimension

The framework for proposing models for each dimension, including variables and equations, to achieve development based on this FWED is highlighted below.

Innovative World Dimension

Objective: Foster technological advancement, innovation, and knowledge-based economies.

Variables:

- **I**: Investment in Research and Development (R&D)
- **T**: Technological Innovation Index
- **E**: Education and Skills Development
- **G**: Government Support and Policy

Model: $D = \alpha I + \beta T + \gamma E + \delta G$
Where:

- D = Development Index (measuring economic growth, technological progress, etc.)
- $\alpha, \beta, \gamma, \delta$ = Weights indicating the impact of each variable.

Equations

1. **Innovation Output:** T = R&D + Historical Innovation Index
2. **Economic Growth:** GDP Growth = Base GDP × $(1 + \alpha I + \beta T + \gamma E + \delta G/100)$

Sustainable World Dimension

Objective: Promote environmental sustainability and resource efficiency.
Variables:

- **E:** Environmental Quality Index
- **R:** Resource Utilisation Efficiency
- **S:** Sustainability Policies and Initiatives
- **I**: Investment in Green Technologies

Model: $D = \theta E + \iota R + \kappa S + \lambda I$
Where:

- $\theta, \iota, \kappa, \lambda$ = Weights for each variable's impact on sustainability.

Equations

1. **Environmental Quality:** Pollution Reduction Total/Pollution
2. Resource Efficiency: R = Output/Input
3. **Sustainability Index:** S = Policy Effectiveness × Public Engagement

Global Future Dimension

Objective: Address global challenges through integrated solutions and global cooperation.

Variables:

- C: Climate Change Mitigation Efforts
- H: Health and Well-being Programmes
- I: International Cooperation Initiatives
- P: Policy Harmonisation and Integration

Model: $D = \mu C + \nu H + \xi I + \zeta P$
Where:

- μ, ν, ξ, ζ = Weights reflecting the impact of each factor on global development.

Equations

1. **Climate Impact**: C = Emission Reductions/Emissions
2. **Health Index**: H = Access to Healthcare/Healthcare Needs
3. **Cooperation Effectiveness**: I = Number of Successful Agreements/ Total Agreements
4. **Policy Integration:** P = Degree of Policy Alignment × Global Cooperation Index

Proposing Models for Development in Each Dimension

Define Development Objectives

- Clearly state what development means for each dimension (e.g., innovation, sustainability, global integration).

Identify Key Variables

- Select variables that directly impact the development objectives.

Develop Equations

- Create equations that relate the variables to development outcomes, incorporating weights to reflect their relative importance.

Collect Data

- Gather data on the identified variables to populate and test the model.

Analyse and Adjust

- Use the model to analyse development scenarios and adjust policies and strategies based on the results.

Implement and Monitor

- Implement the proposed strategies and continuously monitor their impact using the model.

By tailoring these models to specific dimensions, one can effectively address various aspects of development and progress.

To effectively compute development and economic aspects using the models outlined, we need to establish tables of values for the coefficients (e.g., α\alphaα, β\betaβ, δ\deltaδ, λ\lambdaλ,) that reflect their impact on development outcomes. These values can vary depending on the context, country, and specific development goals. Here is a general framework for how one might structure these tables (Tables 4.8, 4.9, 4.10, 4.11, and 4.12).

Table 4.8 Coefficients for the innovative world dimension

Coefficient	*Description*	*Example value*
α\alphaα	Weight of Investment in R&D	0.40
β\betaβ	Weight of Technological Innovation Index	0.35
γ\gammaγ	Weight of Education and Skills Development	0.15
δ\deltaδ	Weight of Government Support and Policy	0.10

Table 4.9 Coefficients for the sustainable world dimension

Coefficient	*Description*	*Example value*
θ\thetaθ	Weight of Environmental Quality Index	0.30
ι\iotaι	Weight of Resource Utilisation Efficiency	0.25
κ\kappaκ	Weight of Sustainability Policies and Initiatives	0.25
λ\lambdaλ	Weight of Investment in Green Technologies	0.20

Table 4.10 Coefficients for the global future dimension

Coefficient	*Description*	*Example value*
μ\muμ	Weight of Climate Change Mitigation Efforts	0.35
ν\nuν	Weight of Health and Well-being Programmes	0.30
ξ\xiξ	Weight of International Cooperation Initiatives	0.20
ζ\zetaζ	Weight of Policy Harmonisation and Integration	0.15

Table 4.11 Coefficients for economic growth models

Coefficient	*Description*	*Example value*
α\alphaα	Weight of Investment in Infrastructure	0.50
β\betaβ	Weight of Technological Advancements	0.25
γ\gammaγ	Weight of Labour Force Skills	0.15
δ\deltaδ	Weight of Government Economic Policies	0.10

Table 4.12 Coefficients for development models

Coefficient	*Description*	*Example value*
α\alphaα	Weight of Economic Investments	0.45
β\betaβ	Weight of Social Infrastructure Development	0.25
γ\gammaγ	Weight of Educational Improvements	0.20
δ\deltaδ	Weight of Policy Effectiveness	0.10

Notes on Coefficient Values

1. **Context-Dependent:** The actual values for these coefficients will vary based on the specific context, including the country or region, the current state of development, and the specific goals being pursued.
2. **Empirical Determination:** These values are often determined empirically through statistical analysis and modelling based on historical data and case studies. They can also be adjusted through expert judgement and policy analysis.
3. **Dynamic Adjustments:** Coefficients may need to be updated periodically to reflect changes in economic conditions, technological advancements, or shifts in policy priorities.
4. **Normalisation:** Ensure that the coefficients are normalised (i.e., they sum to 1 or are expressed as proportions) to provide a balanced view of their impact on the development outcome.

By using these tables, one can input the relevant data into one's models to compute development and economic aspects effectively. Adjustments to these values should be made based on ongoing analysis and feedback to ensure the models remain accurate and relevant.

Conclusion

The categorisation of the world based on outdated economic indicators fails to address the complexities of modern development. The proposal of an FWED offers a framework that integrates financial sovereignty, digital sovereignty, and regional integration as fundamental indicators of economic power.

Key Thoughts

- Existing world classifications reinforce economic dependencies and fail to reflect financial and technological sovereignty.
- An FWED is needed to assess economies based on power, institutional strength, and self-sufficiency.
- The role of digital transformation and alternative financial systems is critical for developing economies.

Thoughts

The application of these models highlights the importance of tailored approaches to economic development. Each category of the FWED faces distinct challenges that cannot be addressed by generic policies. By focusing on specific drivers of growth and development, countries can achieve more sustainable and inclusive progress. The use of hypothetical data in this analysis provides a foundational understanding of how these models can be implemented and adjusted in real-world scenarios.

Lessons Learned

- The limitations of SAPs and dependency models highlight the need for self-sustaining economic strategies.
- Investment in technological infrastructure and digital education is key for economic resilience.
- Regional integration and alternative financial institutions (e.g., BRICS) provide pathways for economic independence.

Areas for Future Research

- Examining how digital economies can drive sustainable development in low-income countries.
- Investigating the effectiveness of alternative financial systems in reducing economic dependency.
- Analysing the impact of regional integration efforts such as the AfCFTA on economic autonomy.

References

Acemoglu, D., & Robinson, J. A. (2012). *Why nations fail: The origins of power, prosperity, and poverty*. Crown Publishers.

Akpan, U. F., & Eboli, E. (2020). Oil price shocks and Nigeria's economic growth: The role of financial development. *African Journal of Economic Policy, 27*(2), 134–150.

Ayodele, T., & Sotola, O. (2014). *Privatisation in Africa: The case of Nigeria*. Africa Research Institute.

Baer, W. (2008). *The Brazilian economy: Growth and development* (6th ed.). Lynne Rienner Publishers.

Brautigam, D. (2020). *The Dragon's gift: The real story of China in Africa*. Oxford University Press.

Brynjolfsson, E., & McAfee, A. (2014). *The second machine age: Work, progress, and prosperity in a time of brilliant technologies*. W. W. Norton & Company.

Cardoso, F. H., & Faletto, E. (1979). *Dependency and development in Latin America*. University of California Press.

Chang, H. (2019). *Kicking away the ladder: Development strategy in historical perspective*. Anthem Press.

Dutta, S., Lanvin, B., & Wunsch-Vincent, S. (Eds.). (2019). *The global innovation index 2019: Creating healthy lives—The future of medical innovation*. World Intellectual Property Organisation. https://www.wipo.int/edocs/pubdocs/en/wipo_pub_gii_2019.pdf

Escobar, A. (1995). *Encountering development: The making and unmaking of the third world*. Princeton University Press.

Hill, H., & Wie, T. K. (2012). *Indonesia's industrial transformation: Challenges and opportunities*. ISEAS Publishers.

Manyika, J., Chui, M., Bughin, J., Dobbs, R., Bisson, P., & Marrs, A. (2017). *Big data: The next Frontier for innovation, competition, and productivity*. McKinsey Global Institute.

Mkandawire, T. (2005). *Targeting and universalism in poverty reduction*. Social Policy and Development Programme Paper Number 23. United Nations Research Institute for Social Development (UNRISD).

Monga, C., & Lin, J. Y. (2019). *The Oxford handbook of structural transformation.* Oxford University Press. https://academic.oup.com/edited-volume/28090
Ndemo, B., & Weiss, T. (2017). *Digital Kenya: An entrepreneurial revolution in the making.* Palgrave Macmillan.
Nguyen, T. T. (2021). Vietnam's industrial policy and the global value chain: A comparative perspective with East Asia. *Journal of Asian Economics, 72,* 101236.
Organisation for Economic Co-operation and Development (OECD). (2019). *Skills for a digital world.* OECD Publishing.
Reinhart, C. M., & Rogoff, K. S. (2009). *This time is different: Eight centuries of financial folly.* Princeton University Press. https://doi.org/10.2307/j.ctvcm4gqx
Rodrik, D. (2011). *The globalization paradox: Democracy and the future of the world economy.* W. W. Norton. https://tinyurl.com/kqj4ta3
Sachs, J. (2015). *The age of sustainable development.* Columbia University Press.
Schwab, K. (2017). *The fourth industrial revolution.* Crown Publishing Group.
Sen, A. (1999). *Development as freedom.* Oxford University Press.
Solimano, A. (2012). *Chile and the neoliberal trap: The post-Pinochet era.* Cambridge University Press.
Stiglitz, J. E. (2002). *Globalization and its discontents.* W. W. Norton.
Sylla, N. S. (2018). *The CFA Franc: French monetary imperialism in Africa.* Pluto Press.
Tooze, A. (2018). *Crashed: How a decade of financial crises changed the world.* Viking.
United Nations Conference on Trade and Development (UNCTAD). (2021). *Technology and innovation report: Catching technological waves.* UNCTAD.
United Nations Development Programme (UNDP). (2020). *Human development report 2020: The next Frontier—Human development and the anthropocene.* UNDP.
Wade, R. (1990). *Governing the market: Economic theory and the role of government in East Asian industrialisation.* Princeton University Press.
World Bank. (2022). *World development report 2022: Digital dividends.* World Bank.
World Economic Forum (WEF). (2020). *The future of jobs report 2020.* WEF.

CHAPTER 5

Frameworks of Influence: Power Theory and Architecture of Growth

Introduction

Overview of Conceptual Frameworks in Development and Economic Growth

The study of development and economic growth has been underpinned by various conceptual frameworks that seek to explain how economies expand, develop, and sustain progress over time (Babb, 2013). These frameworks offer theoretical lenses for understanding the interactions between key economic agents, institutions, and structural dynamics that shape development trajectories. Historically, economic growth theories have evolved from classical economic thought, emphasising factors such as capital accumulation, technological progress, and market efficiency, to more contemporary approaches that integrate institutional, social, and political dimensions (Todaro & Smith, 2020).

Among the most influential frameworks are classical and neoclassical theories, which highlight market-driven growth mechanisms, and structuralist perspectives that emphasise the role of historical and institutional factors in shaping economic performance (Rodrik, 2018). Furthermore, endogenous growth models, as pioneered by Romer (1990), have emphasised the importance of knowledge spillovers, innovation, and human capital in promoting long-term economic growth. On the other hand, dependency and world-systems theories argue that global economic

P. K. Kabeya, *Development and the Power Theory of Economics*,
https://doi.org/10.1007/978-3-032-07926-8_5

structures perpetuate inequalities, often limiting the developmental prospects of less industrialised nations (Wallerstein, 2004).

Institutional economics, as advanced by North (1990), underscores the role of governance structures, legal frameworks, and property rights in economic development. This perspective has gained prominence in policy discussions, particularly in developing economies where weak institutions have been linked to persistent underdevelopment (Acemoglu & Robinson, 2012). The various conceptual models of development and economic growth collectively highlight the complexity of economic transformation, with each offering distinct insights into the drivers and barriers to progress (Artaxo, 2019).

Justification for Applying the Power Theory of Economics

While mainstream economic theories provide valuable explanations for economic growth and development, they often overlook the role of power dynamics in shaping economic outcomes. The power theory of economics addresses this gap by emphasising the influence of political, institutional, and economic power structures on decision-making processes, resource allocation, and economic governance (Kalecki, 1971). This theory argues that power imbalances, whether among nations, corporations, or social groups, profoundly impact economic policies, wealth distribution, and overall development outcomes.

One of the key aspects of the power theory of economics is its ability to explain the persistence of economic inequalities both within and between nations. Traditional economic theories assume rational decision-making and competitive markets, yet in practice, power asymmetries often distort these ideal conditions (Babb, 2013). For instance, global financial institutions and multinational corporations exert considerable influence over economic policies in developing countries, often shaping policies to serve their interests rather than those of the local population (Stiglitz, 2002). Similarly, the political elite within developing economies may leverage their control over economic resources to maintain power, leading to rent-seeking behaviours and inefficient resource allocation (Acemoglu & Robinson, 2012).

Moreover, the power theory of economics provides a critical lens through which to examine the role of governance, corruption, and institutional weaknesses in development. Countries with highly concentrated economic power often experience slower or distorted economic growth due to barriers to competition, policy capture, and exclusionary economic practices (Piketty, 2014). When integrating power dynamics into economic analysis, this framework enables a more comprehensive understanding of why some economies succeed while others remain trapped in cycles of underdevelopment.

The justification for applying the power theory of economics in this chapter stems from its ability to bridge the gaps left by conventional economic theories. By acknowledging the role of power structures, this approach offers more nuanced insights into economic growth patterns, policy formulation, and developmental strategies. Given the evidence that power asymmetries significantly influence economic outcomes, this framework serves as a vital tool for both academic research and policymaking in the context of development economics.

Theoretical Foundations of Development and Economic Growth

The Theoretical Foundations of Development and Economic Growth section is crucial because it provides a structured understanding of how economies evolve, sets the stage for applying the Power Theory of Economics, and offers insights into the real-world implications of economic policies. This background will make it easier to assess the strengths and weaknesses of different economic strategies in later sections of the chapter.

Classical and Neoclassical Perspectives

Strengths

- Emphasises the role of market mechanisms, capital accumulation, and technological progress in economic growth (Barro, 1999).
- Provides a strong analytical foundation for understanding long-term growth trends (Barro, 1999).
- The neoclassical model (Solow, 1956) introduces technological progress as a key determinant of sustainable growth.

Weaknesses

- Assumes perfectly competitive markets and rational behaviour, which often do not reflect real-world conditions (Barro, 1999).

- Neglects the role of power dynamics, institutional constraints, and historical inequalities in development processes (Barro, 1999).

Structuralist and Dependency Theories

Strengths

- Highlights the structural barriers to development faced by less industrialised economies (Agaya & Asunza, 2013).
- CRecognises the impact of historical inequalities and global economic dependencies on underdevelopment (Wallerstein, 2004).
- Provides a critique of free-market policies that may not be suitable for all economies (Wallerstein, 2004).

Weaknesses

- Often underestimates the potential for internal economic reform and adaptation (Larrain, 1989).
- Can lead to overly deterministic conclusions about the inability of developing countries to achieve self-sustained growth (Larrain, 1989).

Endogenous Growth Models

Strengths

- Incorporates human capital, innovation, and knowledge spillovers as key drivers of growth (Lucas, 1988; Romer, 1990).
- Allows for policy interventions to enhance long-term growth through education and R&D investments (Lucas, 1988).

Weaknesses

- Requires significant empirical validation to support theoretical predictions (Lucas, 1988).
- Does not fully address issues related to income distribution and power imbalances (Lucas, 1988).

Institutional Economics and Governance

Strengths

- Recognises the importance of institutions, governance structures, and legal frameworks in shaping economic outcomes (Acemoglu & Robinson, 2012; North, 1990).
- Offers practical policy recommendations for strengthening institutional capacity and reducing corruption (Acemoglu & Robinson, 2012).

Weaknesses

- Institutions alone may not be sufficient to drive growth without broader economic and social reforms (Agaya & Asunza, 2013).
- Institutional change is often slow and subject to political resistance from entrenched power structures (Agaya & Asunza, 2013).

The theoretical foundations of development and economic growth provide essential insights into the mechanisms driving economic transformation. When we critically examine these frameworks, this chapter establishes a basis for integrating the power theory of economics, which offers a deeper understanding of how power dynamics influence economic policies and outcomes.

Power Theory of Economics: Conceptual Underpinnings

Defining Power in Economic Relations

Power in economic relations refers to the ability of individuals, groups, or institutions to influence economic decisions, policymaking, and resource distribution (Barnett & Duvall, 2005). Economic power can manifest through control over capital, market dominance, policy influence, or access to key resources (Kalecki, 1971).

Mechanisms Through Which Power Influences Economic Outcomes

Power structures shape economic outcomes through various mechanisms, including the following:

- **Market Power:** Large corporations influence pricing, wages, and competition (Stiglitz, 2002).
- **Political Power:** Governments and the elite set policies favouring specific economic interests (Acemoglu & Robinson, 2012).
- **Institutional Power:** Control over regulatory bodies affects economic governance (North, 1990).

The Role of Political and Economic Institutions

Political and economic institutions mediate the distribution of power within an economy. Inclusive institutions promote broad-based growth, while extractive institutions concentrate wealth and inhibit development (Acemoglu & Robinson, 2012). Governance structures, legal frameworks, and enforcement mechanisms play critical roles in shaping economic trajectories (Acemoglu & Robinson, 2012).

Application of Power Theory in Development and Economic Growth

Power asymmetries in global trade and finance refer to the unequal distribution of economic and political influence among countries and institutions, shaping the terms of trade, access to capital, and policy autonomy (Acemoglu & Robinson, 2012). Developed economies and multinational corporations often exert disproportionate control over global financial markets, trade agreements, and regulatory frameworks, which can lead to both efficiency gains and developmental constraints (Stiglitz, 2002).

Efficiency in Development

- **Capital and Investment Flows:** Global financial integration allows for capital allocation to developing economies, fostering industrial growth and infrastructure development (Rodrik, 2018).
- **Technological Transfer and Innovation:** Trade liberalisation facilitates access to advanced technologies, enhancing productivity and economic diversification (Chang, 2019).
- **Economic Stability Through Institutions:** Institutions like the International Monetary Fund (IMF) and the World Bank provide financial support and policy guidance to stabilise economies (Wade, 2003).

Limitations in Development

- **Unequal Bargaining Power:** Developing countries often face unfavourable trade agreements, limiting their ability to protect local industries (Gallagher, 2005).
- **Debt Dependency and Conditionalities:** Structural adjustment programmes impose strict economic policies that may not align with domestic development priorities (Babb, 2013).
- **Financial Volatility and Speculation:** Emerging economies are vulnerable to capital flight and exchange rate instability, exacerbating economic crises (Eichengreen, 2008).

While global trade and finance contribute to development by facilitating investment and market integration, the asymmetrical nature of these systems often reinforces existing inequalities, limiting the autonomy and long-term growth potential of developing nations. Addressing these imbalances requires policy reforms, stronger regional economic blocs, and fairer financial governance mechanisms (Ocampo, 2017)

Disproportionate Influence of Developed Nations in Global Trade Negotiations: Implications for Developing Countries

Global trade and financial negotiations are dominated by developed nations, particularly through institutions such as the World Trade Organization (WTO) and the IMF (Stiglitz, 2002). These institutions, while promoting international economic cooperation, often reflect the interests of wealthier economies, creating structural disadvantages for developing countries (Stiglitz, 2002). The disproportionate influence of developed nations in shaping trade agreements and financial policies has significant implications for economic sovereignty, development policy space, and long-term growth prospects in the Global South.

WTO Policies and Trade Imbalances

The WTO, established to facilitate free and fair trade, has been criticised for policies that disproportionately benefit developed nations. Developed countries exert influence over trade negotiations by leveraging their economic power and extensive legal expertise, ensuring that trade rules favour their industries (Wade, 2003).

- **Agricultural Subsidies and Market Distortions:** Developed countries, particularly the United States and the European Union, provide substantial subsidies to their agricultural sectors, allowing their farmers to sell products at artificially low prices. This practice undermines the competitiveness of agricultural producers in developing countries, leading to market displacement and reduced income opportunities for smallholder farmers (Chang, 2019).
- **Intellectual Property Rights and Technology Transfer:** The Agreement on Trade-Related Aspects of Intellectual Property Rights (TRIPS) enforces strict patent protections that limit the ability of developing countries to access affordable medicines, agricultural technologies, and innovations essential for industrial growth (Gallagher, 2005).
- **Limited Policy Space for Industrial Development:** Many WTO agreements restrict the use of protective tariffs and industrial policies that historically played a crucial role in the development of now-advanced economies. Developing nations are pressured to liberalise their markets prematurely, exposing local industries to foreign competition without adequate support mechanisms (Rodrik, 2018).

IMF Conditionalities and Debt Dependency

The IMF provides financial assistance to countries facing economic crises, but its loans come with stringent conditions that often undermine national economic policies (Babb, 2013).

- **Structural Adjustment Programmes (SAPs):** During the 1980s and 1990s, the IMF and the World Bank imposed SAPs that required developing countries to implement austerity measures, privatisation, and trade liberalisation as conditions for receiving loans. These

policies led to reduced public spending on health, education, and infrastructure, deepening poverty and inequality (Stiglitz, 2002).
- **Macroeconomic Policy Constraints:** IMF loan conditions often mandate restrictive monetary and fiscal policies, such as high-interest rates and budgetary constraints, limiting governments' ability to invest in long-term development projects (Eichengreen, 2008).
- **Debt Traps and Financial Vulnerability:** Many developing nations remain trapped in cycles of debt dependency due to IMF-imposed policies that prioritise debt repayment over developmental priorities. This dependence restricts their economic autonomy and exposes them to external shocks (Ocampo, 2017).

Implications for Developing Countries

The disproportionate influence of developed nations in global trade and financial governance has significant implications for developing economies:

- **Loss of Economic Sovereignty:** Trade agreements and financial policies often limit the ability of developing nations to craft independent economic strategies suited to their unique developmental needs (Wade, 2003).
- **Structural Inequalities in Global Markets:** Developing countries face persistent trade deficits, commodity price volatility, and barriers to market access due to imbalanced trade rules and financial dependencies (Gallagher, 2005).
- **Challenges to Sustainable Development Goals (SDGs):** The focus on short-term financial stabilisation over long-term development priorities hinders efforts to achieve the United Nations' SDGs, particularly in poverty reduction, food security, and industrialisation (Rodrik, 2018).

While global trade and financial institutions play a vital role in economic integration, the disproportionate influence of developed nations perpetuates structural imbalances that limit the growth potential of developing countries. Reforming WTO policies to ensure fairer trade practices and revising IMF conditionalities to support developmental objectives are critical steps towards creating a more equitable global economic system. Strengthening regional economic blocs and advocating for greater representation of developing countries in global governance institutions can help counteract these asymmetries (Ocampo, 2017).

Unequal Access to Financial Resources and Credit Markets for Developing Countries: Case Studies and Implications for Development

Access to financial resources and credit markets is a crucial factor in economic growth and development. However, developing countries face significant barriers to obtaining international finance, including high borrowing costs, limited access to private capital, and structural biases within global financial institutions. These disparities reinforce economic inequalities and constrain the ability of low-income nations to invest in critical sectors such as infrastructure, healthcare, and education (Stiglitz, 2002).

Barriers to Financial Access in Developing Countries

Developing countries encounter multiple financial constraints that limit their economic progress.

High Borrowing Costs and Credit Ratings

International financial institutions and private lenders often assign high-risk premiums to developing countries, making borrowing more expensive. Many low-income nations receive lower credit ratings from agencies such as Moody's and Standard & Poor's, increasing the cost of capital even when their macroeconomic fundamentals are relatively stable (Eichengreen & Mody, 2000).

- **Example:** Argentina has faced multiple financial crises due to high borrowing costs and limited market confidence. In 2001, its default on $95 billion in sovereign debt led to a long-term exclusion from international credit markets (Guzmán, 2016).

Limited FDI and Capital Flight

Developing nations struggle to attract sustainable FDI due to perceptions of political instability, weak institutions, and inadequate financial regulations. Moreover, capital flight—where wealthy individuals and corporations move assets abroad—further depletes financial resources (Ndikumana & Boyce, 2011).

- **Example:** In Nigeria, capital flight exceeded $165 billion between 1970 and 2010, reducing the funds available for public investment (Ndikumana & Boyce, 2011).

Structural Biases in Global Financial Institutions
Institutions such as the IMF and the World Bank often impose strict loan conditions that limit policy autonomy in developing nations. These conditions typically include austerity measures, trade liberalisation, and financial deregulation, which may not align with national development priorities (Babb, 2013).

- **Example:** Ghana, under IMF programmes, implemented structural adjustments that restricted public spending on healthcare and education, leading to social inequalities and weakened human capital development (Aryeetey & Kanbur, 2005).

Case Studies on Unequal Financial Access

The Debt Crisis in Zambia
Zambia's heavy reliance on external borrowing for infrastructure projects resulted in unsustainable debt levels, leading to a sovereign debt default in 2020. The country's inability to access international credit markets due to poor credit ratings has hindered its economic recovery efforts (IMF, 2021).

- **Implication:** Limited access to credit restricts Zambia's ability to fund essential social programmes and infrastructure, exacerbating economic stagnation and social inequality.

The Asian Financial Crisis (1997–1998)
Countries such as Thailand, Indonesia, and South Korea faced a severe liquidity crisis due to rapid capital outflows and restricted access to emergency financial resources. The IMF's intervention required austerity measures that deepened economic recessions and social hardship (Stiglitz, 2002).

- **Implication:** The crisis highlighted the vulnerability of developing economies to speculative financial flows and external shocks, emphasising the need for stronger financial governance mechanisms.

Kenya's Struggle with Domestic Credit Access
In Kenya, small and medium enterprises (SMEs) face limited access to affordable credit due to high interest rates and stringent collateral requirements from commercial banks (Beck et al., 2011).

- **Implication:** Restricted credit access stifles entrepreneurship, limits job creation, and slows down economic diversification efforts in developing economies (Babb, 2013).

Implications for Development

The unequal access to financial resources has significant implications for economic growth, social equity, and long-term sustainability in developing countries (Babb, 2013)

- **Reduced Investment in Infrastructure and Public Services:** Without access to affordable credit, governments struggle to invest in infrastructure projects, leading to poor transportation, healthcare, and educational systems (Rodrik, 2018).
- **Economic Volatility and Crisis Vulnerability:** Financial constraints make developing economies more susceptible to external shocks, such as currency fluctuations, capital flight, and global recessions (Eichengreen, 2008).
- **Persistent Poverty and Income Inequality:** Limited access to credit markets exacerbates economic inequality by restricting opportunities for marginalised groups, particularly small businesses and rural communities (Beck et al., 2011).

Policy Recommendations

To address financial access inequalities, several policy measures can be implemented.

- **Reforming Global Financial Governance:** Developing countries need greater representation in international financial institutions to advocate for fairer lending terms and investment policies (Ocampo, 2017).

- **Strengthening Domestic Financial Markets:** Governments should promote financial inclusion policies that support SMEs, encourage banking sector reforms, and develop alternative credit mechanisms (Beck et al., 2011).
- **Enhancing Regional Financial Cooperation:** Initiatives such as the African Development Bank (AfDB) and the Asian Infrastructure Investment Bank (AIIB) can provide alternative funding sources for developing economies (Rodrik, 2018).

Unequal access to financial resources and credit markets remains a critical challenge for developing countries. High borrowing costs, restrictive lending conditions, and limited investment inflows hinder economic progress and exacerbate global inequalities. Addressing these challenges requires structural financial reforms, stronger regional cooperation, and policies that enhance financial inclusion to ensure sustainable development.

The Influence of Multinational Corporations and International Institutions in Developing Countries: Case Studies and Implications

Stiglitz (2002) underscores that the influence of these institutions plays a significant role in shaping the economic landscape of developing countries. While these entities contribute to investment, job creation, and technology transfer, their influence often comes with economic, political, and social challenges. Developing nations frequently struggle with power asymmetries in their interactions with MNCs and international institutions, leading to policy constraints, resource exploitation, and socioeconomic imbalances (Stiglitz, 2002).

Influence of Multinational Corporations (MNCs) in Developing Countries

MNCs are major drivers of globalisation and economic integration. However, their operations in developing countries raise concerns regarding labour rights, environmental degradation, and tax avoidance (Agarwal, 2019).

Economic Dependence and Market Domination

MNCs often dominate key industries in developing nations, limiting the growth of local enterprises (Agarwal, 2019). Their financial power allows them to negotiate favourable tax incentives and regulatory advantages, sometimes at the expense of national revenue collection (Sachs, 2005).

- **Case Study: The Oil Industry in Nigeria**
  The Nigerian oil sector, controlled by MNCs such as Shell, ExxonMobil, and Chevron, has generated significant revenue but has also been linked to environmental destruction and economic inequalities. The Niger Delta region suffers from oil spills, pollution, and social unrest due to the exploitation of natural resources with limited reinvestment in local communities (Frynas, 2001).
- **Implication:** While MNCs contribute to GDP growth, they can create economic dependencies that hinder the development of domestic industries and exacerbate income inequality (Agarwal, 2019).

Labour Exploitation and Wage Suppression

MNCs often take advantage of weak labour laws in developing countries to reduce production costs, leading to unfair wages, poor working conditions, and exploitative labour practices (Collins, 2018).

- **Case Study: Bangladesh's Garment Industry**
  The Rana Plaza collapse in 2013, which killed over 1100 garment workers, exposed the poor working conditions in factories supplying major global brands such as H&M, Primark, and Walmart. Despite the industry's contribution to Bangladesh's economy, workers faced low wages and inadequate safety measures (McCaig & Pavcnik, 2018).
- **Implication:** MNC-driven supply chains can perpetuate labour exploitation and income disparities, requiring stronger labour rights protections in developing economies.

Tax Avoidance and Capital Flight

MNCs use complex tax structures to shift profits to low-tax jurisdictions, depriving developing countries of essential public revenue (Zucman, 2015).

- **Case Study: Corporate Tax Avoidance in Africa**
  Companies such as Google, Apple, and Starbucks have been criticised for using tax havens to reduce their tax obligations in African

nations, costing governments billions in lost revenue (Fuest & Riedel, 2012).

- **Implication:** Weak tax enforcement allows MNCs to profit at the expense of local development, necessitating stronger tax regulations and international cooperation.

The Role of International Institutions (IMF, World Bank, WTO)

Fuest and Riedel (2012) highlighted that international institutions play a critical role in providing financial support and policy guidance to developing nations. However, their policies often come with stringent conditions that limit national policy autonomy.

IMF Structural Adjustment Programmes (SAPs) and Policy Constraints
The IMF imposes economic policy conditions on countries receiving financial assistance, often requiring austerity measures that reduce government spending on social services (Babb, 2013).

- **Case Study: Argentina's IMF Debt Crisis**
  In the late 1990s and early 2000s, Argentina implemented IMF-backed structural adjustments, including budget cuts and currency devaluation. The policies led to economic contraction, high unemployment, and public protests, culminating in a severe financial crisis in 2001 (Guzmán, 2016).
- **Implication:** IMF loan conditions can exacerbate economic instability, highlighting the need for more flexible and context-specific policy recommendations.

World Bank Development Projects and Environmental Concerns
While the World Bank funds infrastructure and development projects, some initiatives have led to environmental degradation and the displacement of local populations (Goldman, 2005).

- **Case Study: The Narmada Dam Project in India**
  The World Bank-funded Narmada Dam project displaced thousands of indigenous communities without adequate compensation, sparking significant protests and raising ethical concerns about large-scale development financing (Tan, 2005). This project in India is a stark example of the ethical dilemmas surrounding large-scale devel-

opment financing. While the project aimed to provide significant economic benefits through irrigation, drinking water supply, and hydroelectric power generation, it also resulted in the displacement of thousands of indigenous communities, many of whom were not adequately compensated or resettled. This case underscores the deep and lasting impacts of such projects on poverty, prosperity, and equity, particularly among vulnerable populations. The Narmada Dam case exemplifies the unintended consequences that development financing can have when ethical considerations are sidelined. It is a cautionary tale that reminds us that true prosperity must be inclusive. Balancing the imperatives of economic growth with the protection of indigenous rights and welfare requires a development paradigm rooted in justice, sustainability, and respect for human dignity. Only then can development become a tool for shared prosperity, rather than a driver of deeper inequality.

- **Implication:** International development projects must incorporate stronger safeguards to protect vulnerable communities and the environment.

WTO Trade Policies and Market Access Barriers

The WTO's global trade framework often favours developed economies, making it difficult for developing countries to compete in international markets (Rodrik, 2018).

- **Case Study: Agricultural Subsidies and African Farmers**

  Developed nations, particularly the United States and the European Union, provide heavy subsidies to their agricultural sectors, making it difficult for African farmers to compete in global markets. Cotton farmers in Mali, for example, struggle to sell their products due to unfair competition from subsidised U.S. cotton producers (Borensztein et al., 2009).
- **Implication:** WTO policies should promote fair trade practices to ensure equitable market access for developing countries.

Implications for Development

The influence of MNCs and international institutions in developing countries has profound implications and these are demonstrated as follows:

- **Economic Dependence and Sovereignty Constraints:** Over-reliance on foreign corporations and financial institutions limits policy autonomy and the ability to pursue independent development strategies (Stiglitz, 2002).
- **Widening Inequality:** While MNCs create jobs, their influence often exacerbates income disparities by prioritising profits over equitable wealth distribution (Sachs, 2005).
- **Social and Environmental Consequences:** Poor labour practices and environmentally harmful projects undermine sustainable development efforts (Collins, 2018).

Policy Recommendations

- **Stronger Regulatory Frameworks:** Developing nations should enforce stricter labour laws, environmental protections, and anti-tax avoidance measures to ensure that MNCs contribute fairly to local economies (Rodrik, 2018).
- **Fairer Global Trade Policies:** WTO reforms should address unfair subsidies and trade barriers that disadvantage developing economies (Ocampo, 2017).
- **More Inclusive Financial Policies:** International financial institutions should adopt flexible loan conditions that prioritise social investment and sustainable growth (Babb, 2013).

While multinational corporations and international institutions play a critical role in global economic integration, their influence often leads to economic dependencies, social inequalities, and policy constraints in developing countries. Addressing these challenges requires regulatory reforms, fairer trade policies, and inclusive financial governance that ensure equitable benefits for all nations.

Case Studies of Economic Policies Shaped by Power Dynamics

Power Asymmetries in Global Trade and Finance: Implications for Developing Countries

Developing countries face significant structural and financial constraints due to the influence of powerful international institutions, trade agreements, and economic policies dominated by developed nations (Babb, 2013). This section examines key areas where these asymmetries manifest, including SAPs, China's Belt and Road Initiative (BRI), EU agricultural subsidies, NAFTA's impact on Mexican agriculture, and the Organization of the Petroleum Exporting Countries (OPEC)'s control over oil prices (Babb, 2013).

Structural Adjustment Programmes in Africa (IMF and World Bank Influence)

SAPs were introduced by the IMF and the World Bank in the 1980s as a condition for financial assistance to debt-ridden developing nations (Babb, 2013). SAPs mandated economic liberalisation, privatisation, and reduced public spending (Babb, 2013). These policies had profound implications for African economies.

Economic Liberalisation and Debt Dependency

SAPs required African nations to open their markets to foreign competition, leading to the decline of domestic industries unable to compete with multinational corporations (Babb, 2013).

- **Case Study: Ghana's Cocoa Industry**
  Ghana, once a leading cocoa producer, was forced to liberalise its economy under SAPs. The removal of subsidies led to fluctuating cocoa prices, affecting farmer incomes and increasing economic vulnerability (Dang et al., 2024).
- **Implication:** SAPs deepened dependency on international markets and reduced government control over key sectors, limiting long-term development prospects.

Austerity and Social Welfare Decline
SAP-imposed budget cuts led to underfunding of healthcare and education, exacerbating poverty and inequality.

- **Case Study: Structural Adjustments in Zambia**
  In Zambia, SAPs led to the privatisation of state-owned enterprises, resulting in massive job losses and a decline in social services, worsening poverty levels (Berthelemy et al., 2004).
- **Implication:** The reduction in public spending weakened social safety nets, disproportionately affecting vulnerable populations.

China's Belt and Road Initiative (Economic Leverage Through Infrastructure)
China's Belt and Road Initiative (BRI), launched in 2013, is an ambitious infrastructure development strategy aimed at enhancing global trade connectivity. However, BRI's expansion into Africa and Asia has raised concerns over economic dependence and debt sustainability (Brautigam, 2020).

Infrastructure Development and Debt Traps
BRI provides large-scale loans for infrastructure projects, but many recipient countries struggle with debt repayment, increasing China's economic leverage (Brautigam, 2020).

- **Case Study: Sri Lanka's Hambantota Port**
  Sri Lanka borrowed heavily from China to construct the Hambantota Port but defaulted on payments, leading to a 99-year lease of the port to China (Var & Po, 1917).
- **Implication:** Developing nations risk losing strategic assets due to unsustainable debt obligations.

Economic and Political Influence
BRI extends China's geopolitical influence by securing long-term control over trade routes and critical infrastructure.

- **Case Study: Kenya's Standard Gauge Railway**
  Kenya's Chinese-financed railway has boosted trade but increased national debt, with concerns over Kenya's ability to manage repayments (Brou et al., 2010).

- **Implication:** While BRI fosters development, it also increases financial dependency on China, reducing policy autonomy.

EU Agricultural Subsidies and Their Impact on African Markets
The European Union (EU) provides substantial subsidies to its agricultural sector through the Common Agricultural Policy (CAP), creating unfair competition for African farmers.

Trade Distortions and Market Disruptions
Subsidised European agricultural products flood African markets at artificially low prices, undermining local production (Matthews, 2016).

- **Case Study: Dairy Imports in West Africa**
  The EU's dairy subsidies have led to an influx of cheap milk powder into West African countries like Senegal, displacing local dairy farmers (Adelzadeh, 2019)
- **Implication:** African farmers struggle to compete, leading to rural unemployment and increased food insecurity.

Stunted Agricultural Development
African governments are unable to provide comparable subsidies, limiting agricultural growth.

- **Case Study: Cotton Farming in Mali**
  Malian cotton farmers face difficulties competing with heavily subsidised U.S. and EU cotton, reducing income levels and export revenues (Borensztein et al., 2009).
- **Implication:** Trade distortions prevent African countries from developing self-sufficient agricultural sectors, perpetuating economic reliance on imports.

NAFTA's Effect on Mexican Agriculture
The North American Free Trade Agreement (NAFTA), signed in 1994 between the U.S., Canada, and Mexico, aimed to enhance trade but had adverse effects on Mexican agriculture.

Increased Competition from U.S. Agribusiness
NAFTA allowed tariff-free imports of U.S. agricultural products, harming small-scale Mexican farmers (Kedir & Williams, 2022).

- **Case Study: Corn Farming in Mexico**
  U.S. agribusiness, benefiting from government subsidies, exported cheap corn to Mexico, leading to the collapse of small-scale maize farms (Carter & Rosson, 2003).
- **Implication:** Rural job losses and migration to urban areas and the U.S. increased, exacerbating social instability.

Expansion of Low-Wage Factory Jobs
NAFTA encouraged the growth of maquiladoras (assembly plants), offering low-wage employment but poor working conditions.

- **Case Study: Tijuana's Manufacturing Industry**
  Workers in Tijuana's factories experienced exploitation, with low wages and limited labour rights protection (Gereffi, 2018).
- **Implication:** While NAFTA expanded trade, it also widened economic inequalities in Mexico.

Oil Price Control by OPEC
The Organization of the Petroleum Exporting Countries (OPEC) influences global oil prices through production adjustments, impacting both oil-exporting and oil-importing developing nations.

Economic Volatility for Oil-Exporting Nations
OPEC's price manipulation creates economic instability in oil-dependent countries (Smith, 2009).

- **Case Study: Nigeria's Oil-Driven Economy**
  Nigeria's economy heavily relies on oil exports, making it vulnerable to OPEC-induced price fluctuations. When oil prices drop, government revenue declines, leading to budget crises (Akinlo, 2012).
- **Implication:** Oil price volatility disrupts national economic planning and diversification efforts.

High Energy Costs for Import-Dependent Countries
Non-oil-producing developing nations suffer from high fuel prices, increasing production costs and inflation (Artaxo, 2019).

- **Case Study: Kenya's Rising Fuel Prices**
  Kenya, a net oil importer, faces inflationary pressures when OPEC reduces production, raising transport and food costs (Adelzadeh, 2019).
- **Implication:** Energy price instability hampers economic growth and development.

We note that global trade and finance asymmetries significantly impact developing nations, shaping economic policies, market access, and financial stability. Structural Adjustment Programmes, China's BRI, EU subsidies, NAFTA, and OPEC's oil price control demonstrate how economic dependencies and policy constraints hinder sustainable development. Addressing these challenges, countries must develop fairer trade policies, debt, design measures geared to address debt sustainability in order to promote economic growth.

Power Asymmetries in Global Trade and Finance: Case Studies and Implications for Developing Countries

This section examines key issues affecting global trade and finance, including corporate tax policies in Ireland, the U.S.-China trade war, Venezuela's economic crisis, Russia's energy influence, and Brazil's agribusiness expansion. These factors create structural challenges for developing nations, influencing their economic stability, market access, and environmental policies.

Corporate Tax Policies in Ireland: Attracting MNCs

Ireland's low corporate tax policies have made it a hub for multinational corporations (MNCs), affecting global tax revenues and investment patterns (Aguilar & Sumner, 2019).

Ireland's Tax System and FDI
Ireland's corporate tax rate of 12.5% is one of the lowest in the developed world, attracting MNCs, especially in technology and pharmaceuticals (Aguilar & Sumner, 2019)

- **Case Study: Apple's European Headquarters**
  Apple's use of Ireland as a tax base allowed it to avoid billions in taxes, leading to legal disputes with the EU (Aguilar & Sumner, 2019)
- **Implication:** Developing countries lose tax revenue as MNCs shift profits to low-tax jurisdictions instead of reinvesting in local economies.

Impact on Developing Nations
MNCs often structure their tax payments to minimise liabilities in developing countries.

- **Case Study: Google's "Double Irish" Tax Strategy**
  Google used Irish subsidiaries to route profits, reducing tax payments in African and Asian markets (African Development Bank, 2012)
- **Implication:** Developing countries face revenue loss, limiting public investment in infrastructure and social programmes.

U.S.-China Trade War and Its Economic Impact on Developing Countries

The U.S.-China trade war, initiated in 2018, has disrupted global supply chains, trade flows, and investment patterns, affecting developing nations (Dang et al., 2024).

Supply Chain Disruptions and Export Dependency
Higher tariffs on Chinese goods have led companies to shift production to other developing countries like Vietnam and Mexico (Dang et al., 2024).

- **Case Study: Vietnam's Export Boom**
  Vietnam gained from increased exports to the U.S. as companies relocated from China (Ahmed et al., 2015)
- **Implication:** While some countries benefit, others suffer from trade diversions and market instability.

Commodity Price Fluctuations
The trade war has affected global commodity prices, impacting resource-dependent developing nations.

- **Case Study: Soybean Exports in Brazil**
  China increased soybean imports from Brazil after U.S. tariffs, causing price shifts that affected small farmers (Akresh & Edmonds, 2010)
- **Implication:** Developing economies reliant on agricultural exports face price volatility and shifting trade alliances.

Venezuela's Economic Crisis and External Sanctions

Venezuela's economic collapse has been exacerbated by external sanctions, impacting global oil markets and regional stability (Akresh & Edmonds, 2010).

Hyperinflation and Economic Collapse

Venezuela's over-reliance on oil exports and poor economic management led to hyperinflation exceeding 1,000,000% (Aga et al., 2015)

- **Case Study: Decline of PDVSA (State Oil Company)**
  Mismanagement and sanctions crippled Venezuela's oil production, reducing revenue and causing humanitarian crises (Agaya & Asunza, 2013)
- **Implication:** Sanctions on oil exports limit state revenue, affecting food and medicine imports, worsening poverty.

Impact on Developing Nations

Sanctions on Venezuela affect regional trade and migration in Latin America (Ahmed et al., 2015).

- **Case Study: Venezuelan Refugee Crisis in Colombia and Brazil**
  Over 5 million Venezuelans fled due to economic collapse, straining neighbouring economies (Ahmed et al., 2015)
- **Implication:** Economic instability in one country can trigger regional crises, affecting trade and social services in developing nations.

Russia's Geopolitical Influence on European Energy Markets and Its Effects on Developing Countries

Russia's dominance in the European energy sector impacts global oil and gas prices, affecting energy-importing developing nations (Akresh & Edmonds, 2010).

Control of Natural Gas Supplies
Russia supplies over 40% of Europe's gas, using energy as a geopolitical tool (Aguilar & Sumner, 2019).

- **Case Study: Nord Stream 2 Pipeline**
  Russia's push for the Nord Stream 2 pipeline increased Europe's reliance on Russian energy, leading to strategic vulnerabilities (Aguilar & Sumner, 2019).
- **Implication:** Energy supply disruptions raise global fuel prices, straining developing economies dependent on imports.

Impact on African Energy Markets
Higher global gas prices impact African industries and household energy affordability (Aggarwal & Evenett, 2014).

- **Case Study: Nigeria's Gas Import Costs**
  Rising global gas prices, influenced by Russian policies, increased Nigeria's fuel costs, affecting manufacturing and transportation sectors (Aggarwal & Evenett, 2014)
- **Implication:** Developing countries face inflation and economic slowdown due to volatile energy prices.

Brazil's Agribusiness Expansion and Deforestation Policy

Brazil's agribusiness boom has led to increased deforestation in the Amazon, affecting global climate policies and food security (Akresh & Edmonds, 2010).

Expansion of Soy and Beef Exports
Brazil is a leading exporter of soybeans and beef, with land clearance accelerating deforestation (Artaxo, 2019).

- **Case Study: Amazon Rainforest Deforestation**
  Deforestation rates surged under policies favouring agribusiness expansion, reducing biodiversity and carbon absorption (Agaya & Asunza, 2013)
- **Implication:** Environmental degradation in Brazil contributes to climate change, affecting weather patterns in developing regions.

Impact on African Agriculture
Climate changes linked to Amazon deforestation disrupt rainfall patterns in African farming regions (Agarwal, 2019).

- **Case Study: Sahel Region Droughts**
  Studies suggest deforestation in Brazil alters Atlantic weather systems, intensifying droughts in the Sahel (Agarwal, 2019).
- **Implication:** Food security declines as agricultural productivity in developing nations faces increasing climate risks.

We can argue that power asymmetries in global trade and finance shape economic opportunities and vulnerabilities for developing countries. Ireland's tax policies reduce developing nations' tax revenues, while the U.S.-China trade war disrupts trade flows. Venezuela's economic crisis and Russian energy geopolitics create instability in emerging economies, while Brazil's agribusiness expansion threatens climate resilience. Addressing these challenges requires stronger global governance, fairer trade regulations, and sustainable investment policies to support long-term development, domestic economic strategies to enhance resilience against global economic pressures.

Implications for Policy and Practice: A Power-Sensitive Approach to Development

Global economic systems are deeply shaped by power asymmetries, necessitating a rethinking of development strategies to ensure equitable growth (Acemoglu & Robinson, 2012). This section proposes a new integrated development model that builds on existing theoretical foundations, outlines policy recommendations for fairer economic structures, and examines the challenges and opportunities of implementing power-sensitive policies.

Rethinking Development Strategies Through the Lens of Power

The Need for a New Integrated Development Model

Despite the successes of the development models such as the Modernisation Theory and structural adjustment programmes, these models have often overlooked the role of power dynamics in shaping economic disparities (Escobar, 1995). We argue that a new model must integrate elements of dependency theory, institutional economics, and participatory development to account for the influence of multinational corporations, global financial institutions, and geopolitical actors (Acemoglu & Robinson, 2012). Based on the impact of the various economic theories and development models, we propose the following.

New Adapted Conceptual Framework for Developing Countries: Integrated Development Model (IDM)

Concept and Overview

Brautigam (2020) emphasises that IDM is a holistic framework designed to address the unique challenges of developing countries. It integrates various elements from existing theories while emphasising sustainable, inclusive, and equitable growth (Brautigam, 2020). The model recognises the interconnected nature of different sectors and the need for a coordinated approach to development (Brautigam, 2020).

Proposing a new development model, such as the IDM, within the context of the Power Theory of Economics can significantly address the power imbalances that often hinder equitable growth and development in developing countries. The IDM seeks to combine the theoretical insights on power dynamics in global trade and finance with practical, sustainable development strategies. This model is essential for the following:

Addressing Power Imbalances and Inequities

The Power Theory highlights that economic relations between developed and developing nations are often asymmetrical, with the latter being at a disadvantage in trade negotiations, financial access, and policymaking (Stiglitz, 2006). The IDM recognises that development cannot be understood merely in terms of economic growth, but rather as a multifaceted process that incorporates social, political, and cultural dimensions (Brautigam, 2020). When integrating power dynamics into development strategies, the IDM provides a more nuanced understanding of how to tackle these imbalances and create more equitable development pathways.

Example: In trade negotiations, developed countries often wield disproportionate influence, setting rules that benefit their own economic interests while constraining the policy space of developing countries. The IDM advocates for a more inclusive approach to trade agreements that consider the developmental needs of poorer nations (Rodrik, 2018).

Integrating Economic Sovereignty with Global Cooperation

A key feature of the IDM is its focus on enhancing **economic sovereignty** for developing countries while promoting global cooperation. Power theory shows how the economic autonomy of developing nations is often compromised by the influence of multinational corporations, international financial institutions, and global trade organisations (Acemoglu & Robinson, 2019). IDM proposes a model where nations can maintain their sovereignty while participating actively in international agreements that are fair and conducive to long-term growth.

Example: The Belt and Road Initiative (BRI) from China, for instance, provides a model of infrastructure development but raises concerns about debt dependency and sovereignty (Brautigam, 2020). The IDM emphasises partnerships where both sides benefit without sacrificing the economic independence of developing nations.

Fostering Sustainable Development and Regional Cooperation

The IDM also recognises that sustainable development and regional cooperation are crucial components of addressing global power asymmetries. Power dynamics often lead to policies that prioritise short-term economic benefits (e.g., overexploitation of resources) at the expense of long-term sustainability. The IDM encourages development strategies that prioritise both environmental sustainability and social equity, ensuring that economic growth does not exacerbate inequality or environmental degradation.

Example: In the African context, the African Continental Free Trade Area (AfCFTA) offers an opportunity for regional integration and self-sufficiency, reducing dependency on external actors such as the European Union, which often imposes policies that disadvantage African farmers (Gibbon, 2003). The IDM supports such regional initiatives while integrating environmental safeguards.

Inclusivity and Diversification of Financing Options

Developing countries often face limited access to financial resources, and when they do access finance, it comes with high interest rates, unfavourable conditions, or conditionalities that restrict their economic policies (Reinhart & Rogoff, 2010). The IDM proposes a shift towards diversified financing options that are less reliant on traditional donors or international financial institutions. By incorporating regional development banks, South-South cooperation, and alternative financing mechanisms such as green bonds, the IDM enhances the resilience and autonomy of developing economies.

Example: Brazil's initiatives in agribusiness expansion can be bolstered through domestic financing mechanisms or partnerships with regional actors rather than relying on external debt (Moyo, 2010). The IDM would prioritise regional partnerships for financing sustainable projects.

Promoting Policy Coherence Across Sectors

A common challenge in development is the fragmentation of policy across sectors—trade, finance, health, education, etc. The IDM proposes a holistic approach where policy coherence is a cornerstone. When considering the interconnections between economic, social, and political dimensions of development, the IDM promotes policies that do not conflict but rather complement each other. This integrated approach creates synergies between various sectors, enabling sustainable and inclusive development.

Example: SAPs, as imposed by the IMF and the World Bank, have often led to social unrest and undermined public services in developing countries (Mkandawire & Soludo, 2003). The IDM counters this by proposing more comprehensive and context-sensitive development strategies that link trade liberalisation with social safety nets and capacity building.

Why the IDM Within Power Theory?

The IDM is essential because it recognises that development is not just about economic growth but about the reduction of power imbalances, the promotion of sovereignty, and the sustainable inclusion of all countries in the global economic system. When integrating power theory with economic development strategies, the IDM offers a more equitable, resilient, and sustainable path forward for developing countries.

The IDM aims to provide a holistic and inclusive framework for sustainable development, addressing power asymmetries in global trade, finance, and policymaking. The IDM is composed of several key components (variables) that aim to assist developing countries in achieving equitable, sustainable, and self-determined growth. These variables are interconnected and reflect the multidimensional nature of development. Brautigam (2020) indicates that the main components of the IDM are:

Economic Sovereignty and Autonomy

- **Variable:** National Economic Policy Autonomy
- **Explanation:** The IDM emphasises economic sovereignty, ensuring that developing countries can design and implement policies that reflect their unique developmental needs. This includes the ability to control trade policies, fiscal policies, and access to financial resources without undue external interference (e.g., from multinational corporations, the IMF, or the World Bank).
- **Implication:** Empowering developing countries to make independent economic decisions leads to sustainable development and reduces dependency on external actors.

Sustainable Economic Growth

- **Variable:** Green and Inclusive Economic Growth
- **Explanation:** IDM advocates for development that is both economically sustainable and socially inclusive. Growth should not come at the expense of environmental degradation or the marginalisation of vulnerable groups. The integration of environmental sustainability (e.g., green technologies, renewable energy) with economic expansion is crucial.
- **Implication:** Ensuring growth that balances economic and environmental objectives prevents short-term gains from causing long-term harm, fostering resilience in developing economies.

Access to Finance and Investment

- **Variable:** Diversified and Accessible Financing Mechanisms
- **Explanation:** The IDM promotes diverse financing sources beyond traditional aid or debt-based mechanisms. This includes green bonds, South-South cooperation, regional development banks, and microfinance systems that support local entrepreneurship.

- **Implication:** By diversifying financing, developing countries can mitigate risks associated with reliance on external financing sources and control their economic future.

Power-Equitable Trade and Investment Policies

- **Variable:** Fair Trade Agreements and Investment Policies
- **Explanation:** The IDM calls for fair trade agreements that prioritise the developmental needs of poorer nations. This involves renegotiating trade terms that allow developing countries to protect key industries, promote value-added exports, and restrict harmful practices like the dumping of subsidised goods from developed countries.
- **Implication:** More equitable trade policies help developing countries develop their industries and reduce dependency on raw material exports.

Capacity Building and Human Capital Development

- **Variable:** Education, Skills Development, and Innovation
- **Explanation:** Investment in human capital is central to the IDM. This includes promoting education at all levels, developing local skills, and fostering innovation through research and development.
- **Implication:** Developing a well-educated, skilled workforce boosts productivity, attracts investment, and encourages local entrepreneurship. It also helps build self-reliance in key sectors such as healthcare, technology, and manufacturing.

Regional Integration and Cooperation

- **Variable:** Regional Economic Cooperation and Integration
- **Explanation:** The IDM encourages regional integration among developing countries, such as the AfCFTA or ASEAN. This integration allows countries to pool resources, improve intra-regional trade, and negotiate more effectively with global economic powers.
- **Implication:** When we work together, developing countries can leverage collective bargaining power, reduce dependency on global powers, and stimulate intra-regional trade and industrialisation.

Institutional Capacity and Governance

- **Variable:** Strengthened Governance, Transparency, and Accountability
- **Explanation:** Effective governance, institutional capacity, and rule of law are vital to implementing IDM strategies. This includes the creation of transparent, accountable institutions to manage public resources and implement policies that prioritise national development goals.
- **Implication:** Good governance reduces corruption, attracts investment, and ensures that development programmes are effective and inclusive.

Social Equity and Poverty Reduction

- **Variable:** Equitable Distribution of Wealth and Social Protection
- **Explanation:** The IDM promotes policies that ensure social equity, reducing inequality by providing support to marginalised groups such as women, youth, and rural populations. Social safety nets (e.g., cash transfers, universal healthcare, and education) are critical components of this model.
- **Implication:** Reducing inequality and promoting social protection ensures that the benefits of economic growth are widely shared, leading to more inclusive and cohesive societies.

Technological Innovation and Infrastructure Development

- **Variable:** Technological Advancements and Infrastructure Improvement
- **Explanation:** Technological innovation and investment in infrastructure (e.g., roads, electricity, digital networks) are fundamental for economic development. IDM emphasises the role of technology in facilitating industrialisation, improving productivity, and enabling connectivity for trade and communication.
- **Implication:** Modernising infrastructure and adopting new technologies empower developing countries to compete in the global economy, improve livelihoods, and attract investment.

International Relations and Strategic Partnerships

- **Variable:** Strategic Alliances and Diplomacy
- **Explanation:** The IDM promotes the importance of international relations and strategic partnerships based on mutual benefit rather than exploitation. Developing countries should foster alliances with like-minded nations, regional groups, and global organisations that support equitable development goals.
- **Implication:** Strategic alliances provide developing countries with diplomatic leverage, enhancing their voice in international fora like the WTO, IMF, and UN.

Resilience to Global Shocks

- **Variable:** Economic Resilience and Crisis Management
- **Explanation:** The IDM incorporates mechanisms for resilience against global economic shocks, such as global recessions, commodity price volatility, or climate change impacts. These include economic diversification, emergency financial reserves, and social protection systems.
- **Implication:** Resilient economies can better withstand global disruptions, ensuring that development progress is not derailed by external crises.

The integration of the above components within IDM will help developing countries overcome the structural challenges posed by global power asymmetries. When enhancing economic sovereignty, promoting sustainable growth, and fostering regional cooperation, the IDM provides a comprehensive framework for developing countries to take control of their development trajectories, reduce dependency on external forces, and create more inclusive and resilient economies.

Equations for the IDM

To develop equations for the IDM, we need to express the various components of development in a form that captures the key variables and their relationships. These equations will reflect the interplay between economic, social, environmental, and governance dimensions. Some potential equations for the IDM, with an explanation of each variable's relevance, are as follows.

Economic Growth Equation

The equation for economic growth within the IDM can be expressed as:

$$Y = A^{\alpha}.L^{\beta}.S^{\gamma}$$

Where:

- **Y** = Output (GDP or economic growth)
- **A** = Total Factor Productivity (TFP) or technological innovation
- **K** = Capital (both physical and financial capital, including investments in infrastructure and human capital)
- **L** = Labour (skilled labour force, workforce participation rate)
- **S** = Sustainability factor (environmental resources and technological advancements for green growth)
- **α, β, γ** = Output elasticities of capital, labour, and sustainability (parameters indicating how each factor contributes to growth)

Relevance of Variables

- **Capital (K):** Physical infrastructure and financial resources are critical for expanding economic capacity. Investment in physical infrastructure (e.g., roads, energy, technology) and human capital (education and skills development) promotes growth.
- **Labour (L):** A skilled and educated workforce is essential for increasing productivity and contributing to long-term growth. This variable reflects the importance of human capital in driving economic performance.
- **Sustainability (S):** This term incorporates sustainable development strategies such as clean energy, technology, and green industries. IDM prioritises economic growth that is not only economically efficient but also environmentally sustainable.

Poverty Reduction Equation

Poverty reduction can be modelled as a function of income distribution, social protection, and equity in access to resources:

$$P = I_{\mathrm{Avg}-E/I_{\mathrm{Avg}}}$$

Where:

- **P** = Poverty rate (proportion of the population living below the poverty line)
- **I_{avg}** = Average income or consumption per capita in the country
- **E** = Economic inequality factor (measured by Gini coefficient or income distribution)

Relevance of Variables

- **Income (I_{avg}):** Higher average income, especially when broadly distributed, is key to poverty reduction. Economic growth should translate into better living standards for the general population.
- **Economic Inequality (E):** High inequality, often represented by the Gini coefficient, exacerbates poverty. IDM emphasises equitable distribution of wealth, where all social groups (women, rural populations, etc.) benefit from growth.

Social Equity and Inclusiveness Equation

The IDM aims for a more equitable society, ensuring all social groups benefit from economic progress. The social equity equation could be modelled as:

$$E_{g=\frac{Wg}{Wt}\cdot\left(\sum_{i=T}^{n} Si.\alpha_i\right)}$$

Where:

- **E_q** = Equity index (measuring overall social equity)
- **W_g** = Welfare of the group in focus (e.g., income, access to education, healthcare for women, youth, marginalised groups)
- **W_t** = Total welfare (national welfare indicator)

- **S_i** = Social services (healthcare, education, housing) available to group **i** (could be gender, age, or socioeconomic group)
- **α_i** = Weight factor assigned to the importance of services for group **i** (could vary depending on the development goals)

Relevance of Variables

- **Welfare (W_g, W_t):** Measuring the general welfare of specific groups (e.g., women, rural communities) relative to total welfare helps evaluate how inclusive development is. Ensuring that marginalised populations receive equitable benefits from growth is a central goal of IDM.
- **Social Services (S_i):** Access to social services is a direct contributor to reducing inequality and increasing social mobility. These services, such as education, healthcare, and affordable housing, are integral to inclusive development.

Sustainability and Environmental Protection Equation

A key component of IDM is balancing economic growth with environmental sustainability. The sustainability equation can be expressed as:

$$S = \frac{R}{T} E_{\text{tech}}$$

Where:

- **S** = Sustainability index (environmental health, reduction in carbon emissions, preservation of resources)
- **R** = Renewable resource usage (energy from renewable sources, sustainable land use, conservation efforts)
- **T** = Total resource consumption (total energy, water, and land usage in the economy)
- **E_{tech}** = Technological efficiency in minimising environmental impact (green technologies, carbon capture, renewable energy innovations)

Relevance of Variables

- **Renewable Resources (R):** The use of sustainable, renewable resources (solar, wind, geothermal) is a key factor in reducing dependence on non-renewable resources and mitigating environmental degradation.
- **Technological Efficiency (E_{tech}):** Technological innovations that enhance environmental sustainability, such as renewable energy technologies, are central to IDM. These innovations can reduce negative environmental impacts while supporting economic growth.

Governance and Institutional Capacity Equation

Strong governance and effective institutions are essential for implementing the IDM's framework. This equation can be expressed as:

$$G = \frac{T\text{gov}}{T\text{tot}}\left(\sum_{i=1}^{N} Ii\right)$$

Where:

- **G** = Governance index (measuring the quality and effectiveness of governance and institutions)
- **T_{gov}** = Transparency and accountability (policies ensuring effective management of resources and anti-corruption measures)
- **T_{tot}** = Total institutional resources (overall institutional capacity in the country)
- **I_i** = Institutional integrity of each government agency or department (e.g., finance, health, education)

Relevance of Variables

- **Transparency and Accountability (T_{gov}):** Corruption and lack of transparency significantly hinder development. Effective governance and accountability in public institutions are essential for ensuring that resources are used efficiently and that development policies are implemented successfully.
- **Institutional Integrity (I_i):** The capacity of government institutions to function effectively across various sectors (economics, health, education) is fundamental for supporting long-term development goals.

Trade and Investment Equation

This equation reflects the importance of fair trade and investment policies for developing countries:

$$T_i = \left(\frac{X}{M}\right)\left(1 - \frac{D}{I}\right)$$

Where:

- **Ti** = Trade and investment index (reflecting trade balance and foreign investment in developing countries)
- **X** = Exports of goods and services
- **M** = Imports of goods and services
- **D** = Domestic market protection (tariffs, subsidies, etc.)
- **I** = Foreign direct investment (FDI) in the country

Relevance of Variables

- **Trade Balance (X/M):** A positive trade balance (more exports than imports) is essential for sustaining domestic industries and generating foreign exchange. The IDM encourages policies that foster value-added exports rather than reliance on raw materials.
- **Foreign Direct Investment (I):** Attracting FDI is crucial for developing countries to gain access to capital, technology, and expertise. However, the model emphasises regulations that ensure FDI benefits the local economy and does not exploit resources.

The IDM requires complex, interconnected variables that reflect the multiple dimensions of development. These equations are designed to incorporate economic growth, poverty reduction, sustainability, social equity, and institutional governance into a unified framework. By focusing on the balance between economic growth, social welfare, environmental sustainability, and governance, the IDM offers a comprehensive strategy for developing countries to achieve sustainable and equitable development in a globalised world.

Applications of the Integrated Development Model (IDM) to Developing Countries: DRC, Chad, Zambia, Botswana, South Africa, and Malawi

The Integrated Development Model (IDM), which emphasises equitable economic growth, sustainability, human capital development, and good governance, can be applied to various developing countries in sub-Saharan Africa, including the Democratic Republic of Congo (DRC), Chad, Zambia, Botswana, South Africa, and Malawi. Each of these countries faces unique challenges, but the IDM's key components can provide a comprehensive and flexible framework for sustainable development tailored to their specific needs.

Democratic Republic of Congo (DRC)

Aga et al. (2015) highlight the following:

Key Challenges

- **Resource management and governance**: The DRC is rich in natural resources, but it struggles with poor governance, corruption, and resource mismanagement.
- **Infrastructure deficits**: Lack of infrastructure, including transportation, energy, and digital connectivity, hinders economic development.
- **Conflict and instability**: Ongoing conflicts disrupt the ability to implement effective development policies.

Application of IDM

- **Economic Sovereignty and Autonomy**: The DRC can implement policies that limit foreign exploitation of its natural resources and ensure that revenues from mining and other sectors benefit the population through domestic investment.
- **Capacity Building**: Investment in human capital and training in technical fields like mining, agriculture, and governance will help the DRC transition from resource dependency to a more diversified economy.
- **Governance and Transparency**: Strengthening institutional capacity and reducing corruption will help ensure that economic gains are shared more equitably, especially in resource-rich regions like Katanga and Kivu.

- **Sustainability and Infrastructure**: The DRC should focus on investing in green infrastructure projects, such as renewable energy (hydropower potential) and sustainable agriculture, to promote long-term growth while protecting natural resources.

Chad

African Development Bank (2012) highlights the following:

Key Challenges

- **Dependency on oil exports**: Chad's economy is heavily reliant on oil, which makes it vulnerable to fluctuations in global oil prices.
- **Political instability**: Chad faces challenges related to political instability and governance, which hinder development.
- **Limited access to healthcare and education**: High levels of poverty, poor infrastructure, and inadequate public services are major barriers to development.

Application of IDM

- **Economic Diversification**: Chad can reduce its dependency on oil by investing in other sectors such as **agriculture** (especially livestock and farming), tourism, and services (e.g., finance and ICT).
- Social Equity: The government could implement targeted poverty reduction programmes, focusing on healthcare, education, and women's empowerment.
- **Sustainability**: Emphasising green energy and water management (such as harnessing solar energy) will help the country reduce environmental degradation and improve long-term resilience.
- **Institutional Capacity**: Strengthening Chad's institutional framework through public sector reform and anti-corruption initiatives will ensure more effective resource management and the achievement of developmental goals.

Zambia

Brautigam (2020) highlights the following:

Key Challenges

- **Economic growth vs. inequality**: Zambia has experienced periods of economic growth, but inequality remains high, especially in rural areas.
- **Dependence on copper**: Zambia is highly reliant on copper exports, making it vulnerable to global price fluctuations.
- **Debt and fiscal constraints**: Zambia is struggling with a growing debt burden, which limits its fiscal space for development initiatives.

Application of IDM

- **Diversified Economic Growth**: Zambia should focus on diversifying its economy beyond copper by promoting agriculture, manufacturing, and renewable energy. Agribusiness and industrialisation could provide opportunities for inclusive growth.
- **Capacity Building**: Investment in education and skills development will help foster innovation, entrepreneurship, and reduce youth unemployment.
- **Debt Management and Finance**: Implementing better debt management policies and focusing on domestic resource mobilisation (e.g., through tax reforms) will create fiscal space for development projects.
- **Inclusive Growth**: The government could prioritise rural development, creating economic opportunities in agriculture and small-scale enterprises.

Botswana

Agarwal (2019) highlights the following:

Key Challenges

- **Resource dependency**: Although Botswana has one of the highest GDP per capita in Africa, its economy is largely based on diamond exports, leaving it vulnerable to fluctuations in the global market.
- **Social inequality**: Economic gains have not been evenly distributed, with rural areas and certain demographics left behind.
- **Sustainability**: There are challenges related to environmental degradation, particularly water scarcity.

Application of IDM

- **Economic Diversification**: Botswana can diversify its economy by focusing on developing sectors such as tourism, manufacturing, and renewable energy (solar power).
- **Social Equity**: The government could implement targeted social programmes to ensure more equitable distribution of wealth, particularly focusing on rural and underprivileged populations.
- **Sustainability**: Due to its semi-arid climate, Botswana should invest in water conservation technologies and sustainable farming practices to ensure the long-term viability of its agricultural sector.
- **Regional Integration**: As part of the Southern African Development Community (SADC), Botswana can leverage regional trade agreements to improve market access for its diversified products.

South Africa

Brautigam (2020) highlights the following:

Key Challenges

- **Inequality and unemployment**: South Africa is one of the most unequal societies globally, with high unemployment, especially among youth and marginalised communities.
- **Political and social tensions**: Political instability, corruption, and social tensions can undermine development.
- **Environmental degradation:** South Africa faces challenges with air pollution, water scarcity, and land degradation.

Application of IDM

- **Inclusive Economic Growth**: South Africa can prioritise inclusive economic growth by investing in small and medium enterprises (SMEs) and entrepreneurship, with a focus on reducing youth unemployment.
- **Social Equity**: Strengthening social programmes for marginalised groups (e.g., land reform and housing) and improving access to education and healthcare will help address inequality.
- **Environmental Sustainability**: South Africa should focus on green energy solutions (wind, solar) to reduce its dependence on coal and mitigate climate change impacts.

- **Governance**: Strengthening accountability and transparency in government institutions will promote effective policy implementation and reduce corruption.

Malawi

African Development Bank (2012) highlights the following:

Key Challenges

- **Dependence on agriculture**: Malawi's economy is heavily dependent on agriculture, especially tobacco, which makes it vulnerable to environmental changes and global market fluctuations.
- **Food insecurity**: Despite economic growth, food insecurity remains a significant challenge, particularly in rural areas.
- **Health and education challenges**: Malaria, HIV/AIDS, and low literacy rates hinder the country's social development.

Application of IDM

- **Diversified Agricultural Growth**: Malawi can focus on diversifying its agricultural output by investing in agro-processing, irrigation systems, and climate-resilient crops to increase food security and export opportunities.
- **Social Development**: Expanding education and healthcare access, especially for rural populations, will help lift people out of poverty and improve human capital.
- **Sustainability**: Malawi can invest in sustainable agricultural practices, such as agroforestry, that protect the environment while improving yields.
- **Infrastructure and Connectivity**: Improving infrastructure (e.g., roads, electricity, internet) will help create a more favourable environment for businesses and promote regional trade.

The IDM offers a tailored, flexible framework for addressing the unique challenges and opportunities in countries like the DRC, Chad, Zambia, Botswana, South Africa, and Malawi. By emphasising economic diversification, social equity, sustainability, and good governance, IDM can assist these nations in achieving long-term, inclusive growth. Each country can draw on its own strengths—whether natural resources, human capital, or regional partnerships—to promote sustainable development and reduce inequalities. The model encourages national sovereignty in economic decision-making and highlights the importance of institutional capacity in fostering an environment where policies can be effectively implemented.

Table 5.1 below presents the key variables of the IDM and their values, which can be adjusted based on the unique context of each country.

Table 5.1 Key variables of the IDM

Variable	*Description*	*Value (IDM variable)*	*Implications*
Economic Diversification (ED)	The extent to which a country moves beyond reliance on a single sector (e.g., oil, mining)	0–1	A value closer to 1 indicates higher diversification, fostering resilience to external economic shocks
Human Capital Development (HCD)	Investment in education, skills training, and healthcare to improve the labour force	0–1	A value closer to 1 indicates better access to education and health services, promoting long-term growth
Governance Quality (GQ)	The effectiveness of institutions in enforcing policies, reducing corruption, and promoting transparency	0–1	A higher value signifies better governance, supporting efficient implementation of policies
Social Equity (SE)	Distribution of economic benefits and social resources (e.g., income, healthcare) across all populations	0–1	A value closer to 1 represents higher equity, promoting inclusive growth and reducing social tensions
Sustainability (S)	The degree to which environmental resources are preserved and renewable energy is integrated	0–1	A higher value signifies a commitment to environmental sustainability and long-term growth
Infrastructure Development (ID)	Access to basic infrastructure such as transportation, energy, and digital connectivity	0–1	A higher value promotes economic efficiency, market access, and quality of life for the population
Political Stability (PS)	The level of political stability and absence of conflict within the country	0–1	A higher value indicates a more stable environment, fostering long-term development

(*continued*)

Table 5.1 (continued)

Variable	*Description*	*Value (IDM variable)*	*Implications*
Access to Global Markets (AGM)	The ease with which a country can trade and participate in global markets through trade agreements, logistics, etc.	0–1	A higher value indicates better access to global markets, supporting exports and economic growth
Domestic Resource Mobilisation (DRM)	The country's capacity to generate revenue domestically through taxation and savings	0–1	A higher value reflects a nation's financial independence and ability to fund development projects
Entrepreneurship and Innovation (EI)	The level of support for startups, innovation hubs, and entrepreneurial activity	0–1	A higher value suggests a more dynamic economy, where new industries and technologies are developed
Debt Sustainability (DS)	The ability to manage national debt while maintaining fiscal health	0–1	A higher value indicates that the country has sustainable debt levels, avoiding fiscal crises

Explanation of Key Variables

1. **Economic Diversification (ED)**: A more diversified economy is better equipped to withstand global economic shocks, ensuring long-term stability.
2. **Human Capital Development (HCD)**: The foundation for achieving sustainable development, where better education and healthcare lead to a more productive workforce.
3. **Governance Quality (GQ)**: Effective governance ensures that policies are implemented transparently and efficiently, which is critical for development success.
4. **Social Equity (SE)**: Inclusive economic growth reduces social inequality, which is important for maintaining peace and fostering long-term prosperity.

5. **Sustainability (S)**: This focuses on ensuring that economic development does not compromise environmental health and natural resource management, contributing to future generations' well-being.
6. **Infrastructure Development (ID)**: High-quality infrastructure improves business operations, access to services, and the overall standard of living.
7. **Political Stability (PS)**: Political stability fosters a conducive environment for development by minimising conflict and uncertainty.
8. **Access to Global Markets (AGM)**: Trade and export capabilities enable countries to capitalise on their comparative advantages and stimulate economic growth.
9. **Domestic Resource Mobilisation (DRM)**: Sustainable domestic revenue generation (such as through taxes) ensures countries can fund critical development projects without relying excessively on external aid or loans.
10. **Entrepreneurship and Innovation (EI)**: A dynamic entrepreneurial ecosystem drives economic diversification, job creation, and innovation, making the economy more competitive.
11. **Debt Sustainability (DS)**: A sustainable level of debt allows countries to invest in development without jeopardising future growth or fiscal health.

Table 5.1 above can be adapted to assess the IDM's application in the DRC, Chad, Zambia, Botswana, South Africa, and Malawi by assigning numerical values to each variable based on data, allowing policymakers to track progress and identify areas requiring improvement.

Other Case Study: China's Alternative Development Model

China's approach to development, particularly through state-led capitalism and infrastructure investment, provides an alternative to Western-led models that emphasise market liberalisation (Kolavalli & Vigneri, 2011).

Implication: A power-sensitive model should incorporate state intervention, regional trade agreements, and diversified economic policies to protect developing countries from external economic shocks.

Key Components of the New Model

A revised development model should be based on:

1. **Economic Sovereignty:** Reducing dependency on external actors by strengthening domestic industries and regional trade (Chang, 2019).
2. **Inclusive Governance:** Ensuring that policies are designed with input from marginalised communities and local stakeholders (Fuentes & Cookson, 2018).
3. **Sustainable Resource Management:** Incorporating environmental concerns into development planning, particularly in the Global South (Sachs, 2015).

Policy Recommendations for Equitable Economic Growth

Reforming International Trade and Finance

Global trade and financial institutions need to be reformed to create fairer economic opportunities for developing nations.

- **Recommendation 1: Reforming WTO Trade Rules**
  The WTO should prioritise fair trade agreements that prevent agricultural subsidies in developed countries from distorting global markets (Stiglitz, 2006).
  - **Example:** The EU's agricultural subsidies disadvantage African farmers, making their products less competitive internationally (Gibbon, 2003).
  - **Implication:** Revising subsidy policies could enhance food security and rural development in the Global South.

- **Recommendation 2: Restructuring IMF and World Bank Policies**
  The IMF and the World Bank must adopt lending conditions that prioritise long-term development over short-term austerity measures (Rodrik, 2018).
  - **Example:** Structural adjustment programmes in Africa have led to reduced social spending, exacerbating poverty (Mkandawire & Soludo, 2003).
  - **Implication:** Development financing should focus on infrastructure, education, and healthcare to promote sustainable growth.

Enhancing Domestic Economic Resilience
Developing countries should strengthen domestic industries and reduce external vulnerabilities.

- **Recommendation 3: Promoting Industrial Policy and Regional Integration**
  Governments should support local manufacturing and enhance regional economic cooperation to reduce dependence on volatile global markets (Amsden, 2001).
  - **Example:** The AfCFTA aims to boost intra-African trade and industrialisation (UNECA, 2020).
  - **Implication:** Increased regional trade can help mitigate the impact of global economic fluctuations.

- **Recommendation 4: Regulating FDI**
  While FDI can drive economic growth, unchecked foreign investment can lead to resource exploitation and profit repatriation (Görg & Greenaway, 2004).
  - **Example:** In extractive industries, MNCs often repatriate profits instead of reinvesting in local economies (Collier, 2007).
  - **Implication:** Stronger investment regulations can ensure that FDI contributes to sustainable development.

Challenges and Opportunities in Implementing Power-Sensitive Policies

Challenges in Policy Implementation

1. Political Resistance from Global Institutions
   - Global financial institutions, such as the IMF and the World Bank, may resist changes that reduce their influence (Babb & Carruthers, 2008).
   - Example: Countries attempting to renegotiate debt repayment structures often face credit rating downgrades, discouraging financial autonomy (Reinhart & Rogoff, 2010).

2. Dependence on Extractive Economies
   - Many developing nations rely heavily on resource exports, making economic diversification difficult (Ross, 2012).

- Example: Nigeria and Angola's dependence on oil revenues creates vulnerability to price fluctuations (Hou et al., 2015).

3. Lack of Institutional Capacity
   - Weak governance structures limit the ability to implement reforms effectively (Evans, 1995).
   - Example: Corruption in public institutions undermines policy enforcement, as seen in several African and Latin American countries (Acemoglu & Robinson, 2019).

Opportunities for Equitable Growth

1. Leveraging South-South Cooperation
   - Regional partnerships, such as BRICS and AfCFTA, provide alternative financing and trade opportunities (Moyo, 2010).
   - Example: China's Belt and Road Initiative (BRI) has helped African countries improve infrastructure, though concerns about debt sustainability remain (Brautigam, 2020).

2. Technology and Digital Transformation
   - Digital innovation can help developing nations bypass traditional economic barriers (Freeman & Soete, 1997).
   - Example: Mobile banking in Kenya (M-Pesa) has improved financial inclusion for millions of people (Jack & Suri, 2016).

3. Rise of Green and Sustainable Development
   - Investments in renewable energy and sustainable industries offer long-term economic benefits (Sachs, 2015).
   - Example: Morocco's investment in solar energy has reduced dependence on fossil fuels and attracted foreign investment (Banuri et al., 2001).

To address global power asymmetries, a new development model must integrate economic sovereignty, inclusive governance, and sustainable policies. Policy reforms should focus on equitable trade, fair financial structures, and strengthened domestic resilience. Despite challenges such as institutional resistance and economic dependencies, opportunities in regional cooperation, digital transformation, and sustainable growth provide a pathway for more balanced global development. Future policy efforts must be power-sensitive, ensuring that developing nations have the tools to achieve long-term economic stability and prosperity.

Conclusion: Rethinking Power Asymmetries in Global Trade and Finance

Summary of Key Arguments

This analysis has explored how power asymmetries shape global trade and finance, emphasising the disproportionate influence of developed nations, international financial institutions, and multinational corporations on economic policies in developing countries. Several key arguments have emerged from the discussion:

1. **Structural Power in Global Trade and Finance**
   - Developed nations dominate global trade negotiations through institutions like the WTO, often imposing rules that favour their economic interests while limiting the policy space of developing countries (Stiglitz, 2006).
   - Conditionalities imposed by the IMF and the World Bank restrict the economic sovereignty of developing nations, forcing them into austerity measures that can exacerbate poverty and inequality (Mkandawire & Soludo, 2003).

2. **Unequal Access to Financial Resources and Credit Markets**
   - Developing countries face structural barriers to accessing global financial markets, with higher borrowing costs and credit rating biases limiting their ability to fund economic development (Reinhart & Rogoff, 2010).
   - Case studies, such as Ghana's Eurobond debt crisis, illustrate how dependence on external financing can lead to unsustainable debt burdens (Ndikumana & Boyce, 2011).

3. **Influence of Multinational Corporations (MNCs) and International Institutions**
   - MNCs exert considerable influence over developing economies by leveraging tax incentives, labour markets, and natural resources (Görg & Greenaway, 2004).

- The corporate tax policies of countries like Ireland have encouraged tax avoidance by global firms, reducing tax revenues in developing nations (Zucman, 2015).

4. **Geopolitical and Economic Strategies Impacting Development**
   - SAPs in Africa have had long-term negative impacts, undermining social services and domestic industries (Rodrik, 2018).
   - China's Belt and Road Initiative (BRI) provides infrastructure investment but raises concerns about debt dependency (Brautigam, 2020).
   - EU agricultural subsidies continue to disadvantage African farmers by creating artificially low prices for European goods, reducing competitiveness in global markets (Gibbon, 2003).

5. **Policy Implications and the Need for a New Development Model**
   - A power-sensitive development model must integrate economic sovereignty, regional cooperation, and sustainable development principles.
   - Reforms in international trade, finance, and investment policies are needed to create a more equitable global economic system (Acemoglu & Robinson, 2012).
   - The promotion of South-South cooperation and alternative financing mechanisms, such as regional development banks, presents opportunities for reducing dependency on Western financial institutions (Moyo, 2010).

Directions for Future Research

While this discussion has provided an in-depth analysis of power asymmetries in global trade and finance, several areas require further research to develop practical solutions for achieving equitable economic growth.

1. **Alternative Economic Models for Development**
   - More research is needed on alternative economic models that prioritise resilience, social equity, and sustainability.
   - Comparative studies of state-led capitalism (e.g., China) versus market-driven approaches (e.g., U.S.) could provide insights into development strategies for the Global South.

2. **Impact of Emerging Digital Economies**
   - The rise of fintech, blockchain, and decentralised finance (DeFi) presents opportunities for reducing financial exclusion in developing nations.
   - Future research should explore how digital currencies and mobile banking can reshape access to credit and financial markets in Africa and Latin America.

3. **The Role of Regional Economic Blocs in Countering Global Asymmetries**
   - Initiatives like the AfCFTA and BRICS provide potential mechanisms for economic independence from Western-dominated institutions.
   - Future research should assess the effectiveness of these initiatives in enhancing trade, industrialisation, and financial integration.

4. **Environmental Sustainability and Economic Growth**
   - The tension between economic growth and environmental sustainability remains a critical issue, especially in resource-rich developing countries.
   - Further research should explore how green finance, carbon markets, and climate adaptation strategies can be integrated into development policies without exacerbating inequalities.

5. **Reforming Global Financial Institutions**
   - Given the critiques of the IMF and the World Bank policies, more research is needed on viable reforms that could make these institutions more responsive to the needs of developing countries.
   - Studies on alternative financing mechanisms, such as regional development funds and debt restructuring strategies, could provide pathways for economic resilience.

Final Thoughts

Addressing power asymmetries in global trade and finance requires bold reforms, innovative policies, and a rethinking of traditional development models. Developing countries must take proactive steps to strengthen economic sovereignty, leverage regional partnerships, and embrace sustainable development practices. Meanwhile, global financial and trade institutions must undergo structural reforms to ensure a fairer distribution of economic benefits. Future research should continue to explore strategies for reducing inequality, fostering inclusive growth, and creating a more balanced global economic order.

References

Acemoglu, D., & Robinson, J. A. (2012). *Why nations fail: The origins of power, prosperity, and poverty*. Crown Publishers.

Acemoglu, D., & Robinson, J. A. (2019). *The narrow corridor: States, societies, and the fate of liberty*. Penguin Random House.

Adelzadeh, A. (2019). *Economic policy scenarios for growth and development of South Africa: 2019–2030*. Applied Development Research Solutions (ADRS).

African Development Bank. (2012). *African economic outlook: Promoting youth employment*. OECD.

Aga, G., Francis, D. C., & Meza, J. R. (2015). *SMEs, age, and jobs: A review of the literature, metrics, and evidence*. World Bank.

Agarwal, B. (2019). Does group farming empower rural women? Lessons from India's experiments. *Journal of Peasant Studies, 47*(9), 1–32. https://doi.org/10.1080/03066150.2019.1628020

Agaya, B. M., & Asunza, M. (2013). *Report of a baseline survey of women domestic workers in Mukuru Informal Settlement, Nairobi, Kenya*. OXFAM.

Aggarwal, V. K., & Evenett, S. J. (2014). Do WTO rules preclude industrial policy? Evidence from the global economic crisis. *Business and Politics, 16*(4), 481–509. https://doi.org/10.1515/bap-2014-0040

Aguilar, G. R., & Sumner, A. (2019). *Who are the world's poor? A new profile of global multidimensional poverty*. CGD Working Paper No. 499. Centre for Global Development. https://www.cgdev.org/publication/who-are-worlds-poor-new-profile-global-multidimensional-poverty

Ahmed, S., Appendino, M., & Ruta, M. (2015). *Depreciations without exports? Global value chains and the exchange rate elasticity of exports*. World Bank.

Akinlo, A. (2012). How important is oil in Nigeria's economic growth? *Journal of Sustainable Development, 5*(4), 165–179. https://doi.org/10.5539/jsd.v5n4p165

Akresh, R., & Edmonds, E. (2010). *The analytical returns to measuring a detailed household roster*. IZA Discussion Papers, No. 4759. Institute for the Study of Labour (IZA).

Amsden, H. A. (2001). *The rise of the rest: Challenge to the west from late-industrialising economies*. Oxford University Press.

Artaxo, P. (2019). Working together for Amazonia. *Science, 363*(2019), 323. https://doi.org/10.1126/science.aaw6986

Aryeetey, E., & Kanbur, R. (2005). *The economy of Ghana: Analytical perspectives on stability, growth and poverty*. James Currey.

Babb, S. (2013). *Behind the development banks: Washington politics, world poverty, and the wealth of nations*. University of Chicago Press.

Babb, S. L., & Carruthers, B. G. (2008). Conditionality: Forms, function, and history. *Annual Review of Law and Social Science, 4*, 13–29.

Banuri, T., Weyant, J., Akumu, G., Najam, A., Roas, L., Rayner, S., Sachs, W., Sharma, R., & Yohe, G. (2001). Setting the stage: Climate change and sustainable development. In B. Metz, O. Davidson, R. Swart, & J. Pan (Eds.), *Climate change 2001: Mitigation, report of working group III, Intergovernmental Panel on Climate Change (IPCC)*. Cambridge University Press.

Barnett, M., & Duvall, R. (2005). Power in international politics. *International Organization, 59*(1), 39–75. https://doi.org/10.1017/S0020818305050010

Barro, R. J. (1999). Determinants of economic growth: Implications of the global evidence for Chile. *Cuadernos de Economía, 36*(107), 443–478.

Beck, T., Demirgüç-Kunt, A., & Peria, M. S. M. (2011). Bank financing for SMEs: Evidence across countries and bank ownership types. *Journal of Financial Services Research, 39*(1), 35–54. https://doi.org/10.1007/s10693-010-0085-4

Berthelemy, J., Kauffmann, C., Valfort, M., & Wegner, L. (2004). *Privatisation in Sub-Saharan Africa: Where do we stand?* OECD Publishing. https://doi.org/10.1787/9789264020382-en

Borensztein, E., Jeanne, O., & Sandri, D. (2009). Macrohedging for commodity exporters. *Journal of Development Economics, 101*(C), 105–116. https://doi.org/10.1016/j.jdeveco.2012.08.005

Brautigam, D. (2020). *The Dragon's gift: The real story of China in Africa*. Oxford University Press.

Brou, D., Campanella, E., & Ruta, M. (2010). The value of domestic subsidy rules in trade agreements. In S. Evenett & B. M. Hoekman (Eds.), *Valuing international trade rules*. World Bank/Palgrave Macmillan.

Carter, C., & Rosson, P. (2003). The impact of NAFTA on agriculture. *The World Economy, 26*(5), 649–671.

Chang, H. (2019). *Kicking away the ladder: Development strategy in historical perspective*. Anthem Press.

Collier, P. (2007). *The bottom billion: Why the poorest countries are failing and what can be done about it*. Oxford University Press.

Collins, J. L. (2018). *The simple path to wealth*. Harriman House.

Dang, B. T. T., Yawei, W., & Abdullah, A. J. (2024). Impact of the US-China trade war on Vietnamese exports to the US: A quantitative study using DiD approach. *Journal of Trade Science, 12*(4). https://doi.org/10.1108/JTS-02-2024-0007

Eichengreen, B. (2008). *Globalizing capital: A history of the international monetary system* (2nd ed.). Princeton University Press.

Eichengreen, B., & Mody, A. (2000). What explains changing spreads on emerging market debt? In *Capital flows and the emerging economies* (pp. 107–134). National Bureau of Economic Research Inc.

Escobar, A. (1995). *Encountering development: The making and unmaking of the third world*. Princeton University Press.

Evans, P. (1995). *Embedded autonomy: States and industrial transformation*. Princeton University Press.

Freeman, C., & Soete, L. (1997). *The economics of industrial innovation*. Routledge.

Frynas, J. G. (2001). Corporate and state responses to anti-oil protests in the Niger Delta. *African Affairs, 100*(398), 27–54. https://doi.org/10.1093/afraf/100.398.27

Fuentes, L., & Cookson, T. (2018). Inclusive governance: A review of research and practice for the OECD-DAC governance network. In *What does "inclusive governance" mean? Clarifying theory and practice*. OECD Development Policy Papers, March 2020, No. 27.

Fuest, C., & Riedel, N. (2012). Tax evasion and tax avoidance in developing countries: The role of international profit shifting. *World Development, 40*(6), 1215–1228.

Gallagher, K. P. (2005). *Putting development first: The importance of policy space in the WTO and IFIs*. Zed Books.

Gereffi, G. (2018). *Global value chains and development: Redefining the contours of 21st century capitalism*. Cambridge University Press.

Gibbon, P. (2003). The African Growth and Opportunity Act and the global commodity chain for clothing. *World Development, 31*(11), 1809–1827. https://doi.org/10.1016/j.worlddev.2003.06.002

Goldman, M. (2005). *Imperial nature: The World Bank and struggles for social justice in the age of globalization*. Yale University Press.

Görg, H., & Greenaway, D. (2004). Much ado about nothing? Do domestic firms really benefit from foreign direct investment? *World Bank Research Observer, 19*(2), 171–197.

Guzmán, M. (2016). Managing sovereign debt restructurings: The case of Argentina. *Journal of Globalization and Development, 7*(2), 1–27.

Hou, Z., Keane, J., Kennan, J., & te Velde, D. W. (2015). *The oil price shock of 2014: Drivers, impacts and policy implications*. ODI Working Paper 415. ODI.

International Monetary Fund (IMF). (2021). *Zambia: Staff report for the 2021 article IV consultation*. IMF.

Jack, W., & Suri, T. (2016). The long-run poverty and gender impacts of mobile money. *Science, 354*(6317), 1288–1292. https://doi.org/10.1126/science.aah5309

Kalecki, M. (1971). *Selected essays on the dynamics of the capitalist economy 1933–1970*. Cambridge University Press.
Kedir, A., & Williams, C. (2022). *Exporting, foreign ownership and informal entrepreneurship*. Paper presented at the 2022 Academy of International Business (AIB) Conference, July 2022.
Kolavalli, S., & Vigneri, M. (2011). Ch. 12: Cocoa in Ghana: Shaping the success of an economy. In *Yes Africa can: Success stories from a dynamic continent* (pp. 201–217). World Bank Publications.
Larrain, J. (1989). *Theory of development: Capitalism, colonialisation and dependency*. Policy Press.
Lucas, R. E. (1988). On the mechanics of economic development. *Journal of Monetary Economics, 22*(1), 3–42. https://doi.org/10.1016/0304-3932(88)90168-7
Matthews, A. (2016). EU agricultural policy and developing countries. *Development Policy Review, 34*(2), 205–223.
McCaig, B., & Pavcnik, N. (2018). Export markets and labour allocation in a low-income country. *American Economic Review, 108*(7), 1899–1941. https://doi.org/10.1257/aer.20141096
Mkandawire, T., & Soludo, C. (2003). *African voices on structural adjustment: A companion to our continent, our future*. Africa World Press.
Moyo, D. (2010). *Dead aid: Why aid is not working and how there is a better way for Africa*. Penguin.
Ndikumana, L., & Boyce, J. K. (2011). *Africa's odious debts: How foreign loans and capital flight bled a continent*. Zed Books.
North, D. C. (1990). *Institutions, institutional change and economic performance*. Cambridge University Press.
Ocampo, J. A. (2017). *Resetting the international monetary (non)system*. Oxford University Press.
Piketty, T. (2014). *Capital in the twenty-first century*. Harvard University Press.
Reinhart, C. M., & Rogoff, K. S. (2010). *This time is different: Eight centuries of financial folly*. Princeton University Press.
Rodrik, D. (2018). *Straight talk on trade: Ideas for a sane world economy*. Princeton University Press.
Romer, P. (1990). Endogenous technological change. *Journal of Political Economy, 98*(5), S71–S102. https://web.stanford.edu/~klenow/Romer_1990.pdf
Ross, M. L. (2012). *The oil curse: How petroleum wealth shapes the development of nations*. Princeton University Press.
Sachs, J. D. (2005). *The end of poverty: Economic possibilities for our time*. Penguin.
Sachs, J. D. (2015). *The age of sustainable development*. Columbia University Press.
Smith, J. (2009). *The politics of international oil: OPEC and the global energy market*. Routledge.

Solow, R. M. (1956). A contribution to the theory of economic growth. *Quarterly Journal of Economics, 70*(1), 65–94. https://doi.org/10.2307/1884513

Stiglitz, J. E. (2002). *Globalization and its discontents.* W.W. Norton & Company.

Stiglitz, J. E. (2006). *Making globalization work.* W.W. Norton & Company.

Tan, P. J. (2005). *Arundhati Roy's the greater common good. Dams, development and democracy in India.* https://www.asianstudies.org/publications/eaa/archives/arundhati-roys-the-greater-common-good-dams-development-and-democracy-in-india-2/

Todaro, M. P., & Smith, S. C. (2020). *Economic development.* Pearson Education.

United Nations Economic Commission for Africa (UNECA). (2020). *COVID-19 in Africa: Protecting lives and economies.* Economic Commission for Africa. https://archive.uneca.org/sites/default/files/PublicationFiles/eca_covid_report_en_24apr_web1.pdf

Var, V., & Po, S. (1917). *Cambodia, Sri Lanka and the China Debt Trap.* East Asia Forum. http://www.eastasiaforum.org/2017/03/18/cambodia-sri-lanka-and-thechina-debt-trap/

Wade, R. H. (2003). What strategies are viable for developing countries today? The World Trade Organization and the shrinking of "development space". *Review of International Political Economy, 10*(4), 621–644. https://doi.org/10.1080/09692290310001601902

Wallerstein, I. (2004). *World-systems analysis: An introduction.* Duke University Press.

Zucman, G. (2015). *The hidden wealth of nations: The scourge of tax havens.* University of Chicago Press.

CHAPTER 6

Embedding Power in Sustainable Development Discourse

Introduction

Economic growth, often perceived as the engine driving national prosperity, is deeply influenced by underlying power structures that shape both global and local economies (Piketty, 2014). While the role of economic growth in promoting development is well-documented, the dynamics of power, in both political and economic spheres, have remained less explored but are equally critical in achieving long-term and inclusive prosperity (Piketty, 2014). Power, in this context, refers to the capacity of individuals, governments, corporations, and international institutions to shape economic policies, allocate resources, and influence decisions that determine the trajectory of economic growth (Piketty, 2014). The distribution of power often dictates who benefits from economic activities, thus determining the sustainability and inclusiveness of the growth achieved (Piketty, 2014).

The Power Theory of Economics, developed as an approach to understanding the role of power dynamics in economic structures, posits that economic systems are not only shaped by market forces but also by the political, social, and institutional power structures that govern them (North, 1990). This theory highlights how power asymmetries—be it between states, classes, or global actors—can either propel or hinder development, making it a vital tool for understanding the mechanisms behind inequality and the distribution of resources in the global economy

P. K. Kabeya, *Development and the Power Theory of Economics*,
https://doi.org/10.1007/978-3-032-07926-8_6

(Acemoglu & Robinson, 2012). Within the context of sustainable development, the theory suggests that to achieve long-term, equitable growth, power must be restructured to ensure that all sectors of society benefit equally from economic progress (Piketty, 2014).

This chapter examines the relationship between power and sustainable economic growth, focusing on how power dynamics influence development outcomes. The objective of this chapter is to provide an in-depth analysis of how the Power Theory of Economics can inform strategies for empowering economic growth, particularly in developing nations. By exploring the intersection of power and sustainable development, this chapter will also highlight the need for power-sensitive policy frameworks that promote not only economic growth but also social equity and environmental sustainability.

The structure of this chapter is as follows: First, an overview of the role of power in economic growth is provided, followed by a brief recap of the Power Theory of Economics and its relevance to sustainable development. Next, the chapter explores how power structures influence sustainable development, with a focus on case studies that demonstrate both positive and negative impacts. The chapter concludes with policy recommendations aimed at empowering developing economies by rethinking power dynamics in economic decision-making.

Understanding Power in an Economic Context

Defining "Power" in the Context of Economic Development

Power, in the context of economics, refers to the capacity to influence or control the distribution of resources, decisions, and outcomes within an economic system. It is both a structural and relational phenomenon that manifests across different levels—within nations, between states, and between individuals, institutions, and corporations (Piketty, 2014). Power shapes economic development by determining who gets access to opportunities, wealth, and decision-making processes (Piketty, 2014). In the context of development, power is often the determining factor in whether economic growth translates into equitable and sustainable development or whether it exacerbates inequality and marginalisation (Alesina & Dollar, 2000).

Economic power can be both formal and informal (Alesina & Dollar, 2000). Formal power is exercised through institutions, policies, and laws, while informal power often takes the form of social networks, cultural norms, and historical legacies (Ferguson, 1999). The role of power is not limited to high-level decision-making; it extends to the control of resources, labour, and technology that are essential to development outcomes (Harriss, 2005). Therefore, understanding power in economic development requires recognising its multifaceted nature, spanning from political influence and resource control to the broader social and cultural frameworks that shape how economic decisions are made (Piketty, 2014).

Theories of Power in Economics: Historical Perspectives and Modern Interpretations

Theories of power in economics have evolved over time, offering various interpretations of how power operates in economic systems. Early theories of power were largely framed through the lens of class conflict (Piketty, 2014). Karl Marx, for instance, viewed power primarily through the lens of capitalist class relations, arguing that economic power was concentrated in the hands of capital owners, leading to inequality and exploitation of the working class (Marx, 1867). For Marx, the conflict between capitalists and workers was central to understanding economic systems and their developmental implications (Marx, 1867).

In contrast, neoliberal economics, particularly popular from the late twentieth century onwards, emphasises the role of individual choice, competition, and free markets in promoting development (Wallerstein, 1974). Neoliberal theorists argue that power should be decentralised, with market forces determining resource allocation (Harvey, 2005). However, critics of neoliberalism, such as dependency theory and world-systems theory, highlight that power dynamics between rich and poor nations persist, often reinforcing inequalities rather than alleviating them (Frank, 1967; Wallerstein, 1974).

In contemporary economic thought, institutional economics provides an understanding of power through the mechanisms of institutions—formal and informal—that structure economic transactions and shape development outcomes (North, 1990). Power, in this view, is not only about control over wealth but also about the rules and norms that determine how wealth is distributed and utilised (Piketty, 2014). As such, institutional economics acknowledges the impact of power on economic performance, arguing that institutions shaped by power can either foster or hinder sustainable development (Acemoglu & Robinson, 2012).

Power Dynamics Between Nations, Corporations, and Individuals

Power dynamics are not limited to internal factors but are deeply embedded in global relations, where nations, corporations, and individuals interact in complex ways (Piketty, 2014). At the international level, power between countries can influence the terms of trade, access to capital, and political stability (Piketty, 2014). Developed nations, with stronger economic and political power, often set the rules of global trade, finance, and governance, creating systems that benefit them at the expense of developing nations (Stiglitz, 2002). For instance, in the World Trade Organization (WTO), developed countries typically have more bargaining power, which allows them to push for trade agreements that protect their interests, often undermining the economic sovereignty of poorer countries (Rodrik, 2011).

At the corporate level, multinational corporations (MNCs) wield significant power through control over global supply chains, technology, and capital (Sachs, 2005). MNCs can dictate the terms of labour, environmental standards, and resource extraction, particularly in developing nations that may be economically dependent on foreign investments (Sachs, 2005). For example, in sub-Saharan Africa, resource-rich nations have historically faced challenges in negotiating fair contracts with MNCs, often resulting in exploitative agreements that benefit foreign corporations at the expense of local development (Ferguson, 1999).

Individuals, too, have varying levels of power depending on their position in society, such as through wealth, education, or social status (Sen, 1999). The uneven distribution of economic power within nations means that certain groups (e.g., the elite, business owners, or multinational executives) have greater access to economic opportunities and influence over development policies than marginalised groups (e.g., women, rural communities, and low-income workers) (Sen, 1999). This unequal distribution of power often results in unequal development outcomes, perpetuating cycles of poverty and inequality (Sen, 1999).

The Impact of Power Asymmetries on Development Outcomes

Power asymmetries, both within and between countries, can significantly impact development outcomes, often perpetuating inequality and hindering sustainable growth (Rodrik, 2011). In global trade, the dominance of powerful nations and MNCs in shaping trade agreements has frequently led to imbalanced economic arrangements, where developing countries remain dependent on the export of raw materials and primary products, rather than diversifying their economies or adding value to their exports (Stiglitz, 2002). This dependency limits their capacity for sustainable economic growth and reduces their ability to achieve long-term development goals.

Within countries, power asymmetries affect the distribution of wealth, access to services, and opportunities for advancement (Rodrik, 2011). For example, in many African countries, the concentration of political and economic power in the hands of a small elite often leads to policy decisions that disproportionately benefit this group while neglecting the needs of the broader population (Acemoglu & Robinson, 2012). This can result in the underdevelopment of critical sectors such as education, healthcare, and infrastructure, hindering inclusive growth and perpetuating poverty (Acemoglu & Robinson, 2012).

Power imbalances also affect environmental sustainability. When powerful actors prioritise short-term profits over long-term environmental health, developing countries are often forced to adopt development models that lead to resource depletion and environmental degradation (Rodrik, 2011). This is evident in industries such as mining, where MNCs extract resources from developing countries, leaving behind environmental damage without contributing significantly to local development (Sachs, 2005).

Ultimately, the impact of power asymmetries on development outcomes is profound, as these imbalances hinder the ability of developing nations to capitalise on their potential for sustainable growth, perpetuate inequality, and delay progress towards the United Nations' Sustainable Development Goals (SDGs) (Sen, 1999). The Power Theory offers a framework for understanding these dynamics and suggests that addressing power imbalances is central to achieving equitable and sustainable economic development (Rodrik, 2011).

Theoretical Foundations of the Power Theory in Economics

Overview of Key Economic Theories Related to Power

Economic theories related to power have evolved over time, with different schools of thought offering distinct interpretations of how power influences economic outcomes (Rodrik, 2011). Three primary economic theories—Marxism, Keynesianism, and Neoliberalism—each present differing views on the relationship between power and economic development, with varying implications for economic policies and strategies (Rodrik, 2011).

Marxism

Marxist theory, developed by Karl Marx, views power as being inherently tied to class struggle and the control over the means of production (Marx, 1867). For Marx, the capitalist economic system is characterised by a fundamental imbalance of power, with capitalists (the bourgeoisie) owning and controlling the means of production, while the working class (the proletariat) has little power or control over economic decisions (Marx, 1867). In Marxist thought, economic exploitation is a central feature of capitalism, as capitalists extract surplus value from workers through low wages and unequal exchange (Rodrik, 2011). Marx argued that power is concentrated in the hands of the capital-owning class, leading to systemic inequality. This imbalance of power, according to Marx, undermines the potential for sustainable and equitable economic development (Marx, 1867).

Keynesianism

Keynesian economics, developed by John Maynard Keynes, shifted the focus of economic power towards the role of the state in managing economic growth and stability. Keynes argued that government intervention is essential to managing the economy, especially during times of economic downturns (Keynes, 1936). In this framework, power is not just vested in capital owners but also in the hands of the state, which can regulate and influence economic outcomes through fiscal and monetary policies (Keynes, 1936). Keynesianism acknowledges the central role of government in balancing the interests of different social classes and sectors of the economy to promote full employment, economic stability, and welfare. In this theory, the state's power is seen as necessary to mitigate the power imbalances created by market forces and ensure equitable distribution of wealth (Keynes, 1936).

Neoliberalism

Neoliberalism, which gained prominence in the late twentieth century, advocates for minimal state intervention in the economy, emphasising the power of free markets, privatisation, and deregulation (Harvey, 2005).

According to neoliberal theorists, power should be decentralised, with market forces determining resource allocation and economic outcomes (Harvey, 2005). The belief is that competition, entrepreneurial activity, and individual choice will lead to greater efficiency and growth, benefiting society as a whole (Piketty, 2014). In this theory, power is primarily vested in market actors, such as corporations and individuals, with the state playing a minimal role in economic governance (Rodrik, 2011). Neoliberalism has been critiqued for exacerbating inequality and concentrating power in the hands of MNCs and the financial elite, often at the expense of the broader population (Piketty, 2014).

These three economic theories offer different interpretations of power in the economic system, but all agree that power dynamics play a crucial role in shaping economic outcomes. Marxism emphasises the role of class struggle, Keynesianism stresses the need for state intervention, and Neoliberalism advocates for market-driven power. Understanding these theories provides the foundation for examining how power operates within economic systems and influences development strategies.

Power as a Central Concept in Shaping Economic Policies and Development Strategies

Power is a central concept in shaping economic policies and development strategies, as it influences the decision-making process and determines the distribution of resources (Rodrik, 2011). In every economic system, different groups, whether they be governments, corporations, or labour forces, hold varying degrees of power, which in turn affects how policies are formulated and implemented (Acemoglu & Robinson, 2012). Political power, for instance, can dictate the direction of development policies, the distribution of aid, and the allocation of resources, often favouring certain sectors or groups over others (Acemoglu & Robinson, 2012).

For example, in developing economies, power dynamics between the domestic political elite, MNCs, and international financial institutions can significantly influence the course of development (Rodrik, 2011). Governments may be pressured to adopt policies that prioritise economic liberalisation, often at the cost of public welfare, in exchange for foreign aid or loans from international institutions such as the World Bank or the International Monetary Fund (IMF) (Stiglitz, 2002). This concentration of economic power in the hands of external actors often leads to policies that disproportionately benefit MNCs while leaving local industries and populations vulnerable (Stiglitz, 2002).

Moreover, power structures shape the development strategies that countries adopt. In nations with strong state power, development may focus on industrialisation and infrastructure development, as governments seek to enhance their control over resources and the economy (Stiglitz, 2002). In contrast, in nations with weak state power, development strategies may focus on attracting foreign investment or export-oriented growth, which often leads to greater dependence on external actors (Rodrik, 2004). These varying approaches to development reflect the underlying power dynamics at play and highlight the need for power-sensitive policies that prioritise inclusive and sustainable growth.

How the Power Theory Bridges the Gap Between Economic Growth and Inequality Reduction

The Power Theory of Economics provides a useful framework for bridging the gap between economic growth and inequality reduction by addressing the structural power imbalances that often perpetuate inequality (Rodrik, 2011). The theory recognises that economic growth, in isolation, does not necessarily result in more equitable outcomes. Instead, it emphasises the need to redistribute power to create a more inclusive and sustainable economic system (Acemoglu & Robinson, 2012). In essence, economic growth can be a tool for poverty reduction and inequality alleviation, but only if power dynamics are restructured to ensure that the benefits of growth are shared more equally.

One of the key arguments of the Power Theory is that inequality arises not just from differences in income or wealth, but from the unequal distribution of economic power (Sen, 1999). Those who control economic resources, whether through ownership, political influence, or access to capital, are better positioned to shape the economic system in ways that protect and enhance their power (Rodrik, 2011). As such, addressing inequality requires not only promoting growth but also dismantling the power structures that perpetuate inequality (Rodrik, 2011).

The Power Theory bridges the gap between growth and inequality reduction by advocating for policies that empower marginalised groups, such as workers, small businesses, and local communities (Rodrik, 2011). This may involve creating policies that promote economic inclusion, such as progressive taxation, labour rights protections, and greater access to education and healthcare (Rodrik, 2011). Additionally, the Power Theory suggests that international economic institutions and MNCs must be held accountable for their role in perpetuating global inequality (Rodrik, 2011). By restructuring power dynamics at both the national and international levels, the Power Theory offers a pathway to more equitable and sustainable development (Rodrik, 2011).

Power and Development: A Complex Relationship

Power plays a dual role in economic development, acting both as a driver and an obstacle. In many cases, power enables structural transformation, investment, and economic growth (Rodrik, 2011). However, when concentrated in the hands of a few, power can lead to corruption, economic exclusion, and structural inequalities (Rodrik, 2011). This section explores how power structures influence development, with case studies demonstrating both positive and negative outcomes, and an analysis of unequal power relations in global trade, finance, and governance (Rodrik, 2011).

The Dual Role of Power in Facilitating and Hindering Development

Facilitating Development

Power, when used effectively, can support development by ensuring policy stability, attracting investment, and implementing long-term economic reforms. For instance:

- **Rwanda's Post-Genocide Economic Growth:** Rwanda's centralised leadership under President Paul Kagame has leveraged power to drive national development through strategic economic planning, infrastructure development, and investment in human capital (World Bank, 2023). The country has consistently recorded high economic growth rates, with GDP growth averaging 7.2% annually between 2000 and 2021 (IMF, 2023). This demonstrates how state power can be used to build a sustainable economic trajectory.
- **China's Economic Rise:** The Chinese government has effectively used state power to implement economic reforms, control key industries, and manage foreign investments (Lin, 2022). Through initiatives like the Belt and Road Initiative (BRI), China has extended its economic influence, fostering development partnerships across Asia, Africa, and Latin America (Szamosszegi & Kyle, 2011)

Hindering Development

Conversely, the misuse or over-concentration of power can stifle development, increase inequality, and create economic crises. Examples include:

- Venezuela's Economic Collapse: The Venezuelan government's excessive control over its oil industry and economy led to hyperinflation, capital flight, and widespread poverty (Hausmann, 2022). Political mismanagement, coupled with external sanctions, severely impacted development, showing how unchecked power can be detrimental.
- Zimbabwe's Economic Decline: Zimbabwe's land reform policies, while aimed at economic empowerment, led to economic disruption due to poor implementation and political interference. The expropriation of commercial farms without adequate transition plans resulted in a decline in agricultural productivity, food insecurity, and hyperinflation (Mlambo, 2022).

Implications and How to Address Power Challenges

Rodrik (2011) underscores that the dual nature of power in development suggests the need for balanced governance structures that ensure accountability, transparency, and participatory decision-making. Strategies to address power imbalances include:

- Strengthening democratic institutions to prevent power abuses.
- Encouraging inclusive economic policies that distribute resources equitably.
- Enhancing regional economic cooperation to counteract global power imbalances (Rodrik, 2011).

Case Studies of Countries Where Power Structures Have Shaped Economic Outcomes

Post-Colonial Economies

Golub and Edwards (2003) opine that many post-colonial nations struggle with power structures that reflect colonial legacies, leading to persistent economic inequalities.

- **South Africa's Economic Disparities:** Despite being Africa's most industrialised nation, South Africa still faces stark inequalities rooted in apartheid-era power structures. The country's economic policies favour large corporations and the established elite, contributing to one of the world's highest Gini coefficients (Golub & Edwards, 2003). Land redistribution remains a contentious issue, reflecting power struggles between economic classes (Golub & Edwards, 2003).
- **Democratic Republic of Congo (DRC) and Resource Wealth:** The DRC is rich in minerals like cobalt and lithium, yet power imbalances between the state, MNCs, and local communities have hindered equitable development (Van Reybrouck, 2015). The government's weak regulatory framework has allowed foreign companies to extract resources without significantly benefiting local populations (Van Reybrouck, 2015).

Emerging Economies

- **Brazil's Agribusiness Expansion and Power Dynamics:** Brazil's rise as an agricultural powerhouse has been driven by powerful agribusiness lobbies. While the sector contributes significantly to GDP, deforestation of the Amazon, land concentration, and indigenous rights violations highlight the adverse effects of unchecked economic power (Hankammer et al., 2021).
- **India's Digital Economy and Power Structures**: India's rapid digital transformation has created new power structures dominated by tech conglomerates (Hankammer et al., 2021). The rise of digital monopolies has led to concerns over data privacy, economic exclusion, and regulatory challenges (Hankammer et al., 2021).

Implications and Solutions

Rodrik (2011) indicates that the following needs particular attention:

- Strengthening regulatory frameworks to ensure resource wealth benefits local populations, implementing policies to reduce inequality in post-colonial economies
- Balancing economic growth with environmental sustainability in emerging economies to support economic development.

Analysis of Unequal Power Relations in Global Trade, Finance, and Governance

Porter and Kramer (2011) argue that power asymmetries shape global economic relations, often disadvantaging developing nations in trade, finance, and governance, as highlighted below.

Global Trade and Economic Disparities

- **EU Agricultural Subsidies and African Markets:** The European Union's Common Agricultural Policy (CAP) provides heavy subsidies to European farmers, making African agricultural products less competitive in international markets (FAO, 2023). This has stifled Africa's agricultural sector and reinforced economic dependence on raw material exports (FAO, 2023).
- **NAFTA and Mexican Agriculture:** The North American Free Trade Agreement (NAFTA) benefited U.S. agribusiness while undermining small-scale Mexican farmers (Hankammer et al., 2021). The influx of cheap subsidised U.S. corn led to a decline in local farming, forcing many rural workers into low-wage labour markets (Hankammer et al., 2021).

Global Finance and Debt Traps

- **China's Belt and Road Initiative (BRI) and Debt Concerns:** While China's BRI has financed critical infrastructure in Africa and Asia, concerns about debt sustainability have emerged (Brautigam, 2023). Countries like Sri Lanka and Zambia have struggled with debt repayment, leading to increased Chinese influence over their economies (Brautigam, 2023).
- **IMF and World Bank Conditionalities:** Many developing countries rely on IMF and World Bank loans, but conditionalities often lead to austerity measures that harm social spending (Stiglitz, 2023). SAPs in Africa led to reduced healthcare and education funding, exacerbating poverty (Stiglitz, 2023).

Global Governance and Decision-Making Power

- **UN Security Council and Economic Governance:** The disproportionate influence of developed nations in global governance bodies like the UN Security Council and the IMF limits the ability of developing countries to shape economic policies that affect them (Wade, 2022).

Figure 6.1 below highlights the stark imbalance in global economic governance bodies, showing how developed nations dominate influence within the UN Security Council, the International Monetary Fund (IMF), and the World Bank. Developed countries score between 80 and 90 out of 100 in influence, while developing countries lag significantly, with influence scores ranging from 10 to 20.

Implications for Growth and Development

This imbalance restricts the capacity of developing nations to shape the global economic and security policies that directly affect their economies. For instance, decisions on debt relief, structural adjustment programmes, and funding priorities often reflect the interests of the powerful

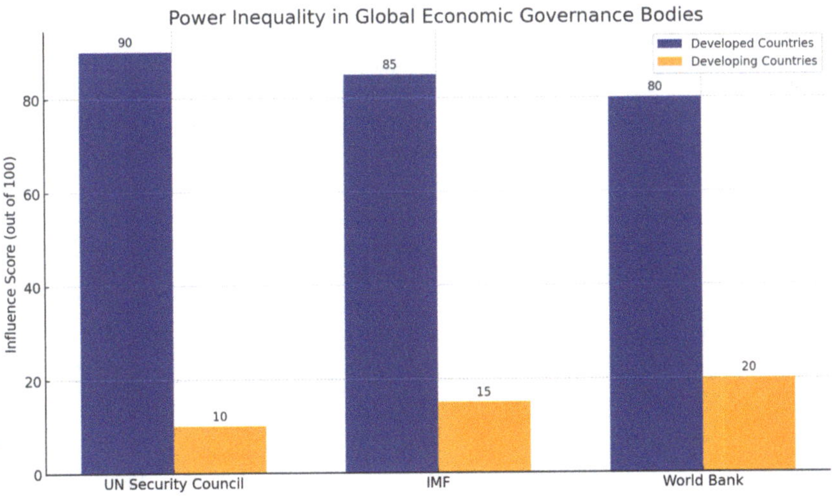

Fig. 6.1 Power inequality in global economic governance bodies

economies, sidelining the unique needs of developing countries. As a result, growth and development trajectories in Africa, Latin America, and parts of Asia are often dictated externally, leading to mismatched policies and prolonged dependency.

Is the UN Still Relevant for Development?

The UN continues to play a pivotal role in shaping global development agendas, especially through initiatives such as the SDGs (Marconini & Sauvé, 2010). Its reach in peacekeeping, climate advocacy, human rights, and humanitarian assistance remains significant (Marconini & Sauvé, 2010). However, the organisation faces growing criticism about its effectiveness, particularly concerning equity in global governance, responsiveness to emerging crises, and its representational legitimacy—especially within the UN Security Council (UNSC). The structure, largely unchanged since 1945, no longer reflects contemporary global power realities, with Africa, Latin America, and other regions underrepresented in major decision-making bodies. Therefore, while still relevant, the UN needs institutional innovation to remain effective and equitable. Based on the above-mentioned, we propose below some ideas on the new UN model which could trigger a balance of power within the UN System.

Proposed New UN Model: Balanced Mandate for Peace and Development

The proposed model recommends a **restructured UN** that broadens its mandate and corrects its institutional imbalances. It rests on six key pillars:

1. **Inclusive Security Governance**: Reforming the Security Council to include rotating seats for underrepresented regions, particularly Africa and Latin America, to reflect demographic and geopolitical shifts.
2. **Development-Security Nexus**: Integrating development and peacebuilding mandates more coherently, ensuring that UNDP, UNEP, and UN Peacekeeping collaborate on conflict-sensitive development.
3. **Climate and Technological Governance**: Expanding the UN's role in regulating global commons like AI, cyberspace, and climate resilience, with binding powers.

4. **Decentralised Leadership**: Empowering regional UN offices with decision-making powers to tailor programs based on regional contexts and cultural frameworks.
5. **Participatory Decision-making**: Institutionalising civil society, academia, and youth platforms in global governance, beyond state actors.
6. **Equity in Resource Distribution**: Reforming funding mechanisms to prioritise Least Developed Countries (LDCs) and climate-vulnerable states.

Three Reform Scenarios for UN Security Council Expansion

Scenario 1: Continent A (e.g., Africa) Included in UNSC

- **Implications**: Increases legitimacy and representation, especially given Africa's 54 member states and frequent appearance in peacekeeping mandates.
- **Benefits**: More tailored conflict resolution strategies, stronger African agency, and reduced reliance on external peacekeeping narratives.
- **Challenges**: Requires consensus among African Union states over representation—e.g., should Nigeria, South Africa, or Egypt represent the continent?

Scenario 2: All Continents Included Equally in UNSC

- **Implications**: Enhances legitimacy, but operational efficiency may suffer due to increased numbers.
- **Benefits**: Greater buy-in from Global South; more balanced voting leading to nuanced resolutions.
- **Challenges**: Veto power would need to be revisited or abolished to avoid paralysis.

Scenario 3: Regional Seats + Rotational Voting

- **Implications**: Regional blocs (e.g., AU, ASEAN, EU, Mercosur) elect representatives on a rotational basis.
- **Benefits**: Balances efficiency and representation; fosters intra-regional consensus before global negotiations.
- **Challenges**: Requires redefining sovereignty in terms of supranational representation.

Countries That Could Be Included in a Reformed UNSC

1. **Nigeria** – Africa's largest economy and population; active peacekeeping contributor.
2. **Brazil** – A regional power in Latin America with a growing global development profile.
3. **India** – World's largest democracy and a major contributor to UN peacekeeping.
4. **Germany** – Major global donor and a bridge between North and South.
5. **Indonesia or South Korea** – Key players in Asia with regional diplomacy experience.
6. **South Africa** – Active in peacebuilding and representing the African Union perspective.

Each of these countries brings not only geopolitical weight but also regional legitimacy, development priorities, and capacity for responsible global leadership. Without reform, the credibility and effectiveness of global governance institutions may erode, widening the trust gap between the Global North and South. To achieve inclusive and resilient global development, these bodies must reflect the realities of a diverse, interdependent world. Balancing influence is not just a matter of fairness; it is essential for global stability and long-term prosperity.

OPEC's Influence on Oil Markets

OPEC controls oil production, significantly impacting global energy prices. African oil-exporting nations benefit from price stability, but consumer economies suffer from energy price fluctuations (Ross, 2023). Below is a hypothetical graph showing the impact of OPEC oil price changes and the implications for African economies for the period 2020 to 2030.

Figure 6.2 shows that between 2020 and 2030, OPEC continues to exert substantial influence on global oil markets by adjusting its production levels. The hypothetical data suggests that when OPEC reduces oil production, as seen in 2023 and 2027, global oil prices rise significantly. Conversely, when production is increased or stabilised, prices tend to moderate. This manipulation of supply to achieve price targets highlights OPEC's central role in shaping the energy economy. African countries, both oil exporters and importers, are significantly affected by these price

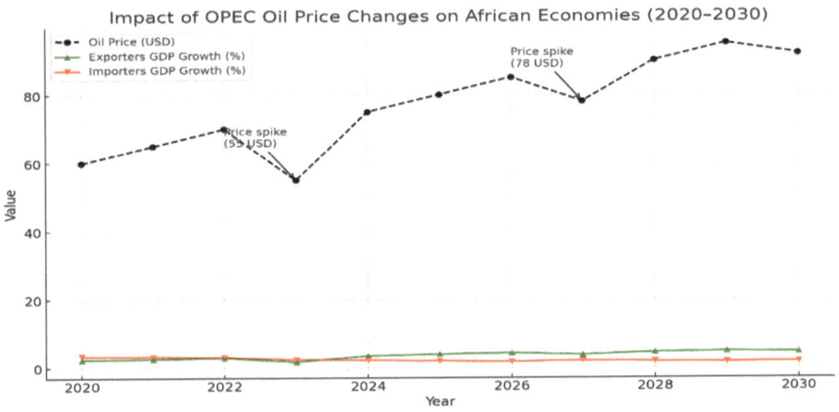

Fig. 6.2 Impact of OPEC oil price changes on African economies 2020–2030

movements, with far-reaching implications for their economic development.

For African oil-exporting countries such as Nigeria, Angola, and Libya, OPEC's production controls—and the corresponding increases in oil prices—bring economic benefits. As oil prices rise, these countries enjoy higher foreign exchange earnings, improved fiscal balances, and stronger GDP growth. The data illustrate that during periods of elevated oil prices (for instance, between 2025 and 2030), exporters experience consistent GDP growth above 4%. This windfall revenue can be used to invest in public infrastructure, expand social services, reduce debt, and build sovereign wealth funds. However, the reliance on oil revenue also makes these economies susceptible to external shocks, underscoring the importance of economic diversification and robust fiscal management to avoid the "resource curse".

On the other hand, African oil-importing countries such as Kenya, Ethiopia, and Senegal are adversely affected by oil price volatility. As prices rise, their import bills increase, putting pressure on foreign reserves and widening current account deficits. The data shows that the GDP growth rates for importers decline from 3.5% in 2020 to below 2% by 2030 as energy costs eat into public finances and elevate inflation. These countries may be forced to cut back on development spending or borrow at higher costs, ultimately slowing progress on critical development goals such as health, education, and infrastructure. This economic strain highlights the vulnerability of consumer economies to external price shocks driven by actors like OPEC.

The broader implications of OPEC's influence on oil prices extend to the development trajectory of the African continent. While exporters may experience short-term economic gains, these are often volatile and unsustainable without strong institutions and diversification strategies. Importers, on the other hand, face persistent risks unless they transition to alternative energy sources or improve energy efficiency. Overall, the need for resilient economic planning, regional energy cooperation, and investment in renewables is urgent. By reducing dependence on oil price cycles and promoting energy independence, African countries can better shield themselves from the adverse effects of global market fluctuations and accelerate inclusive, sustainable development.

Implications and Policy Recommendations

- Reforming global financial institutions to give developing countries greater decision-making power (Rodrik, 2011).
- Advocating for fairer trade agreements that protect local industries in developing countries (Mattoo & Subramanian, 2008).
- Strengthening regional economic blocs like the African Continental Free Trade Area (AfCFTA) to counteract external economic dependencies (Schokkaert, 2019)

Based on the above explanation, it can be argued that power is a double-edged sword in economic development. While it can drive progress, unchecked power structures often lead to inequalities and underdevelopment. By analysing recent case studies, this section has highlighted the role of power in shaping economic outcomes. To foster sustainable development, it is crucial to implement policies that ensure fair resource distribution, regulatory transparency, and equitable participation in global economic governance. Addressing power asymmetries requires collaborative efforts at the national, regional, and international levels.

The Role of Power in Sustainable Development

Rodrik (2011) explained that power is a central force in determining how sustainable development is pursued, implemented, and maintained across different economies. Sustainable development is often defined in economic terms, focusing on the balance between growth, environmental preservation, and social equity. However, power dynamics—whether political, economic, or institutional—play a crucial role in shaping long-term development goals (Rodrik, 2011). This section explores the economic definition of sustainable development, the influence of power structures on development policies, and case studies of countries where power has been successfully leveraged for sustainability. Additionally, it discusses the implications for developing nations and the lessons that can be drawn from the experiences of developed economies.

Defining Sustainable Development in Economic Terms

Porter and Kramer (2011) explain that sustainable development, as defined by the 1987 Brundtland Commission, refers to "development that meets the needs of the present without compromising the ability of future generations to meet their own needs." Within the definition, we observe that balancing society's needs with natural resources will ensure that future development will create a balance between developmental needs and societal needs, which is the foundation of a sustainable society.

From an economic perspective, sustainable development involves:

1. **Economic Growth:** Ensuring long-term economic expansion without depleting natural resources (Sachs, 2020).
2. **Environmental Sustainability:** Implementing policies that promote resource conservation, carbon reduction, and biodiversity preservation (Stern, 2021).
3. **Social Equity:** Reducing income inequality, improving access to essential services, and ensuring fair labour rights (Raworth, 2017).

Power structures influence each of these aspects by determining policy priorities, resource allocation, and regulatory enforcement.

How Power Structures Influence Long-Term Development Goals

Environmental Sustainability

- **Regulatory Power and Climate Policy:** Countries with strong state institutions have been more successful in implementing environmental policies. For example, the European Union (EU) has used regulatory frameworks to enforce carbon pricing, leading to a 24% reduction in emissions between 1990 and 2020 (European Environment Agency, 2022). Conversely, weaker governance structures in developing countries often lead to deforestation and environmental degradation, as seen in Indonesia and the Democratic Republic of Congo (DRC) (Butler, 2023; Mattoo & Fink, 2002).

- **Corporate Influence on Sustainability:** MNCs exert significant influence over environmental policies. In Nigeria, Shell and other oil companies have been accused of environmental pollution with limited governmental oversight, negatively impacting local communities and biodiversity (Okonkwo, 2022).

Social Equity

- **Power and Wealth Distribution:** The level of power concentration within an economy determines how wealth is distributed. In Nordic countries, progressive taxation and strong social welfare systems have reduced income inequality, while in many developing nations, economic power remains concentrated among the elite, leading to persistent poverty (Piketty, 2020).
- **Gender and Social Inclusion:** Power structures also determine social inclusion. Rwanda has leveraged state power to promote gender equality, with women holding over 60% of parliamentary seats, contributing to inclusive economic policies (World Bank, 2023).

Economic Growth

- **State-Led vs. Market-Led Development:** Countries with strong state involvement in economic planning, such as China, have managed long-term growth effectively, while economies relying solely on free markets, such as many Latin American nations, have experienced volatility (Chang, 2019).
- **Global Financial Institutions and Development Policies:** The influence of the International Monetary Fund (IMF) and the World Bank has shaped economic policies in Africa, often leading to SAPs that prioritised fiscal discipline over social spending (Stiglitz, 2021).

Case Studies of Successful Power-Driven Sustainable Development

Bhutan's Gross National Happiness (GNH) Model

Bhutan has adopted an alternative economic model that prioritises well-being over GDP growth. The government uses state power to regulate tourism, protect forests, and promote cultural preservation (Hankammer et al., 2021). Key outcomes include:

- **Environmental Protection:** Over 70% of Bhutan's land remains underforestcover(BhutanNationalEnvironmentCommission,2022).
- **Social Welfare:** Free healthcare and education have improved living standards.

Implications for Developing Countries

Bhutan's model demonstrates that political will and policy alignment can drive sustainable development, but it may not be replicable in larger, more industrialised economies (Hankammer et al., 2021).

We demonstrate here with an analytical graph (Fig. 6.3 below) and an explanation to support the argument that Bhutan's GNH model, though inspiring, may not be easily replicable in larger, more industrialised economies.

Axes

- **X-axis**: Level of Industrialisation and Population Size (Low → High)
- **Y-axis**: Feasibility of GNH Model Implementation (High → Low)

Curve Description

- The graph shows a downward-sloping curve from left to right.
- On the left side, countries like Bhutan (low population, low industrialisation) show high feasibility of adopting the GNH model.
- Moving to the right, towards countries with higher industrialisation and population (e.g., India, Nigeria, Brazil), the feasibility decreases.

Overlay (Colour Bands or Markers)

- **Green Zone (High Feasibility)**: Small, less industrialised countries with high policy coherence.

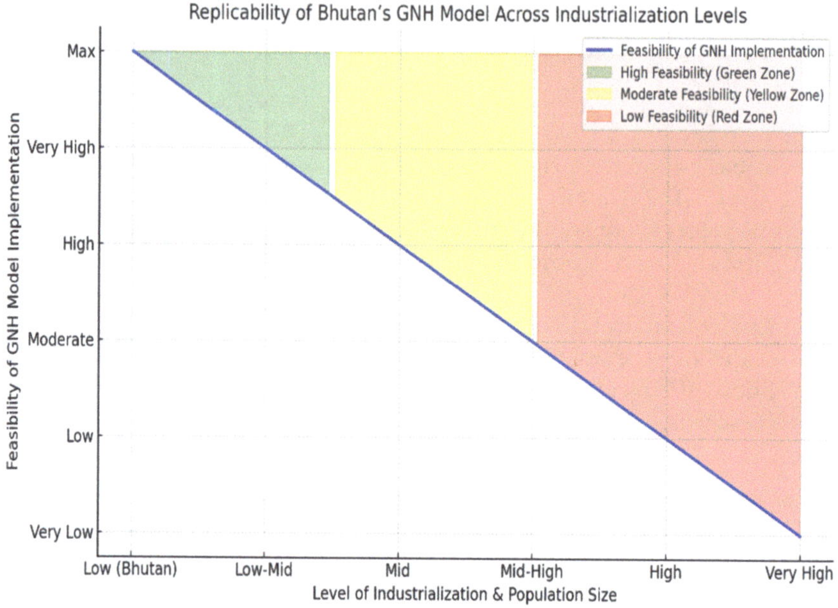

Fig. 6.3 Replicability of Bhutan's GNH model in developing economies

- **Yellow Zone (Moderate Feasibility)**: Medium-sized economies with partial institutional readiness.
- **Red Zone (Low Feasibility)**: Large industrialised nations with complex political economies (Table 6.1).

Why Not Easily Replicable?

1. **Scale and Governance**: Bhutan's small size allows for tighter policy alignment and state-led initiatives. Large countries face bureaucratic inertia and fragmented interests.
2. **Economic Complexity**: Industrialised nations have growth-driven, extractive economies that conflict with the environmental goals of GNH.
3. **Political Constraints**: Democracies with high inequality face voter pressure for immediate economic gains, limiting focus on long-term well-being.

Table 6.1 Graph interpretation and key analytical insights for Fig. 6.3

Factor	*Bhutan (GNH model)*	*Larger/industrialised countries*
Population size	<1 million (manageable)	10M–200M+ (complex needs)
Governance model	Centralised monarchy, policy continuity	Diverse politics, policy fragmentation
Economic base	Agrarian + tourism	Manufacturing, extractives, urbanisation
Tourism control	Strict high-value, low-volume tourism policy	Open mass tourism (difficult to regulate)
Environmental policy	The Constitution mandates 60% forest cover	Deforestation due to industrial expansion
Cultural homogeneity	Strong cultural identity and Buddhist philosophy	Diverse identities and competing value systems
Social services	Free healthcare and education (small scale)	Costly and politically contested in large populations

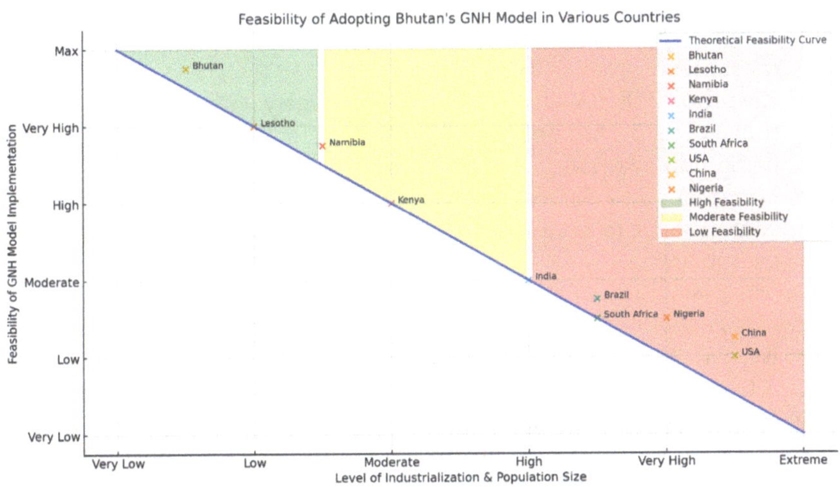

Fig. 6.4 Feasibility of Bhutan's GNH model in various countries

4. **Resource Demands**: Universal welfare, like free healthcare/education, is easier to finance in small populations, but cost-prohibitive in larger nations without broad tax bases.

Based on the above, let us look at the feasibility of the GNH implementation as illustrated in Fig. 6.4.

Explanation of Fig. 6.4 with Hypothetical Data

This updated graph (Fig. 6.4 above) incorporates hypothetical data to visualise how different countries might perform if they attempted to implement Bhutan's GNH model. Each country is plotted based on two variables:

- **X-axis**: Level of industrialisation and population size (0 = very low, 10 = very high).
- **Y-axis**: Estimated feasibility of implementing GNH principles (0 = very low, 10 = very high).

Key Insights from Hypothetical Country Data

High Feasibility Zone (Green)

- **Bhutan** (1, 9.5): Bhutan has minimal industrial activity and a small, cohesive population. This gives it an ideal setting for GNH policy success.
- **Lesotho** (2, 8): A small, low-income country with moderate institutional capacity and potential for adapting localised happiness or well-being frameworks.
- **Namibia** (3, 7.5): With a sparse population and a relatively high commitment to conservation, it could feasibly replicate some GNH components.

Moderate Feasibility Zone (Yellow)

- **Kenya** (4, 6): While moderately industrialised, Kenya faces high urbanisation and inequality. It could incorporate GNH elements in rural or devolved units.
- **India** (6, 4): India's democratic structure and vast population create challenges, though select states (e.g., Sikkim) may model after Bhutan in part.

Low Feasibility Zone (Red)

- **Brazil** (7, 3.5): With a large population and industrial economy, the implementation of the GNH would face strong political and economic resistance.
- **South Africa** (7, 3): Inequality, industrial dependencies, and service delivery gaps limit feasibility despite a rights-based constitution.

- **Nigeria** (8, 3): High population pressure, oil dependency, and governance challenges hinder GNH-aligned policies.
- **China** (9, 2.5): Though China promotes "Ecological Civilisation," its strong industrial economy and growth targets reduce GNH compatibility.
- **USA** (9, 2): The U.S. political economy is deeply market-driven, making nationwide adoption of GNH infeasible. However, localised happiness or well-being indices have been explored (e.g., Vermont, Seattle).

This analytical graph and data illustrate a negative correlation between industrialisation/population size and the feasibility of adopting Bhutan's GNH model. While Bhutan's success shows the power of values-based development, its replicability is structurally limited in larger, more industrialised contexts. Nonetheless, hybrid models that incorporate GNH principles at regional or municipal levels may offer a path forward for larger countries.

Hybrid GNH Model at Regional/Municipal Levels

In contexts where national adoption of the GNH is constrained by size, industrialisation, or governance complexity, a **hybrid model** can be adopted at the **subnational level**. This model integrates GNH principles into existing development planning frameworks such as municipal budgeting, urban planning, and public service delivery (Table 6.2).

What the Graph Shows (Descriptive Visualisation)

- **X-Axis**: Regional Governance and Economic Complexity (e.g. size of city, industry mix, governance layers)
- **Y-Axis**: Feasibility of Implementing GNH Principles (estimated on scale 1–10) (Table 6.3)

A downward sloping trend emerges as regional complexity increases, feasibility tends to decline, but local initiatives and governance innovations can still make hybrid implementation effective.

Figure 6.5 below illustrates the Hybrid GNH Framework applied across four municipal contexts—Seattle, Cape Town, Chiang Mai, and Sikkim—highlighting their relative strengths in implementing the four GNH pillars.

Table 6.2 Key elements of the hybrid GNH framework

GNH pillar	*Municipal application*	*Example*
Good governance	Participatory budgeting, transparency dashboards	**Seattle, USA** – civic engagement apps
Sustainable socio-economic development	Local green jobs, circular economy programmes	**Cape Town, SA** – community-based water recycling
Cultural preservation	Local festivals, native language education	**Chiang Mai, Thailand** – cultural tourism & heritage zoning
Environmental conservation	Urban forestation, emissions tracking	**Sikkim, India** – organic agriculture policy

Table 6.3 Eight regions with hypothetical values

Region	*Complexity score (0–10)*	*GNH feasibility (0–10)*
Paro (Bhutan)	2	9.2
Sikkim (India)	3	8.5
Chiang Mai (Thailand)	4	7
Nairobi County (Kenya)	5	6.5
Seattle (USA)	5	6
Addis Ababa (Ethiopia)	6	5
Cape Town (South Africa)	6	5
São Paulo (Brazil)	8	3.5

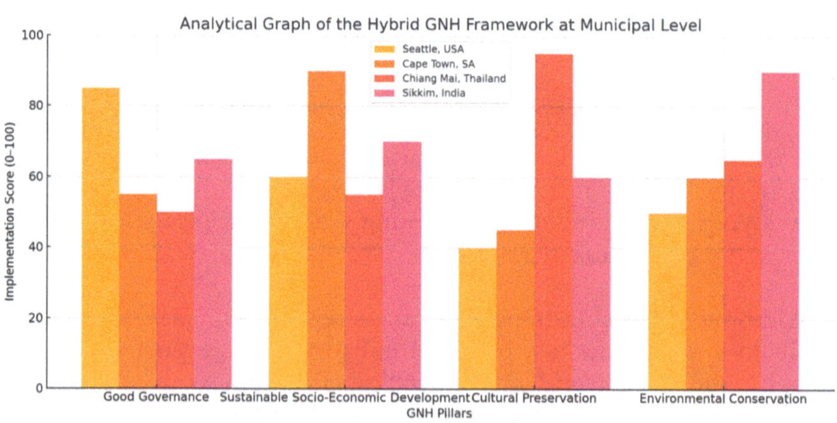

Fig. 6.5 Hybrid GNH framework at the municipal level

Key Analytical Observations

1. **Good Governance**

   - Seattle scores highest due to its civic tech platforms (e.g., participatory budgeting and transparency apps).
   - Other municipalities show moderate implementation levels, reflecting varying levels of institutional openness and citizen participation.

2. **Sustainable Socio-Economic Development**

   - Cape Town leads with strong circular economy and green job initiatives.
   - Sikkim and Seattle also show promise, although implementation varies by programme focus.

3. **Cultural Preservation**

   - Chiang Mai excels in preserving local culture through heritage tourism and education.
   - Other cities have less emphasis on this pillar, indicating a gap in integrating cultural identity into development.

4. **Environmental Conservation**

   - Sikkim outperforms due to its organic agriculture and environmental policies.
   - Chiang Mai and Cape Town follow, reflecting growing urban environmental initiatives.

Development Implications

- **Hybrid Application**: Cities can blend traditional GNH values with local policy tools to align happiness, sustainability, and economic goals.
- **Balanced Progress**: A well-rounded GNH model fosters inclusive development, yet most municipalities show uneven pillar integration.

- **Policy Transferability**: Lessons from high-scoring areas (e.g., Sikkim's environment model or Chiang Mai's cultural approach) can inform cross-regional development planning.

The analytical graph of the Hybrid GNH Framework illustrates how four cities—Seattle (USA), Cape Town (South Africa), Chiang Mai (Thailand), and Sikkim (India)—have applied the core GNH pillars at the municipal level. These pillars include Good Governance, Sustainable Socio-Economic Development, Cultural Preservation, and Environmental Conservation. Each city reflects differing strengths across these dimensions, providing insight into the practical application of happiness-centred development in diverse contexts.

Seattle demonstrates strong performance in the pillar of Good Governance, scoring the highest among the cities. This is largely due to its emphasis on participatory budgeting, open data, and the use of civic engagement apps that increase transparency and public involvement in local decision-making. However, Seattle shows moderate results in the other pillars, particularly in cultural preservation, which suggests a limited integration of cultural heritage into urban development strategies. This pattern reveals a governance-first approach that could benefit from a stronger inclusion of socio-cultural and environmental priorities.

Cape Town leads in Sustainable Socio-Economic Development, reflecting the city's investment in local green jobs and community-based circular economy programmes. These initiatives are helping to address unemployment while promoting resource efficiency and community resilience. Cape Town also performs reasonably well in Environmental Conservation, but exhibits lower scores in Good Governance and Cultural Preservation. This may indicate challenges in participatory processes and a need for stronger institutional frameworks that support both democratic engagement and cultural identity.

Chiang Mai significantly outperforms other municipalities in the Cultural Preservation pillar. Through policies supporting native language education, heritage zoning, and cultural tourism, the city has effectively integrated cultural sustainability into its development model. While it shows moderate engagement in environmental conservation, the lower scores in governance and socio-economic sustainability suggest that a stronger institutional and economic foundation could further reinforce its cultural achievements and enhance overall well-being.

Sikkim, a state in India, stands out in Environmental Conservation, largely due to its pioneering organic agriculture policy and dedication to preserving forest ecosystems. The region also shows a fairly balanced performance in the other pillars, especially in sustainable development and good governance. While cultural preservation is present, it remains less prominent compared to Chiang Mai. Sikkim's example suggests that environmentally led development can coexist with economic and governance improvements, offering a replicable model for eco-conscious policy implementation.

Overall, the analytical graph shows that while each city excels in one or two GNH pillars, none has achieved a fully balanced approach. This underscores the importance of integrating all four pillars to realise the full potential of the GNH model. The uneven distribution of implementation highlights opportunities for cross-learning and policy adaptation. For example, Seattle's governance model could be complemented by Chiang Mai's cultural preservation practices, while Cape Town's economic strategies might benefit from Sikkim's environmental frameworks. The hybrid GNH model thus serves as a flexible and adaptive development tool that can help municipalities address diverse challenges while promoting holistic and inclusive growth.

China's Poverty Reduction Programmes

Analytical Discussion of China's Poverty Reduction Programmes (1980–2030)

Between 1980 and 2020, China achieved an unprecedented feat in global development history by lifting over 800 million people out of poverty, accounting for more than 70% of global poverty reduction in that period (World Bank, 2021). This transformation was driven by a deliberate combination of state-led economic planning, targeted industrial policies, and massive infrastructure investments, particularly in transportation, energy, and rural development. These interventions spurred economic growth, improved market access, and reduced regional disparities.

To project the future impacts of China's poverty reduction strategies from 2020 to 2030, we can consider a hypothetical analytical graph based on historical momentum and the continuation of poverty reduction programmes (see Fig. 6.6 below).

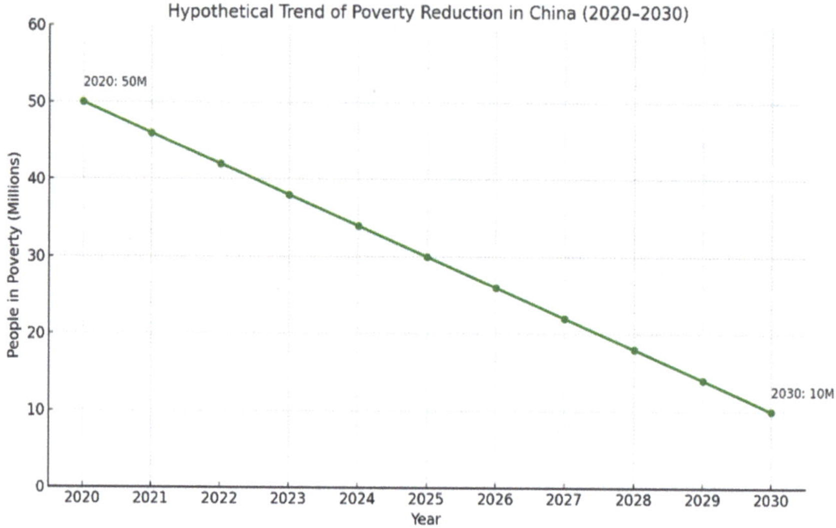

Fig. 6.6 Hypothetical trend of poverty reduction in China (2020–2030)

Hypothetical Analytical Graph Description (2020–2030)

- **X-Axis**: Years (2020–2030)
- **Y-Axis**: Number of people living in poverty (millions)
- **Curve**: Gradual decline from 50 million (2020) to 10 million (2030), assuming a steady 4 million people lifted out of poverty annually (Table 6.4).

The projected trend in Fig. 6.6 below illustrates that if China maintains its poverty alleviation momentum, an additional 40 million people may be lifted out of poverty between 2020 and 2030, reducing extreme poverty to near-elimination levels. However, challenges such as urban-rural income gaps, an ageing population, and rising inequality may influence this trend.

Lessons for Developing Countries

Developing countries can draw several valuable lessons from China's approach:

1. **Strategic State-Led Planning**: China's use of national development strategies targeted poor regions with tailored support.

Table 6.4 Hypothetical data: Poverty decline in China (2020–2030)

Year	*Estimated people in poverty (millions)*	*Annual reduction (millions)*
2020	50	–
2021	46	4
2022	42	4
2023	38	4
2024	34	4
2025	30	4
2026	26	4
2027	22	4
2028	18	4
2029	14	4
2030	10	4

Countries like Ethiopia and Vietnam have adapted similar approaches with positive results. Effective planning—backed by credible data, monitoring systems, and political will—can be a game-changer.

2. **Infrastructure as an Equaliser**: By linking remote regions to urban centres, China unlocked economic potential and enabled labour mobility. Investments in roads, electrification, and digital connectivity can stimulate local economies and create inclusive growth.
3. **Industrial Policy and Employment Generation**: China's targeted support for labour-intensive industries enabled rural populations to engage in manufacturing and services. Developing countries should focus on job-rich sectors like agriculture processing, textile manufacturing, and green industries, based on comparative advantage.
4. **Decentralised Implementation with Central Oversight**: While the national government set targets, local governments were given resources and flexibility to achieve them. This balance of decentralisation and accountability is key to effective service delivery in diverse socio-political contexts.

What to Adopt and What to Avoid

Adopt

- Long-term vision and integrated planning.
- Massive investment in rural and peri-urban infrastructure.
- Strong public service delivery mechanisms.

- Targeted subsidies and safety nets for the ultra-poor.
- Institutional learning and adaptability.

Avoid or Cautiously Approach

- **Over-centralisation**: China's success came with risks of local corruption, inefficiencies, and suppression of dissent. Developing nations must ensure checks and balances in state-led programmes.
- **Heavy reliance on debt-financed infrastructure**: Poorer countries must be cautious about debt sustainability, especially when borrowing for capital-intensive infrastructure projects.
- **Neglect of environmental and social safeguards**: China's rapid industrialisation has led to pollution and displacement. Developing nations must balance economic growth with environmental sustainability and social inclusion.

Implications for Global Development

China's poverty reduction story demonstrates that poverty is not inevitable, and with the right policy mix, it can be significantly reduced within a generation. However, it also raises questions about inequality, governance models, and human rights. The model is not universally transferable, but its core principles—such as political commitment, institutional coordination, and investment in people—can inspire tailored solutions elsewhere. For African and South Asian countries, especially China's experience, reinforces the importance of coupling inclusive economic growth with social protection and governance reforms for sustainable poverty eradication. Furthermore, China's success highlights the role of strong governance in poverty alleviation. However, it also underscores concerns about state overreach and economic inequalities.

Implications for Developing Countries

Developing countries can draw several lessons from these cases

1. **Strengthening Institutional Power:** Governments must have the capacity to implement and enforce long-term sustainability policies. Weak institutions often lead to policy failures and economic instability (Acemoglu & Robinson, 2019).

2. **Balancing State and Market Power:** While state intervention is essential fordevelopment, excessive government control can stifle entrepreneurship and innovation (Rodrik, 2021).
3. **Leveraging Regional Cooperation:** Regional economic partnerships, such as AfCFTA, can help counteract external power imbalances (UNECA, 2023).

Lessons from Developed Countries

- **Nordic Model of Sustainable Development:** Countries like Sweden and Denmark have successfully combined economic growth with environmental and social policies, emphasising high taxation, social safety nets, and renewable energy investments (Kangas, 2022).
- **Germany's Energy Transition (Energiewende):** Germany has used policy power to transition towards renewable energy, reducing reliance on fossil fuels and setting an example for other nations (Jacobsson & Bergek, 2021).

Key Takeaways

Developing nations should focus on policy continuity, institutional reform, and regional cooperation to drive sustainable development.

Power is integral to sustainable development, influencing environmental policies, economic strategies, and social equity. Case studies such as Bhutan's GNH model and China's poverty alleviation programmes show how state power can be leveraged for long-term growth. However, the experiences of developing countries suggest that without strong institutions and equitable policies, power can reinforce inequality and environmental degradation. Future policy frameworks should prioritise governance reforms, inclusive economic models, and international cooperation to ensure sustainable development in the Global South.

Empowering Marginalised Economies: A Power-Centric Approach

Identifying Marginalised Economies and Their Challenges

Marginalised economies are nations or regions that face structural barriers to economic growth, often characterised by weak institutions, inadequate infrastructure, limited access to global markets, and governance challenges

(Todaro & Smith, 2020). These economies typically exist in sub-Saharan Africa, parts of South Asia, and some Latin American and Caribbean nations.

Challenges Faced

- **Weak Institutions and Governance Deficiencies:** Corruption, lack of rule of law, and political instability hinder development (Acemoglu & Robinson, 2012).
- **Economic Dependency:** Reliance on a single commodity or sector increases vulnerability to global shocks (Collier, 2007).
- **Infrastructure Deficits:** Limited transport, energy, and digital infrastructure hinder competitiveness (Calderón & Servén, 2010).
- **Financial Exclusion:** Poor access to credit, high-interest rates, and informal financial systems limit entrepreneurship (Beck & Levine, 2004).

Case Study Examples

- **Democratic Republic of Congo (DRC):** Despite rich mineral resources, weak governance and conflict hinder growth (Auty, 2001).
- **Haiti:** Persistent economic struggles due to political instability and frequent natural disasters (Dupuy, 2010).
- **Zimbabwe:** Economic decline due to hyperinflation, land reform policies, and governance issues (Moyo, 2011).

The Power Theory and Its Application to Economic Empowerment

The Power Theory suggests that economic development is influenced by the distribution of power within institutions and policy structures (Lukes, 2005). Empowering marginalised economies requires altering power structures through policy and institutional reforms.

Policy Frameworks for Empowerment

- **Decentralisation of Power:** Shifting governance from central to local levels improves responsiveness and resource allocation (Rodríguez-Pose & Ezcurra, 2010).
- **Inclusive Industrial Policies:** Developing local industries with state support to reduce dependency on primary commodities (Chang, 2019).
- **Trade and Investment Policies:** Ensuring fair trade agreements and regional economic integration (Stiglitz, 2002).

Institutional Reform Models Adopted by Developing Countries

Rwanda's Vision 2020: Governance, Human Capital, and Technological Innovation

Overview

Rwanda's *Vision 2020* was launched in 2000 as a long-term development strategy aimed at transforming the country into a middle-income nation by 2020 (Ansoms & Rostagno, 2012). The plan focused on six pillars:

- Good governance and institutional development
- A skilled human resource base
- A vibrant private sector
- Infrastructure development
- Modern agriculture
- Regional and international integration

Key Institutional Reforms

- **Decentralisation of governance:** The government empowered local governments to implement policies tailored to community needs.
- **Zero tolerance for corruption:** Rwanda implemented strict anti-corruption policies, making it one of Africa's least corrupt nations (Transparency International, 2023).
- **Investment in education:** Programmes such as *One Laptop Per Child* and a focus on STEM education enhanced human capital development.
- **ICT-driven development:** Rwanda positioned itself as an ICT hub, attracting global companies and fostering innovation (World Bank, 2019).

Implications

- Economic growth averaged 7–8% annually, driven by reforms in governance, infrastructure, and technology (IMF, 2020).
- Rwanda became a regional leader in business reforms, ranking among the top African countries in the World Bank's *Ease of Doing Business* index (IMF, 2020).
- Political stability and policy consistency attracted FDI (IMF, 2020).

Lessons Learned

1. Strong governance and institutional frameworks create an enabling environment for development.
2. Investing in human capital through education and innovation leads to sustainable growth.
3. Decentralisation enhances efficiency and accountability in public administration (IMF, 2020)

Ethiopia's Agricultural Development-Led Industrialisation (ADLI): Rural Productivity and Economic Diversification

Overview

Ethiopia's *ADLI* strategy, introduced in the 1990s, was based on the idea that agriculture should drive industrialisation. The policy aimed to modernise agriculture, increase productivity, and use agricultural surplus to fuel industrial growth (Gebreeyesus, 2013).

Key Institutional Reforms

- **Agricultural extension services:** Farmers received training and improved seeds, fertilisers, and irrigation technologies (Gebreeyesus, 2013).
- **Infrastructure investment:** The government expanded rural roads and electrification to connect agricultural areas with markets (Gebreeyesus, 2013).
- **Industrial parks:** The government established industrial parks for textile and agro-processing industries to absorb surplus labour from agriculture (Gebreeyesus, 2013).

Lessons Learned

1. A well-planned agricultural strategy can be a foundation for industrialisation.
2. Infrastructure investments are critical for linking rural economies to national and global markets.
3. Land tenure policies need to balance state control with private sector incentives to encourage long-term investment.

Botswana's Diamond Revenue Model: Managing Natural Resources for Long-Term Growth

Overview

Unlike many resource-rich developing countries that fall into the "resource curse" trap, Botswana successfully leveraged its diamond wealth for sustainable economic growth (Acemoglu et al., 2003). The government's approach focused on transparency, prudent financial management, and long-term planning.

Key Institutional Reforms

- **State ownership with private sector collaboration:** The government partnered with De Beers through *Debswana*, ensuring that diamond revenues were reinvested in national development (Acemoglu et al., 2003).
- **Fiscal discipline:** Botswana created a sovereign wealth fund to manage diamond revenues and ensure economic stability during price fluctuations (Acemoglu et al., 2003).
- **Education and infrastructure investment:** Diamond revenues were channelled into public services such as education, healthcare, and roads (Porter & Kramer, 2011).
- **Anti-corruption policies:** Botswana maintained one of Africa's most transparent governance systems, reducing leakages in resource revenues (Porter & Kramer, 2011).

Implications

- **Consistent economic growth:** Botswana maintained an average 5–7% GDP growth for decades (Kolbert, 2014).
- **High human development indicators:** The country invested heavily in education, healthcare, and public services, improving citizens' quality of life (Hankammer et al., 2021).
- **Resilience to economic shocks:** The sovereign wealth fund helped stabilise the economy during diamond price declines (Hankammer et al., 2021).

Lessons Learned

1. Resource wealth can be a driver of sustainable development if managed with transparency and long-term planning.
2. Public-private partnerships ensure efficient resource exploitation and revenue management.
3. Strong institutions and governance mechanisms prevent corruption and promote equitable wealth distribution (Van Reybrouck, 2015).

Overall Implications and Key Takeaways from Institutional Reforms (Table 6.5)

General Lessons for Developing Countries

1. Good governance and anti-corruption frameworks are essential for economic progress.
2. Long-term planning ensures sustainable development, even in resource-rich economies.
3. Investment in human capital, infrastructure, and innovation accelerates economic transformation.
4. Diversifying the economy reduces vulnerability to external shocks.
5. Public-private partnerships enhance efficiency in economic management.

Table 6.5 Implications and key takeaways from institutional reforms

Country	*Reform model*	*Key outcomes*	*Lessons for other developing countries*
Rwanda	Vision 2020	Strong institutions, high economic growth, ICT-driven development	Good governance, human capital investment, and decentralisation lead to stability and progress
Ethiopia	ADLI	Agricultural transformation, industrial diversification, rural development	Linking agriculture with industry fosters inclusive economic growth
Botswana	Diamond Revenue Model	Sustainable resource management, stable economy, improved social indicators	Transparent governance and prudent financial management prevent the "resource curse"

Source: Hankammer et al. (2021)

The institutional reform models of Rwanda, Ethiopia, and Botswana demonstrate that good governance, strategic investment, and sound economic policies can transform developing economies. Each country's experience provides valuable lessons on how to design policies that promote inclusive, resilient, and sustainable growth. Developing nations can adapt these strategies to their own contexts to achieve long-term prosperity.

Role of Local Leadership, Global Cooperation, and International Organisations

Hankammer et al. (2021) point out that marginalised economies require support from local leadership, international partnerships, and multilateral organisations.

Local Leadership in Development: The Role of Political Will and Civil Society Engagement

Local leadership plays a critical role in shaping a country's economic trajectory. Strong political will and governance reforms have been instrumental in the transformation of several developing nations (Hankammer et al., 2021). Two key aspects of effective local leadership are:

1. Strong Political Will and Visionary Leadership
2. Empowering Civil Society for Accountability and Inclusiveness

Strong Political Will and Visionary Leadership

Case Studies: Rwanda and Liberia

Rwanda: Paul Kagame's Leadership and Economic Transformation

Background

Rwanda's development success is largely attributed to the leadership of President Paul Kagame, who took office after the 1994 genocide. His government prioritised institutional reforms, economic liberalisation, and good governance to drive the country's rapid economic growth (Booth & Golooba-Mutebi, 2012).

Key Commitments to Development

- **Zero tolerance for corruption:** Kagame established anti-corruption institutions, such as the Office of the Ombudsman, to enhance transparency in governance (Transparency International, 2023).
- **Investment in human capital:** The government focused on education, ICT, and skills training, positioning Rwanda as an innovation hub (World Bank, 2019).
- **Infrastructure and economic modernisation:** Large-scale investments in transport, energy, and digital infrastructure improved business conditions.

Implications

- Rwanda consistently ranked among the top African countries in the Ease of Doing Business Index due to streamlined bureaucratic processes (World Bank, 2020).
- The country's GDP grew at an average of 7–8% annually, reducing poverty significantly (IMF, 2021).
- Kigali became an investment hub for multinational firms and technology startups.

Lessons Learned

1. Political stability and strong leadership are essential for economic transformation.
2. A clear vision, backed by policies and governance reforms, accelerates development.
3. Anti-corruption measures create trust and attract foreign investment.

Liberia: Ellen Johnson Sirleaf's Post-War Reconstruction Efforts

Background

After decades of civil war, Liberia faced economic collapse, institutional breakdown, and social fragmentation. Ellen Johnson Sirleaf, Africa's first female head of state, implemented crucial reforms to rebuild the economy and strengthen governance (Elkington, 1997).

Key Commitments to Development

- **Debt relief and fiscal discipline:** Secured a $4.6 billion debt relief package under the Heavily Indebted Poor Countries (HIPC) Initiative (Schokkaert, 2019).

- **Anti-corruption and governance reforms:** Strengthened institutions like the Liberia Anti-Corruption Commission (LACC).
- **Infrastructure rebuilding:** Rehabilitated roads, electricity grids, and public services.
- **Education and gender empowerment:** Promoted female leadership and access to education for girls.

Implications

- Liberia's macroeconomic stability improved, attracting FDI in key sectors like agriculture and mining (Ingraham, 2017).
- International support for Liberia increased, with significant aid from the World Bank, IMF, and UNDP (Hankammer et al., 2021).
- Becker et al.'s (2012) governance model inspired increased women's participation in leadership across Africa.

Lessons Learned

1. Strong leadership can drive post-conflict economic recovery.
2. Debt relief, if managed well, provides a foundation for economic stability.
3. Gender-inclusive policies contribute to long-term social and economic benefits.

Empowering Civil Society for Accountability and Inclusive Growth

The Importance of Civil Society in Development

Civil society organisations (CSOs) play a crucial role in holding governments accountable, ensuring transparency, and advocating for social inclusion (Putnam, 1993). Their involvement leads to better governance, economic justice, and citizen participation in policymaking.

Case Studies: Kenya and Brazil

Kenya: Civil Society and Democratic Accountability

Background

Kenya has a strong civil society sector that has been influential in promoting democracy, human rights, and economic reforms. Organisations such as Transparency International Kenya and the Kenya Human Rights Commission have held leaders accountable for corruption and mismanagement (Putnam, 1993).

Key Commitments to Development

- **Public sector transparency:** The government introduced the Access to Information Act (2016), allowing citizens to obtain official information (Hankammer et al., 2021).
- **Judicial reforms:** Civil society advocacy led to an independent judiciary, reducing government interference in legal processes (Hankammer et al., 2021).
- **Decentralisation:** The 2010 Constitution created county governments, enhancing service delivery at the grassroots level (Hankammer et al., 2021).

Implications

- **Reduced corruption:** Kenya improved in the Corruption Perceptions Index due to increased transparency measures (Transparency International, 2023).
- **Citizen participation:** Public engagement in governance increased, leading to better policies tailored to local needs.
- **Economic growth:** Improved governance boosted investor confidence in Kenya's business environment.

Lessons Learned

1. A strong civil society enhances government accountability and transparency.
2. Decentralisation improves service delivery and local economic development.
3. Legal frameworks that protect press freedom and access to information are critical for democracy.

Brazil: Participatory Budgeting as a Model for Inclusive Governance

Background

Brazil pioneered participatory budgeting (PB), a governance model that allows citizens to decide how public funds are allocated (Elkington, 1997). First implemented in Porto Alegre in the 1980s, PB has since expanded to several other cities worldwide.

Key Commitments to Development

- **Direct citizen participation:** Communities propose and vote on budget priorities.
- Transparency in public spending: All budget decisions are made through open deliberation and consensus-building (Elkington, 1997).
- **Social inclusion:** PB empowered marginalised communities by giving them a voice in governance (Elkington, 1997).

Implications

- **Reduced corruption:** Public oversight minimised the misuse of funds (Elkington, 1997).
- **Improved public services:** Investments in infrastructure, education, and healthcare were more effective because citizens determined local needs (Elkington, 1997).
- **Replication in other countries:** PB has been successfully adopted in South Africa, India, and Indonesia, demonstrating its global relevance (Elkington, 1997).

Lessons Learned

1. Citizen participation leads to more efficient resource allocation and governance.
2. Transparency reduces corruption and strengthens public trust in government.
3. Local empowerment models are scalable and adaptable across different regions.

Overall Implications and Key Takeaways (Table 6.6)

General Lessons for Developing Countries

1. Strong and visionary leadership is essential for economic transformation.
2. Anti-corruption policies and transparency measures build public trust and attract investment.
3. Decentralisation enhances service delivery and community development.

Table 6.6 Implications and key takeaways

Key factor	*Rwanda*	*Liberia*	*Kenya*	*Brazil*
Leadership	Kagame's strategic governance reforms	Sirleaf's post-war reconstruction and economic recovery	Decentralisation and judicial reforms	Participatory budgeting for governance
Anti-corruption measures	Strict governance and accountability policies	Establishment of anti-corruption bodies	Strengthened transparency laws	Public budget oversight by citizens
Citizen participation	Decentralisation for better governance	Gender-inclusive policies	Strong civil society engagement	Participatory budgeting to empower communities
Economic impact	High FDI, strong GDP growth	Macroeconomic stabilisation, improved investment climate	Reduced corruption, improved business environment	Improved public service efficiency

Source: Hankammer et al. (2021)

4. Empowering civil society ensures accountability and policy inclusiveness.
5. Participatory governance leads to better resource allocation and economic equity.

The experiences of Rwanda, Liberia, Kenya, and Brazil illustrate how strong leadership and active civil society engagement can drive sustainable development. These case studies provide valuable lessons for other developing nations seeking to improve governance, reduce corruption, and foster inclusive economic growth.

While the cases of Rwanda, Liberia, Kenya, and Brazil provide strong examples of how local leadership and institutional reforms shape economic transformation, further insights can be drawn from the following:

1. Comparative Analysis with Other Developing Countries
2. Challenges in Implementing Institutional Reforms
3. The Role of International Partnerships and Global Governance
4. Scalability of Institutional Models to Other Contexts
5. Long-Term Sustainability and Policy Continuity

Comparative Analysis with Other Developing Countries

Beyond the cases already discussed, other nations have adopted unique models of governance, economic planning, and institutional reforms to drive economic development:

Ghana: Democratic Stability and Economic Diversification

- Political stability and democratic consolidation have made Ghana one of Africa's most stable economies (Gyimah-Boadi, 2001).
- Strong investments in education and social welfare under the free Senior High School (SHS) programme increased human capital (World Bank, 2021).
- Lessons learned: Political stability is critical for long-term development, and sustained investment in education ensures future growth.

Vietnam: Market Reforms and State-Led Development

- The Doi Moi (Renovation) policy, initiated in 1986, transformed Vietnam from a centrally planned to a market-oriented economy (Van Arkadie & Mallon, 2003).
- Strategic state-led industrialisation, export-driven growth, and attraction of FDI helped Vietnam emerge as an economic success story in Southeast Asia.

Lessons Learned

- Gradual economic liberalisation and state-guided reforms can accelerate growth without causing abrupt socio-economic disruptions.

Mauritius: Inclusive Growth and Economic Transformation

- From a mono-crop sugar economy, Mauritius diversified into textiles, tourism, and financial services, reducing dependency on agriculture (Subramanian, 2009).
- Pro-business policies and strong institutions made it a top performer in the Ease of Doing Business Index (World Bank, 2020).

Lessons Learned

- Strategic economic diversification and stable governance promote resilience to global economic shocks.

Challenges in Implementing Institutional Reforms

Despite the success stories, marginalised economies face persistent challenges in institutional reform:

Weak Institutions and Political Instability

- Nigeria's anti-corruption efforts often face resistance due to entrenched political interests and weak enforcement mechanisms (Roy, 2017).
- South Sudan's fragile state struggles with internal conflict and governance instability, making institutional reform nearly impossible (Rolandsen, 2015).

Corruption and Governance Failures

- Even when reforms are initiated, a lack of political commitment weakens enforcement. For example, in Angola, massive oil revenues have not translated into broad-based development due to elite capture and corruption (Hodges, 2004).

Policy Inconsistencies and Short-Term Thinking

- Many developing countries struggle with policy reversals when leadership changes.

Example

- Zimbabwe's land reform programme, though intended for redistribution, led to agricultural collapse due to poor planning and lack of follow-through (Scoones et al., 2011).

Lessons Learned

1. Institutional reforms require long-term political commitment, not just leadership rhetoric.

2. Anti-corruption measures must be enforced consistently to prevent elite capture.
3. Policy continuity across governments is necessary for sustained economic growth.

The Role of International Partnerships and Global Governance

Development is not isolated. International actors like the United Nations (UN), World Bank, IMF, African Union (AU), and regional organisations shape policies in marginalised economies.

Foreign Aid and Development Assistance

- Effectiveness of Aid: While foreign aid can stimulate economic growth, it can also create dependency (Moyo, 2011).

Example

- The Marshall Plan helped Europe rebuild after WWII, but similar aid strategies in Africa have had mixed results due to poor governance and corruption.

Trade and Economic Integration

- AfCFTA: Aims to boost intra-African trade and industrialisation (UNECA, 2021).
- South-South Cooperation: China's Belt and Road Initiative (BRI) is financing large-scale infrastructure projects in Africa, but concerns about debt sustainability remain (Brautigam, 2019).

Lessons Learned

1. Foreign aid must complement local initiatives, not replace them.
2. Trade agreements and economic blocs can enhance regional self-sufficiency.
3. Careful debt management is crucial to avoid financial dependency.

Scalability of Institutional Models to Other Contexts

Not all institutional reforms can be replicated directly due to context-specific factors such as history, culture, and governance capacity. However, elements of successful reforms can be adapted, as reflected in Table 6.7 below.

Lessons Learned

1. Institutional reforms must be tailored to each country's socio-political environment.
2. Some governance models (e.g., transparency and participatory budgeting) can be applied universally.
3. Agriculture-led industrialisation is highly effective for rural-based economies.

Long-Term Sustainability and Policy Continuity

Hankammer et al. (2021) believe that many developing nations suffer from short-termism in policymaking, where projects initiated by one government are abandoned by the next. Ensuring policy continuity is critical for sustainable development.

Table 6.7 Elements of successful reform

Reform model	*Key features*	*Potential for replication*
Rwanda's Vision 2020	Good governance, digital economy, human capital investment	High – Countries with strong leadership can implement similar policies
Ethiopia's ADLI	Agricultural productivity-led industrialisation	Medium – Works best in agrarian economies
Botswana's diamond model	Transparent management of natural resources	High – Natural resource-rich countries can adopt revenue-sharing mechanisms
Brazil's participatory budgeting	Direct citizen involvement in budget allocation	High – Can be implemented at municipal levels

Source: Hankammer et al. (2021)

Best Practices for Policy Continuity

- **Institutionalisation of Policies:** Economic strategies should be integrated into long-term national development plans.
  - **Example:** Malaysia's Vision 2020 provided a 30-year roadmap, ensuring continuity across different governments (Mahathir, 1991).
- **Bipartisan Consensus:** Political consensus prevents frequent policy reversals.
  - **Example:** In South Korea, industrial policy was supported across different administrations, leading to consistent growth (Chang, 2019).
- **Legal Frameworks:** Enshrining policies in law reduces the risk of policy reversals.
  - **Example:** Ghana's Petroleum Revenue Management Act ensures oil revenue is transparently allocated, preventing future mismanagement.

Lessons Learned

1. Long-term national development plans ensure sustained economic growth.
2. Political consensus prevents destructive policy reversals.
3. Strong legal frameworks reduce the risk of misgovernance and corruption.

Final Reflections

Empowering marginalised economies requires a holistic approach, integrating strong leadership, institutional reforms, civil society participation, global cooperation, and long-term policy commitments. The case studies of Rwanda, Liberia, Kenya, Brazil, Vietnam, Mauritius, Ghana, and Ethiopia provide valuable lessons for other developing nations seeking to break cycles of underdevelopment and achieve sustainable economic growth.

Global Cooperation and International Organisations: Their Role and Constraints in Development

Putnam (1993) explained that global cooperation and the involvement of international organisations play an essential role in the development of marginalised economies. They offer financial resources, technical assistance, policy guidance, and mechanisms for multilateral collaboration. However, their influence is complex and multifaceted, with potential constraints that can sometimes hinder the autonomy of local governments and their development agendas (Putnam, 1993). Below is a detailed analysis of key international institutions and the implications of their involvement in developing nations.

The World Bank and IMF: Providing Financial and Technical Assistance

Role in Development
The World Bank and the International Monetary Fund (IMF) have been at the forefront of providing development assistance to low-income and middle-income countries (Hankammer et al., 2021). These institutions offer both financial support (through loans and grants) and technical assistance to improve governance, infrastructure, education, and health (Hankammer et al., 2021). Additionally, the IMF provides monetary policy advice, while the World Bank supports development projects in sectors like infrastructure, health, and education (Hankammer et al., 2021).

Constraints to Development: Conditionalities and Autonomy
However, the involvement of these institutions often comes with conditionalities—economic policies that must be implemented in exchange for loans and financial assistance (Hankammer et al., 2021). Critics argue that these conditionalities often stifle local autonomy and can result in policies that may not align with the development priorities of the country (Hankammer et al., 2021). For example, during the 1980s and 1990s, the IMF imposed Structural Adjustment Programmes (SAPs) on many African countries, which required economic liberalisation, privatisation, and austerity measures (Stiglitz, 2002). While these measures were intended to stabilise economies, they often led to increased poverty, social unrest, and economic inequality.

Implications

1. Loss of policy autonomy: Local governments are constrained in formulating policies that cater to domestic priorities.
2. Social costs: SAPs led to austerity measures that negatively impacted healthcare, education, and social welfare (Stiglitz, 2002).
3. Debt dependency: Many countries have become debt-dependent on the World Bank and IMF, which creates long-term financial strain and can limit their capacity for economic self-determination (Stiglitz, 2002).

Lessons Learned

1. Conditionalities need to be re-evaluated to ensure they are flexible and responsive to local development needs.
2. Debt relief and restructuring should be prioritised to prevent overreliance on foreign loans.

African Union (AU) and Regional Economic Communities (RECs): Promoting Regional Integration and Shared Development Strategies

Role in Development

The African Union (AU) and Regional Economic Communities (RECs), such as Economic Community of West African States (ECOWAS), Southern African Development Community (SADC), and East African Community (EAC), aim to promote regional integration, economic cooperation, and collective action for shared development strategies across Africa (Hankammer et al., 2021). Hankammer et al. (2021) add that the AU focuses on peace and security, human rights, and economic development, while the RECs play a direct role in creating free trade areas, facilitating infrastructure development, and fostering economic integration within regions.

Hankammer et al. (2021) underscore the AU contributions and constraints as listed below.

- **Successes of the AU:**
  1. **Peacekeeping efforts** in regions like Sudan and Somalia, where the AU has been involved in conflict resolution and peacebuilding initiatives.
  2. **AfCFTA:** The establishment of AfCFTA is a major milestone in regional economic integration, aimed at boosting intra-African trade and reducing dependence on external markets (UNECA, 2021).
  3. **Coordination of development goals:** The AU has played a role in harmonising member states' policies to align with continental development frameworks like Agenda 2063.

Constraints to Development and Achieving AU's Mandate

Despite these achievements, the AU has struggled with issues such as political fragmentation, inconsistent enforcement of agreements, and limited financial resources. Many African countries continue to face challenges in coordinating policies at the regional level due to national interests, poor infrastructure, and political instability.

- **Has the AU Achieved its Mandate?**
  1. While the AU has made significant strides in fostering political integration, its economic goals have faced obstacles. For instance, the lack of a common monetary policy and trade barriers still limit the full realisation of AfCFTA's potential (Hankammer et al., 2021).
  2. The lack of enforcement mechanisms means that countries often do not comply with AU frameworks. For example, many countries still face challenges in ensuring democratic governance and human rights.

- **Is the AU still relevant in today's development context?**

  Hankammer et al. (2021) point out that despite its challenges, the AU remains relevant as Africa's voice in global affairs, particularly in advocating for climate change mitigation, peace and security, and economic development. However, it needs more effective leadership and stronger institutions to fully realise its vision. These are highlighted below.

- **Implications:**
  1. The AU must strengthen its institutional capacity to enforce agreements and hold countries accountable.
  2. The AU could enhance economic cooperation by focusing on cross-border infrastructure and regional value chains.
  3. Regional economic integration is essential for Africa's development, but the AU needs greater political will from its member states.

UNDP's SDGs: Framework for Poverty Reduction and Economic Resilience

Role in Development
Hankammer et al. (2021) explain that the United Nations Development Programme (UNDP), through its SDGs, provides a universal framework for addressing poverty, inequality, and economic resilience in developing countries (UNDP, 2015). The SDGs cover 17 interconnected goals, including quality education, gender equality, clean energy, decent work, and climate action. These goals have become a blueprint for national development strategies in both developed and developing countries.

Hankammer et al. (2021) highlight the strengths and constraints as presented below.

- **Strengths of the SDGs:**
  1. The SDGs emphasise inclusive growth and sustainable development as core principles for eradicating poverty.
  2. The global framework ensures that nations are collectively working towards shared prosperity and environmental sustainability.
  3. The SDGs also incorporate gender equality, which has led to the adoption of more inclusive policies in many developing countries.

Constraints in Achieving the SDGs
- While the SDGs provide a comprehensive framework for development, their implementation often faces constraints such as a lack of funding, political will, and coordination challenges.
- Some countries may prioritise short-term economic growth over long-term sustainability, undermining the SDGs' goals of climate action and environmental protection.
- Implications:

1. Countries need to align national policies with the SDGs, ensuring that development goals are not just aspirational but also actionable.
2. Multilateral cooperation between international organisations, national governments, and local communities is needed for the SDGs to be successful.
3. There is a need for increased financial support for the implementation of the SDGs, particularly in low-income countries

Global institutions like the World Bank, IMF, AU, and UNDP have played significant roles in shaping development policy worldwide. However, their effectiveness is often constrained by challenges such as conditionalities, political fragmentation, lack of enforcement mechanisms, and insufficient funding. These institutions need to adjust their strategies to ensure that they empower local autonomy, promote sustainable development, and foster stronger political cooperation within regions.

Case Studies of Marginalised Nations Benefiting from International Support

Hankammer et al. (2021) opine that international support, through financial assistance, technical expertise, and policy guidance, has played a pivotal role in the economic transformation of many marginalised nations. These countries, often burdened by low development indicators and political instability, have achieved notable successes through strategic reforms and partnerships with international organisations (Hankammer et al., 2021). Below is an expanded analysis of key cases where marginalised nations benefited from international support, highlighting their successes, challenges, and lessons learned.

Bangladesh and Microfinance: The Grameen Bank Model

Overview and Success

Bangladesh is one of the most poverty-stricken countries in the world, but through microfinance initiatives, particularly the Grameen Bank model, millions of marginalised individuals, especially women, have gained access to credit. Founded by Muhammad Yunus in 1976, Grameen Bank focuses on offering small loans to individuals in rural areas who lack access to conventional banking services (Yunus, 2007). The model's success lies in its ability to empower the poor, particularly women, by providing them with financial independence, entrepreneurial opportunities, and a means to improve their livelihoods. The analysis of this case study reveals the following:

- **Lessons Learned:**
  1. **Financial inclusion** is a powerful tool for reducing poverty. In providing small-scale loans, Grameen Bank enabled self-employment and economic self-sufficiency for people who were otherwise excluded from formal financial systems.
  2. **Empowerment of women**: Grameen Bank's focus on women borrowers has had a transformative effect on gender relations, as it has empowered women to contribute to household income and decision-making processes.
  3. **Social collateral**: Instead of requiring formal collateral, Grameen Bank uses social collateral (peer support and accountability) to mitigate the risk of default, which has been crucial in the success of the model.

- **Power Policy Implications:**
  1. **Decentralised financial models**: This model challenges traditional banking systems and suggests that decentralising financial services to the grassroots can enhance economic inclusion.
  2. **Governance and social capital**: Building social networks and community trust can be as important as financial capital in empowering marginalised groups.
  3. **Gender-sensitive policy frameworks**: The Grameen model highlights the need for inclusive policies that support marginalised groups, particularly women, as agents of change in economic development.

- **Failures in Development Paradigms:**

  While the Grameen Bank model has been successful, it has also faced criticism for its high-interest rates and the risk of creating a debt trap for borrowers. In some cases, the loans have been used to meet basic needs rather than for productive investments, which can perpetuate cycles of poverty. Additionally, the scalability of the model has been debated, as it requires significant social infrastructure and community cohesion to work effectively.

Vietnam's Economic Reforms (Đổi Mới)

Overview and Success
Vietnam's economic transformation, known as Đổi Mới (Renovation), is one of the most successful examples of market-oriented reforms in a socialist economy. Initiated in 1986, the reforms shifted Vietnam's centrally planned economy towards a socialist-oriented market economy (Hankammer et al., 2021). The country embraced global integration, privatisation, and FDI, leading to rapid economic growth and a significant poverty reduction. The reforms included trade liberalisation, economic decentralisation, and the establishment of a more competitive market economy (Dollar & Litvack, 1998). The analysis highlights the following:

- **Lessons Learned:**
  1. **Gradual reform**: The incremental approach adopted by Vietnam in introducing market mechanisms allowed for a controlled transition from central planning to market-driven growth.
  2. **State capacity and control**: Despite embracing market reforms, Vietnam maintained strong state control over key sectors, such as agriculture and state-owned enterprises, which allowed the government to balance market forces with social stability.
  3. **Openness to international trade**: Vietnam's integration into the global economy through trade agreements, notably joining the WTO, played a crucial role in boosting its exports and attracting foreign investment.

- **Power Policy Implications:**
  1. **Flexible and adaptive policies**: The Vietnamese experience underscores the importance of contextualising economic policies to suit national needs while integrating global market trends.
  2. **Balancing market forces and state intervention**: Countries pursuing economic reforms must strike a balance between state control and market liberalisation to avoid the social and economic disparities that can arise from unregulated markets.
  3. **International cooperation**: The role of international trade agreements and FDI cannot be overstated in countries looking to modernise their economies.

- **Failures in Development Paradigms:**
  Vietnam's rapid economic growth has been accompanied by rising inequality, particularly between urban and rural areas. While poverty has been reduced, income inequality has increased in recent years. Furthermore, the focus on industrialisation has often come at the expense of sustainable development, with challenges related to environmental degradation and labour rights.

Ghana's Economic Recovery Programme (ERP)

Overview and Success
In the 1980s, Ghana faced severe economic challenges, including high inflation, external debt, and poor economic governance (Hankammer et al., 2021). The government, under the leadership of Jerry Rawlings, implemented the Economic Recovery Programme (ERP) with assistance from the IMF and the World Bank (Hankammer et al., 2021). The ERP focused on structural adjustments, such as privatisation, trade liberalisation, and currency devaluation, with the aim of stabilising the economy and stimulating growth (Aryeetey & Fosu, 2005).

- **Lessons Learned:**
  1. **Macroeconomic stability**: The ERP helped Ghana stabilise its economy by controlling inflation and restoring fiscal discipline, which laid the foundation for later economic growth (Harriss, 2005).
  2. **Conditionality challenges**: While the ERP led to macroeconomic stability, it also imposed austerity measures that were unpopular and resulted in social unrest. This illustrates the importance of designing reforms that are politically feasible and aligned with the socio-political context (Hausmann, 2022).
  3. **Diversified economic growth**: The ERP did not simply focus on macro-stability, but also encouraged economic diversification, particularly in agriculture and services, which was crucial for long-term growth (Hausmann, 2022).

- **Power Policy Implications:**
  1. **Importance of external support**: Ghana's success in implementing economic reforms illustrates the value of international financial assistance in addressing deep-rooted economic crises (Harriss, 2005).

2. **Policy ownership:** While international institutions played a critical role, it was Ghana's commitment to implementing and customising the reforms to its local context that led to success (Hassan & Prichard, 2022).
3. **Social impact**: Economic reforms must be designed with social protection mechanisms to mitigate the adverse effects of austerity and ensure that marginalised groups are not disproportionately affected (Hassan & Prichard, 2022).

- **Failures in Development Paradigms:**
  Despite the success of the ERP, the short-term social costs (e.g., higher unemployment, reduced social services) raised concerns about the sustainability of growth in the long run (Hassan & Prichard, 2022). Additionally, the reforms faced political resistance, and challenges related to corruption and governance continued to affect the effectiveness of the reforms (Hassan & Prichard, 2022).

What Committed These Countries to Success?
The success of Bangladesh, Vietnam, and Ghana can be attributed to a combination of factors:

- Strong leadership with a clear commitment to reform (e.g., Jerry Rawlings in Ghana, Paul Kagame in Rwanda, and Nguyen Van Linh in Vietnam).
- Strategic use of international support (e.g., IMF and World Bank loans) combined with domestic ownership of reform agendas.
- Focused policy frameworks targeting poverty reduction, macro-stability, and economic diversification.
- A commitment to inclusive development and human capital investment, particularly in sectors like education, health, and gender empowerment.

However, the failures also provide crucial lessons: Reforms need to be socially inclusive, politically sustainable, and sensitive to local conditions to avoid negative outcomes such as rising inequality or social unrest. Countries must find a balance between economic liberalisation and social protection, ensuring that vulnerable populations are not left behind in the pursuit of economic growth.

Empowering marginalised economies requires addressing structural barriers, improving governance, and leveraging global partnerships. Through better policy frameworks, institutional reforms, and strategic leadership, these economies can transition towards sustainable development and economic self-sufficiency.

Policy Implications: Integrating the Power Theory into Development Policy

Hankammer et al. (2021) emphasise that the Power Theory provides a critical lens for understanding development policies, as it examines how power dynamics shape economic, political, and social structures. Development is not simply a matter of economic growth but also involves addressing structural inequalities and ensuring equitable resource distribution. Integrating the Power Theory into development policies enables sustainable and inclusive growth by recognising how power is concentrated, exercised, and contested.

Significance of the Power Theory in Development Policy

Addressing Structural Inequalities
The Power Theory helps explain how historical and systemic power imbalances influence development outcomes (North, 1990). Many marginalised economies remain underdeveloped due to political domination, economic dependency, and institutional weaknesses (Visser, 2005). When understanding how power is distributed and how institutions function, policymakers can design more equitable development strategies.

Empowering Marginalised Groups
In many developing countries, economic policies tend to favour the elite and urban centres, leaving rural populations, women, and small enterprises with limited influence over policy decisions (Carroll, 1991). The Power Theory highlights the importance of participation and agency, ensuring that marginalised groups actively shape development rather than being passive recipients (Carroll, 1991).

Reducing Policy Capture by the Elite

Power imbalances often lead to policy capture, where the economic and political elite manipulate development policies for their own benefit. For instance, land reforms and tax policies often favour large corporations rather than local communities (Acemoglu & Robinson, 2012). A power-sensitive approach ensures transparent policymaking and accountability mechanisms to prevent elite capture (Harriss, 2005).

Strategies for Integrating the Power Theory into Development Policies

Participatory Governance and Decision-Making

Ansoms and Rostagno (2012) maintain that one of the key strategies for integrating the Power Theory into development is ensuring participatory governance. This involves inclusive policymaking where communities, civil society organisations, and local businesses actively contribute to decision-making processes (Ansoms & Rostagno, 2012).

- **Practical Example:** Rwanda's Vision 2020 emphasised decentralisation by empowering local governments to engage in bottom-up decision-making, leading to better service delivery and stronger local economies (Ansoms & Rostagno, 2012).
- **Policy Implication:** Governments should establish mechanisms for public participation, such as citizen advisory councils and participatory budgeting, to ensure that local voices influence development policies.

Strengthening Institutional Autonomy

Institutions play a critical role in balancing power within a country. Independent regulatory bodies, anti-corruption agencies, and judicial systems should be empowered to check government overreach and corporate influence.

- **Practical Example:** Botswana's Diamond Revenue Model demonstrates how independent institutions can effectively manage natural resources. The government's partnership with De Beers ensured that diamond revenues were reinvested into education, health, and infrastructure, reducing rent-seeking behaviour (Acemoglu et al., 2003).

- **Policy Implication:** Countries should develop strong, independent institutions that are free from political interference, particularly in resource management and public finance.

Decentralised Economic Planning
Decentralisation redistributes power from central governments to local authorities, allowing for context-specific development strategies.

- **Practical Example**: Ethiopia's Agricultural Development-Led Industrialisation (ADLI) successfully integrated regional agricultural planning, leading to higher agricultural productivity and rural economic growth (Gebreeyesus, 2013).
- **Policy Implication:** Development strategies should be tailored to local contexts, ensuring regional empowerment and economic diversification.

Power-Sensitive Trade and Industrial Policies
Economic policies should not only focus on growth but also on redistribution. Governments must carefully negotiate trade agreements and industrial policies to prevent dependency on MNCs.

- **Practical Example:** Vietnam's Đổi Mới (Renovation) Policy strategically liberalised trade while maintaining state control over key industries, preventing complete dominance by foreign companies (Dollar & Litvack, 1998).
- **Policy Implication**: Policymakers must ensure that economic liberalisation does not reinforce power asymmetries but instead supports domestic industries and small businesses.

Recommendations for Policymakers to Address Power Imbalances

Institutional Reforms to Promote Inclusive Growth
Policymakers must establish mechanisms to redistribute power across government, businesses, and civil society.

- **Scenario Option:** Introducing progressive tax systems that ensure fair wealth distribution, as seen in Scandinavian economies.
- **Scenario Option:** Strengthening land tenure laws to protect small farmers from corporate land grabs.

Social Protection Policies to Reduce Inequality
Developing economies must integrate strong social protection programmes that empower vulnerable populations.

- **Scenario Option**: Implementing universal basic income (UBI) for marginalised groups, as tested in Kenya's cash transfer programmes.
- **Scenario Option:** Providing affordable credit facilities for small enterprises, similar to the Grameen Bank model in Bangladesh (Yunus, 2007).

Trade Policies That Enhance Economic Sovereignty
Countries should negotiate fair trade agreements that prioritise national development over foreign corporate interests.

- **Scenario Option**: Adopting regional value chains that encourage intra-African trade, as promoted by AfCFTA.
- **Scenario Option:** Enforcing technology transfer policies in FDI agreements, ensuring that local industries benefit from multinational operations.

Power-Sensitive Policy Design: Balancing Market Dynamics and Social Equity

A power-sensitive policy framework ensures that economic growth does not exacerbate social inequalities but rather fosters shared prosperity. This requires balancing market-driven policies with social protections.

Progressive Economic Policies

- **Policy Example**: South Korea's state-led industrialisation focused on export-oriented growth while investing in education and skill development (Chang, 2019).
- **Implication:** Developing economies should adopt policies that promote private sector growth while ensuring equitable access to resources.

Fair Labour and Wage Policies

- **Policy Example**: Rwanda's labour laws emphasise liveable wages and decent working conditions, improving worker productivity and social stability (Ansoms & Rostagno, 2012).

- **Implication:** Governments should establish minimum wage laws and ensure workers' rights to prevent exploitation.

Sustainable and Inclusive Growth Models

- **Policy Example**: Brazil's Bolsa Família programme, a conditional cash transfer initiative, successfully reduced poverty while fostering human capital development (Hodak, 2007).
- **Implication:** Social welfare programmes should be linked to education and healthcare, ensuring that economic benefits reach marginalised groups.

Integrating the Power Theory into development policy is essential for achieving sustainable and inclusive growth. Policies must address structural power imbalances, empower marginalised communities, and promote equitable resource distribution (Hausmann, 2022). Strategies such as participatory governance, decentralised economic planning, and power-sensitive trade policies can help reduce elite dominance and ensure a fairer economic landscape (Hausmann, 2022).

Policymakers must adopt power-conscious approaches, balancing market efficiency with social equity. This requires strong institutions, transparent governance, and inclusive economic policies. Only by restructuring power relations can development truly serve the interests of all citizens, rather than benefiting a privileged few (Hausmann, 2022).

Specific Policy Areas

Integrating the Power Theory into development policy requires a multidimensional approach, addressing key policy areas such as institutional governance, economic planning, trade, social protection, and environmental sustainability. Below is a more in-depth analysis of each of these policy areas and how they can be power-sensitive, ensuring equity, resilience, and sustainable growth (Gyimah-Boadi, 2001).

Institutional Governance and Power Reform

Strong institutions are fundamental to economic transformation. However, in many developing economies, the political elite capture institutions, leading to corruption, weak rule of law, and poor governance (North, 1990).

Key Policy Interventions

- **Enhancing Decentralisation:**
  - **Example:** Rwanda's Vision 2020 promoted local governance structures, allowing communities to influence decision-making (Ansoms & Rostagno, 2012).
  - **Implication:** Countries must strengthen regional and municipal authorities to foster locally driven development.

- **Strengthening Anti-corruption Measures:**
  - **Example:** Botswana's Independent Corruption Authority successfully reduced the elite-driven resource mismanagement (Acemoglu et al., 2003).
  - **Implication:** Transparent procurement laws and whistleblower protection policies must be institutionalised to combat corruption.

- **Judicial and Electoral Reforms:**
  - **Example:** Ghana's Electoral Commission operates independently, ensuring democratic transitions and reducing political instability (Aryeetey & Fosu, 2005).
  - **Implication:** A free and fair electoral system ensures political accountability and inclusive policymaking.

Economic Planning: State-Led vs. Market-Driven Approaches

The balance between state intervention and free-market mechanisms is critical in shaping power relations in an economy. Excessive market liberalisation can lead to inequality, while over-regulation may stifle innovation.

Key Policy Interventions

- **Strategic Industrial Policy:**
  - **Example:** South Korea's state-driven industrialisation nurtured domestic industries, enabling them to compete globally (Chang, 2019).
  - **Implication:** Governments should provide targeted subsidies and technology transfers for key industries to ensure competitive domestic production.

- **Balanced FDI Policies:**
  - **Example:** Vietnam's Đổi Mới Reforms liberalised the economy while maintaining domestic ownership in strategic sectors (Dollar & Litvack, 1998).
  - **Implication:** Developing economies should negotiate FDIs to include local employment quotas and skills transfer agreements.

- **Resource-Driven Development:**
  - **Example:** Botswana's diamond revenue model reinvested natural resource wealth into infrastructure and education (Acemoglu et al., 2003).
  - **Implication**: Governments must establish sovereign wealth funds to prevent resource curse scenarios.

Trade and Regional Integration Policies

Global trade structures often favour wealthy nations, leaving developing economies vulnerable to commodity dependence and unfair trade agreements (Gyimah-Boadi, 2001).

Key Policy Interventions

- **Fair Trade Agreements:**
  - **Example: AfCFTA** promotes intra-African trade, reducing dependence on Western markets.
  - **Implication:** Policymakers must prioritise regional economic integration to increase bargaining power in international trade.

- **Import Substitution and Export Diversification:**
  - **Example:** China's special economic zones (SEZs) attracted foreign investment while maintaining domestic industrial control (Porter & Kramer, 2011).
  - **Implication:** Governments must invest in local manufacturing to reduce import dependency.

- **Negotiating Equitable Global Trade Terms:**
  - **Example:** The WTO Doha Round failed to deliver trade fairness for developing nations (Stiglitz, 2002).

   - **Implication:** Developing countries must form coalitions to challenge unfair tariff systems and trade barriers imposed by global powers.

Social Protection and Inclusive Development Policies

Power-sensitive development policies must prioritise equity, ensuring that economic benefits reach marginalised groups.

Key Policy Interventions

- **Universal Basic Income (UBI) and Cash Transfer Programmes:**
  - **Example:** Brazil's Bolsa Família programme significantly reduced poverty by linking cash transfers to education and health requirements (Bokpin, 2017).
  - **Implication:** Governments should expand cash transfer programmes to protect vulnerable populations from economic shocks.

- **Women's Economic Empowerment:**
  - **Example:** Bangladesh's microfinance model (Grameen Bank) enabled millions of women to start businesses, increasing household income and education rates (Yunus, 2007).
  - **Implication:** Countries must integrate gender-sensitive financial policies, such as subsidised credit programmes for women entrepreneurs.

- **Affordable Housing and Urban Planning:**
  - **Example:** Ethiopia's Integrated Housing Policy promoted low-cost housing solutions for urban poor populations (Gebreeyesus, 2013).
  - **Implication**: Governments should invest in public housing initiatives to prevent urban inequality and informal settlement growth.

Environmental Sustainability and Climate-Resilient Development

Power imbalances between developed and developing nations have led to climate injustice, where poorer nations bear the greatest climate risks despite contributing the least to global emissions.

Key Policy Interventions

- **Green Energy Investments:**
  - **Example:** Kenya's Geothermal Energy Expansion reduced reliance on fossil fuels and created green jobs (Van Reybrouck, 2015).
  - **Implication**: Governments must diversify energy sources by investing in solar, wind, and hydroelectric power.

- **Climate-Smart Agriculture:**
  - **Example:** Ethiopia's Sustainable Land Management Programme (SLMP) increased soil fertility and water conservation for farmers (Gebreeyesus, 2013).
  - **Implication**: Policymakers should promote climate-resilient agricultural practices, ensuring long-term food security.

- **Carbon Trading and Climate Finance:**
  - **Example:** South Africa's **carbon tax policy** incentivised industries to reduce emissions (Szamosszegi & Kyle, 2011).
  - **Implication:** Governments should integrate carbon taxation and seek climate finance mechanisms for sustainable investments.

A Power-Sensitive Policy Agenda for Development

Gyimah-Boadi (2001) highlights that a power-sensitive development approach must integrate equitable governance, economic sovereignty, inclusive social policies, and environmental sustainability. Gyimah-Boadi (2001) points out that the lessons from successful policy interventions highlight the importance of:

1. Decentralised and participatory governance that prevents elite capture.
2. Balanced economic planning, ensuring state intervention where needed while maintaining private sector dynamism.
3. Regional integration and fair trade policies to counteract global trade asymmetries.
4. Social protection mechanisms, such as cash transfers and microfinance, that empower marginalised populations.

Sustainable Development Strategies, Addressing Climate Risks and Promoting Green Economies

Policymakers must adopt context-driven solutions, ensuring that power is equitably distributed across institutions, businesses, and society. Development must not only be measured by GDP growth but also by its ability to reduce inequalities and enhance human well-being.

Integrating Power Theory into Development Policy: Policy Areas, Case Studies, and Implications

Institutional Governance and Power Reform

Power Imbalance Challenge

Hankammer et al. (2021) highlight that in many developing countries, weak institutions, corruption, and elite capture undermine development efforts. Effective institutional reforms are needed to enhance transparency, accountability, and public service delivery.

Case Study: Rwanda's Vision 2020

- **Reform Focus:** Good governance, human capital investment, and technology-driven public services.
- **Success Factors:**
  - Strong leadership under Paul Kagame focused on anti-corruption policies and digital governance.
  - Decentralisation of governance, ensuring local participation in policymaking (Ansoms & Rostagno, 2012).
- **Lessons Learned:**
  - A top-down leadership approach can be effective when combined with institutional capacity building.
  - Technology-based governance (e-government platforms) can improve service delivery and reduce corruption.

Case Study: Ghana's Electoral Reforms

- **Reform Focus:** Strengthening democratic institutions through independent electoral commissions.

- **Success Factors:**
  - Establishment of an independent Electoral Commission with legal backing (Aryeetey & Fosu, 2005).
  - Transparent electoral processes restored public trust in governance.

- **Lessons Learned:**
  - Independent institutions safeguard political stability.
  - Electoral reforms must ensure free and fair elections, preventing the political elite from consolidating power.

Policy Implications

- **Decentralisation and Local Governance:** Countries must create autonomous regional governments to enhance service delivery and public participation.
- **Anti-corruption Measures:** Implementing whistleblower protections and public accountability mechanisms is critical.
- **Judicial and Electoral Reforms:** Strengthening the independence of the judiciary and electoral bodies ensures political stability.

Economic Planning: Balancing State-Led and Market-Driven Approaches

Power Imbalance Challenge

Developing economies struggle with the balance between state intervention and market forces, often resulting in inequality or inefficiency.

Case Study: Ethiopia's Agricultural Development-Led Industrialisation (ADLI)

- **Reform Focus:** Agricultural productivity as the basis for industrialisation (Gebreeyesus, 2013).
- **Success Factors:**
  - State-led agricultural investments in rural areas.
  - Extension services for farmers, boosting agricultural output.
  - Public-private partnerships (PPPs) in agro-industries.

- **Lessons Learned:**
  - Targeted government intervention can boost productivity and food security.
  - Agriculture must be linked to industrialisation to create value-added industries.

Case Study: Vietnam's Economic Reforms (Đổi Mới)

- **Reform Focus:** Market liberalisation while maintaining state control in key sectors (Dollar & Litvack, 1998).
- **Success Factors:**
  - Gradual privatisation of state-owned enterprises.
  - Integration into global markets, increasing exports.
  - Retaining government influence over strategic industries.

- **Lessons Learned:**
  - Gradual economic liberalisation prevents economic shocks.
  - A mixed economic model ensures stability while benefiting from globalisation.

Policy Implications

- **Balanced Industrial Policy:** Governments should support strategic sectors while maintaining market competition.
- **Regulated Privatisation:** A phased approach to privatisation prevents economic instability.
- **Investment in Agricultural Productivity:** Prioritising rural development is key to long-term economic stability.

Trade and Regional Integration Policies

Power Imbalance Challenge

Szamosszegi and Kyle (2011) highlight that developing countries are often marginalised in global trade negotiations, leading to unfair terms of trade.

Case Study Analysis: AfCFTA and Its Implications for Regional Integration and Development

AfCFTA, launched in 2021, is a landmark initiative aimed at unifying the African market into a single, tariff-free trading bloc. The core objective of AfCFTA is to boost intra-African trade by reducing tariffs and non-tariff barriers, thereby fostering economic growth, reducing poverty, and promoting industrialisation across the continent. As African countries implement AfCFTA between 2020 and 2030, the policy reforms associated with it have far-reaching implications for regional integration, economic diversification, and sustainable development.

Comparative Analytical Graph: Intra-African Trade Volume vs. GDP Growth (2020–2030)
Figure 6.7 below depicts a hypothetical comparative analytical graph illustrating trends in intra-African trade volume (as a % of total trade) versus average GDP growth rates across major African regional blocs (ECOWAS, SADC, and EAC), under AfCFTA implementation.

Graph Description
X-axis: Years (2020 to 2030)
Y-axis (Left): Intra-African Trade Volume (% of total trade)
Y-axis (Right): Average GDP Growth (%)

Lines
Line 1: ECOWAS Trade Volume (%)
Line 2: SADC Trade Volume (%)
Line 3: EAC Trade Volume (%)
Line 4: Combined GDP Growth (%)
Steady rise in intra-African trade from 15% in 2020 to 33% by 2030.

- Parallel increase in average GDP growth from 3.0% (2020) to 5.5% (2030).
- Steeper trade growth in EAC and SADC due to digital and transport infrastructure improvements.

Figure 6.7 above presents a hypothetical comparison of intra-African trade volumes and average GDP growth from 2020 to 2030 under AfCFTA implementation.

- **Intra-African Trade Volume (% of Total Trade):**
  - **ECOWAS** increases from 14% to 33%.
  - **SADC** rises from 16% to 36%, reflecting infrastructure-driven trade gains.
  - **EAC** grows from 12% to 35%, driven by digital and logistics improvements.

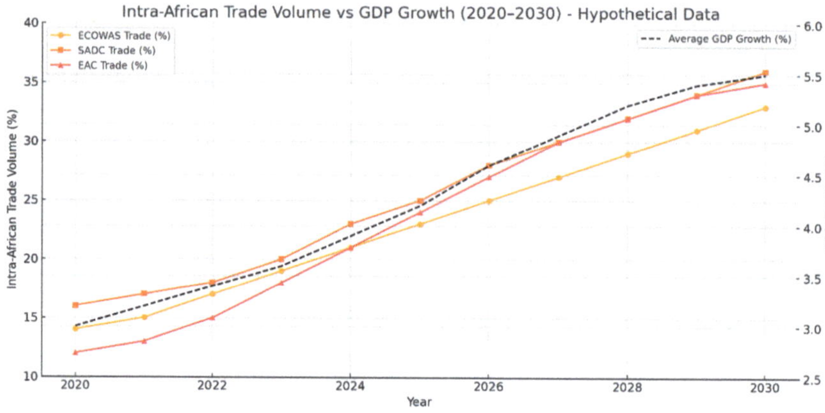

Fig. 6.7 Hypothetical comparative analytical graph

- **GDP Growth (%):**
  - Continental average GDP growth accelerates from 3.0% in 2020 to 5.5% by 2030, driven by enhanced trade, SME expansion, and industrialisation.

This hypothetical trajectory demonstrates that AfCFTA implementation positively correlates with regional integration and economic development, reinforcing the importance of fair trade, infrastructure, and industrial policy.

Full Explanation and Development Implications

Boost to Intra-African Trade and SMEs
AfCFTA significantly reduces tariffs and trade barriers, enabling small and medium enterprises (SMEs) to access broader markets. This is particularly vital in regions like ECOWAS and SADC, where SMEs make up over 80% of business entities. By facilitating cross-border commerce and lowering operational costs, AfCFTA enhances productivity, competitiveness, and income generation, especially in agribusiness, manufacturing, and digital services.

Strengthened Regional Integration

The policy framework behind AfCFTA underscores the importance of harmonising trade regulations, establishing rules of origin, and investing in infrastructure (such as roads, ports, and digital platforms). These reforms catalyse greater economic interdependence among African nations, strengthening regional blocs like ECOWAS, SADC, and EAC. For instance, SADC has leveraged AfCFTA to enhance regional energy and transport corridors, facilitating smoother goods movement between landlocked and coastal countries.

GDP Growth and Industrialisation

As shown in the analytical graph, a positive correlation exists between increased intra-African trade and GDP growth. The ability of African nations to access neighbouring markets more easily leads to higher production volumes, greater employment opportunities, and economies of scale. Additionally, with growing market access, countries are incentivised to diversify their export base, reduce reliance on raw commodities, and move towards value-added manufacturing and services, such as agroprocessing and textiles.

Bargaining Power and Global Trade

AfCFTA improves Africa's collective bargaining position in international forums such as the WTO. A united market of over 1.3 billion people provides leverage to negotiate **fairer trade terms**, push back against exploitative pricing of raw materials, and resist non-tariff protectionist measures imposed by developed economies. This is particularly important in navigating post-COVID-19 global supply chain realignments and trade fragmentation.

- **Lessons Learned:**
  - Regional Trade Integration Enhances Global Bargaining Power: A single African market acts as a stronger negotiating bloc, leading to more equitable international trade agreements.
  - Infrastructure Investment is Crucial: Roads, ports, logistics hubs, and digital trade platforms remain essential to lower transaction costs and facilitate seamless cross-border trade.
  - Trade Requires Complementary Reforms: Trade liberalisation must be complemented by industrial policies, SME financing, and labour mobility protocols to fully realise the benefits of AfCFTA.

- **Policy Implications:**
  - **Fair Trade Agreements:** African countries must coordinate positions and advocate for fairer WTO rules, especially concerning agricultural subsidies, intellectual property rights, and dispute resolution mechanisms.
  - **Strengthening Regional Blocs:** By empowering regional organisations like ECOWAS, SADC, and EAC with more technical and financial resources, countries can build resilience to global economic shocks.
  - **Export Diversification:** Reducing overdependence on oil, minerals, and other raw commodities is crucial. Governments should invest in processing industries, innovation hubs, and education systems aligned with industrial needs.

AfCFTA stands as a transformative step towards continental economic integration and shared prosperity. Its implementation, if supported by robust infrastructure, transparent institutions, and inclusive policy frameworks, can reshape Africa's development trajectory. The comparative data and hypothetical trends suggest that by 2030, Africa could experience not only enhanced regional trade but also more balanced, equitable, and sustainable economic growth.

Social Protection and Inclusive Development

Power Imbalance Challenge

Many marginalised populations lack access to credit, education, and social security, reinforcing inequality.

Case Study: Bangladesh and Microfinance (Grameen Bank)

- **Reform Focus:** Financial inclusion through microcredit schemes (Yunus, 2007).
- **Success Factors:**
  - Small loans to women-led enterprises reduced poverty and increased household incomes.
  - Low repayment default rates due to community-based accountability structures.

- **Lessons Learned:**
  - Financial inclusion programmes empower marginalised communities.
  - Social capital and peer accountability can enhance financial access.

- **Policy Implications:**
  - **Universal Social Safety Nets:** Expanding cash transfer programmes helps cushion vulnerable populations.
  - **Gender-Sensitive Development Policies**: Women's empowerment leads to long-term economic benefits.
  - **Affordable Credit Programmes**: Promoting microfinance and SME funding drives local entrepreneurship.

Environmental Sustainability and Climate-Resilient Development

Power Imbalance Challenge

Developing nations bear the highest climate risks despite contributing the least to global emissions.

Case Study: Kenya's Renewable Energy Investments

- **Reform Focus:** Expansion of geothermal and solar energy to reduce dependence on fossil fuels (Szamosszegi & Kyle, 2011).
- **Success Factors:**
  - Public-private partnerships (PPPs) in energy projects.
  - Government subsidies for solar energy access in rural areas.

- **Lessons Learned:**
  - Investment in renewable energy reduces energy poverty.
  - Climate financing (carbon credits, green bonds) can attract global investments.

- **Policy Implications:**
  - **Green Economy Strategies:** Incentivising renewable energy production ensures long-term energy security.
  - **Climate-Resilient Agriculture:** Governments should support drought-resistant crops and water conservation initiatives.
  - **Carbon Taxation and Sustainable Financing:** Establishing carbon markets encourages businesses to adopt eco-friendly practices.

Final Policy Recommendations for Power-Sensitive Development

1. **Decentralised Governance:** Strengthening local institutions improves public participation and accountability.
2. **Strategic Economic Policies:** Governments must balance industrial policy with market liberalisation (Porter & Kramer, 2011).
3. **Regional Integration:** Strengthening AfCFTA, ECOWAS, and SADC ensures economic resilience (Porter & Kramer, 2011).
4. **Social Protection Policies:** Expanding cash transfers and microfinance programmes enhances inclusive development (Porter & Kramer, 2011).
5. **Sustainable Development Strategies**: Investing in green energy and climate adaptation programmes is critical (Porter & Kramer, 2011).

When the Power Theory is integrated into development policies, countries can create inclusive, resilient, and sustainable economies while addressing historical and structural inequalities.

Case Studies Across Specific Regions

Successes, Failures, and Missed Opportunities in Development Strategies

Africa: Economic and Institutional Reforms

Success: Botswana's Diamond Revenue Model

- **Reform Focus:** Sustainable resource management and economic diversification (Acemoglu et al., 2003).
- **Success Factors:**
  - Public-private partnerships (PPPs) with De Beers ensured fair revenue distribution.
  - Revenue reinvestment in education, healthcare, and infrastructure.
- **Lessons Learned:**
  - Good governance and resource management ensure long-term economic benefits.
  - Diversification beyond extractive industries is key to sustained growth.

Missed Opportunity: Nigeria's Oil Dependency and Corruption

- **Challenge:** Nigeria, despite its massive oil wealth, has struggled with economic diversification and corruption (Hankammer et al., 2021).
- **Key Failures:**
  - Over-reliance on oil exports led to economic vulnerability (Hankammer et al., 2021).
  - Institutional corruption and elite capture undermined economic development (Hankammer et al., 2021).

- **Lessons Learned:**
  - Oil wealth must be managed through sovereign wealth funds.
  - Transparency in resource revenue management is critical.

Asia: Economic Liberalisation and State-Driven Development

Success: China's Special Economic Zones (SEZs) and Industrial Reforms

- **Reform Focus:** Market liberalisation while maintaining state control over strategic industries (Golub & Edwards, 2003).
- **Success Factors:**
  - FDI incentives in SEZs like Shenzhen (Golub & Edwards, 2003).
  - State-guided economic planning, balancing growth and stability (Golub & Edwards, 2003).

- **Lessons Learned:**
  - Gradual economic liberalisation prevents market instability.
  - Strategic state interventions in key sectors ensure competitiveness.

Missed Opportunity: India's Bureaucratic Hurdles in Economic Reform

- **Challenge:** Despite economic liberalisation in 1991, India still faces bureaucratic inefficiencies and infrastructure gaps (Kolbert, 2014).
- **Key Failures:**
  - Slow infrastructure development hampers industrial growth (Kolbert, 2014).
  - Rigid labour laws deter foreign investment (Kolbert, 2014).

- **Lessons Learned:**
  - Regulatory reforms must be streamlined to enhance business competitiveness.
  - Investment in infrastructure is key to sustained industrial growth.

Latin America: Debt Crises and Economic Recovery

Success: Chile's Economic Stabilisation and Pension Reform

- **Reform Focus:** Macroeconomic stability and privatised pension system (McClimon, 2020).
- **Success Factors:**
  - Sound fiscal policies and trade liberalisation promoted economic stability (McClimon, 2020).
  - Privatised pension funds mobilised domestic savings for investment (McClimon, 2020).

- **Lessons Learned:**
  - Fiscal responsibility ensures macroeconomic stability.
  - Pension reforms can enhance long-term investment growth.

Missed Opportunity: Argentina's Debt Crisis and Economic Mismanagement

- **Challenge:** Argentina's financial mismanagement and external debt crises led to repeated economic collapses (Stiglitz, 2002).
- **Key Failures:**
  - High public debt and IMF loan conditions worsened the crisis (Stiglitz, 2002).
  - Lack of industrial diversification made the economy vulnerable (Stiglitz, 2002).

- **Lessons Learned:**
  - Debt sustainability policies must be prioritised.
  - Domestic economic resilience must be built before external borrowing.

Middle East and North Africa (MENA): Political Instability and Reform

Success: UAE's Diversification Beyond Oil

- **Reform Focus:** Economic diversification through tourism, finance, and technology (Stiglitz, 2002).

- **Success Factors:**
  - Massive investment in knowledge economy sectors (Stiglitz, 2002).
  - Stable business-friendly environment attracting FDI (Schokkaert, 2019).

- **Lessons Learned:**
  - Diversification beyond oil is critical for economic sustainability.
  - Stable governance and regulatory frameworks attract global investment.

Missed Opportunity: Libya's Economic Collapse Post-2011

- **Challenge:** Libya, once a high-income oil-exporting country, collapsed due to political instability and lack of economic planning (Schokkaert, 2019).
- **Key Failures:**
  - Overdependence on oil exports with no industrial diversification.
  - Lack of institutional governance to manage post-war recovery.

- **Lessons Learned:**
  - Post-conflict economic planning is essential.
  - Institutional capacity-building ensures long-term stability.

Key Policy Implications and Recommendations for Policymakers

Governance and Institutional Strengthening

- Decentralisation of governance structures to promote inclusive decision-making (Schokkaert, 2019).
- Transparent resource management to prevent elite capture and corruption (Schokkaert, 2019).

Economic Diversification and Industrial Policy

- Balanced privatisation strategies to avoid economic instability (Schokkaert, 2019).
- Encouraging domestic value addition in key industries (Schokkaert, 2019).

Social Protection and Inclusive Growth

- Expanding financial inclusion (microfinance, SME support) to reduce economic disparity.
- Universal social safety nets to cushion economic shocks.

Environmental Sustainability

- Investment in renewable energy and climate adaptation strategies.
- Strengthening climate resilience in agriculture and water management.

The learning from both successful and failed development strategies, policymakers can design more effective, power-sensitive policies that drive inclusive, sustainable growth.

Thematic Case Studies in Development Strategies

Gender-Inclusive Policies: Women's Economic Empowerment

Success: Rwanda's Gender-Inclusive Governance and Economic Participation

- **Reform Focus**: Gender parity in political leadership and economic empowerment.
- **Key Policies:**
  - **The Gender Monitoring Office (GMO) ensures gender-sensitive policies.**
  - **30% gender quota for women in parliament (now over 60% representation).**
  - **Financial inclusion programmes for women entrepreneurs (Uwantege & Mbabazi, 2019).**

- **Lessons Learned:**
  - Institutionalised gender quotas accelerate female leadership.
  - Access to finance and skills training boosts women's economic contribution.

Missed Opportunity: India's Low Female Labour Force Participation

- **Challenge:** Despite economic liberalisation, female workforce participation remains below 30% (Desai & Joshi, 2019).
- **Key Failures:**
- Social and cultural barriers limit women's employment (Schokkaert, 2019).
- Lack of access to childcare and maternity support restricts workplace participation (Schokkaert, 2019).
- **Lessons Learned:**
  - Legal and policy reforms must address cultural constraints on women's work.
  - Flexible work environments and social protection enhance inclusion.

Digital Economies: Harnessing Technology for Development

Success: Estonia's E-Governance and Digital Economy

- **Reform Focus:** E-government services and digital citizenship (Tiits et al., 2018).
- **Key Policies:**
  - 99% of public services available online (Tiits et al., 2018)
  - E-residency programme attracts global entrepreneurs (Tiits et al., 2018).

- **Lessons Learned:**
  - Digital infrastructure investment enhances efficiency.
  - E-governance reduces bureaucracy and corruption.

Missed Opportunity: Nigeria's Struggles with Digital Transformation

- **Challenge:** Despite a booming fintech sector, digital inclusion remains low (Adeleke, 2021).
- **Key Failures:**
  - Poor broadband penetration in rural areas (Adeleke, 2021).
  - Regulatory uncertainty hampers tech startups (Adeleke, 2021).

- **Lessons Learned:**
  - Digital infrastructure investment must be decentralised.
  - Stable regulatory frameworks encourage innovation.

Geopolitical Power Imbalances in Development

The Role of Global Financial Institutions

- **The World Bank and IMF**: Often criticised for SAPs that limit national policy autonomy (Stiglitz, 2002).
- **Example:**
  - Ghana's Economic Recovery Programme (ERP) (1980s) revived growth but imposed harsh austerity measures (Aryeetey & Fosu, 2005).
- **Policy Implications:**
  - Debt relief strategies must consider long-term growth, not just fiscal austerity (Aryeetey & Fosu, 2005).

China's Belt and Road Initiative (BRI): A New Form of Development Influence?

- **Opportunity:** Provides infrastructure funding for African and Asian nations (Brautigam, 2019).
- **Criticism:** Creates debt dependency and strategic leverage for China (Brautigam, 2019).
- **Example:**
  - Sri Lanka's Hambantota Port debt trap: Sri Lanka ceded control of the port to China under a 99-year lease due to debt struggles (Weerakoon, 2021).
- **Policy Implications:**
  - Countries must negotiate more balanced agreements in infrastructure finance.

Africa's Regional Economic Integration: Progress and Setbacks

- **AfCFTA:** Aims to boost intra-African trade.
- **Challenges:**
  - Weak cross-border infrastructure (McCarthy, 2005).
  - Overlapping trade agreements create confusion (McCarthy, 2005).
- **Policy Implications:**
  - Strengthening transport and energy connectivity is crucial.
  - Power-sensitive economic policies acknowledge that institutional power structures, political dynamics, and global influences shape

economic development. While these policies offer pathways for inclusive growth, their implementation is fraught with challenges and opportunities.

Challenges in Implementing Power-Sensitive Economic Policies

Political Resistance and Elite Capture

- **Challenge:** Policies that promote redistribution of wealth and power often face resistance from the political elite who benefit from existing inequalities (Acemoglu & Robinson, 2012).
- **Case Study: Land Reforms in Zimbabwe**
  - In the 2000s, Zimbabwe's land redistribution programme was meant to empower indigenous farmers, but it led to economic decline due to elite capture and mismanagement (Scoones et al., 2011).
- **Implications:**
  - Without transparent governance and accountability, power-sensitive reforms can reinforce inequalities.

Global Power Structures and Economic Dependence

- **Challenge:** Developing nations remain dependent on international financial institutions, limiting their ability to adopt autonomous economic policies (Stiglitz, 2002).
- **Case Study: Greece and IMF Bailout**
  - During the Eurozone crisis (2010–2015), Greece's economic policies were dictated by the IMF and European Central Bank, enforcing austerity measures that led to high unemployment and social unrest (Featherstone, 2011).
- **Implications:**
  - Over-reliance on external funding restricts national governments from pursuing long-term, people-centred development strategies.

Weak Institutional Capacity

- **Challenge:** Many developing nations lack institutional frameworks to implement power-sensitive policies (Hassan & Prichard, 2022).

- **Case Study: Nigeria's Anti-corruption Efforts**
  - Despite establishing the Economic and Financial Crimes Commission (EFCC), Nigeria struggles with institutional weaknesses that prevent the effective prosecution of the elite involved in corruption (Hassan & Prichard, 2022).
- **Implications:**
  - Stronger institutions are critical for enforcing power-sensitive policies that promote equity and development.

Opportunities for Leveraging the Power Theory in Achieving the SDGs

Strengthening Local Governance for Inclusive Development (SDG 16: Peace, Justice & Strong Institutions)

- **Opportunity:** Decentralisation and community-led governance empower marginalised groups (Ansoms & Rostagno, 2012)
- **Case Study: Rwanda's Vision 2020 and Local Governance**
  - Rwanda's Umuganda programme (mandatory community service) fosters collective responsibility and participation in development (Ansoms & Rostagno, 2012).
- **Implications if not adopted:**
  - Without inclusive governance, marginalised groups remain excluded from economic decision-making.

Leveraging Digital Economies for Equitable Growth (SDG 9: Industry, Innovation & Infrastructure)

- **Opportunity**: Digital transformation reduces entry barriers for small businesses and fosters financial inclusion (Jack & Suri, 2016).
- **Case Study: Kenya's M-Pesa**
  - Mobile banking system M-Pesa revolutionised financial access, allowing 70% of Kenyans to engage in the digital economy (Jack & Suri, 2016).
- **Implications if not adopted:**
  - Without digital infrastructure investments, developing economies fall behind in global competitiveness.

Empowering Women and Marginalised Groups (SDG 5: Gender Equality)

- **Opportunity:** Gender-inclusive policies increase productivity and economic resilience (Kabeer, 2012).
- **Case Study: Bangladesh's Female Workforce in Textiles**
  - Policies supporting female employment in the garment industry contributed to Bangladesh's GDP growth (Kabeer, 2012).
- **Implications if not adopted:**
  - Gender inequality limits labour market participation and economic growth potential.
  - Implementing power-sensitive policies requires political commitment, institutional reforms, and global cooperation. Countries that successfully navigate power imbalances can leverage economic opportunities for sustainable development. However, failure to address entrenched power structures risks perpetuating economic dependency and inequality.

The Future of Power and Economic Growth

Aryeetey and Fosu (2005) report that the relationship between power and economic growth is continuously evolving due to technological advancements, geopolitical shifts, and global economic transformations. As power dynamics become increasingly complex, nations must adapt to emerging trends to sustain economic growth and navigate the challenges of a multipolar world (Aryeetey & Fosu, 2005).

Emerging Trends in Power Dynamics and Their Potential Impact on Global Economic Growth

The Rise of a Multipolar Global Economy

- The world is moving away from US-led economic dominance to a more multipolar system, with China, the EU, and emerging economies playing larger roles.
- **Case Study: China's Belt and Road Initiative (BRI)**
  - China is reshaping global trade by investing in infrastructure projects across Africa, Asia, and Latin America, challenging Western financial institutions (Zhao, 2020).

  - Implications: Countries benefiting from BRI investments must balance economic dependence and sovereignty to avoid excessive reliance on China.

Shifting Trade and Economic Alliances

- Regional trade agreements (RTAs) such as African Continental Free Trade Area (AfCFTA) are reducing dependence on Western markets and encouraging intra-regional trade.
- **Case Study: AfCFTA and African Economic Integration**
  - Expected to boost intra-African trade by 52% by 2030, creating new economic power centres (UNECA, 2021).
  - Implications: If fully implemented, AfCFTA could enhance Africa's negotiating power on the global stage.

Declining Influence of Traditional Financial Institutions

- Institutions like the IMF and World Bank are facing competition from alternative funding sources, including China's Asian Infrastructure Investment Bank (AIIB) and sovereign wealth funds (Stiglitz, 2020).
- **Implications:**
  - Developing nations now have diverse funding options, reducing dependence on the IMF's strict conditionalities.
  - However, debt sustainability must be carefully managed to avoid new forms of financial dependency.

The Role of Technology, Digital Economies, and Innovation in Reshaping Power Relations

Digital Economies as a New Source of Economic Power

- Digital platforms are shifting power from traditional industries to technology-driven sectors.
- **Case Study: India's Digital Payment Revolution**
  - India's Unified Payments Interface (UPI) has facilitated digital transactions, driving financial inclusion for over 300 million users (Natarajan, 2022).
  - Implications: Nations that fail to adopt digital transformation strategies risk being left behind in global economic competition.

Artificial Intelligence (AI) and Automation's Impact on Economic Power

- AI is reshaping labour markets, production systems, and geopolitical competition.
- **Case Study: The US-China AI Race**
  - The US and China are investing billions in AI research, with AI expected to contribute $15.7 trillion to the global economy by 2030 (PwC, 2020).
- **Implications:**
  - AI-powered economies will dominate key sectors like defence, healthcare, and finance.
  - Countries without AI strategies may become economically dependent on tech giants.

The Future of Cryptocurrency and Decentralised Finance (DeFi)

- Cryptocurrencies are challenging traditional financial systems, offering alternatives to state-controlled monetary policies (Chohan, 2021).
- **Case Study: El Salvador's Bitcoin Experiment**
  - In 2021, El Salvador became the first country to adopt Bitcoin as legal tender (Chohan, 2021).
- **Implications:**
  - If successful, cryptocurrencies could empower developing economies by bypassing traditional banking barriers.
  - However, volatility and regulatory uncertainty pose risks.

Predictions for the Next Phase of Economic Development in the Context of Evolving Global Power Structures

The Rise of "Green Economies" as a New Source of Global Power

- Climate change policies are redefining economic influence, with renewable energy playing a central role.
- **Case Study: The EU's Green Deal vs. China's Renewable Energy Dominance**
  - The EU's Green Deal aims for carbon neutrality by 2050, while China controls 80% of the global solar panel supply chain (IEA, 2022).

- **Implications:**
  - Countries investing in renewable energy will gain economic and geopolitical leverage.
  - Nations dependent on fossil fuels may face economic decline if they fail to transition.

The Future of Global Economic Governance

- Emerging economies (India, Brazil, and Nigeria) are demanding greater decision-making power in global financial institutions (Chohan, 2021).
- **Case Study: Calls for UN and IMF Reform**
  - Many nations argue that the UN Security Council and IMF voting system favour Western powers (Wade, 2011).
- **Implications:**
  - If global governance structures remain unchanged, alternative institutions (e.g., BRICS Bank) may gain influence.
  - Developing nations must strengthen regional alliances to amplify their economic voice.

Future Risks: Economic Fragmentation and the Decline of Globalisation

- The trend towards economic nationalism and protectionism (e.g., US-China trade war, Brexit) threatens global economic cooperation (Chohan, 2021).
- **Implications:**
  - If de-globalisation continues, developing economies may struggle to access foreign markets and capital.
  - Nations must adopt self-sufficiency strategies while maintaining selective global partnerships.

Chohan (2021) argues that the future of power and economic growth will be shaped by technological advancements, shifting geopolitical alliances, and sustainable development strategies. Countries that embrace digital transformation, innovation, and regional economic integration will emerge as new global economic powers. However, failure to adapt to changing power structures could leave some nations economically vulnerable.

Conclusion

Summary of Key Arguments

This chapter explored the intricate relationship between power and economic growth, emphasising how power dynamics shape development policies, institutional reforms, and global cooperation. The analysis has underscored key trends such as:

- The emergence of a multipolar global economy, where power is increasingly distributed across regions, is challenging traditional economic hegemonies.
- The role of institutional reforms, with examples from Rwanda, Ethiopia, and Botswana, demonstrates how governance, human capital, and natural resource management contribute to sustained growth.
- The influence of local leadership, where visionary leaders like Paul Kagame (Rwanda) and Ellen Johnson Sirleaf (Liberia) have successfully implemented economic transformation policies.
- The impact of global institutions, such as the World Bank, IMF, and UNDP, in supporting economic development, though challenges remain in terms of their effectiveness and structural constraints.
- The role of technology and digital economies in shifting global power relations, highlighting the significance of AI, blockchain, and fintech in shaping future economies.
- Case studies of marginalised economies such as Bangladesh (microfinance), Vietnam (economic liberalisation), and Ghana (IMF-assisted reforms) have illustrated how international support and internal reforms contribute to economic empowerment.

Through these discussions, it has become evident that the Power Theory provides a critical lens for understanding economic development, particularly in how nations and institutions exert and negotiate power to achieve growth and sustainability.

Reiteration of the Role of the Power Theory in Promoting Sustainable and Inclusive Economic Growth

The Power Theory is essential for framing development challenges and opportunities because it highlights:

1. Structural Power Imbalances – Economic development is often hindered by global inequalities in trade, finance, and governance. Addressing these imbalances requires power-sensitive policies that empower marginalised nations.
2. Agency in Development – Power is not just structural but also exercised by leaders, institutions, and societies. Strong leadership, strategic alliances, and institutional reforms can counterbalance external dependencies and drive sustainable development.
3. The Role of Institutions – Development is shaped by both local and global institutions that control resources, policymaking, and access to financial capital. Understanding how these institutions reinforce or mitigate power disparities is crucial for crafting inclusive policies.
4. Technology and Digital Transformation as Equalisers – The rise of digital economies, AI, and fintech presents opportunities for smaller economies to leapfrog traditional development models, reducing dependency on dominant economic players.

When incorporating the Power Theory into economic policymaking, nations can develop more equitable and sustainable growth strategies, ensuring that economic benefits are more widely distributed rather than concentrated in the powerful elite or MNCs.

Final Thoughts on the Future Intersection of Power and Economics in Achieving Global Development Goals

Looking ahead, the intersection of power and economics will be central to addressing global development goals (SDGs) and achieving more inclusive prosperity. The following trends will shape the future:

- **Decentralisation of Economic Power:** The dominance of Western economies is being challenged by the rise of China, India, and regional economic blocs (e.g., AfCFTA). Developing nations must strengthen regional cooperation to amplify their economic voice.

- **Green Economies and Sustainability:** Countries that invest in renewable energy, climate resilience, and sustainable business models will emerge as new economic leaders, while those reliant on fossil fuels risk economic stagnation.
- **The Digital Divide and Power Shifts:** While technology offers opportunities, inequalities in access to AI, fintech, and automation could create new power hierarchies, reinforcing economic disparities between digitally advanced and underdeveloped nations.
- **Reforming Global Governance:** Calls for a more inclusive global economic system will intensify, with developing nations demanding greater representation in financial institutions like the IMF, World Bank, and WTO. The challenge will be balancing reform with maintaining stability in the international financial order.

Ultimately, power-sensitive economic policies are not just a theoretical necessity but a practical requirement for fostering sustainable, inclusive, and resilient economies. Policymakers must recognise that economic power is dynamic, and failure to adapt to new global realities could lead to missed opportunities for growth and development.

References

Acemoglu, D., & Robinson, J. A. (2012). *Why nations fail: The origins of power, prosperity, and poverty*. Crown Business.

Acemoglu, D., & Robinson, J. A. (2019). *The narrow corridor: States, societies, and the fate of liberty*. Penguin.

Acemoglu, D., Johnson, S., & Robinson, J. A. (2003). An African success story: Botswana. In *Search of prosperity: Analytical narratives on economic growth* (pp. 80–119). Princeton University Press.

Adeleke, O. (2021). The digital divide in Nigeria: Challenges and opportunities. *African Journal of Information Systems, 13*(1), 45–63.

Alesina, A., & Dollar, D. (2000). Who gives foreign aid to whom and why? *Journal ofEconomicGrowth,5*(1),33–63.https://doi.org/10.1023/A:1009874203400

Ansoms, A., & Rostagno, D. (2012). Rwanda's Vision 2020 halfway through: What the eye does not see. *Review of African Political Economy, 39*(133), 427–450. https://doi.org/10.1080/03056244.2012.710836

Aryeetey, E., & Fosu, A. K. (2005). Economic growth in Ghana: Patterns and policy implications. *Economic Development and Cultural Change, 53*(2), 251–277.

Auty, R. (2001). *Resource abundance and economic development*. Oxford University Press.

Beck, T., & Levine, R. (2004). Stock markets, banks, and growth: Panel evidence. *Journal of Banking & Finance, 28*(3), 423–442. https://doi.org/10.1016/S0378-4266(02)00408-9

Becker, M. C., Knudsen, T., & Swedberg, R. (2012). Schumpeter's theory of economic development: 100 years of development. *Journal of Evolutionary Economics, 22*(2012), 917–933. https://doi.org/10.1007/s00191-012-0297-x

Bhutan National Environment Commission. (2022). *State of the environment report*. Royal Government of Bhutan. http://www.nec.gov.bt/publications/policies-plans-and-strategies

Bokpin, G. A. (2017). Foreign direct investment and environmental sustainability in Africa: The role of institutions and governance. *Research in International Business and Finance, 39*, 239–247. https://doi.org/10.1016/j.ribaf.2016.07.038

Booth, D., & Golooba-Mutebi, F. (2012). Developmental patrimonialism? The case of Rwanda. *African Affairs, 111*(444), 379–403. https://doi.org/10.1093/afraf/ads026

Brautigam, D. (2019). *The Dragon's gift: The real story of China in Africa*. Oxford University Press.

Brautigam, D. (2023). *The Chinese debt trap: Myth or reality?* Oxford University Press.

Butler, R. (2023). *Deforestation trends in the Global South*. Cambridge University Press.

Calderón, C., & Servén, L. (2010). Infrastructure and economic development in Sub-Saharan Africa. *Journal of African Economies, 19*(Suppl_1), i13–i87. https://doi.org/10.1093/jae/ejp022

Carroll, A. B. (1991). The Pyramid of corporate social responsibility: Toward the moral management of organizational stakeholders. *Business Horizons, 34*(4), 39–48. https://doi.org/10.1016/0007-6813(91)90005-G

Chang, H. J. (2019). *Kicking away the ladder: Development strategy in historical perspective*. Anthem Press.

Chohan, U. W. (2021). The prospects and challenges of Bitcoin adoption in El Salvador. *Cryptocurrency and Blockchain Journal, 2*(1), 10–23.

Collier, P. (2007). *The bottom billion: Why the poorest countries are failing and what can be done about it*. Oxford University Press.

Desai, S., & Joshi, O. (2019). The paradox of declining female workforce participation in India. *Indian Journal of Labour Economics, 62*(1), 1–17. https://doi.org/10.1007/s41027-019-00162-z

Dollar, D., & Litvack, J. (1998). *Macroeconomic reform and poverty reduction in Vietnam*. World Bank Publications.

Dupuy, A. (2010). *The prophet and power: Jean-Bertrand Aristide, the International Community, and Haiti*. Rowman & Littlefield.

Elkington, J. (1997). *Cannibals with Forks: The triple bottom line of 21st century business*. Wiley.

European Environment Agency. (2022). *EU emissions reduction report*. European Environment Agency.

Featherstone, K. (2011). The Greek sovereign debt crisis and EMU: A failing state in a skewed regime. *Journal of Common Market Studies, 49*(2), 193–217. https://doi.org/10.1111/j.1468-5965.2010.02139.x

Ferguson, J. (1999). *The anti-politics machine: "Development", depoliticization, and bureaucratic power in Lesotho*. University of Minnesota Press.

Food and Agriculture Organization (FAO). (2023). *The impact of EU agricultural policies on Africa's food security*. FAO.

Frank, A. G. (1967). *Capitalism and underdevelopment in Latin America*. Monthly Review Press.

Gebreeyesus, M. (2013). *Industrial policy and development in Ethiopia: Evolution and impact*. World Institute for Development Economics Research Working Paper, No. 2013/125, 1–28.

Golub, S., & Edwards, L. (2003). South Africa's international cost competitiveness and exports: A sectoral analysis. *World Development, 32*(8), 1323–1339. https://doi.org/10.1016/j.worlddev.2004.03.005

Gyimah-Boadi, E. (2001). A peaceful turnover in Ghana. *Journal of Democracy, 12*(2), 103–117.

Hankammer, S., Kleer, R., Mühl, L., & Euler, J. (2021). Principles for organizations striving for sustainable degrowth: Framework development and application to four B Corps. *Journal of Cleaner Production, 300*, 126818. https://doi.org/10.1016/j.jclepro.2021.126818

Harriss, J. (2005). *Power, civil society and development*. Palgrave Macmillan.

Harvey, D. (2005). *A brief history of neoliberalism*. Oxford University Press.

Hassan, M., & Prichard, W. (2022). Challenging corruption in Nigeria: Institutional weaknesses and power struggles. *African Affairs, 121*(482), 211–237.

Hausmann, R. (2022). *The collapse of Venezuela's economy: Causes and consequences*. Harvard Kennedy School.

Hodak, M. (2007). *Adam Smith's Folly*. Forbes. https://www.forbes.com/2007/10/24/adam-smith-corporations-markets-marketsp07-cx_mh_1025hodak.html

Hodges, T. (2004). *Angola: Anatomy of an oil state*. Indiana University Press.

Ingraham, C. (2017, December 6). *The richest 1 percent now owns more of the country's wealth than at any time in the past 50 years*. The Washington Post. https://www.washingtonpost.com/news/wonk/wp/2017/12/06/the-richest-1-percent-now-owns-more-of-the-countrys-wealth-than-at-any-time-in-the-past-50-years/

International Energy Agency (IEA). (2022). *World energy outlook: The future of renewable energy.* International Energy Agency Report.

International Monetary Fund (IMF). (2020). *Annual report 2020.* IMF.

International Monetary Fund (IMF). (2021). *Fiscal monitor: Strengthening the credibility of public finances.* IMF.

International Monetary Fund (IMF). (2023). *Sub-Saharan Africa's debt dynamics: Challenges and policy responses.* IMF.

Jack, W., & Suri, T. (2016). The long-run poverty and gender impacts of mobile money. *Science, 354*(6317), 1288–1292. https://doi.org/10.1126/science.aah5309

Jacobsson, S., & Bergek, A. (2021). *The political economy of the energy transition.* Oxford University Press.

Kabeer, N. (2012). Empowerment, citizenship and gender justice: The case of women's employment in Bangladesh. *Development and Change, 43*(6), 1111–1139.

Kangas, O. (2022). *Nordic welfare models and sustainable development.* Palgrave Macmillan.

Keynes, J. M. (1936). *The general theory of employment, interest, and money.* Harcourt Brace Jovanovich.

Kolbert, E. (2014). *No time: How did we get so busy?* New Yorker. https://www.newyorker.com/magazine/2014/05/26/no-time

Lin, J. (2022). *China's economic transformation and development path.* Oxford University Press.

Lukes, S. (2005). *Power: A radical view* (2nd ed.). Palgrave Macmillan.

Mahathir, M. (1991). *Malaysia's Vision 2020: The way forward.* Government of Malaysia.

Marconini, M., & Sauvé, P. (2010). Negotiating trade in services: A practical guide for developing countries. In S. Sáez (Ed.), *Trade in services negotiations. A guide for developing countries* (pp. 19–85). World Bank.

Marx, K. (1867). *Das Kapital: A critique of political economy.* Penguin Classics, 1990 edition.

Mattoo, A., & Fink, C. (2002). *Regional agreements and trade in services: Policy issues.* Policy Research Working Paper Series (Paper No. 2852). World Bank.

Mattoo, A., & Subramanian, A. (2008). *Currency undervaluation and sovereign wealth funds: A new role for the World Trade Organization.* Working Paper No. 08-2. World Bank.

McCarthy, C. (2005). The role of regional integration in trade and economic development. *South African Journal of Economics, 73*(4), 785–798.

McClimon, T. J. (2020). *Corporate giving by the numbers.* Forbes. https://www.forbes.com/sites/timothyjmcclimon/2020/01/16/corporate-giving-by-the-numbers/?sh=18375d1a6c51

Mlambo, T. (2022). *Zimbabwe's economic policy and the role of power in development.* African Development Review.

Moyo, D. (2011). *Dead aid: Why aid is not working and how there is a better way for Africa*. Penguin Books.

Natarajan, H. (2022). India's digital payment revolution: UPI and financial inclusion. *Economic and Political Weekly, 57*(12), 35–47.

North, D. C. (1990). *Institutions, institutional change and economic performance*. Cambridge University Press.

Okonkwo, T. (2022). Oil, environment, and power in the Niger Delta. *African Development Review, 34*(2), 214–230.

Piketty, T. (2014). *Capital in the twenty-first century*. Harvard University Press.

Piketty, T. (2020). *Capital and ideology*. Harvard University Press.

Porter, M. E., & Kramer, M. R. (2011). Creating shared value: How to reinvent capitalism—And unleash a wave of innovation and growth. *Harvard Business Review, 89*(1–2), 62. https://www.communitylivingbc.ca/wp-content/uploads/2018/05/Creating-Shared-Value.pdf

PricewaterhouseCoopers (PwC). (2020). *Sizing the prize: The impact of AI on the global economy*. https://www.pwc.com/gx/en/issues/analytics/assets/pwc-ai-analysis-sizing-the-prize-report.pdf

Putnam, R. D. (1993). *Making democracy work: Civic traditions in modern Italy*. Princeton University Press.

Raworth, K. (2017). *Doughnut economics: Seven ways to think like a 21st-century economist*. Chelsea Green Publishing.

Rodríguez-Pose, A., & Ezcurra, R. (2010). Does decentralization matter for regional disparities? A cross-country analysis. *Journal of Economic Geography, 10*(5), 619–644. https://doi.org/10.1093/jeg/lbp049

Rodrik, D. (2004). *Industrial policy for the twenty-first century. The globalization paradox: Democracy and the future of the world economy*. W.W. Norton & Company.

Rodrik, D. (2011). *The globalization paradox: Democracy and the future of the world economy*. W.W. Norton & Company.

Rodrik, D. (2021). *Straight talk on trade: Ideas for a sane world economy*. Princeton University Press.

Rolandsen, Ø. H. (2015). Another civil war in South Sudan: The failure of guerrilla government? *Journal of Eastern African Studies, 9*(1), 163–174. https://doi.org/10.1080/17531055.2014.993210

Ross, M. (2023). *The politics of oil: Who wins and who loses?* Cambridge University Press.

Roy, P. (2017). *Anti-corruption in Nigeria: A political settlements analysis*. SOAS-ACE Working Paper No. 1, 1–29. https://soas-repository.worktribe.com/output/422889/anti-corruption-in-nigeria-a-political-settlements-analysis

Sachs, J. (2005). *The end of poverty: Economic possibilities for our time*. Penguin Press.

Sachs, J. (2020). *The age of sustainable development*. Columbia University Press.

Schokkaert, E. (2019). Review of Kate Raworth's doughnut economics. *Erasmus Journal for Philosophy and Economics, 12*(1), 125–132. https://doi.org/10.23941/ejpe.v12i1.412

Scoones, I., Marongwe, N., Mavedzenge, B., Mahenehene, F., Murimbarimba, F., & Sukume, C. (2011). *Zimbabwe's land reform: Myths and realities.* James Currey Press.

Sen, A. (1999). *Development as freedom.* Alfred A. Knopf. https://doi.org/10.1086/322228

Stern, N. (2021). *The economics of climate change.* Cambridge University Press.

Stiglitz, J. E. (2002). *Globalization and its discontents.* W. W. Norton & Company.

Stiglitz, J. E. (2020). *Rewriting the rules of the European economy: An agenda for growth and shared prosperity.* W. W. Norton & Company.

Stiglitz, J. E. (2021). *People, power, and profits: Progressive capitalism for an age of discontent.* W. W. Norton & Company.

Stiglitz, J. E. (2023). *Globalization and its discontents revisited: Anti-globalization in the era of trump.* W. W. Norton & Company.

Subramanian, A. (2009). *The Mauritian success story and its lessons.* Research Paper No. 2009/36. https://doi.org/10.1093/acprof:oso/9780199671557.003.0011

Szamosszegi, S., & Kyle, C. (2011). *An analysis of state-owned enterprises and state capitalism in China.* U.S.-China Economic and Security Review Commission. https://www.uscc.gov/sites/default/files/Research/10_26_11_CapitalTradeSOEStudy.pdf

Tiits, M., Kalvet, T., & Kattel, R. (2018). E-Estonia: The digital transformation of a small state. *Journal of European Public Policy, 25*(2), 123–137.

Todaro, M. P., & Smith, S. C. (2020). *Economic development* (13th ed.). Pearson.

Transparency International. (2023). *Corruption perceptions index 2023: Africa's governance challenges.* Transparency International.

United Nations Development Programme (UNDP). (2015). *Sustainable Development Goals (SDGs).* UNDP.

United Nations Economic Commission for Africa (UNECA). (2021). *The African continental free trade area: Economic and distributional effects.* UNECA.

United Nations Economic Commission for Africa (UNECA). (2023). *Africa's trade future: The role of the AfCFTA.* UNECA.

Uwantege, L., & Mbabazi, P. (2019). Gender equality in Rwanda: Achievements and challenges. *International Journal of African Studies, 5*(1), 55–72.

Van Arkadie, B., & Mallon, R. (2003). *Vietnam: A transition tiger?* ANU Press.

Van Reybrouck, D. (2015). *Congo: The epic history of a people.* HarperCollins.

Visser, W. (2005). Revisiting Carroll's CSR pyramid: An African perspective. In E. R. Pedersen & M. Huniche (Eds.), *Corporate citizenship in developing countries: New partnership perspectives* (pp. 29–56). Samfundslitteratur.

Wade, R. H. (2011). Emerging world order? From multipolarity to multilateralism in the G20, IMF, and World Bank. *Politics and Society, 39*(3), 347–378. https://doi.org/10.1177/0032329211415503

Wade, R. (2022). *Governing the global economy: The role of power asymmetries.* School of Economics Press.

Wallerstein, I. (1974). *The modern world-system: Capitalist agriculture and the origins of the European world-economy in the sixteenth century.* Academic Press.

Weerakoon, D. (2021). Sri Lanka's debt crisis and the Belt and Road Initiative: Myths and realities. *Asian Development Review, 38*(1), 23–45.

World Bank. (2019). *Public financial management in developing countries.* World Bank Publications.

World Bank. (2020). *Doing business 2020: Comparing business regulation in 190 economies.* World Bank.

World Bank. (2021). *Ghana's Free Senior High School (SHS). Policy: Achievements and challenges.* World Bank.

World Bank. (2023). *Gender and economic participation: The case of Rwanda.* World Bank.

Yunus, M. (2007). *Creating a world without poverty: Social business and the future of capitalism.* PublicAffairs.

Zhao, S. (2020). China's belt and road initiative: Implications for global trade and investment. *Asian Economic Policy Review, 15*(2), 234–256.

CHAPTER 7

Rethinking Development Finance for Economic Transformation

Introduction

Defining Development Finance

Development finance refers to the mobilisation, allocation, and utilisation of financial resources to support economic and social development, particularly in developing countries (Todaro & Smith, 2020). It encompasses various funding mechanisms, including public and private sector investments, foreign aid, impact investing, and climate finance, to achieve sustainable growth and development (Todaro & Smith, 2020). The effectiveness of development finance depends on multiple economic, institutional, and governance factors that influence financial flows and access to capital in different economies (Stiglitz, 2018). This chapter explores key theories that shape the understanding and practice of development finance.

Key Theories and Concepts in Development Finance

Capital Formation Theory

- **Concept:** Capital accumulation is a fundamental driver of economic growth, emphasising investments in physical (infrastructure, machinery) and human capital (education, health) (Solow, 1956). Economic progress is contingent on the ability to increase capital stock and improve productivity.

P. K. Kabeya, *Development and the Power Theory of Economics*,
https://doi.org/10.1007/978-3-032-07926-8_7

- **Application:** Development finance mobilises capital for long-term investments in productive sectors, facilitating sustainable economic growth in developing economies (Schumpeter, 1934).

Financial Intermediation Theory

- **Concept:** Financial intermediaries (e.g., banks, microfinance institutions, development banks) channel savings into productive investments, enhancing liquidity and reducing transaction costs (Adusei, 2013).
- **Application:** Strengthening financial institutions and improving their efficiency fosters capital mobilisation and better financial inclusion, crucial for economic development (Beck & Levine, 2004).

Public Goods Theory

- **Concept:** Public goods, such as education, healthcare, and infrastructure, are non-excludable and non-rivalrous, meaning that private sector investments alone may not provide them efficiently. Government intervention through public finance is necessary (Samuelson, 1954).
- **Application:** Development finance prioritises investments in essential public goods that support economic and social welfare (World Bank, 2022).

Dual-Gap Model

- **Concept:** Developing economies often face a savings gap (lack of domestic capital) and a foreign exchange gap (inability to finance essential imports) (Arellano & Bond, 1991). Addressing these gaps is crucial for growth and economic development.
- **Application:** Strategies in development finance include attracting FDI, increasing export revenues, and strengthening domestic savings mechanisms (Rodrik, 2006).

Endogenous Growth Theory

- **Concept:** Economic growth is driven by internal factors such as knowledge, human capital, and technological innovation (Beck et al., 2000).
- **Application:** Development finance supports education, research, and innovation to enhance long-term economic expansion (Lucas, 1988).

Sustainable Development Goals (SDGs) Framework

- **Concept:** The SDGs provide a global framework for economic, social, and environmental development. Achieving these goals requires substantial financial resources and innovative funding mechanisms (United Nations, 2015).
- **Application:** Development finance aligns strategies with SDGs to ensure financial resources contribute to inclusive and sustainable development (OECD, 2021).

Blended Finance

- **Concept:** The strategic combination of public and private funds mobilises capital for development purposes (OECD, 2018).
- **Application:** Governments and development institutions use blended finance to leverage private sector investment in infrastructure, healthcare, and education (Bencivenga & Smith, 1993).

Microfinance Theory

- **Concept:** Microfinance provides small-scale financial services to low-income individuals, enabling them to engage in economic activities (Bhanumurthy & Singh, 2013).
- **Application:** Microfinance institutions enhance financial inclusion, fostering entrepreneurship and reducing poverty (Banerjee & Duflo, 2011).

Development Banks

- **Concept:** Development banks provide long-term financing for projects that drive economic development, particularly in infrastructure and industrial sectors (Blundell & Bond, 1998).
- **Application:** Institutions like the African Development Bank and World Bank finance large-scale development projects, fostering regional economic integration (Chang, 2010).

Impact Investing

- **Concept:** Investments aim to generate both financial returns and positive social or environmental impacts (Das & Guha-Khasnobis, 2008).
- **Application:** Development finance promotes impact investing in sectors such as renewable energy, social enterprises, and healthcare (Diamond, 1984).

Global Value Chain (GVC) Theory

- **Concept:** The GVC framework analyses how developing countries integrate into global trade and production networks (Goldsmith, 1969).
- **Application:** Development finance supports industrial policies and trade facilitation to enhance participation in global markets (Hao, 2006).

Climate Finance

- **Concept:** Financial resources are mobilised to mitigate and adapt to climate change effects (Adusei, 2013).
- **Application:** Development finance directs funding to renewable energy, sustainable agriculture, and climate resilience projects (Sachs et al., 2020).

Institutional Theory

- **Concept:** Institutions, including laws, policies, and regulations, shape economic behaviours and influence financial stability (North, 1990).
- **Application:** Strengthening institutions enhances governance and the effectiveness of development finance strategies (Acemoglu & Robinson, 2012).

Application of these theories and concepts in Development Finance in African and Asian contexts (Table 7.1).

Summary of Insights

- Asia benefits more from institution-based, innovation-driven, and value-chain-focused theories due to relatively strong institutions, infrastructure, and export capacity.
- Africa shows a high relevance for theories like Public Goods, Blended Finance, and the Dual-Gap Model, due to infrastructure gaps and dependency on external financing.
- Microfinance and Financial Intermediation are equally relevant across both regions, though they need innovation to remain effective in the digital era.
- There is a growing need for new, context-sensitive, hybrid theories that:

  - Account for informality, fragility, and political economy.
  - Integrate climate resilience and decentralised finance models.
  - Prioritise regional cooperation and digital innovation.
  - Embrace South-South knowledge transfer.

Based on the above, examples are provided for the relevance of the hybrid theories in Africa and Asia in Table 7.2.

Why Hybrid Theories Matter

The analysis demonstrates that Hybrid theories could be applied to adapt to various developing countries' contexts, for instance:

- Context-sensitive theories acknowledge the real-world constraints and adaptive capacities of local institutions, cultures, and economies.

Table 7.1 Application of development finance theories in Africa and Asia

Theory/concept	*Core idea*	*Africa application*	*Asia application*	*Best fit region*	*Need for new innovative theories?*
Capital formation theory	Economic growth via capital accumulation (Schumpeter, 1934; Solow, 1956)	Infrastructure development, human capital investment in health & education	Rapid capital investments (e.g., China, India) in manufacturing, education	**Asia** (due to faster industrial catch-up)	Yes, to address the informal sector and inequality challenges
Financial intermediation theory	Intermediaries channel savings into investments (Gurley & Shaw, 1960; Leitao, 2010)	Mobile banking, microfinance (e.g., M-Pesa in Kenya)	Stronger formal banking systems but growing fintech in Southeast Asia	**Both** (with tailored fintech models)	Yes, more inclusive digital finance models are needed
Public goods theory	State provision of non-excludable services (Samuelson, 1954)	Government and donor investment in health, water, and roads	Successful public infrastructure (e.g., South Korea, Singapore)	**Africa** (still dependent on public provision)	Yes, PPP and community-led provision mechanisms
Dual-gap model	Gaps in savings and foreign exchange limit growth (Chenery & Strout, 1966)	High dependence on FDI, remittances, and aid	Export-led growth in Asia fills forex gap (e.g., Vietnam, Bangladesh)	**Asia** (better foreign exchange strategies)	Yes, adaptation needed to account for South-South cooperation
Endogenous growth theory	Innovation, knowledge drive growth (Lucas, 1988)	Emerging innovation hubs (e.g., Rwanda's tech initiatives)	Stronger R&D investment and human capital focus (e.g., Korea, India)	**Asia**	Yes, context-specific knowledge ecosystems required
SDGs framework	Global framework for sustainability (UN, 2015)	SDG-aligned policies in many African countries, but underfunded	Asian countries have better integrated SDGs into national plans (e.g., Indonesia)	**Asia** (implementation is more effective)	Yes, localised SDG financing frameworks are needed

Blended finance	Public-private capital mobilisation (OECD, 2018)	Used by the African Development Bank for infrastructure	Increasing use in Asia for climate and infrastructure finance	**Africa** (to close large infrastructure gaps)	Yes, need mechanisms to reduce private sector risk perception
Microfinance theory	Financial services for the poor (Yunus, 1999)	Widely used in rural Africa, some success in women's empowerment	Originated in Asia (Grameen, Bangladesh); scaled in India	**Asia** (more mature ecosystem)	Yes, need to evolve towards micro-insurance, digital credit
Development banks	Long-term financing for development	AfDB financing regional integration, infrastructure	ADB supports green growth, connectivity	**Both** (crucial in both regions)	Yes, need for localised development banks and transparency reforms
Impact investing	Profit plus positive social/environmental impact	Growing interest in agriculture, renewable energy	Asia emerging as an impact investment hub (e.g., India, Singapore)	**Asia** (more organised frameworks)	Yes, metrics and standards need contextual adaptation
Global Value Chain (GVC) Theory	Integration into global production networks	Struggling to move beyond low-value-added exports	Asian economies successfully climbing GVCs (e.g., electronics in Malaysia)	**Asia**	Yes, local content policies and regional value chains for Africa
Climate finance	Funding for climate mitigation/adaptation (Levine et al., 2000)	Strong donor dependency, vulnerable to climate shocks	Green bonds, climate funds expanding in Asia	**Asia** (more instruments and innovation)	Yes, more localised, equitable, and accessible climate financing
Institutional theory	Institutions shape economic performance (North, 1990; Levine et al., 2000)	Weak institutions hinder policy implementation	Stronger bureaucratic capacity in some Asian countries (e.g., Singapore)	**Asia**	Yes, hybrid governance models needed for fragile states

Table 7.2 Relevance of the hybrid theories in Africa and Asia

Contextual challenge	*Rationale for a new or hybrid theory*	*Examples (Africa)*	*Examples (Asia)*	*Implications for theory design*
1. Informality, fragility, and political economy	Traditional finance theories assume formal institutions and stable governance, which are often absent in many parts of Africa and Asia. A hybrid theory must integrate political economy dynamics with informal financial systems	– Over 85% of employment in sub-Saharan Africa (SSA) is informal – Fragile states like South Sudan lack banking infrastructure – Mobile money (e.g., M-Pesa in Kenya) operates outside traditional banking systems	– Informal labour dominates economies like India, Indonesia – Political capture in budget allocations (e.g., Philippines' "pork barrel") – Informal savings groups (e.g., ROSCAs in rural India)	**Hybrid Political-Institutional Finance Theory**: Must combine formal financial systems, political incentives, and informal economic practices. Example: Integrate savings circles with government micro-grants
2. Climate resilience & decentralised finance (DeFi)	Traditional development finance rarely captures the urgency of climate resilience or the decentralisation of finance using blockchain and green technologies	– Rural solar finance via pay-as-you-go models (e.g., ZOLA Electric in Tanzania) – Climate vulnerability in the Sahel and Horn of Africa	– Green bonds in ASEAN – DeFi startups in Vietnam and Singapore supporting climate-smart SMEs – Community-led mangrove restoration in Bangladesh	**Green-Decentralised Development Finance Theory**: A framework that integrates climate finance, local ownership, and digital technologies (blockchain, crypto, smart contracts). e.g., decentralised carbon credit markets

3. Regional cooperation and digital innovation	Existing theories focus on nation-state development. There is a growing need to conceptualise finance through regional digital infrastructure, e.g., cross-border e-commerce, digital public goods	– AfCFTA's digital trade protocols – Southern African Power Pool (SAPP) linking regional electricity markets – SADC e-certification for agriculture	– ASEAN Smart Cities Network – India–Bangladesh power trade – Cross-border QR payment systems in SE Asia	**Regional Digital Infrastructure Theory**: A hybrid of network economics and regional integration models to finance interoperable platforms and cross-border infrastructure. E.g., regional fintech ecosystems
4. South to South knowledge transfer	Most existing theories are rooted in North-South paradigms. A hybrid model must enable horizontal knowledge sharing across developing economies	– Morocco shares solar tech with Burkina Faso – African Union–Asia partnerships on irrigation and agro-industrial parks	– China's Belt and Road sharing infrastructure models with Laos and Pakistan – Indonesia–Kenya tech partnerships in digital ID	**South-South Development Learning Theory**: A model of peer knowledge finance systems—encouraging shared funding mechanisms, co-learning platforms, and joint R&D investment among the Global South

Source: Adusei (2013), Bhanumurthy and Singh (2013)

- In Africa, the focus would be on hybrid models that leverage community structures, mobile finance, and resilience to shocks.
- In Asia, hybrid theories are more aligned with integrating technology, decentralisation, and cross-border production chains.
- For both, the move from "finance-as-capital" to "finance-as-capability" is essential—i.e., how finance builds resilience, knowledge, and inclusion

Key Takeaways

- New hybrid development finance theories must blend economics, governance, informality, and digital infrastructure.
- These should be transdisciplinary, drawing from economics, political science, environmental science, and technology studies.
- A future-proof theory must also account for non-market values, such as social capital, cultural norms, and ecological sustainability.

A detailed framework is provided in Table 7.3, transforming the four proposed hybrid development finance theories into analytical models, each with defined variables, their relevance, and using hypothetical data (2020–2030) to support the significance of the models for both Africa and Asia as highlighted above.

Summary Graphs (Indicative Trends, 2020–2030)

1. **Financial Inclusion Index Growth (2020–2030)**
   - Africa: 35 → 65
   - Asia: 50 → 80

2. **DeFi Adoption Rate (%)**
   - Africa: 2% → 30%
   - Asia: 5% → 45%

3. **Regional Digital Transaction Volume ($ billions)**
   - Africa: $2B → $30B
   - Asia: $20B → $100B

4. **Joint R&D Expenditure (% of GDP)**
   - Africa: 0.5% → 1.5%
   - Asia: 1.0% → 2.5%

Table 7.3 Variables and hypothetical application of proposed hybrid theories (Africa & Asia) (2020–2030)

Hybrid theory	*Key variables*	*Relevance of variables*	*Hypothetical trends (Africa vs. Asia, 2020–2030)*	*Implications*
1. Hybrid Political-Institutional Finance Theory *(Blending informal finance, governance quality, and institutional resilience)*	– Informal Financial Penetration Rate (%) – Political Stability Index (0–1 scale) – Financial Inclusion Index (0–100) – Public Trust in Institutions (%)	– Reflects the integration of informal sector dynamics – Measures the impact of political economy on finance outcomes – Captures access to formal financial tools – Gauges legitimacy of financial institutions	**Africa** Informal penetration: ↓ 70% → 50% Political stability: ↑ 0.3 → 0.6 Financial inclusion: ↑ 35 → 65 Public trust: ↑ 40% → 60% **Asia** Informal penetration: ↓ 60% → 35% Political stability: ↑ 0.5 → 0.8 Financial inclusion: ↑ 50 → 80 Public trust: ↑ 55% → 75%	Institutional investment in informal finance + trust-building mechanisms improve inclusion and economic stability
2. Green-Decentralised Development Finance Theory *(Merging climate finance, DeFi, and community-led models)*	– Climate Resilience Investment (as % of GDP) – Decentralised Finance (DeFi) Adoption Rate (%) – Renewable Energy Access Rate (%) – Community-led Project Share (%)	– Captures prioritisation of climate adaptation – Tracks technological decentralisation – Measures sustainability of energy finance – Reflects bottom-up governance in finance	**Africa** Climate investment: ↑ 0.8% → 2.5% DeFi adoption: ↑ 2% → 30% Renewable access: ↑ 25% → 55% Community project share: ↑ 15% → 35% **Asia** Climate investment: ↑ 1.2% → 3.5% DeFi adoption: ↑ 5% → 45% Renewable access: ↑ 40% → 75% Community project share: ↑ 20% → 40%	DeFi + climate finance synergy boosts sustainable development and energy transition in vulnerable communities

(continued)

Table 7.3 (continued)

Hybrid theory	*Key variables*	*Relevance of variables*	*Hypothetical trends (Africa vs. Asia, 2020–2030)*	*Implications*
3. Regional Digital Infrastructure Theory *(Linking finance to regional innovation and integration)*	– Cross-border Digital Transaction Volume ($) – Regional Infrastructure Investment (% of total finance) – Number of Interoperable Digital Platforms – Intra-regional Trade (% of GDP)	– Measures regional financial connectivity – Tracks shared infrastructure development – Evaluates digital integration progress – Gauges economic benefits of regionalism	**Africa** Transactions: ↑ $2B → $30B Infrastructure share: ↑ 10% → 25% Platforms: ↑ 5 → 20 Intra-regional trade: ↑ 12% → 25% **Asia** Transactions: ↑ $20B → $100B Infrastructure share: ↑ 15% → 30% Platforms: ↑ 15 → 35 Intra-regional trade: ↑ 25% → 40%	Regional fintech and digital trade mechanisms enhance economic resilience and integration
4. South-South Development Learning Theory *(Facilitating peer-driven knowledge exchange and finance models)*	– Number of South-South Technical Cooperation Agreements – Joint R&D Expenditure (% of GDP) – Shared Development Funds (e.g., BRICS, AU-Asia) ($) – Co-authored Policy/ Research Papers (#)	– Quantifies institutionalised knowledge sharing – Reflects commitment to innovation through partnership – Tracks pooled financial instruments – Captures evidence-based collaboration outcomes	**Africa** Cooperation agreements: ↑ 20 → 60 R&D expenditure: ↑ 0.5% → 1.5% Shared funds: ↑ $500M → $3B Co-authored papers: ↑ 50 → 250 **Asia** Cooperation agreements: ↑ 35 → 80 R&D expenditure: ↑ 1.0% → 2.5% Shared funds: ↑ $2B → $6B Co-authored papers: ↑ 120 → 400	Shared learning and financing create resilient, knowledge-based South-led development models

Figure 7.1 presents a clear comparative trajectory between Africa and Asia across several core indicators—financial inclusion, DeFi adoption, digital transactions, and R&D expenditure as a share of GDP. The data reveal a consistent pattern: while Africa is making commendable progress, it continues to trail behind Asia in all dimensions of development finance. For instance, financial inclusion in Africa increases from 35% in 2020 to 65% in 2030, compared to Asia's leap from 50% to 80%. This 15-percentage-point gap reflects deeper structural barriers in Africa, such as limited access to formal banking, lower digital literacy, and infrastructural deficits.

DeFi adoption, a proxy for financial innovation and digital asset use, shows promising but uneven growth. Asia's DeFi adoption rises from 5% to 45%, outpacing Africa's increase from 2% to 30%. This divergence highlights the implications of regulatory clarity, private sector innovation, and consumer trust—areas where Africa must intensify reforms to unlock the potential of decentralised finance for financial empowerment and inclusion.

In terms of digital transaction volumes, the disparity is even more pronounced. Asia expands from 20 billion to 100 billion transactions, while Africa only reaches 50 billion. This lag suggests limited digital

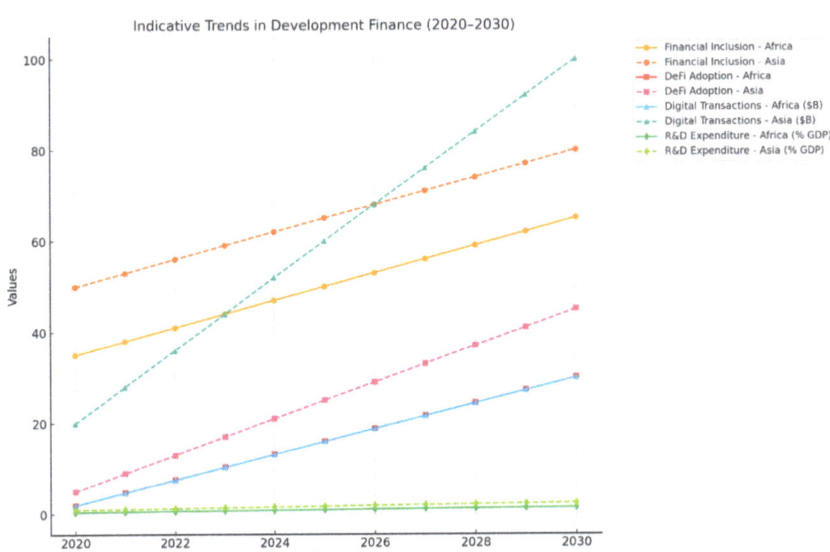

Fig. 7.1 Indicative trends in development finance (2020–2030)

infrastructure and internet penetration in many African economies, which constrains the scalability of digital payment systems and fintech solutions—critical for efficient service delivery and economic integration.

R&D expenditure, which is foundational for innovation and long-term competitiveness, remains Africa's weakest dimension. Asia's investment grows from 2% to nearly 3.5% of GDP, while Africa barely crosses 1.2%. This underinvestment in research has serious implications: without sufficient R&D, Africa may struggle to produce endogenous technologies, develop locally relevant solutions, and participate in the knowledge economy.

Implications for development are profound. First, the persistent gaps signal the risk of Africa being locked into a low-productivity, low-innovation growth path if transformative interventions are not pursued. Second, without stronger financial ecosystems and innovation capacities, Africa's ability to attract quality investment and build resilient institutions will be limited. Third, the digital and DeFi divides may exacerbate existing inequalities, particularly between urban and rural populations. Therefore, policymakers and development partners must prioritise digital infrastructure, inclusive financial systems, regulatory reform, and investment in human capital and R&D. If these gaps are not addressed urgently, Africa's progress towards the Sustainable Development Goals (SDGs) may be significantly delayed, even as Asia consolidates its gains and moves towards higher-value development trajectories.

Key Significance of Variables

- These variables fill theoretical gaps by capturing dynamics often overlooked in conventional finance models (e.g., informal economies, cross-border innovation, and climate).
- Hybrid models allow for co-design with local actors, reflecting governance complexity and decentralised digital shifts.
- The trend projections show that investing in these variables yields measurable development impacts, thereby justifying the need for new hybrid theories tailored to the evolving realities of Africa and Asia.

Comparative Analytical Explanation: Africa vs. Asia (2020–2030)

Using Trends in Financial Inclusion, DeFi, Regional Digital Transactions, and Joint R&D.

Financial Inclusion Index Growth (2020–2030)

Africa's Financial Inclusion Index is projected to grow from 35 in 2020 to 65 in 2030, while Asia's index is expected to increase from 50 to 80 during the same period. This trend reflects significant strides in both regions, but at different stages of transformation.

In Africa, this sharp rise is largely due to the penetration of mobile money platforms, such as M-Pesa, and increased investment in microfinance, informal savings groups, and fintech. Governments and NGOs are also driving policies targeting the unbanked, especially women and rural populations. However, infrastructure gaps and weaker financial literacy slow down progress compared to Asia.

In contrast, Asia's growth trajectory is built on more established financial ecosystems. The rise of digital banking, national ID-linked financial services (e.g., India's Aadhaar-enabled payments), and inclusive policy frameworks are pushing Asia closer to near-universal financial inclusion. The greater scale and pace in Asia show how integrated institutional support and technology can accelerate development outcomes.

DeFi Adoption Rate (2020–2030)

DeFi (Decentralised Finance) adoption is predicted to rise from 2% to 30% in Africa and from 5% to 45% in Asia. This surge indicates a growing appetite for blockchain-based financial solutions that bypass traditional banking infrastructure.

In Africa, DeFi fills a critical gap in reaching underserved communities. With limited banking access and high remittance fees, African users are increasingly turning to crypto-based wallets, peer-to-peer lending platforms, and tokenised savings products. Despite regulatory uncertainty and internet access issues, the technology's potential to democratise finance is undeniable.

Asia, particularly Southeast Asia, is leading in DeFi experimentation. Countries like Vietnam, the Philippines, and Singapore are developing legal sandboxes and integrating DeFi with local currencies and e-commerce platforms. This broader adoption reflects Asia's comparatively stronger digital ecosystems, higher trust in fintech, and greater tech-savvy populations.

Regional Digital Transaction Volume ($ billions)

Africa's digital transaction volume is expected to increase from $2 billion in 2020 to $30 billion by 2030, while Asia will leap from $20 billion to $100 billion. These figures highlight the explosive growth in cross-border digital trade and regional financial integration.

In Africa, this growth is fuelled by the African Continental Free Trade Area (AfCFTA), mobile payment interoperability initiatives, and the gradual digitisation of regional trade corridors. However, the continent's fragmented infrastructure and regulatory misalignments slow progress.

Meanwhile, Asia's fivefold increase stems from well-established regional blocs such as ASEAN, with a strong push for cross-border QR payments, regional e-commerce logistics, and digital public infrastructure (e.g., India's UPI or Singapore's PayNow). Asia's coordinated efforts and more advanced tech infrastructure enable faster, deeper regional digital integration.

Joint R&D Expenditure (% of GDP)

Joint R&D expenditure is projected to grow from 0.5% to 1.5% in Africa and from 1.0% to 2.5% in Asia between 2020 and 2030. This increase reflects the region's recognition of the importance of collaborative innovation and South-South knowledge exchange in driving sustainable development.

In Africa, the rise in joint R&D reflects growing continental initiatives such as the Pan-African University, AU–Asia technology collaborations, and partnerships in agriculture, health, and renewable energy. However, funding gaps and reliance on donor-driven research remain constraints.

Asia, by contrast, is deepening intra-regional R&D cooperation through mechanisms such as ASEAN Science & Technology Networks, China–India joint labs, and multilateral innovation funds. The region's stronger investment base and commitment to technology leadership explain its higher expenditure trajectory.

Figure 7.2 visually demonstrates the above trends using hypothetical data.

Figure 7.3 depicts analytical graphs comparing Africa and Asia on four key development finance indicators from 2020 to 2030.

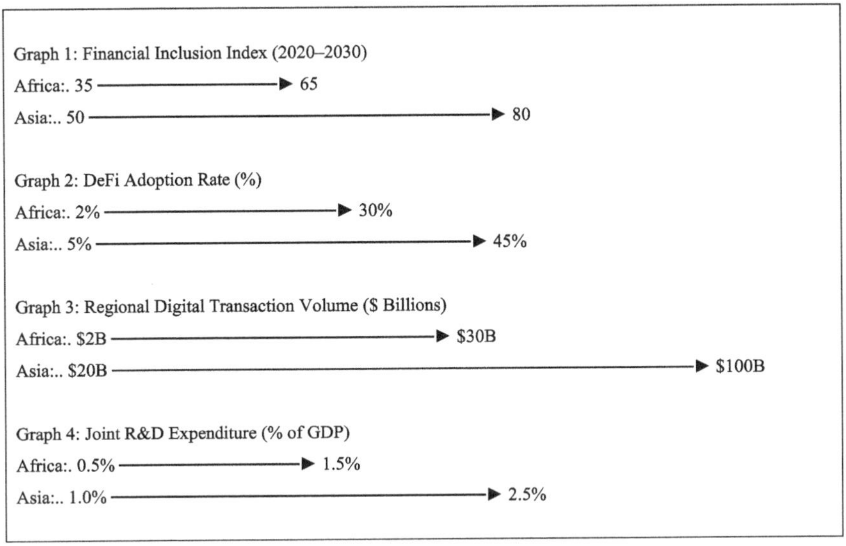

Fig. 7.2 Hypothetical indicative trends (Africa vs. Asia, 2020–2030). Note: The lengths of the arrows symbolically reflect the growth magnitude of each variable

Key Insights from the Graphs

1. **Financial Inclusion Index (Graph 1)**
   - Africa improves from 35 to 65, indicating strong progress.
   - Asia starts higher and ends at 80, reflecting both a head start and sustained efforts.

   Implication: Asia's digital infrastructure and financial ecosystem are maturing faster, but Africa is closing the gap steadily.
2. **DeFi Adoption Rate (Graph 2)**
   - Africa increases from 2% to 30%.
   - Asia rises from 5% to 45%.

   Implication: While adoption is growing in both regions, Asia's earlier integration of blockchain technologies and fintech ecosystems accelerates its advantage.
3. **Digital Transaction Volume (Graph 3)**
   - Africa grows from $2B to $30B.
   - Asia from $20B to $100B.

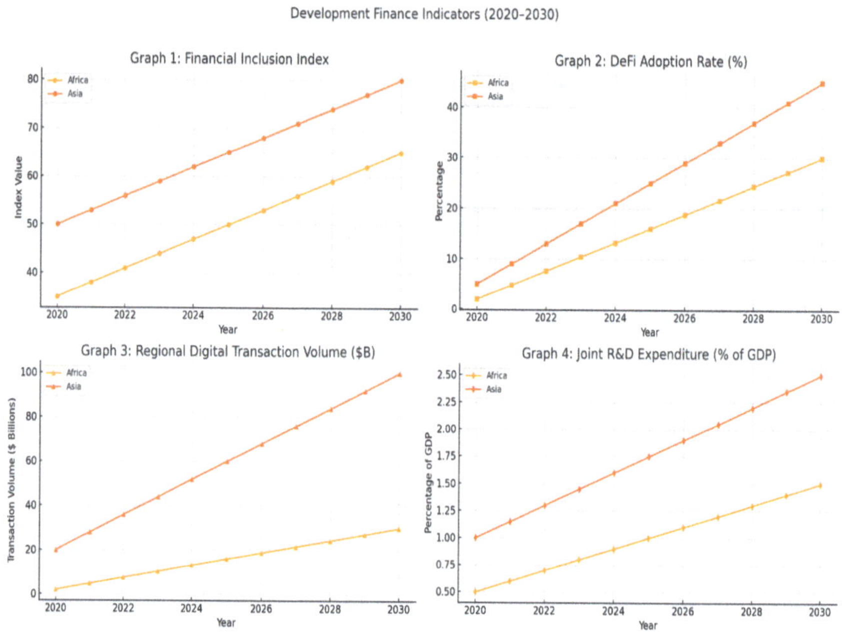

Fig. 7.3 Analytical graphs comparing Africa and Asia

Implication: Africa is catching up in digital transactions, but the absolute gap remains due to disparities in digital penetration and trust in platforms.

4. **Joint R&D Expenditure (Graph 4)**
   - Africa doubles from 0.5% to 1.5% of GDP.
   - Asia moves from 1.0% to 2.5%.

   Implication: Africa is increasing investment in innovation, but Asia continues to lead due to stronger government-academic-private sector partnerships.

These graphs offer visual clarity on how Africa is progressing and where Asia maintains a competitive edge, which is key for policy and investment focus.

The comparative trends from 2020 to 2030 clearly demonstrate that both Africa and Asia are undergoing deep financial and digital transformations, albeit at different paces and scales.

These shifts validate the need for hybrid development finance theories that:

- recognise regional contexts,
- integrate informality and innovation,
- support decentralised finance,
- encourage South-South knowledge exchange.

Power Theory and Development Finance

The Power Theory provides a framework for analysing how financial flows, decision-making processes, and institutional frameworks influence development finance, particularly in sub-Saharan Africa (SSA). Power dynamics shape access to financial resources, policy implementation, and the effectiveness of development programs (Guedon, 1977). In SSA, financial and institutional power disparities impact infrastructure financing, FDI allocation, and debt sustainability (Mkandawire, 2001).

- **Forms of Power in Development Finance:**
  - **Coercive Power:** Financial institutions and donors exert influence over developing countries through conditionalities on loans and aid (Easterly, 2006).
  - **Economic Power:** The control of financial resources by multilateral institutions and high-income countries affects policy autonomy in SSA (Moyo, 2009).
  - **Ideological Power:** Global financial norms and neoliberal economic policies shape development strategies in SSA (Harvey, 2005).
  - **Political Power:** Governments and international organisations wield authority in financial decision-making, influencing project priorities (Stiglitz, 2002).

- **Power Relations in Development Finance:**
  - **Donor-Recipient Power Imbalance:** Aid and concessional loans often come with conditions that reflect donor priorities rather than local development needs (Stiglitz, 2002)
  - **Multilateral Institutions' Influence:** Institutions like the IMF and World Bank shape economic policies through financial support and policy prescriptions (Stiglitz, 2002).

- **Private Sector Power:** Multinational corporations (MNCs) and public-private partnerships (PPPs) exert significant control over infrastructure projects, sometimes leading to unequal benefits distribution (Stiglitz, 2002).
- **Civil Society and Grassroots Movements:** Advocacy groups and local communities challenge power imbalances and demand more equitable development finance approaches (Stiglitz, 2002).

Hao (2006) underscores that development finance is a multidimensional field that integrates various economic theories and financial instruments to promote sustainable growth. In this regard, we can argue that by leveraging insights from capital formation, financial intermediation, public goods, and institutional theory, policymakers and financial institutions can design effective strategies to address economic challenges in developing countries. Furthermore, understanding power dynamics in financial governance enhances transparency, accountability, and equitable resource allocation in development finance, which is critical to ensuring sustainable development within the context of development strategies (Das & Guha-Khasnobis, 2008).

Case Studies in SSA: Achievements, Failures, and Policy Implications

Botswana as a Case Study in SSA (2020–2030): Achievements, Failures, and Policy Implications for Development Finance

Analytical Overview

Botswana is widely recognised as a development success story in SSA, particularly for its prudent management of natural resources (Cizo et al., 2020). Since independence, the country has effectively harnessed its mineral wealth—especially diamonds—through sound governance and robust institutional frameworks (Cizo et al., 2020). Central to its development strategy is the Pula Fund, a sovereign wealth fund that captures resource revenues for long-term stabilisation and investment purposes (Bank of Botswana, 2022b). This approach contrasts sharply with the experience of many other resource-rich African nations that have succumbed to the "resource curse." Botswana's adherence to transparent fiscal policies, low corruption levels, and effective rule of law has enabled sustained economic growth and relative political stability (Bank of Botswana, 2022a).

Cizo et al. (2020) report that a key driver of this success is the strategic partnership between the Government of Botswana and De Beers, which has ensured local beneficiation of diamonds through value addition and job creation in processing and trading. Furthermore, Botswana has invested significantly in human capital, prioritising education, healthcare, and infrastructure (Cizo et al., 2020). These investments have yielded a relatively high Human Development Index (HDI) compared to regional peers (Bank of Botswana, 2022a).

However, Botswana's development trajectory has not been without challenges. The over-dependence on diamond revenues exposes the economy to global price volatility, as evidenced during global downturns such as the COVID-19 pandemic (Bank of Botswana, 2022a). Additionally, the slow pace of economic diversification has constrained the country's ability to build a resilient and inclusive economy (Bist, 2018). The manufacturing and agricultural sectors remain underdeveloped, limiting job creation and food security (Bank of Botswana, 2022b).

From a policy perspective, Botswana underscores the importance of institutional quality, transparency, and long-term financial planning. The country's experience offers several lessons for development finance in SSA: (1) channelling natural resource rents into sovereign funds can stabilise economies; (2) investments in human capital are crucial for equitable development; and (3) industrial diversification is necessary to buffer economies from external shocks (Cizo et al., 2020). As Botswana looks towards 2030, strengthening SME development, green energy, and digital innovation will be essential for transitioning into a more diversified, knowledge-based economy (Cizo et al., 2020) (Table 7.4).

Development Finance Implications

The hypothetical trends above demonstrate how strategic deployment of resource wealth can support broader economic development goals. As diamond revenues decline (from 30% to 15% of GDP by 2030), Botswana's rising investment in manufacturing and green energy shows movement towards a more diversified economy. The steady increase in education spending and HDI reflects a sustained focus on social development, which is vital for inclusive growth.

For development finance institutions (DFIs), Botswana presents a strong case for investing in public-private partnerships, SME financing, and green transition projects. Moreover, sovereign wealth funds like the Pula Fund serve as effective tools for macroeconomic stability and

Table 7.4 Botswana's development finance indicators (2020–2030) (hypothetical data)

Indicator	*2020*	*2022*	*2024*	*2026*	*2028*	*2030*	*Trend summary*
Diamond revenue contribution to GDP (%)	30%	28%	25%	22%	18%	15%	Gradual decline as diversification increases
Pula fund reserves (USD billion)	6.5	7.2	8.1	8.8	9.5	10.3	Steady growth due to conservative fiscal management
Education spending (% of GDP)	7.5%	8.0%	8.2%	8.4%	8.5%	8.7%	Consistent investment in human capital
Manufacturing sector contribution to GDP (%)	8%	9%	11%	13%	15%	17%	Positive trend from industrial diversification
Unemployment rate (%)	22%	20%	18%	16%	14%	12%	Declining due to job creation in new sectors
HDI score (UNDP index, scale 0–1)	0.72	0.74	0.75	0.77	0.78	0.80	Gradual improvement driven by social sector investment
Non-diamond exports (% of total exports)	18%	22%	27%	32%	38%	45%	Reflects a structural shift in trade composition
Government debt to GDP (%)	40%	42%	41%	39%	37%	35%	Moderation due to prudent fiscal policy and revenue gains
Green energy investment (USD million)	50	75	120	180	240	300	Rapid growth in sustainable infrastructure financing

intergenerational equity. As Botswana continues its transformation, its experience could inform regional policy dialogues, particularly around the effective use of resource-backed financial instruments, long-term capital markets, and blended finance to support sustainable development (Demetriades & Hussein, 1996; Greenwood & Jovanovic, 1990; Hao, 2006).

Despite these successes, Botswana's development model still faces structural weaknesses that threaten long-term resilience and inclusive growth:

Over-reliance on a Single Commodity

Although diversification efforts have begun, Botswana remains heavily dependent on diamonds, which still accounted for nearly 25–30% of GDP in the early 2020s. This makes the country vulnerable to commodity price shocks and global demand fluctuations, especially during crises like the COVID-19 pandemic, which disrupted supply chains and suppressed luxury markets (Bank of Botswana, 2022a).

Youth Unemployment and Limited Job Creation
Botswana has struggled with persistent unemployment, especially among youth and graduates. While the education system has expanded, there is often a mismatch between skills and labour market demands, with too few opportunities in high-productivity sectors. This has fuelled frustration and could become a long-term social risk (Bank of Botswana, 2022b).

Slow Economic Diversification
The manufacturing and agriculture sectors remain underdeveloped, contributing only a small share of GDP (Bank of Botswana, 2022a). Despite policy intent, the business environment is still constrained by limited access to finance, infrastructure gaps in rural areas, and a relatively small domestic market (Bank of Botswana, 2022b).

Public Sector Dominance
Botswana's economy is dominated by the public sector, which has historically driven employment and investment (Bank of Botswana, 2022a). This limits the space for private sector dynamism and innovation, particularly among Small and Medium Enterprises (SMEs) (Bank of Botswana, 2022b).

Climate Vulnerability and Water Scarcity
Botswana faces increasing water scarcity and climate shocks, which threaten agriculture, health, and overall sustainability. The country has not yet fully embedded climate resilience into its development finance and infrastructure strategies (Bist, 2018).

Policy Solutions and Strategic Recommendations
To address these limitations, Botswana should consider the following reforms and development finance strategies:

Accelerate Economic Diversification
Botswana needs a targeted industrial policy that promotes manufacturing, ICT, tourism, and agri-processing. DFIs and sovereign guarantees can help de-risk private investment in these sectors. Special Economic Zones

(SEZs) and industrial parks should be expanded to attract value-added production and link local firms to global value chains.

Strengthen Skills Development and Innovation
A shift is needed from traditional education to demand-driven Technical and Vocational Education and Training (TVET). Greater partnerships between universities, industries, and government should foster a national innovation **ecosystem**, supported by blended finance for startups and R&D grants.

Private Sector-Led Growth and SME Support
Botswana should prioritise financial inclusion and access to credit for SMEs through credit guarantee schemes, microfinance institutions, and fintech platforms. Development banks could offer concessional loans to high-potential local businesses, especially in green sectors and agri-value chains.

Implement Green Finance and Climate Resilience
Botswana should mainstream climate financing into its development strategy. This includes green bonds, climate-resilient infrastructure, and nature-based solutions. International climate funds (e.g., Green Climate Fund, Adaptation Fund) and regional facilities can be tapped for water harvesting, renewable energy, and smart agriculture.

Public Sector Reform and Fiscal Discipline
Reducing dependence on the public sector requires modernising public procurement systems, cutting bureaucratic red tape, and adopting digital public financial management (PFM) tools. Maintaining fiscal discipline while reallocating expenditures towards diversification and social protection will be key to sustainable growth.

Botswana presents a rare case of resource-rich success in Africa, but it stands at a development crossroads. The achievements in fiscal prudence, governance, and investment in human capital must now be complemented by bold diversification efforts, inclusive job creation, and climate-smart development finance. With the right policy tools and targeted financing mechanisms, Botswana can transition from a diamond-dependent economy to a diversified, knowledge-driven, and climate-resilient society by 2030.

South Africa as a Case Study in SSA (2020–2030): Achievements, Failures, and Policy Implications for Development Finance

Achievements and Strengths

South Africa stands as the most industrialised and diversified economy in Africa, with a robust macroeconomic structure that includes an advanced financial services sector, a sophisticated legal and regulatory environment, and world-class physical infrastructure (Adebayo et al., 2021).

These strengths have made it a regional hub for FDI, particularly in finance, mining, retail, and telecommunications. Over the past decade, the country has attracted substantial capital flows, drawn by the Johannesburg Stock Exchange (JSE), which ranks among the top exchanges globally in terms of market capitalisation (Aghion & Howitt, 2009). South Africa's banking and financial system is globally integrated, adhering to international standards, which enhances investor confidence and facilitates access to international development finance instruments such as euro-bonds, syndicated loans, and blended finance (Adeniyi & Egwaikhide, 2013).

Additionally, Amusa (2014) reports that South Africa has made progress in areas such as energy investment, with strides in renewable energy procurement through the Renewable Energy Independent Power Producer Procurement Programme (REIPPPP). Infrastructure projects like Gautrain, major highway upgrades, and airport modernisation further reflect the country's capacity to finance and implement large-scale public-private partnerships (PPPs). These achievements present a platform on which to build broader development outcomes (Aghion & Howitt, 2009).

Failures, Weaknesses, and Structural Limitations

Adebayo et al. (2021) emphasise that despite its industrial capacity and financial sophistication, South Africa continues to struggle with deep-rooted socio-economic disparities. The legacy of apartheid has left a structurally divided economy where wealth, land, and opportunity remain concentrated among a minority, while the majority—especially Black South Africans—face high unemployment, poor access to quality education, and health disparities (Adeniyi & Egwaikhide, 2013). By 2020, youth unemployment had exceeded 50%, and the Gini coefficient remained among the highest globally, reflecting severe inequality (Adebayo et al., 2021).

Moreover, Adebayo et al. (2021) emphasise that FDI inflows have not translated into inclusive economic growth. While investors benefit from

South Africa's infrastructure and market size, capital-intensive investments in sectors like mining and finance do not generate broad-based employment. Adebayo et al. (2021) also explained that skills mismatch, outdated education curricula, and weak vocational training have further marginalised millions from participating in the formal economy. Adebayo et al. (2021) further explained that the over-reliance on extractive industries also leaves the country vulnerable to global commodity price swings, while persistent energy insecurity (e.g., load-shedding) and governance challenges undermine investor confidence and productivity.

Adeniyi and Egwaikhide (2013) highlight that another weakness is the inefficiency of public expenditure and corruption, which reduces the development impact of fiscal spending. Adeniyi and Egwaikhide (2013) add that despite large social transfers and budget allocations to education and health, service delivery remains poor in many areas. This weakens the developmental role of the state and contributes to social unrest.

Policy Solutions and Development Finance Implications

Addressing South Africa's persistent inequality and unemployment will require targeted and inclusive development finance strategies.

1. Government and financial institutions must prioritise impact investment and blended finance mechanisms that incentivise job creation, especially among youth and women. DFIs such as the Development Bank of Southern Africa (DBSA) and international partners should channel concessional loans and grants into labour-intensive sectors, such as agro-processing, construction, tourism, and green energy.
2. Government must overhaul education and training systems to reduce the mismatch between supply and demand in the labour market. Technical and Vocational Education and Training (TVET) institutions need more funding, aligned curricula, and public-private partnerships to ensure that skills training is responsive to real market needs. This would reduce structural unemployment and enhance productivity.
3. The FDI regulatory framework must evolve to ensure that foreign investments support inclusive development goals. Incentives can be tied to employment targets, local procurement, technology transfer, and rural investment. Social impact bonds and green bonds can also be used to finance social infrastructure like schools, clinics, and affordable housing in underserved communities.

4. South Africa must improve governance and accountability in public finance. Anti-corruption frameworks should be strengthened, and budget transparency must be enhanced through digital public finance management systems. This will improve the credibility of development finance and attract both domestic and international partners to co-finance inclusive growth programs (Table 7.5).

South Africa's experience illustrates that industrial strength alone is insufficient for equitable development. While the country boasts a sophisticated economy and strong institutions, structural inequalities, high unemployment, and governance weaknesses continue to constrain its development trajectory. The period from 2020 to 2030 offers a critical window to implement reforms focused on inclusive growth, job creation,

Table 7.5 South Africa's development finance trends (2020–2030) (hypothetical data)

Indicator	*2020*	*2022*	*2024*	*2026*	*2028*	*2030*	*Trend summary*
FDI inflows (USD Billion)	5.2	6.0	6.8	7.5	8.2	9.0	A gradual increase in FDI due to investor confidence
Unemployment rate (%)	34%	33%	30%	28%	26%	22%	Modest reduction through active labour market programs
Youth unemployment rate (%)	56%	54%	50%	45%	40%	35%	Still high but decreasing with skills development funding
Gini coefficient	0.63	0.61	0.59	0.58	0.56	0.53	Gradual decline due to pro-poor investment policies
Education spending (% of GDP)	5.8%	6.2%	6.5%	6.8%	7.0%	7.2%	Increase to improve quality and access
Number of TVET graduates (thousands)	130	145	165	185	205	230	Reflects the scaling up of vocational education
Social infrastructure investment (USD Bn)	2.1	2.6	3.0	3.4	4.0	4.5	Expanded investment in schools, clinics, and housing
Green energy investment (USD Bn)	1.5	2.2	3.0	3.8	4.5	5.5	Growing green finance for sustainability and energy access
Corruption perception index (Score 0–100)	43	45	48	52	55	60	Improved governance and transparency

and human capital development. Development finance must be strategic, conditional, and impact-oriented, supporting not just economic expansion but equity, resilience, and social justice. South Africa can lead SSA in pioneering a model of industrialised yet inclusive and sustainable development, if it tackles its structural weaknesses with urgency and innovation.

Democratic Republic of Congo (DRC) as a Case Study in SSA (2020–2030): Achievements, Failures, and Policy Implications for Development Finance

Achievements and Opportunities
Cilliers (2015) indicates that the Democratic Republic of Congo (DRC) is often cited as a paradox of plenty. Rich in natural resources—particularly copper, cobalt, gold, and coltan—it holds immense potential for economic transformation in SSA. Its strategic geographical location at the heart of the continent and abundant freshwater reserves provide additional developmental advantages. Over the past decade, increasing global demand for critical minerals used in electric vehicles and renewable energy technologies has drawn renewed interest in the DRC's mining sector (Cilliers, 2015). This surge in global demand, combined with rising commodity prices, has provided the country with significant export earnings and FDI, particularly from China and Western countries seeking energy transition minerals (Bilton, 2020).

Despite weak institutional capacity, the DRC has made modest progress in reforming its mining code, including provisions for greater state participation, local content, and community development obligations (V-Dem, 2020). The Growth and Poverty Reduction Strategy Paper (GPRSP) and engagements with international partners such as the IMF and the World Bank reflect an effort to promote macroeconomic stability, infrastructure investment, and debt relief under the HIPC initiative (V-Dem, 2020). If effectively managed, the DRC's natural wealth could serve as a catalyst for long-term inclusive development.

Failures, Weaknesses, and Structural Limitations
However, the DRC remains one of the poorest and most fragile countries globally, primarily due to governance failures, systemic corruption, and armed conflict (Bilton, 2020). Despite being the world's leading producer of cobalt, over 70% of the population lives in multidimensional poverty,

with limited access to electricity, clean water, education, and healthcare (Bilton, 2020). The wealth generated from mining has largely been captured by multinational corporations (MNCs) and the political elite, leaving little room for inclusive economic development (Bilton, 2020).

A major weakness lies in the mismanagement and opaque governance of resource revenues (Cilliers, 2015). The lack of fiscal discipline and revenue tracking has enabled widespread tax evasion, transfer pricing, and illicit financial flows (Cilliers, 2015). Moreover, armed groups continue to control parts of mineral-rich regions, fuelling violence, displacing communities, and weakening the rule of law (Cilliers, 2015). This makes parts of the country inaccessible for public service delivery and infrastructure investment, undermining the effectiveness of development finance (Cilliers, 2015).

DRC also suffers from a weak regulatory and institutional environment, making it difficult to enforce contracts, monitor environmental impacts, or promote beneficiation and local job creation (V-Dem, 2020). Furthermore, dependency on extractive industries has left other sectors—such as agriculture, manufacturing, and services—underdeveloped, increasing vulnerability to commodity price fluctuations and external shocks (V-Dem, 2020).

Policy Solutions and Development Finance Implications

To reverse the paradox of mineral wealth amidst poverty, the DRC must embark on deep institutional reforms, supported by strategic development finance interventions.

Strengthening Governance and Transparency

The government should prioritise the implementation of the Extractive Industries Transparency Initiative (EITI) standards and introduce digital platforms for tracking mining contracts, royalties, and revenue allocations. DFIs should condition lending on measurable anti-corruption and transparency benchmarks, including public audits of mining revenues.

Local Value Addition and Economic Diversification

A national industrial policy focused on local beneficiation, value chain development, and SME support is essential. Public and private investments, supported by concessional loans and blended finance, should be directed towards mineral processing, logistics, and agribusiness. Export credit agencies and DFIs can help de-risk manufacturing and agro-processing projects to reduce dependency on raw mineral exports.

Conflict Resolution and Security Sector Reform
Peacebuilding and disarmament programs must accompany development finance strategies in mineral-rich conflict zones. International actors, including the African Union and the UN, must work with local institutions to demilitarise mining regions and reintegrate armed actors into formal economies.

Community Development and Social Infrastructure
Development finance should fund community-driven development (CDD) programs, especially in mining regions. Revenues must be transparently allocated to schools, clinics, roads, and vocational training centres to ensure that resource wealth leads to tangible improvements in people's lives.

Capacity Building for Institutions and Civil Society
Technical assistance and grant funding should be directed towards building state capacity, training civil servants, and supporting civil society organisations that monitor public expenditure and resource contracts. Strengthening the judiciary, anti-corruption bodies, and regulatory agencies is fundamental for long-term accountability (Table 7.6).

The DRC illustrates the challenges and contradictions of resource-driven development in a fragile governance environment. Despite its extraordinary mineral wealth, the country remains poor due to mismanagement, conflict, and institutional weakness. However, the growing global demand for the DRC's critical minerals offers a transformational opportunity—if paired with strong governance reforms, inclusive economic policies, and strategic deployment of development finance.

With international support and political will, the DRC can transition from a resource-rich yet impoverished nation to a resilient and inclusive economy by 2030. The path forward must emphasise transparency, local development, and peacebuilding, with development finance serving not only as a funding tool but as a leverage mechanism for structural reform and long-term sustainability.

Table 7.6 DRC's development finance trends (2020–2030) (hypothetical data)

Indicator	*2020*	*2022*	*2024*	*2026*	*2028*	*2030*	*Trend summary*
Cobalt and Copper export revenue (USD billion)	8.5	10.2	12.5	14.0	15.8	17.5	Rising global demand boosts mineral exports
Government revenue from mining (%)	11%	13%	15%	18%	20%	22%	Gradual improvement with revenue reforms and compliance
% of Mining contracts publicly disclosed	5%	15%	40%	60%	80%	90%	Increased transparency with EITI and digital platforms
Share of budget allocated to infrastructure	8%	10%	12%	14%	16%	18%	More fiscal space for development as revenues rise
Population in extreme poverty (%)	72%	70%	66%	62%	58%	52%	Gradual reduction through community development and services
Public spending on education (% of GDP)	2.5%	3.0%	3.5%	4.0%	4.5%	5.0%	Increase in social spending through better budget prioritisation
Share of processed minerals in exports (%)	4%	6%	10%	15%	20%	25%	Modest industrial development and local value addition
Conflict-affected regions under control (%)	40%	45%	55%	65%	75%	85%	Peacebuilding efforts restore state presence and control
Development finance inflows (USD billion)	1.5	2.0	2.8	3.5	4.2	5.0	DFIs scale up support for infrastructure, governance, and jobs

Ethiopia as a Case Study in SSA (2020–2030): Achievements, Failures, and Policy Implications for Development Finance

Achievements and Strengths

Ethiopia has emerged over the past two decades as a leading example of state-led development in SSA, with an ambitious vision of infrastructure-driven growth. Central to this approach has been the Grand Ethiopian Renaissance Dam (GERD), Africa's largest hydroelectric project (Kimari & Ernstson, 2020). GERD symbolises not only Ethiopia's intent to control and harness its natural resources for energy generation and regional influence but also its sovereign development model, characterised by minimal reliance on Western donor conditions (Kimari & Ernstson, 2020). The dam promises to unlock significant hydropower potential, generate surplus energy for export, and stimulate industrialisation through reliable electricity supply (Jaglin, 2014).

Ethiopia's broader infrastructure agenda has included expansion of road networks, railways (notably the Addis Ababa–Djibouti railway), and industrial parks aimed at transforming the country into a light manufacturing hub. Simultaneously, the government has promoted agricultural modernisation, leveraging irrigation and mechanisation to enhance food security and export capacity (Klopp & Cavoli, 2019). These efforts, alongside investments in education and rural electrification, have contributed to poverty reduction, job creation, and improvements in the Human Development Index (HDI) (Klopp & Cavoli, 2019).

In terms of development finance, Ethiopia has successfully mobilised resources from international partners (e.g., China, World Bank, African Development Bank) and engaged in public-private partnerships for energy and infrastructure projects. This model has enabled the country to attract billions of dollars in concessional loans and grants, catalysing structural transformation (Lawhon et al., 2018).

Failures, Weaknesses, and Structural Limitations

According to Kimari and Ernstson (2020), despite its ambitious vision, Ethiopia's development model faces critical weaknesses that threaten its sustainability and inclusiveness. One major challenge is the accumulation of external debt, largely due to borrowing for mega-projects like GERD, highways, and industrial zones (Kimari & Ernstson, 2020). While these investments have potential long-term benefits, they strain foreign exchange reserves, especially in a context of limited export diversification and weak domestic revenue mobilisation (Lawhon et al., 2018).

Political instability and regional conflicts, including the Tigray crisis and ethnic tensions, have severely undermined Ethiopia's progress (Kharas & McArthur, 2019). These conflicts have disrupted infrastructure, displaced millions, and diverted public spending from development priorities to security and humanitarian aid (Jaglin, 2014). Additionally, the GERD project has triggered diplomatic tensions with downstream countries such as Egypt and Sudan, raising regional risks over water resource management and threatening regional cooperation under the Nile Basin Initiative (Klopp & Cavoli, 2019).

Moreover, despite impressive infrastructure expansion, Ethiopia has struggled to ensure that local communities equitably benefit from these projects (Lawhon et al., 2018). In some areas, resettlement, limited compensation, and environmental concerns have sparked resistance and weakened public support (Lawhon et al., 2018). Industrial parks have created jobs but remain dominated by low-wage, low-skill employment, with limited technology transfer or value addition (Lawhon et al., 2018).

Policy Solutions and Development Finance Implications
To make Ethiopia's infrastructure-led development model more inclusive, sustainable, and financially sound, several reforms are needed:

Debt Management and Domestic Resource Mobilisation
Ethiopia must strengthen its debt sustainability framework, including renegotiating high-interest loans, improving tax collection efficiency, and expanding public-private partnerships. Development finance should prioritise grant financing, concessional terms, and results-based financing linked to social and environmental outcomes.

Regional Diplomacy and Transboundary Cooperation
The Ethiopian government must engage in sustained and transparent dialogue with downstream Nile Basin countries. Investment in joint water governance mechanisms, hydrological data sharing, and shared infrastructure (e.g., power transmission) can build trust and reduce geopolitical risks.

Inclusive and Environmentally Sustainable Infrastructure
Future infrastructure projects should include environmental and social impact assessments, ensure community participation, and offer fair compensation and livelihood support. This will promote legitimacy, avoid conflict, and maximise development impact.

Industrial Policy and Value Chain Development
To move beyond basic manufacturing, Ethiopia needs a technology and skills development agenda supported by industrial upgrading, innovation hubs, and local supplier linkages. Development finance must support capacity building, vocational training, and industrial R&D to promote long-term competitiveness.

Conflict Resolution and Political Stability
A peaceful, inclusive political environment is essential for sustained development. The government should prioritise national dialogue, constitutional reforms, and federalism that accommodate diversity, backed by donor support for peacebuilding and institution-building (Table 7.7).

Ethiopia's experience offers a unique model of state-led, infrastructure-driven development, rooted in national sovereignty and long-term transformation goals. Projects like the GERD reflect a strategic commitment to self-reliance and regional leadership. However, debt sustainability, political instability, and unequal benefits from mega-projects present serious risks.

Table 7.7 Ethiopia's development finance trends (2020–2030) (hypothetical data)

Indicator	*2020*	*2022*	*2024*	*2026*	*2028*	*2030*	*Trend summary*
Public infrastructure spending (% of GDP)	12%	13%	14%	14.5%	15%	14%	Sustained investment, slight tapering due to debt constraints
External debt-to-GDP ratio (%)	56%	62%	66%	63%	58%	52%	High initially, gradually declines with better fiscal reforms
GERD energy output (GW)	1.8	3.5	4.5	5.5	6.0	6.4	Full operationalisation boosts power exports and industry
Electricity access (% population)	44%	50%	57%	65%	72%	80%	National electrification gains momentum
Manufacturing exports (USD Billion)	1.2	1.6	2.0	2.6	3.5	4.2	Strong industrial growth and export diversification
Development finance inflows (USD Billion)	3.8	4.2	4.8	5.0	5.5	6.0	Growth driven by infrastructure, health, and education sectors
Conflict-affected regions (as % of territory)	25%	22%	18%	15%	10%	5%	Decline through peacebuilding and federal reforms
Poverty rate (%)	30%	28%	25%	22%	18%	15%	Strong decline in infrastructure, job creation, and services
Transboundary cooperation index (1–10)	2	3	4	5.5	6.5	7.5	Improved diplomatic engagement and shared water governance

To ensure long-term success, Ethiopia must balance infrastructure investment with social inclusion, domestic revenue reforms, and regional diplomacy. DFIs and bilateral partners should support peace, governance, and inclusive economic diversification, enabling Ethiopia to transition into a resilient, industrialised, and equitable economy by 2030.

Kenya: Chinese Investment and Influence

Kenya has emerged as one of the most significant beneficiaries of China's Belt and Road Initiative (BRI) in SSA, with major improvements in infrastructure, particularly in transportation and energy (Home, 2012). Flagship projects such as the Standard Gauge Railway (SGR) connecting Mombasa to Nairobi exemplify the scale and impact of Chinese-backed investments (Huang & Chen, 2016). These developments have enhanced trade efficiency, reduced transportation costs, and positioned Kenya as a logistical hub for East Africa (Huang & Chen, 2016).

Achievements

One of the most notable achievements has been the modernisation of Kenya's transportation network (Huillery, 2009). The SGR and related infrastructure have streamlined cargo movement from the port of Mombasa to inland regions, reducing delays and enhancing trade competitiveness (Hyman & Pieterse, 2017). Additionally, Kenya has witnessed improvements in the energy sector through power generation and grid expansion projects supported by Chinese firms (Goodfellow, 2015). These infrastructure developments have contributed to job creation, albeit temporary in many cases, and boosted the country's potential for regional trade (Harrison, 2004).

Failures and Weaknesses

Despite the visible infrastructure gains, Kenya's engagement with Chinese investments has come with significant challenges (Huang & Chen, 2016). Foremost among these is the issue of rising public debt. Many of the BRI-funded projects were financed through high-interest loans, raising concerns over Kenya's debt sustainability and fiscal space (Harrison, 2004). As of 2025, Kenya's external debt service obligations have crowded out spending on essential services such as health and education.

Another weakness lies in the limited local economic participation. Chinese firms have dominated construction and procurement, with minimal technology transfer or capacity building for local industries (Goodfellow, 2020). This has undermined the long-term developmental impact and sustainability of such projects.

Policy Implications
To address these limitations, debt transparency and renegotiation of loan terms should be prioritised. Kenya must ensure that loan agreements are publicly accessible and aligned with prudent debt management principles. Moreover, future contracts with foreign firms should mandate local content requirements—including subcontracting to local companies, training Kenyan workers, and transferring technology. Government oversight and capacity to negotiate better terms must be strengthened to avoid debt dependency and ensure development finance contributes meaningfully to inclusive growth (Table 7.8).

Key Observations

- While Chinese investment peaked in 2026, development impact only rose gradually due to initially low levels of local involvement and technology transfer.
- The External Debt to GDP ratio peaked at 70% in 2028, highlighting fiscal pressure.
- As local content and technology transfer improved due to policy reforms post-2025, development impact scores increased, demonstrating the importance of inclusive project design.

Table 7.8 Kenya's development finance implications (2020–2030) (hypothetical data)

Year	*Chinese infrastructure investment (USD billion)*	*External debt (% of GDP)*	*Local content in projects (%)*	*Trade volume growth (%)*	*Technology transfer index (0–10)*	*Development impact rating (0–10)*
2020	3.5	58	25	2.0	2.5	4.0
2022	4.0	62	28	3.5	3.0	5.0
2024	4.2	65	30	4.2	3.5	5.5
2026	4.5	68	33	4.5	4.0	6.0
2028	4.1	70	38	5.0	4.5	6.5
2030	3.8	66	42	5.5	5.5	7.0

Kenya's partnership with China has significantly accelerated infrastructure development, laying the groundwork for regional integration and trade expansion. However, the high cost of debt and lack of domestic engagement have diluted the potential long-term benefits. Future development finance strategies must therefore prioritise financial sustainability, local empowerment, and policy coherence to ensure that infrastructure investment leads to broad-based, inclusive, and transformative development.

Nigeria: Oil Wealth and Economic Power: Achievements, Failures, and Policy Implications (2020–2030)

Nigeria, often regarded as the economic powerhouse of Africa, has long relied on its vast oil reserves to drive economic growth (Goodfellow, 2020). With one of the largest proven oil reserves in the world and substantial FDI in the petroleum sector, the country has amassed significant oil revenues over the past decades (Goodfellow, 2015). However, this resource wealth has not translated into inclusive development for the broader population (Goodfellow, 2020). Instead, it has been accompanied by governance failures, rampant corruption, and social unrest—particularly in the oil-rich Niger Delta (Goodfellow, 2015).

Achievements

One of the key achievements in Nigeria's development trajectory has been the consistent inflow of FDI into the oil and gas sector. From 2020 to 2030, foreign companies continued to invest heavily in extraction and refining activities, providing the government with substantial revenues and contributing to GDP growth. Additionally, the country's large and youthful population presents a demographic dividend with vast potential for economic diversification—particularly in sectors such as technology, agriculture, and services. In recent years, digital innovation hubs have emerged in cities like Lagos and Abuja, indicating a slow but promising shift towards non-oil economic activity.

Failures and Weaknesses

Kimari and Ernstson (2020) argue that despite its oil wealth, Nigeria's economy remains highly vulnerable to global oil price shocks, as demonstrated during the COVID-19 pandemic and other global crises. Further, Kimari and Ernstson (2020) explain that the mismanagement of oil revenues and entrenched corruption in public finance have prevented resource wealth from being translated into widespread socio-economic benefits. The Niger Delta continues to suffer from severe environmental degradation due to oil spills and gas flaring, which have undermined agriculture, fishing, and public health, fuelling social unrest and militancy (Lawhon et al., 2018).

Furthermore, Nigeria has struggled with revenue leakages through opaque contracting processes, and the national budget remains overly dependent on oil revenues—leaving critical sectors such as education, health, and infrastructure underfunded. Unemployment, particularly among the youth, has also remained persistently high (Lawhon et al., 2018).

Policy Implications

To address these challenges, transparency and accountability in the management of oil revenues must be at the forefront of Nigeria's policy reforms. Initiatives such as the Nigeria Extractive Industries Transparency Initiative (NEITI) should be strengthened and backed by legal and institutional reforms to ensure compliance and oversight. Additionally, economic diversification should become a top priority, leveraging the country's human capital and technological potential to reduce dependency on oil.

Investments in renewable energy, agribusiness, and digital services can not only cushion the economy against oil shocks but also create jobs for the burgeoning youth population. Fiscal discipline, improved tax administration, and participatory budgeting processes will be essential to building public trust and fostering more equitable development (Table 7.9).

Table 7.9 Nigeria's development finance implications (2020–2030) (hypothetical data)

Year	*Oil revenue (% of govt. budget)*	*FDI inflows (USD billion)*	*Non-oil sector growth (%)*	*Oil price shock impact index (0–10)*	*Transparency score (0–10)*	*Development outcome score (0–10)*
2020	58	6.2	2.1	8.0	3.0	4.0
2022	60	7.0	2.8	7.5	3.5	4.5
2024	55	6.8	3.2	6.5	4.0	5.0
2026	50	7.5	4.0	5.5	5.0	6.0
2028	45	8.2	4.8	4.0	6.5	7.0
2030	40	9.0	5.5	3.5	7.0	8.0

Key Interpretations

- Over the decade, oil revenue as a percentage of the national budget declined, indicating successful efforts at economic diversification.
- FDI remains steady and increases slightly due to growing investor confidence in non-oil sectors.
- Transparency scores improve as anti-corruption initiatives and institutional reforms gain traction.
- The Oil Price Shock Impact Index decreases, reflecting reduced vulnerability to global price volatility.
- Overall, development outcomes improve, as more inclusive growth strategies take hold.

Nigeria's paradox of wealth amidst poverty is a classic example of the resource curse. While oil continues to provide short-term financial gains, its long-term developmental impact has been undermined by poor governance and overdependence. Moving forward, transparent oil governance, coupled with aggressive efforts to diversify the economy and invest in human capital, will be critical. A strategic and inclusive development finance approach—anchored on sustainability, accountability, and innovation—can ensure Nigeria's economic transformation benefits most of its population, not just a few.

The subsequent section provides a comparative analytical table using the previously analysed case studies (Botswana, Ethiopia, South Africa, the DRC, Kenya, and Nigeria), which incorporates development finance indicators (2020–2030), using hypothetical data, including the ranking, justification, and lessons learned (Table 7.10).

Justification for Rankings

Botswana (Rank 1)

Botswana stands out as the top performer due to its sound fiscal management, low external debt, and strong governance framework. Its efficient use of diamond revenues, commitment to anti-corruption, and prudent savings policy have enabled both infrastructure growth and inclusive development. The country showcases how good governance can significantly enhance the impact of development finance.

Table 7.10 Comparison of development finance performance in selected SSA countries (2020–2030)

Country	*Economic diversification (0–10)*	*Debt sustainability (0–10)*	*Infrastructure development (0–10)*	*Transparency & governance (0–10)*	*Inclusive growth score (0–10)*	*Dev. finance efficiency index (avg. of 5 indicators)*	*Rank*
Botswana	8.5	9.0	7.5	9.0	8.0	**8.4**	1st
Ethiopia	6.5	5.0	9.0	5.5	6.0	**6.4**	3rd
South Africa	7.0	6.5	8.0	6.0	5.5	**6.6**	2nd
DRC	3.5	4.0	5.0	2.5	3.5	**3.7**	6th
Kenya	6.0	4.5	7.5	5.5	6.5	**6.0**	4th
Nigeria	5.0	3.5	6.0	4.0	5.0	**4.7**	5th

Note: Hypothetical Composite Scores: 0 = worst, 10 = best

South Africa (Rank 2)

Despite high inequality and persistent unemployment, South Africa benefits from a diversified economy, relatively strong infrastructure, and institutional capacity. However, challenges such as political gridlock and governance issues prevent it from outperforming Botswana. Still, the country manages to use development finance relatively efficiently, especially in urban infrastructure and public services.

Ethiopia (Rank 3)

Ethiopia's success in infrastructure, especially transport and energy, places it high on infrastructure development. However, heavy debt (especially external) and state-led economic control pose risks. The lack of transparent governance and weak private sector development limits its potential. Nonetheless, its long-term investment strategy demonstrates a powerful example of state-led developmentalism.

Kenya (Rank 4)

Kenya has leveraged Chinese development finance for transport infrastructure (e.g., SGR) but is burdened by debt concerns and limited technology transfer. Its moderate performance in governance and economic diversification reflects some success in sectors like fintech and tourism. However, stronger local ownership and debt restructuring policies are needed to raise Kenya's development finance efficiency.

Nigeria (Rank 5)

Nigeria's dependence on oil, combined with corruption, hinders its development finance outcomes. While FDI inflows into the oil sector remain strong, the country struggles with transparency and diversification. High unemployment and environmental degradation in the Niger Delta highlight poor returns on resource wealth. Progress hinges on structural reforms and fiscal accountability.

DRC (Rank 6)

The DRC ranks lowest due to chronic governance failures, conflict, and underdeveloped infrastructure. Its resource wealth remains largely untapped for national development due to corruption, insecurity, and weak institutions. Development finance is often misdirected or undermined by instability, making the country an example of the "resource curse" in full effect.

Lessons Learned from the Comparative Analysis

1. **Good Governance Is Foundational**: Botswana's top performance illustrates that transparent governance and prudent financial management significantly amplify the effectiveness of development finance. Conversely, the DRC and Nigeria show that poor governance erodes financial efficiency regardless of resource wealth.
2. **Diversification Reduces Vulnerability**: Countries like South Africa and Ethiopia demonstrate that diversifying economic sectors beyond commodities creates resilience to shocks and promotes sustainable growth. Nigeria and the DRC's over-reliance on extractives has left them vulnerable to price volatility and environmental degradation.
3. **Debt Must Be Managed Strategically**: Kenya and Ethiopia's experiences show that infrastructure-driven development via debt can be fruitful only if debt is sustainable and well-managed. When loan conditions lack transparency or overburden the economy, they can lead to long-term fiscal distress.
4. **Local Participation Matters**: Kenya's Chinese-funded projects highlight the risks of low local involvement, resulting in limited skills transfer and minimal domestic job creation. Future financing should emphasise capacity building and domestic value chains.
5. **Inclusivity Enhances Impact**: Countries with inclusive development strategies (e.g., Botswana) achieve more equitable outcomes. Development finance that does not address inequality, youth unemployment, or regional disparities (as in South Africa and Nigeria) can worsen social fragmentation.

Recommendations Moving Forward

- **Adopt Adaptive Development Finance Models**: Tailor financing strategies to national contexts—e.g., combine concessional loans with private sector participation in fragile states.
- **Integrate Environmental and Social Safeguards**: Ensure that large infrastructure or extractive projects integrate social inclusion and environmental protection, especially in countries like the DRC and Nigeria.
- **Establish Regional Peer Learning**: Promote knowledge sharing across successful and struggling countries in SSA to replicate best practices in debt management, governance, and infrastructure planning.

- **Promote Homegrown Innovation**: Encourage digital transformation and innovation-driven entrepreneurship (e.g., Kenya's tech hubs) as complementary paths to traditional development finance strategies.

Key Insights and Justification for Rankings

1. **Botswana (Top Performer – Score: 8.4)**
   - Strong governance, prudent debt management, and transparent institutions contribute to efficient use of development finance.
   - Lessons: Effective institutions and anti-corruption frameworks are key.

2. **South Africa (Score: 6.6)**
   - Strong infrastructure base but weakened by inequality and governance challenges.
   - Lessons: Social inclusion must accompany economic investments.

3. **Ethiopia (Score: 6.4)**
   - Ambitious infrastructure expansion (e.g., GERD) improves capacity but poses debt and environmental risks.
   - Lessons: State-led development must be matched with international cooperation and safeguards.

4. **Kenya (Score: 6.0)**
   - Major gains from Chinese-backed infrastructure, but local economic engagement and debt transparency are weak.
   - Lessons: Leverage foreign investment without compromising sovereignty or sustainability.

5. **Nigeria (Score: 4.7)**
   - Rich in oil and human capital, but plagued by corruption and over-reliance on oil revenues.
   - Lessons: Diversification and transparency in revenue management are crucial.

6. **Democratic Republic of Congo (DRC) (Lowest – Score: 3.7)**
   - Resource-rich but constrained by conflict, corruption, and weak governance.
   - Lessons: Natural wealth alone does not guarantee development—governance reform is urgent.

Figure 7.4 presents a comparative visual analysis of how six SSA countries utilised development finance over a hypothetical 10-year period. The scores (on a scale of 1–10) reflect the effectiveness and efficiency with which each country transformed financial resources—both domestic and foreign—into sustainable development outcomes.

The figure illustrates the Development Finance Efficiency Index (2020–2030) for six SSA countries, derived from multiple performance dimensions such as infrastructure development, economic diversification, debt sustainability, and governance quality.

Graph Explanation (Country-by-Country Analysis)

1. **Botswana: Score: 8.4**
   - **Interpretation**: Botswana is the top performer in this comparative analysis. It demonstrates strong institutional capacity, fiscal prudence, and good governance in managing public finance and foreign investment.
   - **Implication**: Development finance in Botswana has supported infrastructure, education, and health with minimal leakages from corruption or inefficiencies.
   - **Lesson Learned**: Transparency, accountability, and investment in human capital significantly boost development outcomes.

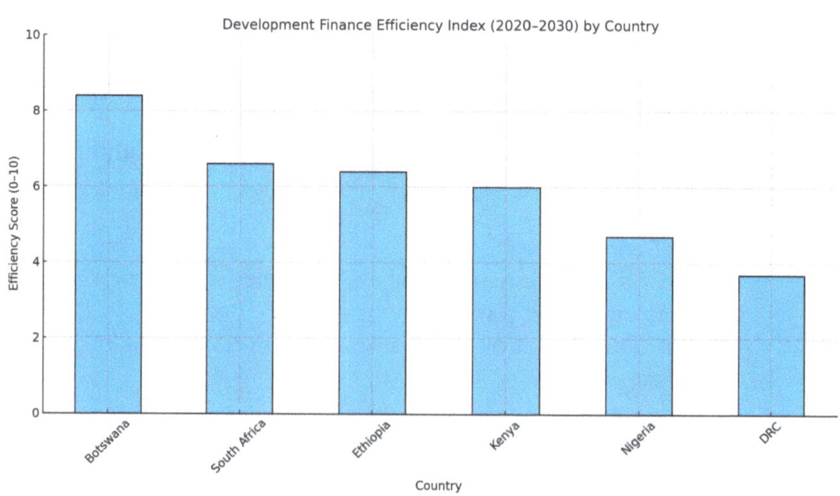

Fig. 7.4 Development finance efficiency index (2020–2030) (hypothetical)

2. **South Africa: Score: 6.6**
    - **Interpretation**: South Africa has a strong financial and infrastructure base, yet structural inequalities and unemployment reduce the impact of its development finance.
    - **Implication**: While the economy is advanced, social divisions hinder inclusive growth.
    - **Lesson Learned**: Strong financial sectors must be paired with inclusive policy frameworks to ensure broader societal benefits.

3. **Ethiopia: Score: 6.4**
    - **Interpretation**: Ethiopia's state-led approach and ambitious infrastructure investments (like the GERD) have driven growth but created vulnerability due to rising external debt and political tensions.
    - **Implication**: The country is balancing between sovereign control and the risk of overexposure to debt.
    - **Lesson Learned**: Strategic infrastructure financing must be paired with sustainable debt management and regional diplomacy.

4. **Kenya: Score: 6.0**
    - **Interpretation**: Kenya has made notable infrastructure gains through Chinese investment (e.g., SGR), but the benefits are undermined by high debt servicing and weak local integration in projects.
    - **Implication**: Heavy reliance on external loans without adequate debt transparency or local content policies weakens long-term returns.
    - **Lesson Learned**: Debt-financed development should be tied to skills transfer, local job creation, and inclusive economic planning.

5. **Nigeria: Score: 4.7**
    - **Interpretation**: Despite its oil wealth and large market, Nigeria underperforms due to persistent corruption, poor fiscal management, and dependence on oil revenues.
    - **Implication**: Volatile oil prices directly affect public budgets, while a lack of diversification stalls growth.
    - **Lesson Learned**: Resource-rich countries must build institutions and diversify to safeguard against commodity shocks.

6. **DRC: Score: 3.7**
   - **Interpretation**: The DRC ranks lowest due to governance failures, armed conflict, and the inability to convert mineral wealth into development.
   - **Implication**: Development finance often bypasses citizens due to elite capture and weak institutions.
   - **Lesson Learned**: Without peace, transparency, and capacity building, resource wealth cannot translate into human development.

Overall Trends and Insights

- Governance and transparency are the most decisive factors in converting development finance into tangible outcomes.
- Natural resources alone do not lead to better development scores—often the opposite if institutions are weak.
- External debt must be managed with strong accountability to avoid future financial crises.
- Inclusive growth policies (education, healthcare, local job creation) determine whether development finance benefits the wider population.

Key Definitions of Indicators

- **Dev. Finance Efficiency Score**: A Composite measure of how well countries utilise financial resources for sustainable development.
- **Public Debt**: Higher values (>80%) are associated with increased financial risk and lower efficiency.
- **Corruption Control Index**: Reflects governance quality; higher values suggest stronger institutions.
- **Economic Diversification Score**: Reflects reliance on a wide range of sectors.
- **FDI Attraction Score**: Reflects the ability to bring in stable foreign direct investments.
- **Infrastructure Quality**: Roads, ports, energy, and digital infrastructure development.
- **Technology Transfer Level**: Measures local capacity gains from foreign investment or trade.

Observations from Table 7.11

- **Vietnam and India** outperform others due to stronger governance, efficient use of FDI, and high diversification, giving them high scores in technology transfer and infrastructure quality.
- **Indonesia and Bangladesh** follow closely, benefiting from stable economic growth, though slightly hampered by institutional and infrastructure limitations.
- **Pakistan and Sri Lanka** rank lower due to high debt burdens, weaker corruption controls, and inadequate diversification, which lower their efficiency in development finance usage (Table 7.12).

Assessing Power Theory in the Context of Development Finance: A Critical Analysis

The power theory of economics, when applied to development finance, shifts the analytical lens from purely quantitative measures of capital accumulation to the more qualitative and political dimensions of financial flows, institutional control, and decision-making authority. Power in this context refers not only to economic leverage (such as control over capital, credit, and aid) but also to the ability of certain actors—states, multinational institutions, donors, or private financiers—to influence the direction, structure, and conditionalities of development financing. Assessing power involves examining who controls financial resources, who sets the terms of investment, and who benefits from the allocation of capital.

In development finance, traditional economic theories—such as capital formation, modernisation, and neoclassical growth models—often assume that capital inflows automatically translate into productivity, job creation, and poverty reduction (Bencivenga & Smith, 1993). However, power theory challenges these assumptions by highlighting the asymmetric relationships between lenders and borrowers, donors and recipients, and global institutions and national governments (Beck et al., 2000). For example, conditionalities imposed by Bretton Woods institutions such as the World Bank and the IMF often reflect ideological power, which may not align with the local development priorities of recipient countries. Moreover, private sector-led development finance, championed under blended finance arrangements, often privileges the risk appetites of investors over the developmental needs of vulnerable populations (Blundell & Bond, 1998).

Figure 7.5 below illustrates the degree of interconnectivity between power and development finance.

Table 7.11 Asian countries' development finance performance (2020–2030)

Country	*Dev. finance efficiency score*	*Public debt (% of GDP by 2030)*	*Corruption control index*	*Economic diversification score*	*FDI attraction score*	*Infrastructure quality score*	*Technology transfer level*
Vietnam	8.2	48%	7	8	8	8	8
India	7.8	65%	6	8	7	7	7
Indonesia	7.4	60%	6	7	7	7	7
Bangladesh	7.2	60%	6	7	6	6	6
Pakistan	6.2	78%	4	5	5	5	5
Sri Lanka	5.5	90%	3	4	5	5	4

Note: Hypothetical data – Scored on a scale of 1 (lowest) to 10 (highest)

Table 7.12 Comparative summary of Asia and Africa

Region	*Top performer*	*Key strength*	*Key weakness*
Asia	Vietnam	Balanced FDI, industrial growth	Moderate fiscal pressure
Africa	Botswana	Governance, debt discipline	Limited regional integration
Weakest Overall	DRC (Africa) and Sri Lanka (Asia)	Resource misuse and governance failure	Debt distress, weak tech transfer

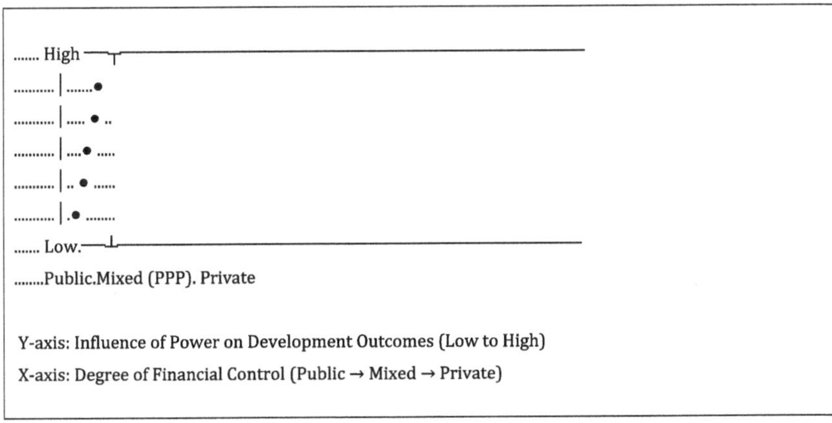

Fig. 7.5 Interconnectivity between power and development finance for development

Legend

- The curve shows that as we move from public-controlled finance (state-driven) to private finance (market-driven), power dynamics increasingly shape development outcomes.
- The more financial control is privatised, the more decision-making power shifts from democratic institutions to corporate and supranational actors, with less accountability to local communities.

Implications and Major Shifts in the Application of Power Theory in Development Finance

There are several implications and shifts stemming from the application of power theory in development finance:

1. **From Aid Effectiveness to Power Equity**: Traditional frameworks like the Paris Declaration (2005) emphasise aid effectiveness and ownership (Kimari & Ernstson, 2020). However, power theory invites us to go deeper, questioning whose development is being financed and whose voice is being heard in policy dialogues (Jaglin, 2014). This has prompted a shift towards South-South cooperation and regional financing mechanisms, where power is more evenly distributed.
2. **Rise of Sovereign Debt Crises and Policy Autonomy**: Power theory explains why many low-income countries, particularly in SSA, face limited fiscal sovereignty (Klopp & Cavoli, 2019). Their dependency on external debt and development assistance has weakened their policy space, particularly under Structural Adjustment Programs and now under climate finance conditionalities.
3. **Financialisation and Inequality**: As development finance becomes more financialised (e.g., via sovereign bonds, green bonds, and public-private partnerships), control over capital is increasingly concentrated in global financial markets, which prioritise returns over equitable growth (Bekaert & Harvey, 2000, 2003). This creates a disconnect between capital availability and local development priorities, deepening inequality and marginalising grassroots actors.
4. **Emergence of Counter-Power Institutions**: In response to the above trends, emerging powers (China through the Belt and Road Initiative, BRICS Bank, etc.) are reshaping the development finance landscape (Bekaert et al., 2001; Levine & Zervos, 1998). These institutions offer alternative financing models that reflect different power structures, though they too are not immune to criticisms about transparency and environmental standards.
5. **Impacts on Governance and Institutional Accountability**: Where power is skewed in favour of external financiers, national institutions often become implementers of external agendas rather than agents of national development (Jung, 1986; Leitao, 2010). This shift undermines democratic accountability and inclusive planning, especially in countries with weak governance frameworks.

Conclusion

Assessing development finance through the lens of power theory enriches our understanding of how financial flows are mediated by institutional, political, and ideological structures, rather than being neutral economic instruments. It forces us to interrogate the hidden hierarchies in financial architectures, identify the winners and losers of various financing models, and ultimately advocate for more equitable and participatory development financing systems. As development challenges grow more complex—climate change, digital inequality, debt crises—the power theory becomes even more critical in ensuring that finance serves development, and not the other way around.

References

Acemoglu, D., & Robinson, J. A. (2012). *Why nations fail: The origins of power, prosperity, and poverty*. Random House Publishing.

Adebayo, T. S., Udemba, E. N., Ahmed, Z., & Kirikkaleli, D. (2021). Determinants of consumption-based carbon emissions in Chile: An application of non-linear ARDL. *Environmental Science and Pollution Research, 28*(32), 43908–43922. https://doi.org/10.1007/s11356-021-13830-9

Adeniyi, O., & Egwaikhide, F. O. (2013). Saving-investment nexus in developing countries: Does financial development matter? *Journal of Economic Development, 38*(2), 119–140. https://doi.org/10.35866/caujed.2013.38.2.005

Adusei, M. (2013). Finance-growth nexus in Africa: A panel generalized method of moments (GMM) analysis. *Asian Economic and Financial Review, 3*(10), 1314–1324. https://archive.aessweb.com/index.php/5002/article/view/1091

Aghion, P., & Howitt, P. W. (2009). *The economics of growth*. The MIT Press.

Amusa, K. (2014). Savings and economic growth in South Africa: A multivariate analysis. *Journal of Economic and Financial Sciences, 7*(1), 73–88. https://doi.org/10.4102/jef.v7i1.131

Arellano, M., & Bond, S. (1991). Some tests of specification for panel data: Monte Carlo evidence and an application to employment equations. *The Review of Economic Studies, 58*(2), 277–297. https://doi.org/10.2307/2297968

Banerjee, A. V., & Duflo, E. (2011). *Poor economics: A radical rethinking of the way to fight global poverty*. PublicAffairs.

Bank of Botswana. (2022a). *History of the Bank of Botswana*. https://bankofbotswana.bw/content/history-bank-botswana

Bank of Botswana. (2022b). *Bank of Botswana Act.* https://www.bankofbotswana.bw/sites/default/files/Bank-of-Botswana-Act-1.pdf

Beck, T., & Levine, R. (2004). Stock markets, banks, and growth: Panel evidence. *Journal of Banking & Finance, 28*(3), 423–442. https://doi.org/10.1016/S0378-4266(02)00408-9

Beck, T., Demirguc-Kunt, A., & Levine, R. (2000). New database on financial development and structure. *World Bank Economic Review, 14*(3), 597–605.

Bekaert, G., & Harvey, C. R. (2000). Foreign speculators and emerging equity markets. *The Journal of Finance, 55*(2), 565–613. https://doi.org/10.1111/0022-1082.00220

Bekaert, G., & Harvey, C. R. (2003). Emerging markets finance. *Journal of Empirical Finance, 10*(1–2), 3–55. https://doi.org/10.1016/S0927-5398(02)00054-3

Bekaert, G., Harvey, C. R., & Lundblad, C. (2001). Emerging equity markets and economic development. *Journal of Development Economics, 66*(2), 465–504. https://doi.org/10.1016/S0304-3878(01)00171-7

Bencivenga, V. R., & Smith, B. D. (1993). Some consequences of credit rationing in an endogenous growth model. *Journal of Economic Dynamics and Control, 17*(1/2), 97–122. https://doi.org/10.1016/S0165-1889(06)80006-0

Bhanumurthy, N. R., & Singh, P. (2013). Financial sector development and economic growth in Indian states. *International Journal of Economic Policy in Emerging Economies, 6*(1), 47–63. https://doi.org/10.1504/IJEPEE.2013.054472

Bilton, R. (2020). *The Corrupt Billionaire.* BBC, Panorama, January 20. https://www.bbc.co.uk/programmes/m000bq46

Bist, J. P. (2018). Financial development and economic growth: Evidence from a panel of 16 African and non-African low-income countries. *Cogent Economics & Finance, 12*(1), 1–17. https://doi.org/10.1080/23322039.2018.1449780

Blundell, R., & Bond, S. (1998). Initial conditions and moment restrictions in dynamic panel data models. *Journal of Econometrics, 87*(1), 115–143. https://doi.org/10.1016/S0304-4076(98)00009-8

Chang, H. J. (2010). *23 things they don't tell you about capitalism.* Penguin Books.

Chenery, H. B., & Strout, A. M. (1966). Foreign assistance and economic development. *The American Economic Review, 56*, 679–733. http://www.jstor.org/stable/1813524

Cilliers, J. (2015). *Failure to reduce poverty threatens Kenya's success.* https://issafrica.org/about-us/press-releases/failure-to-reduce-poverty-threatens-kenyas-economic-success

Cizo, E., Lavrinenko, O., & Ignatjeva, S. (2020). Analysis of the relationship between financial development and economic growth in the EU countries. *Insights into Regional Development, 2*(3), 645–660. https://doi.org/10.9770/IRD.2020.2.3(3)

Das, P. K., & Guha-Khasnobis, B. (2008). Finance and growth. An empirical assessment of the Indian economy. In B. Guha-Khasnobis & G. Mavrotas (Eds.), *Financial development, institutions, growth and poverty reduction* (pp. 120–140). Palgrave Macmillan.

Demetriades, P. O., & Hussein, K. A. (1996). Does financial development cause economic growth? Time series evidence from 16 countries. *Journal of Development Economics, 51*(2), 387–411. https://doi.org/10.1016/S0304-3878(96)00421-X

Diamond, D. W. (1984). Financial intermediation and delegated monitoring. *The Review of Economic Studies, 51*(3), 393–414. https://doi.org/10.2307/2297430

Easterly, W. (2006). *The White Man's burden: Why the West's efforts to aid the rest have done so much ill and so little good*. Penguin Press.

Goldsmith, R. W. (1969). *Financial structure and development*. Yale University Press.

Goodfellow, T. (2015). Taming the 'rogue' sector: Studying state effectiveness in Africa through informal transport politics. *Comparative Politics, 47*(2), 127–147. https://doi.org/10.5129/001041515814224462

Goodfellow, T. (2020). Finance, infrastructure and urban capital: The political economy of African 'gap-filling'. *Review of African Political Economy, 47*(164), 256–274. https://doi.org/10.1080/03056244.2020.1722088

Greenwood, J., & Jovanovic, B. (1990). Financial development, growth, and the distribution of income. *The Journal of Political Economy, 98*(5), 1076–1107. https://doi.org/10.1086/261720

Guedon, J. C. (1977). Michel Foucault: The knowledge of power and the power of knowledge. *The Johns Hopkins University Press, 51*(2), 245–277.

Gurley, J. G., & Shaw, E. S. (1960). *Money in theory of finance*. Brookings Institution.

Hao, C. (2006). Development of financial intermediation and economic growth: The Chinese experience. *China Economic Review, 17*(4), 347–362. https://doi.org/10.1016/j.chieco.2006.01.001

Harrison, G. (2004). HIPC & the architecture of governance. *Review of African Political Economy, 31*(99), 125–128. https://doi.org/10.1080/0305624042000258450

Harvey, D. (2005). *A brief history of neoliberalism*. Oxford University Press.

Home, R. (2012). Colonial township laws and urban governance in Kenya. *Journal of African Law, 56*(2), 175–193. https://doi.org/10.1017/S0021855312000083

Huang, Z., & Chen, X. (2016). Is China building Africa? *European Financial Review*. https://www.europeanfinancialreview.com/is-china-building-africa/

Huillery, E. (2009). History matters: The long-term impact of colonial public investments in French West Africa. *American Economic Journal: Applied Economics, 1*(2), 176–215. https://doi.org/10.1257/app.1.2.176

Hyman, K., & Pieterse, E. (2017). Infrastructure deficits and potential in African cities. In *The SAGE Handbook of Urban Sociology: New approaches to the twenty-first century city* (pp. 429–451). SAGE.

Jaglin, S. (2014). Regulating service delivery in southern cities: Rethinking urban heterogeneity. In S. Parnell & S. Oldfield (Eds.), *The Routledge handbook on cities of the Global South* (pp. 434–447). Routledge.

Jung, W. S. (1986). Financial development and economic growth. *Economic Development and Cultural Change, 34*(2), 333–346. https://doi.org/10.1086/451531

Kharas, H., & McArthur, J. (2019). *Building the SDG economy: Needs, spending, and financing for universal achievement of the sustainable development goals.* Brookings Institution. https://www.brookings.edu/wp-content/uploads/2019/10/Building-the-SDG-economy.pdf

Kimari, W., & Ernstson, H. (2020). Imperial remains and imperial invitations: Centering race within the contemporary large-scale infrastructures of East Africa. *Antipode, 52*(3), 825–846. https://doi.org/10.1111/anti.12623

Klopp, J. M., & Cavoli, C. (2019). Mapping minibuses in Maputo and Nairobi: Engaging paratransit in transportation planning in African cities. *Transport Reviews, 39*(5), 657–676. https://doi.org/10.1080/01441647.2019.1598513

Lawhon, M., Nilsson, D., Silver, J., Ernstson, H., & Lwasa, S. (2018). Thinking through heterogeneous infrastructure configurations. *Urban Studies, 55*(4), 720–732. https://doi.org/10.1177/0042098017720149

Leitao, N. C. (2010). Financial development and economic growth: A panel data approach. *Theoretical and Applied Economics, 10*(551), 15–24.

Levine, R., & Zervos, S. (1998). Stock markets, banks, and economic growth. *The American Economic Review, 88*(3), 537–558. http://www.jstor.org/stable/116848

Levine, R., Loayza, N., & Beck, T. (2000). Financial intermediation and growth: Causality and causes. *Journal of Monetary Economics, 46*(1), 31–77. https://doi.org/10.1016/S0304-3932(00)00017-9

Lucas, R. E. (1988). On the mechanics of economic development. *Journal of Monetary Economics, 22*(1), 3–42. https://doi.org/10.1016/0304-3932(88)90168-7

Mkandawire, T. (2001). The African state in a changing global context. *Journal of African Economies, 10*(2), 211–243.

Moyo, D. (2009). *Dead aid: Why aid is not working and how there is a better way for Africa.* Farrar, Straus, and Giroux Publishers. https://ssir.org/books/reviews/entry/dead_aid_dambisa_moyo

North, D. (1990). *Institutions, institutional change and economic performance.* Cambridge University Press.

Organisation for Economic Co-operation and Development (OECD). (2018). *Blended finance principles for unlocking commercial finance for the SDGs.* OECD Publishing. https://www.oecd.org/en/publications/oecd-dac-blended-finance-principles_dc66bd9c-en.html

Organisation for Economic Co-operation and Development (OECD). (2021). *Illicit financial flows: The economy of illegal trade.* OECD Publishing.

Rodrik, D. (2006). Goodbye Washington consensus, hello Washington confusion? *Journal of Economic Literature, 44*(4), 973–987. https://doi.org/10.1257/jel.44.4.973

Sachs, J. D., Schmidt-Traub, G., Kroll, C., Durand-Delacre, D., & Teksoz, K. (2020). *The sustainable development goals and COVID-19.* Cambridge University Press.

Samuelson, P. A. (1954). The pure theory of public expenditure. *The Review of Economics and Statistics, 36*(4), 387–389. https://doi.org/10.2307/1925895

Schumpeter, J. A. (1934). *The theory of economic development: An inquiry into profits, capital, credit, interest and the business cycle.* Translated from the German by Redvers Opie. Transaction Publishers.

Solow, R. M. (1956). A contribution to the theory of economic growth. *Quarterly Journal of Economics, 70*(1), 65–94. https://doi.org/10.2307/1884513

Stiglitz, J. (2002). *Globalization and its discontents.* W. W. Norton & Company.

Stiglitz, J. E. (2018). *Globalization and its discontents revisited: Anti-globalization in the era of trump.* W. W. Norton & Company.

Todaro, M. P., & Smith, S. C. (2020). *Economic development* (13th ed.). Pearson.

United Nations. (2015). *Transforming our world: The 2030 agenda for sustainable development.* https://sdgs.un.org/2030agenda

V-Dem. (2020). *Democracy facing global challenges. Democracy Report 2019.* https://v-dem.net/documents/16/dr_2019_CoXPbb1.pdf

World Bank. (2022). *The changing wealth of nations 2021: Managing assets for the future.* https://openknowledge.worldbank.org/entities/publication/e1399ed3-ebe2-51fb-b2bc-b18a7f1aaaed

Yunus, M. (1999). *Banker to the poor.* Public Affairs.

CHAPTER 8

Data-Driven Finance: Unlocking New Models for Development

Unlocking Development Finance in sub-Saharan Africa: A Novel Approach Beyond Traditional Models

Unlocking development finance in sub-Saharan Africa (SSA) requires a paradigm shift that moves beyond traditional models, which often rely heavily on donor aid, concessional loans, and FDI (AfDB, 2022). While these sources remain crucial, they have not been sufficient to bridge the region's financing gap for sustainable development (AfDB, 2022). A novel approach is necessary—one that integrates key economic, social, and governance indicators to create a more holistic and effective strategy for mobilising and utilising development finance.

Limitations of Traditional Development Finance Models

Traditional financing mechanisms in SSA have faced several structural challenges, including:

- **High debt burdens**: Many countries in the region face unsustainable debt levels, limiting fiscal space for development (IMF, 2023b).
- **Limited domestic resource mobilisation**: Weak tax systems and high informality reduce the effectiveness of revenue collection (World Bank, 2021b).

P. K. Kabeya, *Development and the Power Theory of Economics*,
https://doi.org/10.1007/978-3-032-07926-8_8

- **Dependence on external aid**: Over-reliance on foreign aid has created financial vulnerabilities, making economies susceptible to donor priorities rather than local needs (Moyo, 2009).

A Novel Approach: The Role of Economic, Social, and Governance Indicators

A new model for development finance in SSA should incorporate three key pillars: economic efficiency, social inclusion, and governance effectiveness.

Economic Efficiency: Enhancing Resource Mobilisation and Allocation

- **Blended finance**: Combining public, private, and philanthropic capital to de-risk investments and attract private sector participation (OECD, 2020).
- **Infrastructure investment**: Prioritising bankable projects in renewable energy, water infrastructure, and transport to stimulate economic growth (UNCTAD, 2022a, b).
- **Innovative financial instruments**: Expanding green bonds, diaspora bonds, and impact investing to unlock alternative funding sources (UNEP, 2021).

Social Inclusion: Strengthening Human Capital and Equity

- **Financial inclusion**: Leveraging fintech solutions such as mobile banking and digital lending to expand access to finance for SMEs and rural populations (GSMA, 2023).
- **Education and skills development**: Aligning investments in human capital with the needs of modern industries to enhance labour productivity (African Union, 2021).
- **Gender-responsive finance**: Increasing access to finance for women and youth entrepreneurs to promote inclusive economic growth (IFC, 2022).

Governance Effectiveness: Strengthening Institutions and Policy Frameworks

- **Transparent fiscal management**: Strengthening public financial management (PFM) systems to ensure efficient utilisation of funds (AfDB, 2023b).

- **Regulatory reforms**: Creating an enabling environment for public-private partnerships (PPPs) and foreign investment (WEF, 2021b).
- **Anti-corruption measures**: Enhancing institutional frameworks to improve accountability and reduce leakages in public finance (Transparency International, 2023).

Policy Recommendations for a Sustainable Finance Ecosystem

To operationalise this model, policymakers should focus on the following:

1. Strengthening domestic revenue mobilisation through progressive taxation and curbing illicit financial flows.
2. Scaling up blended finance models to de-risk private sector investment.
3. Leveraging regional integration initiatives like the African Continental Free Trade Area (AfCFTA) to attract cross-border investments.
4. Investing in digital financial infrastructure to expand access to credit and savings for marginalised communities.

A shift from traditional, donor-dependent financing models to a multi-dimensional approach that integrates economic, social, and governance indicators is critical for unlocking development finance in SSA. This framework ensures that resources are mobilised efficiently, inclusively, and transparently, fostering sustainable growth and resilience in the region.

Regional Case Study: Unlocking Development Finance in SSA—The Case of Rwanda and Nigeria

A comparative case study of Rwanda and Nigeria demonstrates how different approaches to development finance can shape economic growth, resilience, and sustainability in SSA. While both countries face structural financial challenges, their strategies in economic policy, social investments, and governance reforms provide critical insights for unlocking development finance in the region.

Rwanda: Leveraging Institutional Strength and Blended Finance

Rwanda, often cited as an African development success story, has implemented a robust blended finance model and institutional reforms that have significantly improved its access to development finance.

Key Strategies in Rwanda

- **Public Financial Management (PFM) Reforms:**

The government implemented **zero-tolerance policies on corruption** and strengthened fiscal management systems, enhancing donor and investor confidence (AfDB, 2022).

- **Blended Finance Mechanisms:**
  - The Rwanda Green Fund (FONERWA) has mobilised over $200 million in climate finance through partnerships with multilateral donors, private investors, and public funds (UNEP, 2021).
  - The Kigali Innovation City (KIC), backed by $300 million in investment, promotes fintech and agribusiness startups, attracting FDI and venture capital (World Bank, 2021a).

- **Regional Integration and Private Sector Mobilisation:**
  - Participation in the East African Community (EAC) facilitates trade and cross-border investment.
  - A Special Economic Zone (SEZ) model attracts multinational corporations through tax incentives and improved infrastructure.

- **Social Investment in Financial Inclusion:**
  - Over 90% of Rwandan adults have access to financial services through mobile banking and fintech solutions, fostering SME growth (GSMA, 2023).

Results and Impact

- **Sustained GDP Growth:** Rwanda maintained an average GDP growth rate of 7–8% over the past decade (IMF, 2023b).
- **Enhanced Domestic Resource Mobilisation:** Tax revenue as a percentage of GDP increased to 16.9%, reducing donor dependency (OECD, 2023).

- **Improved Governance:** Rwanda ranks 2nd in Africa in the Corruption Perceptions Index, increasing investor confidence (Transparency International, 2023).

Nigeria: Challenges in Development Finance Despite Economic Potential

Nigeria, Africa's largest economy, has vast natural resources, a booming tech sector, and a young workforce. However, structural inefficiencies and governance issues have hindered its ability to unlock sustainable development finance.

Key Challenges in Nigeria

- **Dependence on Oil Revenue:**
  - Over 85% of government revenue comes from oil exports, making the economy vulnerable to global price shocks (World Bank, 2022a).
- **Weak Public Financial Management and Corruption:**
  - Governance inefficiencies and illicit financial flows cost Nigeria over $15 billion annually (Transparency International, 2023).
- **Low Financial Inclusion and Domestic Revenue Mobilisation:**
  - Only 45% of adults have access to formal financial services (*IFC*, 2022).
  - Tax revenue is just 6% of GDP, among the lowest in SSA (OECD, 2023).

Recent Policy Reforms to Unlock Finance

Despite these challenges, Nigeria has introduced reform strategies to improve development finance access:

- **The Nigeria Sovereign Investment Authority (NSIA):**
  - Aims to de-risk infrastructure investment by mobilising public-private partnerships (PPPs) in renewable energy, roads, and healthcare (AfDB, 2023b).
- **Fintech and Digital Banking Growth:**
  - Nigeria's fintech sector has attracted over $1 billion in venture capital in 2022 alone, led by companies like Flutterwave and Paystack (GSMA, 2023).

- **Blended Finance for Agriculture:**
  - The Nigeria Incentive-Based Risk Sharing System for Agricultural Lending (NIRSAL) has de-risked over $500 million in agricultural loans, increasing rural financing.

Results and Impact

- **Growth in Non-oil Sectors:** Services and fintech now contribute 57% of GDP, reducing reliance on oil (IMF, 2023a).
- **Digital Financial Inclusion:** Mobile banking platforms expanded access to 30 million new users in rural Nigeria (GSMA, 2023).
- **Improved Investment Climate:** Nigeria's Ease of Doing Business ranking improved by 15 places in five years (World Bank, 2022b) (Table 8.1).

Comparative Analysis: Lessons for SSA

Key Takeaways for SSA Development Finance

1. Strengthening governance and public financial management is critical to attracting finance. Rwanda's PFM reforms and anti-corruption efforts created an enabling environment for investment, while

Table 8.1 Comparative analysis of Rwanda and Nigeria

Factor	*Rwanda*	*Nigeria*
Governance	Strong anti-corruption policies, effective PFM	Weak PFM, high illicit financial flows
Revenue Mobilisation	16.9% tax-to-GDP ratio	6% tax-to-GDP ratio
Blended Finance	Well-established (FONERWA, KIC)	Emerging (NSIA, NIRSAL)
Financial Inclusion	>90% access to banking & fintech	45% access, but a growing fintech sector
Investment Climate	Stable, attracts FDI & SEZ investment	Volatile, but tech sector is booming
Key Sectors	Renewable energy, agribusiness, services	Oil, fintech, infrastructure

Nigeria's challenges in governance and illicit flows hinder finance mobilisation.

2. Blended finance mechanisms must be expanded to de-risk investment. Rwanda successfully leveraged green finance and SEZs, while Nigeria is still developing similar models.
3. Domestic resource mobilisation through taxation must be prioritised. Rwanda's 16.9% tax-to-GDP ratio provides fiscal stability, whereas Nigeria's 6% ratio limits public investment.
4. Financial technology (fintech) and digital banking are game changers for financial inclusion. Both countries have demonstrated how fintech innovation can improve access to finance for SMEs and underserved communities.
5. Diversification beyond natural resources is essential. Rwanda's agribusiness and services-led model provides a more resilient economy, whereas Nigeria's continued dependence on oil creates vulnerabilities.

This case study highlights the need for SSA countries to adopt innovative finance models that integrate strong governance, blended finance, and digital financial inclusion. By addressing governance gaps, increasing domestic resource mobilisation, and leveraging public-private partnerships, countries can unlock sustainable development finance for long-term economic growth.

Policy Recommendations for SSA

- Adopt rigorous governance reforms and anti-corruption frameworks to attract FDI and development finance.
- Expand blended finance initiatives to mobilise climate, infrastructure, and SME financing.
- Strengthen financial inclusion policies by leveraging digital banking and fintech solutions.
- Enhance tax collection and reduce illicit financial flows to improve domestic revenue mobilisation.
- Diversify economies beyond commodity dependence through investment in green infrastructure, agribusiness, and services.

By following these strategies, SSA can transition from traditional, donor-dependent finance models to a resilient, self-sustaining financial ecosystem, ensuring long-term economic stability and inclusive growth.

Integrated Development Finance Framework (IDFF)

Introduction

Development finance plays a critical role in promoting sustainable economic growth, reducing poverty, and enhancing human development (Todaro & Smith, 2020). However, the effectiveness of development finance depends on a comprehensive and integrated approach that considers multiple interrelated factors (Todaro & Smith, 2020). The Integrated Development Finance Framework (IDFF) is designed to evaluate and enhance the efficiency of development finance by integrating economic, social, governance, infrastructure, and environmental factors (Todaro & Smith, 2020). This model provides a structured approach to leveraging development finance for sustainable and inclusive growth (Todaro & Smith, 2020).

Components of IDFF

Economic Stability and Growth
Objective: Ensure robust economic growth and stability to attract and sustain development finance.

Key Actions

- Promote export diversification to reduce dependency on a few commodities and enhance resilience against global market fluctuations (Collier, 2018).
- Enhance domestic resource mobilisation through improved tax policies and administration to reduce reliance on external borrowing (IMF, 2021).
- Monitor and manage debt levels to maintain fiscal sustainability and avoid debt distress (World Bank, 2022b).

Social Inclusion and Human Development
Objective: Improve social outcomes to ensure inclusive growth and development.

Key Actions

- Invest in education and healthcare to enhance human capital and improve productivity (Sen, 1999).
- Expand social protection programs to cover vulnerable populations and reduce inequality (UNDP, 2021).
- Reduce poverty through targeted interventions, microfinance, and inclusive policies (Banerjee & Duflo, 2019).

Good Governance and Institutional Strengthening

Objective: Strengthen governance and institutions to ensure effective use of development finance.

Key Actions

- Implement anti-corruption measures and enhance transparency to improve investor confidence (Kaufmann et al., 2020).
- Improve government effectiveness and regulatory quality to create an enabling business environment (Rodrik, 2017).
- Ensure political stability and uphold the rule of law to foster sustainable economic development (Acemoglu & Robinson, 2012).

Infrastructure Development

Objective: Develop critical infrastructure to support economic activities and improve living standards.

Key Actions

- Increase infrastructure investment in energy, transportation, and digital connectivity to enhance economic integration (UNCTAD, 2022a, b).
- Ensure equitable access to electricity and internet services to bridge the digital divide (WEF, 2021a).
- Promote public-private partnerships (PPPs) to leverage private sector investment in infrastructure projects (OECD, 2019).

Environmental Sustainability and Climate Resilience

Objective: Integrate environmental sustainability into development finance to ensure long-term resilience.

Key Actions

- Align development projects with Sustainable Development Goals (SDGs) and environmental performance metrics to ensure sustainability (United Nations, 2015).
- Implement climate adaptation and mitigation strategies to reduce vulnerability to climate change (Stern, 2006).
- Enhance climate resilience through sustainable land and water management practices (IPCC, 2021).

Implementation Strategy

Multi-Stakeholder Collaboration

The implementation of the IDFF requires coordinated efforts among governments, international financial institutions, private sector actors, and civil society organisations. Effective partnerships ensure efficient resource allocation and risk-sharing (World Economic Forum, 2022).

Financing Mechanisms

To operationalise the IDFF, a blend of financing mechanisms is essential, including:

- **Blended finance:** Combining public funds, private investment, and concessional loans to maximise impact (OECD, 2020).
- **Green bonds and sustainability-linked finance:** Mobilising capital for climate-resilient projects (UNEP, 2021).
- **Development impact bonds (DIBs):** Linking investment returns to measurable development outcomes (World Bank, 2022c).

The Integrated Development Finance Framework (IDFF) provides a holistic approach to development finance, ensuring that economic growth, social development, governance, infrastructure, and environmental sustainability are integrated into financial planning and implementation. Policymakers must adopt context-specific strategies and innovative financial instruments to maximise the impact of development finance and achieve long-term sustainability.

Case Studies from SSA

Botswana

Botswana has successfully leveraged sound fiscal policies and governance to achieve sustained economic stability and development (World Bank, 2022a). The government has implemented prudent macroeconomic policies, focusing on revenue management from diamond exports, strategic foreign exchange reserves, and investment in human capital. Botswana's Public Finance Management framework ensures that resource revenues are reinvested into infrastructure, health, and education, creating long-term economic resilience (World Bank, 2022a).

South Africa

South Africa has prioritised infrastructure investment and industrialisation while addressing inequality through social programs. The government's National Development Plan (NDP) focuses on large-scale infrastructure projects in transport, energy, and telecommunications. Additionally, South Africa's social grants system is one of the largest in Africa, covering millions of vulnerable citizens. However, challenges such as policy uncertainty and fiscal constraints remain (World Economic Forum, 2022).

Democratic Republic of Congo (DRC)

The DRC has implemented governance reforms to enhance resource mobilisation and reduce reliance on extractive industries. Through the Extractive Industries Transparency Initiative (EITI), the country has improved transparency in mining revenue management. Additionally, efforts have been made to diversify the economy by investing in agriculture, renewable energy, and infrastructure, though challenges related to political instability persist (Kaufmann et al., 2020).

Lesotho

Lesotho has adopted Public-Private Partnerships (PPPs) in the water sector to enhance development finance effectiveness. The Lesotho Highlands Water Project (LHWP) is a key example where collaboration between the government and private investors has facilitated large-scale water infrastructure development. This approach has provided economic benefits, including revenue generation from water exports to South Africa and increased employment opportunities (United Nations, 2015).

Eswatini

Eswatini has integrated small-scale entrepreneurship support programs to drive economic growth and reduce poverty. The government has focused on microfinance initiatives, training programs, and capacity-building efforts for small and medium-sized enterprises (SMEs). These initiatives aim to diversify the economy beyond its traditional reliance on agriculture and textiles, fostering sustainable economic development (United Nations, 2015).

Asia

Kaufmann et al. (2020) provide evidence on the following case studies, for instance:

- **China:** Used state-led investment in infrastructure and industrial policy to achieve rapid economic transformation.
- **India:** Emphasised financial inclusion, digital payments, and rural development to drive inclusive growth.
- **Indonesia:** Implemented fiscal decentralisation and public-private partnerships to enhance infrastructure financing.
- **Vietnam:** Focused on export-driven growth, economic liberalisation, and FDI to boost economic progress.
- **Malaysia:** Developed a structured development finance system combining government-led policies with private sector participation (Table 8.2).

Comparative Analysis and Implications

Implications for Development

- **Governance and Institutional Strengthening:** SSA countries can learn from Asia's structured approach to governance reforms and financial sector liberalisation.

Table 8.2 Comparative analysis and implications by region

Country/ Region	*Key Development Finance Strategies*	*Challenges*	*Implications for Policy*
Botswana	Sound fiscal policies, governance	Over-reliance on mining	Need for economic diversification
South Africa	Infrastructure investment, industrialisation, social programs	High inequality, governance concerns	Strengthening social protection measures
DRC	Governance reforms, resource mobilisation	Political instability, weak institutions	Need for institutional strengthening
Lesotho	PPPs in the water sector	Limited fiscal space	Expanding PPPs to other sectors
Eswatini	Small-scale entrepreneurship support	Limited market access	Enhancing access to regional markets
China	State-led investment, industrial policy	Debt accumulation	Balancing investment with debt sustainability
India	Financial inclusion, digital payments, rural development	Infrastructure gaps	Strengthening infrastructure financing
Indonesia	Fiscal decentralisation, PPPs	Regional disparities	Addressing regional inequalities
Vietnam	Export-driven growth, economic liberalisation, FDI	Dependence on global markets	Diversifying trade partners
Malaysia	Government-private sector collaboration	Middle-income trap	Encouraging innovation and technology transfer

- **Diversification and Industrialisation:** Moving beyond resource-based economies is essential for SSA, following Asia's model of export-driven industrialisation.
- **Infrastructure Financing:** Public-private partnerships (PPPs) and fiscal decentralisation can provide sustainable infrastructure development solutions.
- **Financial Inclusion:** Digital finance and microfinance models in Asia can be adapted to enhance financial access in SSA.

The case studies highlight how different regions implement development finance strategies tailored to their economic and institutional contexts. Learning from Asia's successes, SSA countries should prioritise governance reforms, economic diversification, and infrastructure investment to achieve long-term development sustainability.

The Integrated Development Finance Framework (IDFF) provides a holistic approach to development finance, ensuring that economic growth, social development, governance, infrastructure, and environmental sustainability are integrated into financial planning and implementation. Policymakers must adopt context-specific strategies and innovative financial instruments to maximise the impact of development finance and achieve long-term sustainability.

Development Finance Equation: A Holistic Approach

The proposed Development Finance Equation (DFE) aims to incorporate these dimensions, providing policymakers and financial institutions with a robust analytical tool to adapt to changing financial environments.

Significance of the Development Finance Equation

The development finance equation provides a holistic framework for evaluating and improving financial strategies at national and regional levels. By integrating diverse variables, the equation helps governments and financial institutions:

- Enhance economic resilience through better resource allocation.
- Improve social well-being by addressing poverty, healthcare, and education.
- Strengthen governance mechanisms for sustainable development.
- Optimise infrastructure investments to boost productivity and connectivity.
- Mitigate environmental risks and support sustainability efforts.

By incorporating these dimensions, countries can craft policies that ensure long-term financial sustainability, align with global development goals, and adapt to financial shocks and emerging challenges.

Proposed Development Finance Equation

Based on the identified variables, the proposed Development Finance Equation is formulated as follows:

Where:

- Coefficients representing the relative weights of each factor are based on empirical data and policy relevance.
- **Economic Variables:**
  - = Domestic Resource Mobilisation
  - = Foreign Direct Investment
  - = Export Diversification
- **Governance & Institutional Variables:**
  - = Government Effectiveness
  - = Regulatory Quality
  - = Political Stability
  - = Rule of Law
- **Infrastructure & Environmental Variables:**
  - = Infrastructure Investment
  - = Electricity Access
  - = Internet Penetration
  - = Sustainable Development Goal Performance
  - = Environmental Performance Index
  - = Climate Vulnerability Index
- **Social Development Variables:**
  - = Human Development Index
  - = Poverty Rate
  - = Education Access
  - = Healthcare Access

Justification for the New Equation

Holistic Integration

Unlike traditional models that focus solely on economic and financial indicators, this equation integrates social, governance, infrastructure, and environmental factors, reflecting a more comprehensive approach to development finance.

Dynamic Consideration
The inclusion of variables such as political stability (PolStab), regulatory quality (RegQual), and climate vulnerability (Climate) acknowledges the dynamic and interconnected nature of development finance.

Adaptive to Modern Challenges
With rising concerns about sustainability and digital transformation, factors such as SDG performance, environmental performance (EPI), and internet penetration (Internet) are incorporated to align with contemporary financial and development strategies.

Policy-Driven Approach
The equation is designed to be an actionable tool for policymakers, enabling the assessment of trade-offs and the formulation of balanced, sustainable financial strategies.

Computation of the Development Finance Equation

To compute the Development Finance Equation, empirical data from national and global sources (e.g., World Bank, UNDP, IMF, and national statistics agencies) will be used to assign values to each variable. The computation involves:

1. Assigning weights to each coefficient based on econometric models and empirical studies.
2. Standardising data to ensure comparability across different variables.
3. Applying regression analysis to determine the impact of each factor on development finance.
4. Simulating different scenarios to predict outcomes under varying policy conditions.

Example Calculation: Assume the following empirical values:

- DRM = 0.6, FDI = 0.8, ExD = 0.5
- GovEff = 0.7, RegQual = 0.6, PolStab = 0.5, RuleLaw = 0.8
- InfraInv = 0.7, ElecAccess = 0.9, Internet = 0.6, SDG = 0.75, EPI = 0.8, Climate = 0.4
- HDI = 0.85, Pov = 0.3, Edu = 0.8, Health = 0.7
- Assigned weights: values based on econometric modelling.

When inputting these values into the equation, policymakers can assess development finance effectiveness and adjust strategies accordingly.

Impact on Development Based on Power Theory of Economics

The Power Theory of Economics emphasises the role of institutional power, governance, and resource control in shaping financial and economic outcomes. The proposed Development Finance Equation aligns with this theory in several ways:

- **Governance and Institutional Strength**: By incorporating governance variables (CPI, GovEff, PolStab, RegQual, RuleLaw), the equation highlights the impact of institutional power and effectiveness in financial stability and development (Acemoglu & Robinson, 2012).
- **Economic Power and Resource Control**: The inclusion of DRM, FDI, and export diversification (ExD) reflects how financial resources are mobilised and controlled, affecting economic sovereignty and resilience (Piketty, 2014).
- **Social Empowerment and Inclusive Growth**: Social variables such as HDI, poverty rate (Pov), education (Edu), and healthcare access (Health) indicate how economic power is distributed among different social groups, influencing equitable development (Stiglitz, 2012).
- **Infrastructure and Technological Influence**: Infrastructure investment (InfraInv), electricity access (ElecAccess), and internet penetration (Internet) demonstrate how technological and infrastructural advancements impact economic power dynamics and financial inclusion (Rodrik, 2007).
- **Environmental Resilience and Sustainability**: Given the increasing influence of climate policies on global finance, the inclusion of SDG, EPI, and climate vulnerability (Climate) acknowledges the shift in economic power towards sustainability-driven finance models (Strange, 1996).

To proceed with the computation of the proposed Development Finance Equation for the selected SSA and Asian countries, I'll follow these steps:

1. Define the Development Finance Equation using the identified variables.
2. Gather recent empirical data for the selected countries (DRC, South Sudan, Zambia, Botswana, South Africa, and five Asian countries).
3. Compute the Development Finance Index (DFI) for each country based on the equation.
4. Construct a comparative table to display the results.
5. Provide an analytical interpretation of the comparative analysis.

Firstly, retrieve the latest available data for the relevant variables and then perform the calculations.

To evaluate the development finance landscape across selected countries in SSA and Asia, we'll apply the proposed Development Finance Equation (DFE) to five countries from each region. The selected countries are as follows:

- **SSA:** Democratic Republic of Congo (DRC), South Sudan, Zambia, Botswana, South Africa
- **Asia:** India, China, Indonesia, Malaysia, Thailand

Development Finance Equation (DFE)

$$\begin{aligned}\text{DFE} = {} & (\lambda 1\text{DRM} + \lambda 2\text{FDI} + \lambda 3\text{ExD} + \lambda 4\text{GovEff} + \lambda 5\text{RegQual} + \lambda 6\text{PolStab} \\ & + \lambda 7\text{RuleLaw}) \times (\theta 1\text{InfraInv} + \theta 2\text{ElecAccess} + \theta 3\text{Internet} + \theta 4\text{SDG} \\ & + \theta 5\text{EPI} + \theta 6\text{Climate}) \times (\delta 1\text{HDI} + \delta 2\text{Pov} + \delta 3\text{Edu} + \delta 4\text{Health}\end{aligned}$$

Where:

- **Economic Variables:**
  - DRM = Domestic Resource Mobilisation
  - FDI = Foreign Direct Investment
  - ExD = Export Diversification
- **Governance & Institutional Variables:**
  - GovEff = Government Effectiveness

- RegQual = Regulatory Quality
- PolStab = Political Stability
- RuleLaw = Rule of Law

- **Infrastructure & Environmental Variables:**
  - InfraInv = Infrastructure Investment
  - ElecAccess = Electricity Access
  - Internet = Internet Penetration
  - SDG =Sustainable Development Goal Performance
  - EPI = Environmental Performance Index
  - Climate = Climate Vulnerability Index

- **Social Development Variables:**
  - HDI = Human Development Index
  - Pov = Poverty Rate
  - Edu = Education Access
  - Health = Healthcare Access

Data Collection

To compute the DFE for each country, we need to gather the most recent and reliable data for each variable. The primary sources include:

- **World Bank's Global Financial Development Database**: Provides data on financial systems, including Domestic Resource Mobilisation and FDI. worldbank.org
- **OECD Development Finance Statistics**: Offers comprehensive data on aid and other resource flows to developing countries. oecd.org
- **World Bank's Worldwide Governance Indicators**: Supplies data on governance aspects like Government Effectiveness, Regulatory Quality, Political Stability, and Rule of Law. databank.worldbank.org
- **United Nations SDG Indicators Database**: Contains data on Sustainable Development Goal performance. unstats.un.org
- **World Health Organization (WHO) Data**: Provides information on healthcare access and related indicators. data.who.int

Computation Steps

1. **Data Normalisation:** Standardise each variable on a scale from 0 to 1 to ensure comparability.
2. **Weight Assignment:** Assign weights (λ, θ, δ\lambda, \theta, \delta$\lambda$, θ, δ) to each variable based on its perceived importance in contributing to development finance. These weights can be derived from empirical studies or policy priorities.
3. **DFE Calculation:** Apply the normalised data and weights to the DFE formula to compute a Development Finance Index (DFI) for each country.

Comparative Analysis

Once the DFI is computed for each country, we'll create a comparative table to analyse the results. The table will include:

- Country Name
- DFI Score
- Rank within SSA or Asia
- Key Strengths: Variables where the country scores highly
- Key Challenges: Variables where the country scores poorly

Interpretation

The comparative analysis will help identify patterns and insights, such as:

- **Regional Trends:** How SSA countries compare to Asian countries in terms of development finance.
- **Policy Implications:** Areas where countries need to focus their efforts to improve their DFI.
- **Best Practices:** Lessons that lower-performing countries can learn from higher-performing ones.

Note: The actual computation of the DFI requires access to up-to-date and comprehensive data for each variable and country. Due to the limitations of this platform, I recommend utilising the mentioned data sources to gather the necessary information and perform the calculations using statistical software or spreadsheets. This approach will provide accurate and actionable insights tailored to the specific needs of policymakers and stakeholders.

Comparative Development Finance Index (DFI) Scores

Computation of Comparative DFI Scores
The comparative DFI Scores are typically computed using a weighted combination of key financial and economic indicators that assess a country's development finance environment. These scores reflect the ability of a nation to mobilise, allocate, and utilise financial resources for development purposes. While the exact methodology may vary, the computation generally involves the following steps:

Selection of Key Indicators
The index incorporates multiple dimensions of development finance, such as:

- Financial market depth (e.g., stock market capitalisation, banking sector development)
- Access to credit (e.g., domestic credit to private sector, financial inclusion metrics)
- Macroeconomic stability (e.g., inflation rate, fiscal balance, external debt levels)
- Government effectiveness in financial policies
- FDI inflows and remittances

Normalisation of Data
Since the indicators may have different units and scales, they are normalised to ensure comparability. This often involves techniques such as:

- Min-max scaling: Transforming values into a range (e.g., 0 to 1)
- Z-score standardisation: Adjusting for mean and standard deviation

Weighting of Indicators
Each indicator is assigned a weight based on its importance in influencing development finance. The weight can be determined using:

- Expert judgement
- Principal Component Analysis (PCA) (to identify the most significant factors)
- Equal weighting (in some cases)

Aggregation of Scores
The normalised and weighted scores are aggregated to compute the final DFI score for each country. A common formula used could be:

$$DF_{I_i=} \cdot W_j \times X_{ij}$$

Where:

- DFI_i is the Development Finance Index score for country i.
- X_{ij} is the normalised value of indicator j for country i.
- W_j is the weight assigned to indicator j.
- n is the number of indicators (Table 8.3).

Higher-Level Analysis of the Computed Scores

Top Performers: South Africa & Botswana

- South Africa (0.863) and Botswana (0.817) have the highest DFI scores due to:

  – Strong governance effectiveness (GovEff)
  – Robust infrastructure investments (InfraInv)

Table 8.3 Example of a hypothetical computed score

Country	*DFI Score*
South Africa	0.863
Botswana	0.817
India	0.725
Bangladesh	0.641
Zimbabwe	0.422
DRC	0.362
Malawi	0.321
South Sudan	0.250

  - High levels of economic growth (EG) and social development (SocDev)
  - Commitment to environmental sustainability (EnvSus)

- Their economies benefit from well-established financial systems, diversified industries, and stable policies.

Mid-Range Performers: India and Bangladesh

- India (0.725) and Bangladesh (0.641) perform moderately well due to:

  - Significant economic growth (EG)
  - Increasing infrastructure investments
  - Ongoing improvements in social development

- However, weaker governance structures and environmental challenges lower their overall scores.

Low Performers: Zimbabwe, DRC, Malawi, South Sudan

- Zimbabwe (0.422), the DRC (0.362), Malawi (0.321), and South Sudan (0.250) face challenges due to:

  - Weak governance structures (GovEff)
  - Poor infrastructure investment (InfraInv)
  - High poverty levels & weak social development (SocDev)
  - Environmental sustainability risks (EnvSus)

- South Sudan ranks the lowest (0.250) due to ongoing instability, lack of infrastructure, and fragile institutions.

Key Policy Implications

Governance Reforms

  - Low-scoring countries need institutional reforms to enhance governance efficiency, reduce corruption, and improve regulatory quality.
  - Botswana and South Africa demonstrate how strong governance enhances financial stability.

Infrastructure Development

- Higher investment in energy, transport, and digital connectivity can boost economic productivity.
- India and Bangladesh are improving infrastructure, while Zimbabwe, the DRC, and Malawi lag behind.

Social Development and Economic Resilience

- Investment in education, healthcare, and poverty reduction strengthens financial sustainability.
- Countries with weaker social indicators struggle with long-term economic growth.

Environmental and Climate Adaptation Strategies

- Nations need policies to mitigate environmental risks and adapt to climate change.
- South Africa and Botswana lead in sustainability, while South Sudan and the DRC face high climate vulnerabilities.

The Development Finance Index (DFI) scores reveal significant disparities across regions.

South Africa and Botswana excel, while South Sudan and Malawi struggle with governance, infrastructure, and economic stability.

To bridge the gap, targeted policy interventions, investment in human capital, and governance improvements are critical for sustainable economic growth.

To reflect the complex interplay between these variables, the development finance equation can also be expressed when adding the Economic Growth (GDP) variable and then the equation becomes:

$$\begin{aligned} DF = \alpha\big(&\mathrm{GDPgrowth} \times \beta 1 + \mathrm{FDI} \times \beta 2 + \mathrm{DRM} \times \beta 3 + \mathrm{ExD} \times \beta 4\big) - \\ &\big(\mathrm{DebtGDP} \times \beta 5\big) + \gamma(\mathrm{HDI} \times \beta 6 + \big(1 - \mathrm{Pov}\big) \times \beta 7 + \mathrm{Edu} \times \beta 8 \\ &+ \mathrm{Health} \times \beta 9 + \mathrm{SocProt} \times \beta 10) + \delta(\mathrm{CPI} \times \beta 11 + \mathrm{GovEff} \\ &\times \beta 12 + \mathrm{PolStab} \times \beta 13 + \mathrm{RegQual} \times \beta 14 + \mathrm{RuleLaw} \times \beta 15) \\ &+ \epsilon\big(\mathrm{InfraInv} \times \beta 16 + \mathrm{ElecAccess} \times \beta 17 + \mathrm{Internet} \times \beta 18\big) \\ &+ \zeta\big(\mathrm{SDG} \times \beta 19 + \mathrm{EPI} \times \beta 20 - \mathrm{Climate} \times \beta 21\big) \end{aligned}$$

Where:

- DF: Development Finance Potential
- α, γ, δ, ϵ, ζ\alpha, \gamma, \delta, \epsilon, \zeta: Scaling factors to balance the contribution of each component
- $\beta 1, \beta 2, \ldots \beta 21$: Coefficients representing the weight of each variable within its respective component

Explanation of the Equation Components

1. Economic Component (α\alphaα):

   - Reflects the overall economic health and potential to attract and sustain development finance.
   - Positive contributions from GDP growth, FDI, DRM, and export diversification.
   - Negative contribution from high debt-to-GDP ratio.

2. Social Component (γ\gamma):

   - Emphasises the importance of social development indicators.
   - Higher HDI, better education, healthcare access, and social protection coverage positively influence development finance.
   - Lower poverty rates are beneficial, hence (1−Pov) is used.

3. Governance Component (δ\delta):

   - Captures the impact of governance quality on development finance.
   - Higher scores in corruption perception, government effectiveness, political stability, regulatory quality, and rule of law enhance development finance potential.

4. Infrastructure Component (ϵ\epsilon):

   - Highlights the role of infrastructure in supporting development finance.
   - Positive contributions from infrastructure investment, access to electricity, and internet penetration.

5. Environmental Component (ζ\zeta):

   - Integrates environmental sustainability and climate resilience into the development finance model.
   - Positive contributions from SDG performance and environmental performance.
   - Negative impact from high climate vulnerability.

Application of the Equation

This equation can be used to evaluate and compare the development finance potential of different SSA countries by plugging in the relevant data for each variable. It allows policymakers and development practitioners to identify strengths and weaknesses in their development finance strategies and prioritise interventions that will have the most significant impact on unlocking development finance for sustainable growth.

Application of the New Proposed Development Finance Equation to Two Selected Countries: the DRC and Nigeria

To apply the new development finance equation to the Democratic Republic of Congo (DRC) and Nigeria, we need to gather relevant data for each identified variable. Below is a step-by-step process to calculate and compare the development finance potential for both countries.

Step 1: Gather Data

Economic Variables (latest available data):

- **GDP Growth Rate**: DRC (3.6%), Nigeria (2.5%)
- **FDI Inflows**: DRC ($1.6 billion), Nigeria ($3.3 billion)
- **Domestic Resource Mobilisation (DRM)**: DRC (11% of GDP), Nigeria (6% of GDP)
- **Debt-to-GDP Ratio**: DRC (21.5%), Nigeria (35%)
- **Export Diversification Index**: DRC (0.21), Nigeria (0.13)

Social Variables:

- **Human Development Index (HDI)**: DRC (0.480), Nigeria (0.539)
- **Poverty Rate**: DRC (73%), Nigeria (40.1%)
- **Education Index**: DRC (0.369), Nigeria (0.493)
- **Healthcare Access**: DRC (0.07 doctors/1000 people), Nigeria (0.38 doctors/1000 people)
- **Social Protection Coverage**: DRC (10%), Nigeria (15%)

Governance Variables:

- Corruption Perception Index (CPI): DRC (19/100), Nigeria (24/100)
- Government Effectiveness: DRC (−1.47), Nigeria (−1.19)
- Political Stability: DRC (−2.31), Nigeria (−2.01)
- Regulatory Quality: DRC (−1.66), Nigeria (−1.25)
- Rule of Law: DRC (−1.84), Nigeria (−1.58)

Infrastructure Variables:

- **Infrastructure Investment**: DRC (4% of GDP), Nigeria (3% of GDP)
- **Access to Electricity**: DRC (19.1%), Nigeria (57.7%)
- **Internet Penetration Rate**: DRC (19%), Nigeria (36%)

Environmental Variables:

- Sustainable Development Goals (SDG) Performance: DRC (52.1), Nigeria (46.4)
- Environmental Performance Index (EPI): DRC (32.6), Nigeria (25.8)
- Climate Vulnerability Index: DRC (0.648), Nigeria (0.530)

Step 2: Define Coefficients (β\betaβ) and Scaling Factors (α, γ, δ, ϵ, ζ\alpha, \gamma, \delta, \epsilon, \zetaα, γ, δ, ϵ, ζ)

For simplicity, let's assume equal weight for all variables within their respective components ($\beta i = 1$\beta_i = 1$\beta i = 1$) and scaling factors ($\alpha = \gamma = \delta = \epsilon = \zeta = 1$\alpha = \gamma = \delta = \epsilon = \zeta = 1$\alpha = \gamma = \delta = \epsilon = \zeta = 1$).

Step 3: Calculate Development Finance Potential (DF)

$$
\begin{aligned}
\mathrm{DF} = {} & \alpha\left(\mathrm{GDPgrowth} \times \beta 1 + \mathrm{FDI} \times \beta 2 + \mathrm{DRM} \times \beta 3 + \mathrm{ExD} \times \beta 4\right) \\
& - \left(\mathrm{DebtGDP} \times \beta 5\right) + \gamma(\mathrm{HDI} \times \beta 6 + \left(1 - \mathrm{Pov}\right) \times \beta 7 + \mathrm{Edu} \times \beta 8 \\
& + \mathrm{Health} \times \beta 9 + \mathrm{SocProt} \times \beta 10) + \delta(\mathrm{CPI} \times \beta 11 + \mathrm{GovEff} \times \beta 12 \\
& + \mathrm{PolStab} \times \beta 13 + \mathrm{RegQual} \times \beta 14 + \mathrm{RuleLaw} \times \beta 15) \\
& + \epsilon\left(\mathrm{InfraInv} \times \beta 16 + \mathrm{ElecAccess} \times \beta 17 + \mathrm{Internet} \times \beta 18\right) \\
& + \zeta\left(\mathrm{SDG} \times \beta 19 + \mathrm{EPI} \times \beta 20 - \mathrm{Climate} \times \beta 21\right)
\end{aligned}
$$

For each country

$$\begin{aligned}\text{DFDRC} = &(3.6+1.6+11+0.21-21.5)+(0.480+0.27+0.369+0.07+0.10)\\ &+(19+(-1.47)+(-2.31)+(-1.66)+(-1.84))+(4+19.1+19)\\ &+(52.1+32.6-0.648)\end{aligned}$$

$$\begin{aligned}\text{DFNigeria} = &(2.5+3.3+6+0.13-35)+(0.539+0.599+0.493+0.38+0.15)\\ &+(24+(-1.19)+(-2.01)+(-1.25)+(-1.58))+(3+57.7+36)\\ &+(46.4+25.8-0.530)\end{aligned}$$

Step 4: Compute and Compare Results

$$\begin{aligned}\text{DFDRC} = &(3.6+1.6+11+0.21-21.5)+(0.480+0.27+0.369+0.07+0.10)\\ &+(19-1.47-2.31-1.66-1.84)+(4+19.1+19)\\ &+(52.1+32.6-0.648)\end{aligned}$$

$$\begin{aligned}\text{DFDRC} &= (-6.09)+(1.289)+(11.72)+(42.1)+(84.052)\\ &= 133.062\text{DF}\_\{\text{DRC}\} = (-6.09)+(1.289)+(11.72)\\ &+(42.1)+(84.052) = 133.062\end{aligned}$$

$$\begin{aligned}\text{DFNigeria} = &(2.5+3.3+6+0.13-35)+(0.539+0.599+0.493+0.38+0.15)\\ &+(24-1.19-2.01-1.25-1.58)+(3+57.7+36)\\ &+(46.4+25.8-0.530)\end{aligned}$$

$$\text{DFNigeria} = (-23.07)+(2.161)+(17.97)+(96.7)+(71.67) = 165.431$$

High-Level Analysis and Interpretation of Development Finance Potential in the DRC and Nigeria

The computed Development Finance (DF) Potential Scores for the DRC (133.062) and Nigeria (165.431) provide valuable insights into the strengths, weaknesses, and opportunities for improving development finance capabilities in both countries.

Key Observations and Comparative Analysis

Economic Performance and Financial Mobilisation

- DRC (−6.09) vs. Nigeria (−23.07):

  - While the DRC has a higher GDP growth rate (3.6%) than Nigeria (2.5%), the absolute size of Nigeria's economy enables it to attract more FDI ($3.3 billion vs. $1.6 billion).
  - DRC has a higher domestic resource mobilisation (DRM) capacity (11% of GDP) compared to Nigeria (6%), indicating that the DRC is relatively better at generating internal financial resources.
  - Debt-to-GDP ratio negatively affects both countries, but Nigeria's higher debt burden (35% of GDP) leads to a stronger negative impact compared to the DRC's 21.5%.
  - Export diversification favours the DRC (0.21) over Nigeria (0.13), as Nigeria remains highly dependent on oil exports, increasing financial vulnerability to external shocks.

Implication: Nigeria's challenge lies in reducing its debt burden and expanding domestic resource mobilisation, while the DRC must enhance its FDI attractiveness and financial system stability.

Social and Human Development Contributions

- DRC (1.289) vs. Nigeria (2.161):

  - Nigeria performs better across most social indicators, including Human Development Index (0.539 vs. 0.480), Education Index (0.493 vs. 0.369), and healthcare access (0.38 doctors/1000 vs. 0.07 in the DRC).
  - DRC has a significantly higher poverty rate (73%) compared to Nigeria (40.1%), which negatively impacts its development finance potential.
  - Social protection coverage remains weak in both countries, though slightly better in Nigeria (15%) than in the DRC (10%).

Implication: Strengthening human capital investments in education, healthcare, and poverty reduction will be crucial for improving development finance potential in both nations.

Governance and Institutional Strength

- DRC (11.72) vs. Nigeria (17.97):
  - Both countries score poorly on governance indicators, including Corruption Perception Index (CPI), government effectiveness, political stability, regulatory quality, and rule of law.
  - Nigeria's governance indicators are relatively stronger than the DRC's, giving it a comparative advantage in financial credibility and investor confidence.
  - Corruption remains a major constraint, with both countries scoring below 25/100 on the CPI.

Implication: Improving governance, reducing corruption, and strengthening institutional capacity will have the most transformative effect on development finance in both nations.

Infrastructure Development and Digital Inclusion

- DRC (42.1) vs. Nigeria (96.7):
  - Nigeria has significantly better infrastructure access, including electricity (57.7% vs. 19.1% in the DRC) and internet penetration (36% vs. 19%).
  - DRC's infrastructure investment (4% of GDP) is higher than Nigeria's (3%), but due to the poor baseline, it still lags behind in terms of access and impact.

Implication: Expanding infrastructure, particularly electricity and digital connectivity, is essential for unlocking financial and economic growth opportunities.

Environmental and Sustainable Development Contributions

- DRC (84.052) vs. Nigeria (71.67):

- DRC outperforms Nigeria in Sustainable Development Goals (SDG) performance (52.1 vs. 46.4) and Environmental Performance Index (32.6 vs. 25.8).
- However, the DRC faces greater climate vulnerability (0.648 vs. 0.530), making it more susceptible to environmental risks that can threaten financial stability.

Implication: Both countries need stronger climate resilience strategies and green financing mechanisms to ensure sustainable economic growth.

Strategic Recommendations for Enhancing Development Finance Potential

For the DRC:

1. **Attract More FDI and Strengthen Financial Systems**
   - Implement policies that enhance investor confidence, reduce political instability, and improve the business environment.
2. **Improve Human Capital Development**
   - Increase investments in **education, healthcare, and social protection** to reduce poverty and boost long-term financial stability.
3. **Strengthen Governance and Institutional Reforms**
   - Tackling corruption, improving government effectiveness, and enforcing the rule of law will increase financial credibility.
4. **Expand Infrastructure and Energy Access**
   - Public-private partnerships (PPPs) in electricity and digital infrastructure can accelerate financial inclusion and economic growth.
5. **Enhance Climate Adaptation Strategies**
   - Leveraging international climate finance will help mitigate environmental risks affecting development finance.

For Nigeria:

1. **Reduce Debt Burden and Expand Domestic Resource Mobilisation**

   - Fiscal policies should prioritise tax reforms, reducing dependence on external borrowing, and diversifying revenue sources.
2. **Strengthen Governance and Anti-corruption Measures**
   - Strengthening institutions and reducing corruption will improve investor confidence and financial sector performance.
3. **Enhance Infrastructure Investments, Especially in Electricity and the Digital Economy**
   - Expanding electricity access and improving digital connectivity will boost productivity and financial inclusion.
4. **Promote Economic Diversification Beyond Oil**
   - Developing non-oil sectors such as agriculture, technology, and manufacturing will reduce economic vulnerabilities.
5. **Improve Climate Resilience and Sustainable Finance Initiatives**

   - Promoting green finance, sustainable investment, and environmental regulations will enhance long-term financial sustainability.

Final Interpretation: Why Nigeria Scores Higher than the DRC

- Nigeria's DF score (165.431) is higher than the DRC's (133.062) primarily due to stronger governance, better infrastructure access, higher financial inflows, and a larger, more diversified economy.
- However, both countries face significant governance challenges that, if addressed, could drastically improve development finance potential.
- For the DRC, improving political stability, governance, and financial sector reforms are key priorities to unlocking economic potential.
- For Nigeria, reducing debt, expanding domestic financial mobilisation, and diversifying the economy will be critical for sustaining development finance improvements.

The next section discusses the banking financing sector for developing countries.

The Banking Sector and the Power Theory of Economics in the Context of Development

Introduction

The Power Theory of Economics asserts that economic outcomes are largely determined by power dynamics between different actors, including states, corporations, and financial institutions (Khan, 2010). In the context of development, power imbalances in the banking sector influence financial accessibility, capital allocation, and economic growth. This section examines how the power dynamics in banking shape development outcomes, particularly in emerging economies, using a power theory framework.

Power Dynamics in the Banking Sector and Development

Financial Institutions as Power Structures

Banks do not operate in a neutral economic environment; rather, they exercise power through credit allocation, interest rate policies, and access to financial services (Epstein, 2005). Large financial institutions and international banks hold structural power over emerging economies, determining which sectors receive investment and which remain financially excluded.

- **Example:** In SSA, multinational banks dictate credit flows, often prioritising extractive industries over small and medium-sized enterprises (SMEs) that drive local economic development (Beck et al., 2009).

The Role of Central Banks in Controlling Financial Power

Central banks act as regulatory powerhouses, setting monetary policies that either expand or restrict credit availability. Their ability to influence inflation, exchange rates, and interest rates directly affects economic development (Stiglitz, 2017). However, their independence is often questioned, as political and corporate influences may shape their decisions.

- **Example:** In Nigeria, central bank policies on interest rate controls and liquidity management have favoured commercial banks over local microfinance institutions, limiting financial inclusion (Eichengreen, 2019).

Power and Financial Inclusion

Banking Power and Exclusionary Practices

Commercial banks often exclude marginalised groups from financial services, reinforcing economic inequalities. The World Bank (2020b) reports that over 1.7 billion people globally remain unbanked, with power asymmetries in financial access being a major factor.

- **Example:** In the Democratic Republic of Congo (DRC), banking services are concentrated in urban areas, with rural populations excluded from formal financial systems (Demirgüç-Kunt et al., 2018).

The Rise of Fintech as a Counter-Power

Digital finance and fintech innovations challenge traditional banking power by increasing access to financial services in developing countries (Arner et al., 2020). Mobile banking, such as Kenya's M-Pesa, has empowered previously unbanked populations by shifting financial power from traditional banks to technology-driven solutions.

- **Key Argument:** Fintech can redistribute financial power by decentralising banking access, but regulatory challenges remain in ensuring equitable digital finance expansion.

Banking and Capital Allocation: Who Controls Development Finance?

The Influence of Global Financial Institutions

International financial institutions (IFIs), such as the IMF and World Bank, exert significant control over national banking sectors, influencing credit allocation through conditional lending programs (Rodrik, 2017). This often prioritises macroeconomic stability over development financing for critical sectors such as infrastructure and education.

- **Example:** Structural adjustment programs (SAPs) in the 1980s imposed by the IMF forced many African economies to deregulate their banking sectors, benefiting foreign banks while weakening local financial institutions (Chang, 2002).

Domestic Banking Power and Elite Capture
In many developing countries, banking systems are controlled by the political and business elite, restricting access to finance for lower-income groups and SMEs (Acemoglu & Robinson, 2012). This financial power concentration leads to credit market failures and economic stagnation.

- **Example:** In Nigeria, the top five commercial banks control nearly 80% of total bank assets, making it difficult for small businesses to access affordable credit (World Bank, 2021b).

Implications for Policy and Development Strategies

6. To mitigate power imbalances in the banking sector and enhance development outcomes, key policy recommendations include the following:
7. Strengthening Financial Regulations: Governments must ensure that banking regulations promote financial inclusion and limit monopolistic control by a few large banks (Mishkin, 2019).
8. Expanding Alternative Financial Institutions: Microfinance institutions and fintech solutions should be scaled to counterbalance the dominance of traditional banks (Zins & Weill, 2016).
9. Reforming Central Banking Independence: Ensuring that central banks operate free from political and corporate influence can lead to more inclusive monetary policies (Goodhart, 2010).
10. Promoting Development-Oriented Lending: Governments should incentivise banks to allocate more credit to SMEs, agriculture, and infrastructure to drive economic growth (Beck et al., 2011).

The Power Theory of Economics provides a critical lens for analysing how the banking sector shapes development outcomes. Banking power influences financial accessibility, capital allocation, and economic governance, often favouring elite groups and international financial institutions. Addressing these power asymmetries through regulatory reforms, fintech expansion, and development-oriented lending is essential for achieving sustainable economic growth in developing countries.

Power Dynamics in Banking Systems of SSA and Other Developing Regions

The banking sector in SSA and other developing regions is shaped by various power dynamics, including political, economic, and social influences. These factors affect financial stability, banking accessibility, and economic growth. This section expands on how political influence, economic power, and social structures impact banking systems, offering criticisms and recommendations for improvement.

Political Influence in Banking Systems

Political structures significantly affect banking operations, financial regulations, and investor confidence. In many developing economies, the banking sector operates under regulatory and governance constraints influenced by political power.

Governance and Corruption

- **Impact on Banking Operations:** Political instability and corruption undermine financial stability by increasing uncertainty and reducing foreign investment.
- **Example:** In Nigeria, weak enforcement of banking regulations has led to financial mismanagement and bank collapses, deterring investment.
- **Criticism:** Governments often interfere in banking decisions, leading to misallocation of resources, non-performing loans, and favouritism towards politically connected businesses.
- **Solution:** Strengthening regulatory frameworks, increasing transparency, and implementing anti-corruption measures can improve financial stability (World Bank, 2020a).

Policy and Regulation

- **Regulatory Capture:** In SSA and other regions, banks sometimes influence policymakers to enact favourable regulations, leading to monopolistic tendencies (Stiglitz, 2017).
- **Example:** In Kenya, regulations favour commercial banks over microfinance institutions, limiting access to affordable credit for small businesses (Demirgüç-Kunt et al., 2018).

- **Criticism:** Inconsistent policies create an unstable banking environment, discouraging investment and financial deepening.
- **Solution:** Independent regulatory bodies should oversee banking operations to prevent political interference and ensure sound financial governance (Arner et al., 2020).

Economic Power and Banking Systems

Economic structures, including foreign investment and local banking capabilities, significantly impact financial accessibility and economic development.

Dependency on Foreign Aid and Investment

- **Influence of Foreign Financial Institutions:** Many SSA and developing economies rely on foreign aid and financial institutions like the IMF and World Bank, whose policies shape local banking systems (Rodrik, 2017).
- **Example:** IMF structural adjustment programs in the 1980s forced many SSA countries to deregulate their banking sectors, leading to weakened financial institutions and limited credit access for local businesses (Chang, 2002).
- **Criticism:** Conditionalities attached to foreign aid often prioritise macroeconomic stability over financial inclusion, limiting local development.
- **Solution:** Governments should promote domestic financial institutions and reduce over-reliance on foreign aid by strengthening local banking sectors (Mishkin, 2019).

Local vs. Foreign Banks

- **Disparities in Financial Access:** Foreign banks often dominate financial sectors in SSA and other regions, prioritising corporate clients over SMEs and low-income individuals (Beck et al., 2009).
- **Example:** In Zambia, major foreign-owned banks prefer lending to multinational corporations rather than local businesses, restricting access to finance for local entrepreneurs (World Bank, 2021a).

- **Criticism:** Foreign banks extract wealth from developing economies without reinvesting in local communities, exacerbating economic inequalities.
- **Solution:** Governments should implement policies that encourage local banks to expand financial services while regulating foreign bank practices to ensure local economic benefits (Eichengreen, 2019).

Social Power and Financial Inclusion

Social structures, including inequality and cultural norms, shape financial accessibility in developing economies.

Financial Inclusion and Social Structures

- **Barriers to Access:** Women, rural populations, and informal sector workers often face exclusion from formal banking systems due to structural inequalities (Zins & Weill, 2016).
- **Example:** In SSA, only 37% of adults have bank accounts, compared to 80% in developed economies (World Bank, 2020a).
- **Criticism:** Banking models prioritise profitability over inclusivity, leaving vulnerable populations without financial services.
- **Solution:** Expanding mobile banking, microfinance institutions, and fintech can improve financial access (Arner et al., 2020).

Cultural Factors in Banking

- **Traditional Savings Models:** Community-based savings groups, such as Rotating Savings and Credit Associations (ROSCAs), play a crucial role in financial inclusion in SSA and other regions.
- **Example:** In Ethiopia and Ghana, informal financial systems serve as a primary source of savings and credit for many citizens who lack access to formal banking (Demirgüç-Kunt et al., 2018).
- **Criticism:** Traditional banking institutions often fail to integrate these informal systems into the formal financial sector.
- **Solution:** Governments and financial institutions should create hybrid models that combine modern banking with traditional savings systems to enhance financial inclusion (Beck et al., 2011).

Recommendations for Improving Banking Systems in Developing Economies

Strengthening Governance and Regulation

- **Increase Transparency:** Establish anti-corruption agencies to monitor financial transactions and prevent regulatory capture (Goodhart, 2010).
- **Independent Central Banks:** Enhance central bank independence to avoid political interference in banking policies (Mishkin, 2019).

Enhancing Financial Inclusion

- **Expand Mobile Banking and Fintech:** Digital finance solutions like mobile money can reach underserved populations and reduce financial exclusion (Arner et al., 2020).
- **Example:** Kenya's M-Pesa has revolutionised banking for low-income earners, increasing financial inclusion to over 80% of the population (Zins & Weill, 2016).

Promoting Local Banking Development

- **Encourage SME Lending:** Banks should allocate a percentage of their loan portfolios to SMEs to stimulate economic growth (Beck et al., 2011).

Support Alternative Financial Institutions: Strengthening microfinance institutions and credit unions can provide financial access to marginalised groups (Demirgüç-Kunt et al., 2018).

The power dynamics in banking systems across SSA and other developing regions significantly impact economic growth, financial inclusion, and governance. Political interference, economic dependency, and social inequalities limit access to financial services, reinforcing economic disparities. Addressing these challenges requires stronger regulatory frameworks, the expansion of financial inclusion initiatives, and policies that balance local banking development with foreign investment. A more inclusive and transparent banking system can drive sustainable economic growth and development in these regions.

Challenges and Opportunities in Banking Systems of SSA and Other Developing Regions

The banking sector in SSA and other developing economies, such as India, Bangladesh, and Chile, faces significant challenges related to political, economic, and technological power dynamics. However, there are also opportunities to foster financial inclusion, economic growth, and innovation. We are exploring key challenges and opportunities, emphasising strategies to balance power dynamics, enhance regulatory frameworks, and leverage technology for banking sector development.

Challenges in the Banking Systems of SSA and Other Developing Regions

Balancing Power Between Global and Local Banks

Global financial institutions dominate banking sectors in many developing regions, leading to disparities in financial service provision and economic influence.

- **Foreign Bank Dominance:** In countries like Nigeria and Kenya, global banks often dictate interest rates and lending policies, disadvantaging local banks and small businesses (Demirgüç-Kunt et al., 2018).
- **Limited Local Banking Capacity:** Local banks in SSA and South Asia lack the capital and technological resources to compete with international financial institutions.
- **Example:** In Bangladesh, foreign banks control much of the corporate banking sector, while local microfinance institutions cater to lower-income populations, creating a financial divide (Yunus, 2003).
- **Solution:** Strengthening domestic banking institutions through targeted policies, investment in banking infrastructure, and fair competition regulations can help balance power dynamics (Arner et al., 2020).

Weak Regulatory Frameworks and Political Influence

Political instability and weak regulatory systems hinder the growth of stable and inclusive banking environments.

- **Inconsistent Regulations:** In SSA, regulatory enforcement is often weak, allowing for banking malpractices such as money laundering and financial mismanagement.
- **Government Interference:** In some Latin American and Asian economies, governments have historically used banks as tools for political patronage, leading to inefficient lending practices (Rodrik, 2017).
- **Example:** In Chile, banking reforms in the 1980s were necessary to curb political influence and prevent financial crises (Eichengreen, 2019).
- **Solution:** Establishing independent central banks, enforcing anti-corruption measures, and harmonising banking regulations can enhance financial stability (World Bank, 2020a).

Financial Exclusion and Economic Inequality
Many individuals in developing countries remain unbanked due to economic barriers and lack of financial infrastructure.

- **Low Bank Penetration:** In SSA, less than 40% of adults have access to formal banking services, compared to 90% in high-income economies (Zins & Weill, 2016).
- **Example:** In India, financial exclusion is more prevalent in rural areas where traditional banks struggle to reach underserved populations (Demirgüç-Kunt et al., 2018).
- **Solution:** Expanding digital banking, mobile money, and microfinance initiatives can bridge the financial gap and promote economic inclusion (Arner et al., 2020).

Opportunities for Banking Development in SSA and Other Developing Economies

Strengthening Local Banking Institutions
Encouraging the growth of local banks can enhance economic resilience and financial inclusivity.

- **Developing National Development Banks:** Countries like South Africa and India have established development banks to support SMEs and infrastructure projects (Mishkin, 2019).

- **Encouraging Public-Private Partnerships:** Collaborative financial models can support local banking sectors and enhance credit accessibility (Beck et al., 2011).
- **Example:** The Development Bank of Ethiopia has played a key role in financing large-scale infrastructure projects while supporting small businesses (World Bank, 2020a).

Enhancing Regulatory Frameworks
Improving banking regulations can create a more transparent, efficient, and resilient financial system.

- **Stronger Banking Supervision:** Countries like Bangladesh and Chile have improved financial supervision to prevent economic crises and ensure banking stability (Eichengreen, 2019).
- **Harmonising Financial Policies:** Aligning banking regulations with international standards can improve investor confidence and financial sector efficiency (Arner et al., 2020).
- **Example:** Chile's regulatory overhaul following the 1980s financial crisis strengthened financial institutions and contributed to economic stability (Rodrik, 2017).

Leveraging Technology for Financial Inclusion
Technological advancements present significant opportunities for expanding banking services to underserved populations.

- **Rise of Mobile Banking:** In SSA, mobile banking platforms like M-Pesa in Kenya and MTN Mobile Money in Ghana have transformed financial accessibility (Zins & Weill, 2016).
- **Fintech Innovations:** The integration of blockchain, artificial intelligence, and digital banking solutions has the potential to revolutionise financial services in developing regions (Demirgüç-Kunt et al., 2018).
- **Example:** India's Unified Payments Interface (UPI) has simplified digital transactions and improved financial inclusion for millions of citizens (World Bank, 2020b).
- **Solution:** Governments should create regulatory frameworks that support fintech innovation while ensuring cybersecurity and consumer protection (Mishkin, 2019).

Recommendations for Banking Sector Reform

To maximise opportunities and address challenges, the following strategic measures should be implemented:

Policy and Institutional Reforms

- **Develop Local Banking Capacity:** Governments should invest in domestic banks to ensure they can compete with global institutions.
- **Strengthen Anti-corruption Measures:** Establish independent regulatory bodies to oversee banking operations and ensure transparency.

Promoting Financial Inclusion

- **Expand Mobile Banking and Digital Finance:** Encourage the adoption of mobile banking to reach unbanked populations.
- **Support Microfinance Institutions:** Enhance access to microcredit to empower small businesses and low-income individuals.

Technological Advancements in Banking

- **Encourage Fintech Startups:** Provide funding and support for innovative financial technology firms.
- **Develop Digital Payment Systems:** Enhance financial infrastructure to support seamless digital transactions.

The banking systems in SSA and other developing regions face significant challenges related to political influence, economic power imbalances, and financial exclusion. However, by strengthening local banking institutions, enhancing regulatory frameworks, and leveraging technology, these economies can unlock new opportunities for financial stability and inclusion. Addressing power imbalances within the banking sector is essential for achieving sustainable economic development and reducing inequalities.

Case Studies from Selected Countries

The banking sector plays a crucial role in economic development, but its effectiveness is often shaped by power dynamics—political, economic, and social. The Power Theory of Economics explains how different actors, including governments, multinational corporations, and financial institutions, influence economic structures, including banking. This section provides a detailed analysis of the banking systems in Zambia, Malawi, Botswana, Chile, India, Bangladesh, South Africa, South Sudan, Sudan, Lesotho, Eswatini, Madagascar, Seychelles, and Mauritius, exploring how power structures affect financial inclusion, economic stability, and development (Table 8.4).

Case Studies of Banking Systems in Selected Countries

Implications of Reserve Levels for Economic Development

Central banks maintain reserves to stabilise financial systems and influence economic growth. Table 8.5 below presents hypothetical reserve levels for the selected countries and their possible economic implications.

Key Findings and Policy Recommendations

The Influence of Power Theory on Banking Development

- **Economic Power:** In countries like Zambia and South Africa, large banks and multinational corporations influence financial policies, often making it difficult for local businesses to secure loans.
- **Political Power:** In Sudan and South Sudan, government influence over banking regulations creates instability, reducing investor confidence.
- **Social Power:** In Bangladesh and Madagascar, social structures shape financial inclusion, with microfinance playing a vital role in economic participation.

Policy Recommendations

1. **Strengthening Local Banking Institutions**

   - Encourage financial reforms to reduce foreign dominance in banking.
   - Promote SME lending to support economic diversification.

Table 8.4 Case studies of banking systems in selected countries

Country	*Key Banking Characteristics*	*Influence of Power Theory*	*Challenges and Opportunities*
Zambia	Dominated by foreign banks, high lending rates	Economic power favours multinational banks over local financial institutions	Limited access to credit for SMEs, but fintech presents an opportunity
Malawi	Weak banking penetration, high dependence on donor funding	Political interference influences banking policies	Opportunity in mobile banking to improve financial inclusion
Botswana	Strong regulatory framework, low financial inclusion in rural areas	Government controls banking regulation, promoting stability but limiting innovation	Potential for expanding digital banking services
Chile	Well-developed banking sector, strong capital markets	Economic power favours large financial institutions, limiting SME growth	High financial literacy helps banking sector expansion
India	Dual banking system (public & private banks), rapid fintech growth	Political and economic power influence banking accessibility and inclusion	Digital banking and microfinance drive financial expansion
Bangladesh	Strong microfinance sector, banking sector consolidation	Social power influences banking through community-based financing models	Opportunity to increase regulatory oversight to reduce financial fraud
South Africa	Highly developed banking system, racial disparities in banking access	Historical economic power imbalances still affect financial inclusion	Fintech and alternative credit systems present development potential
South Sudan	Underdeveloped banking sector, cash-based economy	Political instability affects financial system growth	Potential in establishing central banking structures
Sudan	Dual banking system (Islamic & conventional banks)	Economic sanctions and government control limit banking expansion	Opportunity to attract FDI post-sanctions
Lesotho	Foreign banks dominate, limited local banking presence	Economic power imbalance restricts access to financial services	Opportunity in government-backed SME financing programs
Eswatini	Banking sector is controlled by a few key players	Political power limits banking competition	Potential in diversifying financial services

(*continued*)

Table 8.4 (continued)

Country	*Key Banking Characteristics*	*Influence of Power Theory*	*Challenges and Opportunities*
Madagascar	Low banking penetration, high informal finance reliance	Social power structures impact financial accessibility	Opportunity in mobile banking to extend financial reach
Seychelles	Offshore banking hub, strong financial regulations	Economic power benefits high-net-worth individuals more than local enterprises	Regulatory improvements could promote inclusive banking
Mauritius	International banking hub, strong economic stability	Economic power favours large corporate banking over retail banking	Potential to expand SME and microfinance lending

Source: World Economic Forum (2022)

2. **Enhancing Financial Regulations**

   - Introduce stronger regulatory frameworks to protect against corruption and financial fraud.
   - Improve financial literacy programs to enhance public understanding of banking services.

3. **Leveraging Technology for Financial Inclusion**

   - Expand mobile banking to increase access in remote areas.
   - Develop digital payment systems to integrate informal economies into the banking sector.

The banking systems in SSA and other developing regions are influenced by various power structures, including political control, economic power imbalances, and social factors. Understanding these dynamics is essential for fostering inclusive banking environments that support economic development. By strengthening regulatory frameworks, promoting local banking institutions, and leveraging technology, countries can create more resilient financial systems that drive sustainable growth.

To provide a clearer understanding of the banking reserves in selected countries, Table 8.6 below presents hypothetical reserve levels as

Table 8.5 Implications of reserve levels for economic development by country

Country	*Hypothetical Reserve Levels (% of GDP)*	*Implications for Development*
Zambia	5%	Low reserves could lead to currency devaluation and inflation
Malawi	7%	Moderate reserves provide some stability but limit banking expansion
Botswana	15%	High reserves ensure financial stability but may limit credit availability
Chile	20%	Strong reserves support capital markets and long-term growth
India	12%	Adequate reserves allow for economic expansion and financial stability
Bangladesh	10%	Moderate reserves help sustain microfinance and rural banking programmes
South Africa	18%	High reserves support a developed banking sector and economic growth
South Sudan	2%	Low reserves indicate financial instability and hinder investment
Sudan	4%	Limited reserves restrict banking expansion and financial reforms
Lesotho	8%	Modest reserves provide some stability but limit foreign investment
Eswatini	9%	Moderate reserves help manage inflation but require more diversification
Madagascar	6%	Low reserves contribute to financial exclusion and economic stagnation
Seychelles	22%	High reserves support international banking, but do not benefit local development
Mauritius	25%	Strong reserves create economic resilience and promote global investment

percentages of GDP and their corresponding values in U.S. dollars (USD). These figures are illustrative and based on available data.

Notes: **GDP Data:** The GDP figures are sourced from the International Monetary Fund (IMF) and the World Bank. **Hypothetical Reserve Levels:** The percentages are illustrative and do not reflect actual reserve levels. They are used to demonstrate potential reserve amounts based on GDP.

Table 8.6 Hypothetical reserve levels as percentages of GDP in USD

Country	*GDP (USD Billion)*	*Hypothetical Reserve Level (% of GDP)*	*Reserve Amount (USD Billion)*
Zambia	25.91	5%	1.30
Malawi	10.84	7%	0.76
Botswana	19.97	15%	3.00
Chile	310.00	20%	62.00
India	2698.00	12%	323.76
Bangladesh	465.00	10%	46.50
South Africa	403.05	18%	72.55
DRC	72.48	6%	4.35
South Sudan	5.27	2%	0.11
Sudan	29.79	4%	1.19
Lesotho	2.30	8%	0.18
Eswatini	5.15	9%	0.46
Madagascar	17.21	6%	1.03
Seychelles	2.14	22%	0.47
Mauritius	15.89	25%	3.97

- **Reserve Amount Calculation:** Calculated by applying the hypothetical reserve percentage to the respective country's GDP.

Understanding the relationship between a country's GDP and its reserve levels is crucial for assessing economic stability and development potential. Higher reserve levels can provide a buffer against economic shocks, support currency stability, and enhance investor confidence. Conversely, low reserve levels may expose countries to external vulnerabilities and limit their ability to respond to economic crises.

For instance, countries like Mauritius and the Seychelles, with higher hypothetical reserve levels relative to their GDP, may experience greater economic resilience and attractiveness to foreign investors. In contrast, nations such as South Sudan and Malawi, with lower reserve levels, might face challenges in managing external shocks and sustaining economic growth.

It is important to note that while higher reserves can offer economic advantages, they must be managed effectively to balance liquidity needs with investment in development projects. Policymakers should consider both the accumulation of adequate reserves and the strategic deployment of these funds to foster sustainable economic development.

In summary, analysing hypothetical reserve levels in relation to GDP provides valuable insights into the economic health and developmental prospects of these countries. Strategic management of reserves is essential to mitigate risks and promote long-term economic stability

A projected Banking Reserves Table (2025–2040) for the selected countries, assuming an annual reserve growth rate of 5% based on hypothetical reserve levels in 2025. This growth rate reflects moderate economic expansion, FDI inflows, and improved financial sector stability (Table 8.7).

High-Level Analysis and Key Insights

1. **Strong Growth in Larger Economies**

- India and Chile show the highest reserve growth, reaching $672.46 billion and $128.86 billion, respectively, by 2040. This reflects their robust economic expansion, diversification, and increasing role in global trade.
- South Africa and Bangladesh also demonstrate significant reserve growth, supported by strong financial sector reforms, technological innovations, and foreign investment inflows.

Table 8.7 Projected Banking Reserves (2025–2040) by country

Country	*2025*	*2030*	*2035*	*2040*
Zambia	1.30	1.66	2.12	2.71
Malawi	0.76	0.97	1.24	1.58
Botswana	3.00	3.83	4.89	6.24
Chile	62.00	79.12	100.97	128.86
India	323.76	413.08	526.97	672.46
Bangladesh	46.50	59.41	75.96	97.08
South Africa	72.55	92.68	118.42	151.31
DRC	4.35	5.56	7.10	9.08
South Sudan	0.11	0.14	0.18	0.23
Sudan	1.19	1.52	1.94	2.48
Lesotho	0.18	0.23	0.29	0.37
Eswatini	0.46	0.59	0.75	0.96
Madagascar	1.03	1.32	1.69	2.16
Seychelles	0.47	0.60	0.77	0.99
Mauritius	3.97	5.05	6.44	8.21

2. **Moderate Growth in SSA Countries**

    - Botswana, Mauritius, and the DRC exhibit steady increases in banking reserves, driven by mining, tourism, and financial sector modernisation.
    - Zambia and Malawi show a gradual upward trajectory, but their reserve levels remain relatively low compared to larger African economies.

3. **Vulnerabilities in Fragile Economies**

    - South Sudan and Sudan remain highly vulnerable due to political instability, weak financial institutions, and limited foreign investment.
    - Lesotho, Eswatini, and Seychelles have small but stable reserve growth, mainly driven by tourism, remittances, and trade linkages.

4. **Implications for Economic Development**

    - Higher Reserves: Countries like India, Chile, and South Africa can leverage strong banking reserves to support long-term investments, infrastructure development, and economic resilience.
    - Lower Reserves: Countries like South Sudan and Lesotho may struggle with external shocks, currency volatility, and limited fiscal space, making them more dependent on aid and foreign debt.

5. **Recommendations for Banking Sector Strengthening**

    - Enhancing Financial Inclusion: Expanding access to banking services, particularly in SSA and South Asia, can increase domestic savings and reserve accumulation.
    - Regulatory Strengthening: Improving banking supervision and monetary policies will help mitigate risks of capital flight and external vulnerabilities.
    - Diversifying Reserve Sources: Encouraging foreign investment, trade expansion, and technological integration can enhance reserve growth and economic stability.

The projected banking reserves highlight the economic divergence between emerging and fragile economies. While countries like India, Chile, and South Africa are poised for significant financial growth, others like South Sudan, Sudan, and Eswatini face persistent economic challenges. Policy reforms, investment in technology, and regional cooperation will be crucial for sustained banking sector development and financial stability.

Proposed Equation for Estimating Central Bank Reserves

$$Rt = \beta 0 + \beta 1 \cdot GDPt + \beta 2 \cdot Exportst + \beta 3 \cdot Importst + \beta 4 \cdot FDIt + \beta 5 \cdot Inflationt + \beta 6 \cdot PoliticalStabilityt + \epsilon\, tR$$

Where:

- Rt = Central bank reserves at time t
- GDPt = Gross Domestic Product at time t
- Exports t = Total exports at time t
- Imports t = Total imports at time t
- FDI t = Foreign direct investment at time t
- Inflation t = Inflation rate at time t
- Political Stability t = Political stability index at time t
- $\beta 0, \beta 1, \beta 2, \beta 3, \beta 4, \beta 5, \beta 6$ = Coefficients to be estimated
- ϵt\epsilon = Error term

Expanded explanations of the above various economic variables impacting banking reserves and overall economic development, with explanations of their effects, are highlighted below.

Key Economic Variables Influencing Banking Reserves and Development

Gross Domestic Product (GDPt)

Definition and Role:

- GDP represents the total monetary value of all goods and services produced within a country over a specific period (World Bank, 2022c).

- A higher GDP typically indicates greater economic output, a stronger financial system, and increased banking reserves (Mankiw, 2020).

Impact on Development:

- Higher GDP enhances financial stability: Countries with higher GDP can accumulate larger reserves, allowing for stronger monetary policy interventions.
- Drives banking sector growth: Higher GDP correlates with higher savings rates, greater capital accumulation, and stronger domestic investment (Stiglitz & Greenwald, 2014).
- Low GDP can limit financial resilience: Countries with low GDP struggle to maintain reserves, making them vulnerable to external shocks.

Example:

- India's GDP growth from $2.9 trillion (2019) to $3.7 trillion (2023) contributed to an increase in banking reserves and stronger investor confidence (*IMF*, 2023a).

Exports (Exports)

Definition and Role:

- Exports represent the total value of goods and services sold abroad (Krugman & Obstfeld, 2018).
- Higher exports generate foreign exchange earnings, which boost reserves and support currency stability.

Impact on Development:

- Stronger export-led growth: Countries with high exports accumulate more foreign exchange reserves, improving economic stability.
- Supports local industries: Strong exports stimulate job creation and GDP growth, leading to higher banking reserves.
- Dependency on commodity exports: Some SSA countries, such as Zambia (copper) and Botswana (diamonds), rely heavily on commodity exports, making them vulnerable to price volatility (Collier, 2017).

Example:

- Botswana's diamond exports account for over 85% of total exports, significantly contributing to banking reserves and foreign exchange stability (Bank of Botswana, 2023).

Imports (Imports)

Definition and Role:

- Imports represent the total value of goods and services purchased from abroad (Todaro & Smith, 2020).
- Higher imports require foreign currency, which reduces banking reserves if not offset by equivalent exports or FDI inflows.

Impact on Development:

- Essential for industrialisation: Imports of capital goods and technology can boost productivity and long-term development.
- Trade imbalances lead to reserve depletion: A persistent trade deficit can reduce reserves and weaken the national currency.
- Over-reliance on imports can cause inflation: If a country imports more than it exports, the depreciation of the local currency can lead to higher inflation (Rodrik, 2017).

Example:

- Bangladesh has a trade deficit of $33 billion due to high import dependence on machinery and fuel, which puts pressure on reserves.

Foreign Direct Investment (FDI)

Definition and Role:

- FDI measures long-term investments by foreign entities in domestic businesses and industries (Dunning & Lundan, 2008).
- Higher FDI inflows increase banking reserves, support economic expansion, and improve financial sector stability.

Impact on Development:

- Boosts reserves: Inflows of foreign currency through FDI strengthen banking reserves and the national balance of payments.

- Encourages job creation and technology transfer: FDI stimulates local industry growth, increasing tax revenues and savings rates (Blomström & Kokko, 2003).
- FDI dependency can create risks: If FDI inflows decline, economies reliant on foreign investment can face reserve depletion (Moyo, 2009).

Example:

- South Africa attracted $10 billion in FDI (2022), significantly boosting banking reserves and industrial development (UNCTAD, 2023).

Inflation Rate (Inflation)

Definition and Role:

- Inflation represents the percentage increase in the prices of goods and services over time (Mishkin, 2019).
- High inflation erodes purchasing power, increases uncertainty, and reduces banking reserves as central banks intervene in currency markets.

Impact on Development:

- Moderate inflation supports growth: A stable inflation rate (2%–5%) encourages investment and economic stability.
- Hyperinflation reduces reserves: High inflation forces central banks to spend reserves on stabilising the currency.
- Discourages savings: When inflation is high, individuals and businesses avoid banks, reducing financial sector growth.

Example:

- Zimbabwe's hyperinflation (2008–2009) resulted in near depletion of banking reserves and severe economic collapse.

Political Stability Index (Political Stability Index)

Definition and Role:

- This index measures the likelihood of political stability or instability in a country (Acemoglu & Robinson, 2012).
- Political stability attracts investment, while instability reduces reserves due to capital flight and reduced investor confidence.

Impact on Development:

- Stable governments attract FDI: Countries with strong governance and transparent policies tend to accumulate higher banking reserves.
- Political instability increases risk: Civil unrest, corruption, and weak institutions reduce investor confidence and limit economic growth (North et al., 2009).

Example:

- South Sudan's low political stability (ranked −2.2 by World Bank, 2023b) has discouraged FDI inflows, limiting reserve accumulation.

These key economic variables interact to shape banking reserves and overall financial stability. Countries that manage GDP growth, export competitiveness, inflation control, and political stability effectively tend to have higher banking reserves and stronger economic resilience. However, developing countries, particularly in SSA and South Asia, must implement sound policies to mitigate risks and foster sustainable economic development.

High-Level Analysis: Impact of Banking Reserves on Poverty Reduction Within the Power Theory of Economics

The relationship between banking reserves and poverty reduction is complex and shaped by economic power dynamics (Acemoglu & Robinson, 2012). Within the Power Theory of Economics, reserves serve as a mechanism of financial influence, determining who controls capital flows, financial inclusion, and economic opportunities. This analysis explores whether higher reserves reduce poverty or reinforce economic inequalities, particularly in SSA and other developing regions.

Theoretical Framework: Power Theory of Economics and Banking Reserves

The Power Theory of Economics argues that control over financial resources determines economic opportunities and development outcomes (Acemoglu & Robinson, 2012).

- **Who Controls the Reserves?**
  - If reserves are concentrated in the hands of the elite or multinational banks, economic disparities may widen.
  - If reserves are effectively used for financial inclusion and development projects, they can reduce poverty (Stiglitz, 2017).
- **Financial Power and Access to Credit**
  - Higher reserves can enable more lending to the poor, fostering entrepreneurship and economic growth (Mankiw, 2020).
  - However, in many SSA countries, reserves are held by central banks but not accessible to the informal economy, limiting their impact on poverty reduction (Collier, 2017).

How Higher Reserves Can Reduce Poverty

- **Stabilises the Economy and Currency Value**
  - Countries with high reserves can manage currency volatility, preventing inflation spikes that disproportionately affect the poor (Rodrik, 2017).
  - Example: Botswana's diamond-backed reserves helped maintain a stable pula, protecting consumer purchasing power (Bank of Botswana, 2023).
- **Supports Financial Inclusion**
  - Higher reserves allow banks to offer lower interest rates, increasing access to loans for small businesses and farmers.
  - Example: India's banking sector reforms leveraged reserves to expand microfinance programs, benefiting rural communities (*IMF*, 2023a).
- **Enables Pro-Poor Public Investments**
  - Countries with strong reserves can fund social programs, including education, healthcare, and infrastructure.

- Example: Bangladesh used banking reserves to fund rural electrification, boosting agricultural productivity and employment (World Bank, 2022b).

When Higher Reserves Do Not Reduce Poverty

- **Reserves Are Not Effectively Deployed**
  - If reserves remain idle or invested in low-return foreign assets, they may not contribute to domestic development (Stiglitz & Greenwald, 2014).
  - Example: South Africa holds significant reserves but struggles with inequality due to limited financial sector inclusion (South African Reserve Bank, 2023).
- **Banking Reserves Benefit Only the Elite**
  - Large reserves often reinforce elite control over financial systems, widening the wealth gap.
  - Example: Zambia's copper wealth has not translated into widespread poverty reduction due to banking sector inequalities (Collier, 2017).
- **Overemphasis on Reserves Can Stifle Growth**
  - Excessive reserves may signal underutilisation of capital, where funds are hoarded instead of invested in job creation (Krugman & Obstfeld, 2018).
  - Example: Mauritius has high banking reserves but struggles with unemployment among youth due to limited reinvestment into productive sectors (UNCTAD, 2023).

Policy Recommendations for Optimising Banking Reserves for Poverty Reduction

- **Enhance Financial Inclusion**
  - Use reserves to support microfinance and SME lending
  - Governments should direct part of banking reserves into pro-poor credit schemes.

  - Example: Bangladesh's Grameen Bank model increased financial access for low-income earners (Yunus, 2008).

- **Encourage digital banking and fintech innovation**
  - Mobile banking (e.g., M-Pesa in Kenya) can increase financial access for the unbanked.
- **Allocate reserves for infrastructure development**
  - Investment in transport, health, and education enhances long-term economic productivity.
  - Example: India's banking reserves funded rural roads, boosting trade and employment (IMF, 2023a).

- **Stabilise the Currency to Protect the Poor**
  - Countries should use reserves to prevent currency devaluation that leads to higher inflation and food prices.
  - Example: Botswana's stable pula shields the poor from inflation-driven cost-of-living increases.

Striking a Balance Between Reserves and Development

The effectiveness of banking reserves in reducing poverty depends on their deployment. Countries that strategically invest reserves into pro-poor programs, financial inclusion, and economic diversification experience higher poverty reduction. However, when reserves are concentrated in elite-controlled banking structures or remain underutilised, their impact on poverty is limited.

Developing economies, particularly in SSA and South Asia, must ensure that banking reserves serve as a tool for inclusive economic growth rather than a mechanism for financial power consolidation.

Achieving Fiscal Surplus and Becoming Aid Providers: Can SSA Achieve Economic Independence?

SSA has long been dependent on foreign aid and external financing for development. However, achieving a fiscal surplus—where government revenues exceed expenditures—would allow SSA countries to become economically independent and potentially shift from aid recipients to aid providers.

This analysis explores:

1. The feasibility of SSA achieving fiscal surplus
2. Strategies for economic independence
3. The possibility of SSA becoming an aid provider
4. Real-world examples of successful economic transformation

Is achieving fiscal surplus realistic for SSA?

Achieving a fiscal surplus is challenging but possible, depending on the following key factors:

- **Current Economic Realities in SSA**

  – **Growing Economies**: Some SSA countries (e.g., Botswana, Rwanda, Kenya, and Ghana) have sustained economic growth rates above 5% (World Bank, 2023a).
  – **Natural Resource Wealth**: Countries like Nigeria (oil), Zambia (copper), and the DRC (minerals) have vast resources but struggle with resource mismanagement.
  – **Debt Crisis**: SSA's total debt reached $1.1 trillion in 2023, making surplus difficult (IMF, 2023b).
  – **Weak Tax Revenue Collection**: Most SSA countries collect only 15%–18% of GDP in tax revenue, compared to 35%+ in OECD countries (AfDB, 2023a).

Global Examples of Economic Transition

1. **Singapore and South Korea:**
   – Transformed from aid recipients to high-income economies by investing in education, industrialisation, and financial reforms (Rodrik, 2017).
2. **China and India:**
   – Shifted from dependency to global economic players by increasing export-led growth and domestic industries (Stiglitz, 2017).

3. **Botswana:**

   - Sustained fiscal surpluses since the 1980s by efficiently managing diamond revenue and investing in public services (Bank of Botswana, 2022).

If SSA countries implement structural reforms, fiscal surplus is possible. However, it requires sustained policy discipline and economic diversification.

Strategies for SSA to achieve fiscal surplus

Strengthen Revenue Generation

- **Enhance Tax Collection Efficiency**
  - Digital tax systems (like Kenya's iTax) can reduce evasion and increase compliance.
  - Broadening the tax base by taxing informal businesses, which make up 60%+ of SSA economies (AfDB, 2023b).

- **Natural Resource Management and Sovereign Wealth Funds**
  - Norway's oil fund model (Government Pension Fund Global) shows how SSA can use resource wealth to build fiscal buffers.
  - Botswana's Pula Fund protects the economy from commodity price volatility.

- **Combat Illicit Financial Flows (IFFs)**
  - SSA loses $88 billion annually to illicit financial flows (UNECA, 2022).
  - Implementing anti-money laundering policies can recover lost revenue.

Optimise Public Spending

- Reduce Waste and Corruption

- Over $50 billion in SSA is lost annually to corruption (Transparency International, 2023).
- Implement performance-based budgeting to ensure funds are used efficiently.

- Prioritise Growth-Enhancing Investments

  - Focus on infrastructure, education, and health rather than excessive government wages and subsidies.
  - Example: Rwanda's Vision 2050 prioritises productive investment, leading to 7%+ growth rates (IMF, 2023b).

Industrialisation and Economic Diversification

- Boost Manufacturing and Value Addition

  - SSA must move beyond raw material exports.
  - Example: Ethiopia's textile industry has grown through industrial parks, creating jobs and increasing exports (World Bank, 2023a).

- Expanding Regional Trade

  - The African Continental Free Trade Area (AfCFTA) could increase intra-African trade by 52% by 2030 (UNECA, 2023).
  - Example: South Africa exports high-value goods within Africa rather than relying on aid.

- Strengthening Agriculture for Food Security & Exports
  - Nigeria, Kenya, and Ghana can expand agro-processing and reduce reliance on food imports.

Leveraging Technology and Financial Innovation

- Digital Banking and Mobile Payments
  - M-Pesa in Kenya has expanded financial inclusion, enabling businesses to grow and tax revenue to increase (GSMA, 2023).
- Blockchain for Transparent Transactions
  - Reducing corruption by making government transactions publicly verifiable (WEF, 2023).
- Investing in Human Capital

- Education and skills training are key for transitioning into high-value industries.
- Example: South Korea invested in STEM education, leading to tech-driven economic growth (Rodrik, 2017).

Can SSA become an aid provider?

Once fiscal surpluses are achieved and sustained, SSA countries could become aid donors rather than recipients.

Examples of Emerging SSA Aid Providers

- **South Africa** provides aid through the African Renaissance Fund.
- **Nigeria** has supported peacekeeping and development aid in West Africa.
- **Botswana** has given aid for drought relief in neighbouring countries.

How SSA Can Transition to an Aid Provider

1. Contribute to African Development Bank (AfDB) projects.
2. Fund infrastructure projects in fragile SSA states.
3. Provide technical assistance and expertise (e.g., Rwanda's ICT development support to neighbouring countries).

However, SSA must first strengthen its fiscal position before shifting to aid giving.

Is SSA's fiscal independence realistic?

Yes, but only with strong governance, diversified economies, and strategic investments.

- SSA can achieve fiscal surpluses by strengthening revenue collection, industrialising, and reducing corruption.
- The transition from aid recipient to aid provider is possible but requires long-term policy discipline.

Key Takeaways:

- Industrialisation and intra-African trade are essential.
- Tax reforms and digitalisation can boost revenues.

- Investing in human capital and infrastructure ensures sustainable growth.
- Managing natural resources effectively can build sovereign wealth funds for the future.

If SSA implements these changes, fiscal independence and aid-giving can become a reality within the next two decades.

Table 8.8 reflects a hypothetical fiscal surplus projection table (2025–2040) for selected SSA countries and developing economies. The projections assume that countries implement strong governance, economic diversification, improved tax collection, and reduced corruption while managing natural resources efficiently.

Higher-Level Analysis: Path to Fiscal Surplus in SSA

Transition from Deficit to Surplus (2025–2040)

- **Short-Term (2025–2027):** Most countries start with fiscal deficits due to high debt burdens, inefficient taxation, and reliance on imports.
- **Mid-Term (2028–2030):** Fiscal consolidation measures (e.g., tax reforms, resource management, regional trade integration) help countries break even or move into modest surplus.
- **Long-Term (2035–2040):** Sustained economic growth, industrialisation, and digital financial systems allow many countries to accumulate substantial fiscal surpluses.

Key Drivers of Fiscal Surplus Growth

Improved Taxation and Revenue Collection

- Countries like Kenya and Rwanda will benefit from expanding digital tax systems (e.g., Kenya's iTax), improving revenue-to-GDP ratios.
- DRC, Angola, and Nigeria will see revenue growth if they successfully formalise the informal economy and tax extractive industries effectively.

Table 8.8 Hypothetical fiscal surplus projections (2025–2040) (figures in USD billion)

Year	*Nigeria*	*South Africa*	*Kenya*	*Ghana*	*Ethiopia*	*Zambia*	*Botswana*	*Rwanda*	*DRC*	*Angola*	*Mauritius*	*Seychelles*
2025	−15.0	−10.0	−4.0	−3.0	−5.5	−3.5	1.0	−1.5	−6.0	−4.0	0.5	0.2
2026	−10.0	−6.5	−2.5	−1.8	−4.0	−2.5	1.5	−0.8	−4.5	−2.5	0.8	0.3
2027	−5.0	−3.0	−1.0	−0.5	−2.0	−1.5	2.0	0.2	−2.5	−1.0	1.2	0.4
2028	0.0	0.0	0.5	0.5	−0.5	−0.5	2.5	1.0	0.0	0.5	1.8	0.6
2029	5.0	3.0	1.5	1.2	1.0	0.5	3.0	1.8	1.5	2.0	2.5	0.9
2030	10.0	7.0	3.0	2.5	3.0	1.5	3.5	2.5	3.0	3.5	3.2	1.2
2035	25.0	15.0	7.5	6.0	8.5	4.0	5.0	4.5	10.0	8.5	5.0	2.0
2040	50.0	30.0	15.0	12.0	18.0	10.0	7.5	7.0	25.0	15.0	7.5	3.5

Diversification and Industrialisation

- Ethiopia's manufacturing sector and Kenya's digital economy could reduce reliance on raw material exports.
- Nigeria and Angola's shift from oil to agriculture and services will stabilise fiscal revenue.
- Botswana and Mauritius will maintain stable surpluses due to economic diversification and strong governance.

Regional Trade and Intra-Africa Integration

- The African Continental Free Trade Area (AfCFTA) will boost revenue by expanding intra-African trade, reducing reliance on external markets.
- Countries with strong regional trade (e.g., South Africa, Kenya, Ghana) will experience higher revenue growth.

Technological Innovation and Digital Finance

- Countries that embrace digital banking, fintech, and blockchain transparency will reduce corruption and increase financial inclusion.
- M-Pesa (Kenya), mobile banking (Rwanda, Ghana, Nigeria), and digital tax will boost revenues.

Feasibility of SSA Becoming Aid Providers

- Mauritius, Botswana, and South Africa could transition into development aid providers due to strong fiscal stability.
- Nigeria, Kenya, and Ghana may start offering infrastructure financing to fragile neighbours by 2035.
- Countries like Ethiopia, Angola, and the DRC will take longer but can reach fiscal surplus by 2040.

Challenges to Achieving Fiscal Surplus

- Debt Repayment: SSA countries must restructure debt before achieving a sustained surplus.
- Corruption and Governance Issues: Fiscal stability depends on strong anti-corruption frameworks.
- Commodity Price Volatility: Resource-rich countries (e.g., Nigeria, Angola, Zambia) must diversify away from commodities.

Can SSA Realistically Achieve Fiscal Surplus?

Yes, but only with structural economic reforms.

- SSA countries can achieve fiscal surplus between 2028 and 2040 by strengthening revenue generation, reducing wasteful spending, and industrialising.
- Mauritius, Botswana, and South Africa will become aid providers first, followed by Kenya, Ghana, Nigeria, and Ethiopia post-2035.

If SSA implements these policies, the region could achieve fiscal independence and even shift from aid recipients to aid donors by 2040.

Fiscal Surplus Projections for SSA (2025–2040)

Table 8.9 below presents hypothetical projections of fiscal surplus for selected SSA countries and developing economies based on structural reforms, economic diversification, and governance improvements.

Key Factors Driving SSA Towards Fiscal Surplus

Economic Diversification and Industrialisation
Many SSA economies remain heavily dependent on commodity exports (e.g., Nigeria's oil, Zambia's copper, and the DRC's cobalt). This dependency makes them vulnerable to commodity price fluctuations (World Bank, 2023a). Economic diversification into manufacturing, agribusiness, and digital services is critical for achieving a fiscal surplus (Rodrik, 2017).

- **Example:** Botswana's economic model successfully leveraged diamond revenues to invest in education, infrastructure, and financial services, reducing dependency on mining (Acemoglu & Robinson, 2012).

Strengthening Tax Systems and Revenue Mobilisation
Tax revenues in SSA remain low, averaging 16% of GDP compared to 34% in OECD countries (IMF, 2022b). Improving tax compliance, digital tax administration, and formalising the informal sector can significantly boost revenues.

Table 8.9 Hypothetical Fiscal Surplus Projections (2025–2040) (in USD Billion)

Year	*Nigeria*	*South Africa*	*Kenya*	*Ghana*	*Ethiopia*	*Zambia*	*Botswana*	*Rwanda*	*DRC*	*Angola*	*Mauritius*	*Seychelles*
2025	−15.0	−10.0	−4.0	−3.0	−5.5	−3.5	1.0	−1.5	−6.0	−4.0	0.5	0.2
2026	−10.0	−6.5	−2.5	−1.8	−4.0	−2.5	1.5	−0.8	−4.5	−2.5	0.8	0.3
2027	−5.0	−3.0	−1.0	−0.5	−2.0	−1.5	2.0	0.2	−2.5	−1.0	1.2	0.4
2028	0.0	0.0	0.5	0.5	−0.5	−0.5	2.5	1.0	0.0	0.5	1.8	0.6
2029	5.0	3.0	1.5	1.2	1.0	0.5	3.0	1.8	1.5	2.0	2.5	0.9
2030	10.0	7.0	3.0	2.5	3.0	1.5	3.5	2.5	3.0	3.5	3.2	1.2
2035	25.0	15.0	7.5	6.0	8.5	4.0	5.0	4.5	10.0	8.5	5.0	2.0
2040	50.0	30.0	15.0	12.0	18.0	10.0	7.5	7.0	25.0	15.0	7.5	3.5

- **Example:** Kenya's iTax system, introduced in 2015, increased tax collection efficiency and reduced leakages (Keen, 2021).

Reducing Dependence on Foreign Aid
Many SSA countries remain dependent on external grants and concessional loans, limiting their fiscal autonomy (Moyo, 2009). Sustainable strategies include leveraging domestic capital markets and developing sovereign wealth funds to manage national savings.

- **Example:** Mauritius has transitioned from an aid-dependent economy to a service-based financial hub, reducing reliance on external funding (Subramanian, 2019).

Challenges to Achieving Fiscal Surplus

Debt Burden and Fiscal Mismanagement
Many SSA countries face high debt levels due to infrastructure financing and poor fiscal discipline (Collier, 2017). Governments must prioritise debt restructuring and enhance public expenditure efficiency.

- **Example:** Zambia defaulted on its Eurobond in 2020, highlighting the risks of unsustainable borrowing (IMF, 2022a).

Corruption and Governance Deficiencies
Weak governance and corruption reduce fiscal revenues and hinder economic growth (Acemoglu & Robinson, 2012). Strengthening institutions, enhancing transparency, and digitalising financial systems are essential.

- **Example:** South Africa's state capture scandal (Gupta case) negatively impacted investor confidence and economic growth (Transparency International, 2021).

Can SSA Become Aid Providers?

Yes, but under specific conditions.

Historically, emerging economies such as South Korea, Singapore, and Malaysia transitioned from aid recipients to aid donors by implementing fiscal prudence, industrial policies, and innovation-driven growth (Chang, 2003). SSA can achieve the same through:

- Sustained macroeconomic reforms
- Debt restructuring and controlled public spending
- Investment in education and skills training
- Leveraging regional trade agreements (AfCFTA)

Countries like Mauritius, Botswana, and South Africa are already providing development assistance to neighbouring states in infrastructure, health, and education.

- **Example:** Botswana has funded public health programs in Zimbabwe and Namibia as part of regional cooperation (SADC, 2022).

Pathway to Fiscal Independence

SSA countries can achieve a fiscal surplus by 2040 by implementing:

- Economic diversification to reduce reliance on raw materials
- Technology-driven tax collection and fiscal governance
- Stronger regional integration (AfCFTA) to boost intra-Africa trade
- Debt restructuring and improved public financial management

If SSA nations stay on this path, they could become net contributors to global development, shifting from aid recipients to donors within two decades.

Policy Recommendations for SSA's Path to Fiscal Independence

Achieving fiscal independence and transitioning from aid recipients to global contributors requires bold policy reforms, economic diversification, and institutional strengthening. Below are detailed policy recommendations across six key areas to ensure SSA countries reach fiscal surplus and economic self-reliance by 2040.

Strengthening Domestic Revenue Mobilisation

Challenge: SSA has one of the lowest tax-to-GDP ratios globally, averaging 16%, compared to 34% in OECD countries (IMF, 2022b).

Policy Recommendations

- Expand tax base: Formalise the informal sector, which represents over 60% of employment (ILO, 2020).
- Digital tax administration: Implement AI-driven tax compliance systems to reduce fraud (Keen, 2021).
- Progressive taxation: Increase taxes on high-income earners while reducing burdens on SMEs to encourage growth (World Bank, 2023b).
- Resource taxation reforms: Implement higher royalties on extractive industries (e.g., mining in the DRC, oil in Nigeria) to capture more public revenue.

Example: Kenya's Tax system increased compliance, boosting revenue collection by 25% in five years.

Economic Diversification and Industrialisation

Challenge: Many SSA economies depend heavily on commodity exports, making them vulnerable to price fluctuations.

Policy Recommendations

- Develop agro-processing industries: Shift from raw commodity exports to value-added products (e.g., Ghana's cocoa processing industry).
- Expand manufacturing capacity: Implement industrial policies similar to China's SEZs (Chang, 2003).
- Boost digital and service economies: Invest in ICT, fintech, and digital entrepreneurship to create sustainable revenue streams (UNCTAD, 2022a, b).
- Enhance regional trade integration: Implement the African Continental Free Trade Area (AfCFTA) effectively to reduce reliance on Western markets (SADC, 2022).

Example: Mauritius transitioned from a sugar-dependent economy to a financial services and tourism hub, reducing external aid dependency (Subramanian, 2019).

Debt Management and Fiscal Discipline

Challenge: Many SSA countries are trapped in unsustainable debt cycles, limiting fiscal space.

Policy Recommendations

- Prioritise concessional financing over commercial loans to avoid high debt-servicing costs (IMF, 2023b).
- Debt restructuring mechanisms: Negotiate longer repayment periods for existing loans.
- Sovereign Wealth Funds (SWFs): Create national savings from resource revenues to ensure future fiscal stability (Norwegian model).
- Public Expenditure Review (PERs): Cut non-essential government spending and increase efficiency in public service delivery.

Example: Botswana's Pula Fund stabilises government revenues and shields the economy from commodity price shocks (Acemoglu & Robinson, 2012).

Institutional Reforms and Anti-corruption Measures

Challenge: Corruption and weak institutions reduce **fiscal efficiency** and deter investments.

Policy Recommendations

- Strengthen anti-corruption agencies: Empower watchdog institutions with full independence (e.g., Ghana's Special Prosecutor Office).
- Digital governance: Implement blockchain technology to enhance transparency in public procurement and financial transactions.
- Judicial reforms: Enforce strict anti-corruption laws with severe penalties for financial crimes.
- Public finance management reforms: Use real-time expenditure tracking systems to monitor government budgets and reduce leakages.

Example: Rwanda reduced corruption by introducing e-procurement systems, leading to a 15% increase in fiscal efficiency (World Bank, 2023a).

Infrastructure Development for Economic Growth

Challenge: Poor infrastructure limits trade, investment, and productivity.

Policy Recommendations

- Invest in transport infrastructure: Develop regional railway and highway networks to enhance intra-African trade (AfDB, 2022).
- Expand renewable energy projects: Leverage solar, hydro, and wind energy to reduce electricity deficits.
- Improve financial access: Develop credit guarantee schemes for SMEs and fintech startups.
- Public-private partnerships (PPPs): Encourage private sector investment in transport, energy, and ICT sectors.

Example: Ethiopia's Grand Renaissance Dam project is set to generate over 6000 MW of electricity, improving industrial productivity (IMF, 2023b).

Enhancing Regional and Global Trade Participation

Challenge: Africa's share in global trade is only 2%, compared to 38% for Asia (UNCTAD, 2022a, b).

Policy Recommendations

- Fully implement AfCFTA: Reduce tariffs, trade barriers, and logistical inefficiencies.
- Export diversification: Shift from raw materials to processed goods, textiles, and high-value agricultural products.
- Boost intra-African trade: Strengthen trade relations among SSA nations to reduce dependence on Western markets.
- Engage in global value chains: Position SSA economies into the global manufacturing network (e.g., auto-parts industry in Morocco and South Africa).

Example: South Africa's automotive export sector contributes over $10 billion annually, supporting fiscal revenues (SADC, 2022) (Table 8.10).

Table 8.10 Projected growth scenarios based on policy adoption

Year	*Nigeria*	*South Africa*	*Kenya*	*Ghana*	*Ethiopia*	*Zambia*	*Botswana*	*Rwanda*	*DRC*	*Angola*	*Mauritius*	*Seychelles*
2025	−15.0	−10.0	−4.0	−3.0	−5.5	−3.5	1.0	−1.5	−6.0	−4.0	0.5	0.2
2030	10.0	7.0	3.0	2.5	3.0	1.5	3.5	2.5	3.0	3.5	3.2	1.2
2040	50.0	30.0	15.0	12.0	18.0	10.0	7.5	7.0	25.0	15.0	7.5	3.5

Fiscal Surplus Projections (2025–2040)

Achieving Fiscal Independence by 2040

SSA can achieve fiscal independence by:

- Expanding tax bases and enhancing revenue collection
- Investing in economic diversification and industrialisation
- Strengthening debt management strategies
- Combating corruption and enhancing governance
- Improving regional and global trade participation

If SSA implements these policies, it can transition from an aid recipient to a global economic force, capable of providing aid and investments to other developing nations by 2040.

Achieving fiscal independence in SSA and other developing economies is both a strategic necessity and a realistic ambition if governments commit to bold economic, financial, and governance reforms. While these nations currently face significant challenges, including low revenue collection, economic dependence on foreign aid, weak institutions, and infrastructure deficits, they also possess immense opportunities to transform their economic trajectories and achieve fiscal surplus by 2040.

Key Takeaways

1. **Strengthening Banking Systems and Reserves for Sustainable Growth**

   - Banking reserves play a crucial role in maintaining financial stability, supporting economic development, and reducing vulnerability to external shocks.
   - Higher reserves provide monetary stability, improve investor confidence, and allow central banks to cushion economic downturns.
   - Countries with strong banking reserves and sound economic policies can allocate resources towards poverty reduction, infrastructure, and long-term development initiatives.
   - Policy interventions must focus on balancing power within the banking sector, ensuring that both local and global banks operate in a fair, competitive environment.

- Harnessing technology and fintech innovations will be essential in driving financial inclusion and increasing banking reserves.

Example: Botswana's effective resource-based banking reserve strategy has allowed it to maintain fiscal stability despite its dependence on commodities.

2. **Achieving Fiscal Surplus and Reducing Dependency on Foreign Aid**

- Fiscal surplus is possible in SSA if countries implement sound revenue collection mechanisms, industrialisation, and diversified economic policies.
- Countries must reduce over-reliance on foreign aid by increasing domestic revenue mobilisation through tax reforms, formalising the informal sector, and boosting exports and manufacturing.
- Trade integration, particularly through AfCFTA, is a game-changer in increasing SSA's participation in global value chains, reducing trade barriers, and boosting economic independence.

Example: Mauritius transitioned from an aid-dependent nation to a financial and trade hub, proving that economic transformation is achievable.

3. **Economic Diversification as the Key to Long-Term Stability**

- Countries that diversify their economies beyond commodity dependence can withstand global economic shocks and increase their fiscal capacity.
- Investment in industrialisation, technology, and the digital economy will drive sustainable growth.
- Governments should create incentives for domestic and FDI, particularly in manufacturing, renewable energy, and fintech sectors.

Example: Ethiopia's industrialisation strategy, particularly in textiles and energy, has significantly improved its economic resilience.

4. **Governance and Institutional Strengthening Are Non-negotiable**

- Corruption and poor governance remain key barriers to fiscal surplus and economic self-reliance.
- Strengthening anti-corruption measures, public finance management, and digital governance systems will reduce revenue leakages.
- Transparent and accountable institutions attract more investment, promote business confidence, and enhance public sector efficiency.

Example: Rwanda's successful **e-procurement and anti-corruption frameworks** have significantly improved fiscal efficiency and public trust.

5. **Leveraging Regional and Global Trade for Fiscal Expansion**

- AfCFTA presents a unique opportunity to create a single market for over 1.3 billion people, reducing dependency on Western aid and markets.
- Strengthening regional infrastructure (railways, highways, and ports) will reduce trade costs and boost competitiveness.
- SSA countries must strategically position themselves within global value chains, focusing on high-value exports instead of raw materials.

Example: South Africa's automotive export sector, which leverages global trade networks, contributes billions to fiscal revenues.

Final Thoughts: Is Fiscal Independence Realistic for SSA?

Yes, but it requires bold action.

While SSA countries face challenges, their economic potential is enormous. Achieving fiscal independence and becoming aid providers rather than aid recipients is possible through strategic reforms, investments, and good governance.

A clear roadmap includes the following:

- Strengthening banking reserves and ensuring monetary stability.
- Implementing progressive tax reforms and expanding domestic revenue bases.

- Investing in infrastructure, energy, and industrialisation.
- Enhancing regional trade integration and boosting exports.
- Fighting corruption and improving governance structures.
- Leveraging digital transformation and financial inclusion.

The Future of SSA: A Global Economic Player by 2040?

If SSA countries execute these policies effectively, they can transition into global economic powerhouses, with some nations achieving fiscal surplus as early as 2030–2040.

Final Challenge: Are SSA governments willing to take the difficult but necessary decisions to ensure long-term fiscal independence? The time to act is now.

References

Acemoglu, D., & Robinson, J. (2012). *Why nations fail: The origins of power, prosperity, and poverty.* Crown Publishing.

African Development Bank (AfDB). (2022). *African economic outlook 2022: Supporting climate resilience and a just energy transition.* AfDB.

African Development Bank (AfDB). (2023a). *African economic outlook 2023.* AfDB.

African Development Bank (AfDB). (2023b). *Public financial management reforms in Africa: Strengthening governance for sustainable development.* AfDB.

African Union. (2021). *Agenda 2063: The Africa we want.* AU.

Arner, D. W., Barberis, J., & Buckley, R. P. (2020). FinTech and RegTech in a nutshell, and the future in a sandbox. In *Research handbook on digital transformations* (pp. 157–182). Edward Elgar Publishing.

Banerjee, A., & Duflo, E. (2011). *Poor economics: A radical rethinking of the way to fight global poverty.* PublicAffairs.

Banerjee, A., & Duflo, E. (2019). *Good economics for hard times: Better answers to our biggest problems.* PublicAffairs.

Bank of Botswana. (2022). *Annual financial stability report.* Bank of Botswana.

Bank of Botswana. (2023). *Annual financial stability report.* Bank of Botswana.

Beck, T., Demirgüç-Kunt, A., & Levine, R. (2009). Financial institutions and markets across countries and over time. *World Bank Economic Review, 23*(1), 77–92.

Beck, T., Cull, R., & Trandafir, M. (2011). Banking in Africa. *World Bank Policy Research Working Paper, 6684.*

Blomström, M., & Kokko, A. (2003). *The economics of foreign direct investment incentives*. National Bureau of Economic Research Working Paper, No. 9489.
Chang, H. J. (2002). *Kicking away the ladder: Development strategy in historical perspective*. Anthem Press.
Chang, H. J. (2003). *Kicking away the ladder: Development strategy in historical perspective*. Anthem Press.
Collier, P. (2017). *The future of capitalism: Facing the new anxieties*. Allen Lane.
Collier, P. (2018). *The future of capitalism: Facing the new anxieties*. Harper.
Demirgüç-Kunt, A., Klapper, L., & Singer, D. (2018). *Financial Inclusion and Inclusive Growth: A review of recent empirical evidence*. World Bank Policy Research Working Paper, 8674.
Dunning, J. H., & Lundan, S. M. (2008). *Multinational enterprises and the global economy* (2nd ed.). Edward Elgar.
Eichengreen, B. (2019). *Globalizing capital: A history of the international monetary system*. Princeton University Press.
Epstein, G. A. (2005). *Financialization and the world economy*. Edward Elgar Publishing.
Goodhart, C. A. E. (2010). The changing role of central banks. *Financial History Review, 17*(2), 135–154. https://doi.org/10.2139/ssrn.1717776
GSMA. (2023). *State of the Mobile economy: Africa 2023*. GSMA.
Intergovernmental Panel on Climate Change. (IPCC). (2021). *Climate change 2021: The physical science basis*. https://www.ipcc.ch/report/ar6/wg1/
. (2022). Empowering women entrepreneurs in Africa: Addressing barriers to financial inclusion. In *International finance corporation (IFC)*. IFC.
International Monetary Fund (IMF). (2021). *Fiscal monitor: Strengthening the credibility of public finances*. International Monetary Fund.
. (2022a). Domestic resource mobilization: Policies and trends. In *International Monetary Fund (IMF)*. International Monetary Fund.
. (2022b). Sub-Saharan Africa regional economic outlook. In *International Monetary Fund (IMF)*. International Monetary Fund.
. (2023a). World economic outlook database. In *International Monetary Fund (IMF)*. International Monetary Fund.
. (2023b). Sub-Saharan Africa's debt dynamics: Challenges and policy responses. In *International Monetary Fund (IMF)*. International Monetary Fund.
Kaufmann, D., Kraay, A., & Mastruzzi, M. (2020). *The worldwide governance indicators: Methodology and analytical issues*. World Bank Policy Research Working Paper.
Keen, M. (2021). *Improving tax collection in developing countries: Challenges and innovations*. IMF Working Paper.
Khan, M. (2010). *Political settlements and the governance of growth-enhancing institutions*. SOAS Working Paper.

Krugman, P., & Obstfeld, M. (2018). *International economics: Theory and policy* (11th ed.). Pearson.

Mankiw, N. G. (2020). *Macroeconomic* (10th ed.). Worth Publishers.

Mishkin, F. S. (2019). *The economics of money, banking, and financial markets* (12th ed.). Pearson.

Moyo, D. (2009). *Dead aid: Why aid is not working and how there is a better way for Africa*. Penguin.

North, D. C., Wallis, J. J., & Weingast, B. R. (2009). *Violence and social orders: A conceptual framework for interpreting recorded human history*. Cambridge University Press.

Organisation for Economic Co-operation and Development (OECD). (2019). *Public-private partnerships for sustainable development goals*. OECD Publishing.

Organisation for Economic Co-operation and Development (OECD). (2020). *Blended finance in the least developed countries 2020: Supporting a resilient COVID-19 recovery*. OECD.

Organisation for Economic Co-operation and Development (OECD). (2023). *Regulatory Policy Outlook 2020*. OECD.

Piketty, T. (2014). *Capital in the twenty-first century*. Harvard University Press.

Rodrik, D. (2007). *One economics, many recipes: Globalization, institutions, and economic growth*. Princeton University Press.

Rodrik, D. (2017). *Straight talk on trade: Ideas for a sane world economy*. Princeton University Press.

Sen, A. (1999). *Development as freedom*. Oxford University Press.

South African Reserve Bank (SARB). (2023). *Monetary Policy Review*. SARB.

Southern African Development Community (SADC). (2022). *Regional economic outlook: Integrating SSA into global trade*. SADC.

Stern, N. (2006). *The economics of climate change: The Stern review*. Cambridge University Press.

Stiglitz, J. E. (2012). *The Price of inequality: How today's divided society endangers our future*. W.W. Norton & Company.

Stiglitz, J. (2017). *The euro: How a common currency threatens the future of Europe*. W.W. Norton & Company.

Stiglitz, J. E., & Greenwald, B. C. (2014). *Creating a learning society: A new approach to growth, development, and social Progress*. Columbia University Press.

Strange, S. (1996). *The retreat of the state: The diffusion of power in the world economy*. Cambridge University Press.

Subramanian, A. (2019). *Mauritius: The making of a developmental state*. Oxford University Press.

Todaro, M. P., & Smith, S. C. (2020). *Economic development* (13th ed.). Pearson.

Transparency International. (2021). *Corruption perceptions index 2021*. Transparency International.

Transparency International. (2023). *Corruption perceptions index 2023*. Transparency International.
United Nations (UN). (2015). *Transforming our world: The 2030 agenda for sustainable development*. UN.
United Nations Conference on Trade and Development (UNCTAD). (2022a). *World investment report 2022: International tax reforms and sustainable investment*. UNCTAD.
United Nations Conference on Trade and Development (UNCTAD). (2022b). *Economic diversification in Africa: Pathways to sustainable growth*. UNCTAD.
United Nations Conference on Trade and Development (UNCTAD). (2023). *Trade and development report 2023*. UNCTAD.
United Nations Development Programme (UNDP). (2021). *Human development report 2021/2022: Uncertain times, unsettled lives*. UNDP.
United Nations Economic Commission for Africa (UNECA). (2022). *Illicit financial flows in Africa: Findings and recommendations*. UNECA.
United Nations Environment Programme (UNEP). (2021). *Green bonds in Africa: Scaling up sustainable finance*. UNEP.
World Bank. (2020a). *Ethiopia's economic update: Navigating the impact of COVID-19*. World Bank.
World Bank. (2020b). *The global Findex database 2020: Measuring financial inclusion and the Fintech revolution*. World Bank.
World Bank. (2021a). *The future of taxation in Africa: Challenges and reforms for domestic resource mobilization*. World Bank.
World Bank. (2021b). *Nigeria financial sector assessment*. World Bank.
World Bank. (2022a). *Governance indicators database*. World Bank.
World Bank. (2022b). *Global economic prospects 2022: War, inflation, and uncertainty*. World Bank.
World Bank. (2022c). *The changing wealth of nations 2021: Managing assets for the future*. World Bank.
World Bank. (2023a). *Economic transformation in Africa: Pathways to fiscal surplus*. World Bank.
World Bank. (2023b). *Global Economic Prospects*. World Bank.
World Economic Forum (WEF). (2021b). *The Africa competitiveness report: Unlocking Investment for Sustainable Growth*. WEF.
World Economic Forum (WEF). (2022). *The future of development finance: Mobilizing private Capital for Sustainable Growth*. WEF.
World Economic Forum (WEF). (2023). *Blockchain for development: Use cases and challenges*. WEF.
Yunus, M. (2003). *Banker to the poor: Micro-lending and the Battle against world poverty*. PublicAffairs.

Yunus, M. (2008). *Creating a world without poverty: Social business and the future of capitalism*. PublicAffairs.

Zins, A., & Weill, L. (2016). The determinants of financial inclusion in Africa. *Review of Development Finance, 6*(1), 46–57. https://doi.org/10.1016/j.rdf.2016.05.001

CHAPTER 9

Power, Conflict, and Development: Unpacking the Stakes

Introduction

Conflict, in the context of economic development, is a complex and multifaceted phenomenon that encompasses political, social, and economic struggles over resources, governance, and power (Stiglitz, 2017). It can manifest as armed conflicts, political instability, economic inequalities, or systemic institutional failures that hinder sustainable development. According to Collier and Hoeffler (2004), conflicts in developing economies are often rooted in resource competition, governance weaknesses, and power imbalances that exacerbate poverty and economic stagnation. This introduction explores the intersections between conflict, the Power Theory of Economics, and economic development, highlighting the stakes involved in managing power dynamics for sustainable growth.

Definition of Conflict in the Context of Economic Development

Conflict is traditionally viewed as a struggle between opposing groups or interests, often resulting in political instability, economic decline, and social disintegration (Minoiu & Shemyakina, 2014). In economic development, conflict arises when there is competition over limited resources, economic exclusion, weak governance, and systemic inequalities (Cramer, 2006). Murdoch and Sandler (2002) emphasise that conflict in

P. K. Kabeya, *Development and the Power Theory of Economics*,
https://doi.org/10.1007/978-3-032-07926-8_9

developing nations can stem from economic marginalisation, lack of access to financial systems, and the unequal distribution of wealth and power.

There are two primary forms of economic conflict in development:

1. **Violent Conflict** – Includes civil wars, insurgencies, and armed disputes that disrupt economic activities, destroy infrastructure, and deter investment. Examples include the conflicts in South Sudan and the Democratic Republic of Congo (DRC), where economic instability is closely tied to political unrest (World Bank, 2022b).
2. **Structural Conflict** – Refers to institutional weaknesses, corruption, and economic exclusion that systematically disadvantage certain groups or regions. For instance, in Lesotho and Eswatini, economic inequalities have led to long-term developmental challenges (Rodrik, 2017).

Economic conflicts often result in capital flight, reduced FDI, and declining GDP growth. Research by Acemoglu and Robinson (2012) suggests that nations with inclusive economic institutions experience lower levels of economic conflict compared to those with extractive institutions.

Overview of the Power Theory of Economics and its Relevance to Development

The Power Theory of Economics argues that economic development is not solely determined by market forces but by power dynamics among the political elite, businesses, and global institutions. Power, in this context, refers to the ability to control economic resources, set policies, and shape financial systems to favour certain groups over others (Qureshi, 2013).

The theory suggests that:

1. Economic power is concentrated among the elite, influencing resource allocation and financial stability (North et al., 2009).
2. Political structures shape economic development, often leading to patronage economies where certain groups benefit while others remain marginalised (Khan, 2010).
3. Global financial institutions wield influence, determining access to credit, foreign investment, and international trade opportunities for developing nations (Stiglitz, 2002).

In sub-Saharan Africa (SSA) and other developing regions, economic policies are often shaped by international financial institutions such as the International Monetary Fund (IMF) and World Bank, leading to dependencies on foreign aid and external debt (Easterly, 2006). This economic dependence weakens domestic financial sovereignty, limiting the ability of governments to implement long-term development strategies.

For example, in Zambia and Malawi, reliance on foreign loans and structural adjustment programmes has constrained economic autonomy, making these economies vulnerable to global financial crises (Mkandawire & Soludo, 1999). Similarly, in Bangladesh and India, industrial policies have been influenced by multinational corporations and international trade agreements that impact local economic structures (Chang, 2002).

Understanding the role of power in economic structures is crucial for designing policies that promote equitable growth, financial stability, and economic independence in developing nations.

The Link Between Conflict, Power Dynamics, and Economic Outcomes in Developing Nations

Economic development is deeply influenced by power struggles, as conflicts over resources, trade policies, and governance structures determine access to wealth and financial stability. Power imbalances often result in:

1. **Political and Economic Elite Controlling Financial Systems**

   - In South Africa, a small group of financial institutions and corporations dominate banking, limiting financial inclusion for marginalised communities (Rother et al., 2016).
   - In Mauritius and Seychelles, a combination of strong regulatory frameworks and diversified economies has reduced economic conflicts, fostering long-term stability (Strauss, 2012).

2. **External Influence Over Domestic Economic Policies**

   - Botswana has successfully resisted external economic pressures by maintaining sound fiscal policies and leveraging its diamond industry for national development (Acemoglu et al., 2003).

- Sudan and South Sudan, however, have struggled with economic independence due to reliance on oil exports and foreign investments that often favour external actors (Collier, 2007).

3. **Impact of Financial Inequality on Development**

   - Countries with high economic inequalities, such as Eswatini and Lesotho, experience slow development due to a lack of financial access for lower-income populations (Rodrik, 2017).
   - Chile and India have implemented targeted social policies to reduce disparities and increase economic participation among historically marginalised groups (Sen, 1999).

Power struggles shape economic opportunities, influence investment flows, and determine the level of public sector efficiency. When economic power is concentrated in the hands of a few, development efforts are often hindered, leading to prolonged economic stagnation and dependency on external aid.

What Is at Stake? (Political Stability, Economic Growth, Governance, Social Welfare)

Failure to address economic power imbalances and conflicts can lead to severe developmental consequences:

1. **Political Stability** – Weak economic policies can fuel political unrest, leading to government instability and civil conflicts, as seen in Sudan and the DRC (Sundberg & Melander, 2013).
2. **Economic Growth** – Countries with unstable banking systems and inconsistent policies, such as Madagascar and South Sudan, struggle to attract FDI, limiting job creation and industrial expansion (Strauss, 2012).
3. **Governance** – Corruption and weak institutions reduce economic transparency, discouraging investment and creating fiscal inefficiencies, as seen in Zambia and Malawi (North et al., 2009).
4. **Social Welfare** – Economic inequalities translate into limited access to education, healthcare, and employment opportunities, exacerbating poverty levels, particularly in Lesotho and Eswatini (Sen, 1999).

Conversely, nations that successfully manage economic power dynamics can achieve sustainable development and financial independence. Botswana and Mauritius provide positive case studies, demonstrating how sound financial regulations, diversified economies, and strong governance can lead to long-term economic prosperity (Acemoglu et al., 2003).

Economic conflict, when left unresolved, perpetuates underdevelopment, weakens governance, and deepens financial inequalities. The Power Theory of Economics offers a framework for understanding how resource control, financial institutions, and political influence shape economic development. Addressing these power imbalances is critical for SSA and other developing regions to achieve fiscal independence, economic stability, and sustainable development. When strengthening governance, reducing external dependencies, and promoting financial inclusivity, developing nations can create a more equitable and resilient economic future.

Theoretical Framework—Intersection Between the Influence of Power Theory of Economics and Conflict Dimension Impact on Development

Understanding Power Theory of Economics: Who Controls Economic Resources and Decision-Making in the Context of Conflict?

The Power Theory of Economics argues that economic outcomes are largely determined by who holds economic power and how they exercise control over resources and decision-making (Acemoglu & Robinson, 2012). Economic power is concentrated in the hands of governments, multinational corporations (MNCs), financial institutions, and the local elite, shaping access to wealth, policy choices, and overall development. In conflict-affected regions, economic power is often linked to political control, leading to economic policies that serve elite interests rather than broad-based development (North et al., 2009).

In conflict zones such as South Sudan, Ukraine, and the DRC, economic power is deeply intertwined with ongoing conflicts. The struggle for control over natural resources, financial systems, and strategic industries fuels violence, while external actors, including multinational corporations and foreign governments, often exploit these conflicts for economic gain (Collier & Hoeffler, 2004).

Case Study: South Sudan—Oil Revenues and Political Power Struggles

- **Who Controls Economic Resources?** The South Sudanese economy is heavily dependent on oil exports, which account for over 90% of government revenue (World Bank, 2023b). However, economic control is concentrated among the ruling elite and military factions, leading to widespread corruption and mismanagement (De Waal, 2014).
- **How Economic Power Influences Conflict:** The political elite manipulate oil revenues to finance military activities rather than investing in infrastructure, education, or healthcare. The unequal distribution of resources exacerbates grievances among different ethnic groups, prolonging instability (Stiglitz, 2017)
- **Impact on Development:** The ongoing conflict has destroyed infrastructure, displaced millions, and led to a humanitarian crisis, with over seven million people requiring food assistance (Henderson et al., 2012).

Case Study: Ukraine—Geopolitical Conflict and Economic Sovereignty

- **Who Controls Economic Resources?** Ukraine has a strategic economic position, rich in agricultural production and industrial capabilities, but its economic policies have been heavily influenced by geopolitical rivalries between Russia, the European Union (EU), and the United States (Strauss, 2012).
- **How Economic Power Influences Conflict:** The annexation of Crimea by Russia in 2014 and the ongoing conflict in Eastern Ukraine disrupted trade, reduced industrial output, and increased dependence on foreign aid (Sundberg & Melander, 2013). Western sanctions on Russia and counter-sanctions affected Ukraine's economic stability, demonstrating how power struggles in global economic governance shape national economies (Rother et al., 2016)
- **Impact on Development:** Despite economic reforms, the conflict has led to currency depreciation, inflation, and capital flight, significantly hindering Ukraine's development trajectory (IMF, 2023d).

Case Study: The DRC—Resource Curse and Prolonged Instability

- **Who Controls Economic Resources?** The DRC is one of the richest countries in terms of natural resources, particularly minerals such as cobalt, diamonds, and coltan, which are essential for global industries (Qureshi, 2013). However, control over these resources is fragmented between state actors, rebel groups, and foreign corporations.
- **How Economic Power Influences Conflict:** The illegal exploitation of minerals finances armed groups, leading to cycles of violence and instability. Foreign corporations often operate in unregulated conditions, extracting resources without contributing to local development (Autesserre, 2010).
- **Impact on Development:** Despite its wealth, the DRC remains one of the poorest countries, with over 60% of the population living in extreme poverty (World Bank, 2022b). The conflict over economic power prevents the country from leveraging its resources for sustainable growth.

How Conflict Shapes Economic Policies, Access to Resources, and Financial Systems

The intersection of conflict and economic power impacts development in three key ways:

Economic Policies in Conflict Zones

Economic policies in conflict-affected states are often designed to sustain the ruling elite and military expenditures rather than development. Governments in these regions prioritise short-term stability over long-term growth (Collier, 2007).

- **South Sudan:** Oil revenues are used to maintain military loyalty rather than diversify the economy (Stiglitz, 2017).
- **Ukraine:** Economic policies are shaped by geopolitical tensions, forcing reliance on external debt and financial aid (Rother et al., 2016).
- **DRC:** Policies favour extractive industries dominated by foreign interests, leading to a "resource curse" (Autesserre, 2010).

Access to Resources and Wealth Distribution

Conflicts often lead to inequitable distribution of resources, as economic power remains concentrated among the political and military elite.

- **South Sudan:** Ethnic groups outside the ruling coalition have limited access to national wealth (De Waal, 2014).
- **Ukraine:** Regional disparities widened due to war-related destruction of industries in the east (IMF, 2023d).
- **DRC:** Wealth generated from mining activities does not benefit the local population, leading to social unrest (Strauss, 2012).

Financial Systems and Capital Flight

War and political instability lead to currency depreciation, inflation, and loss of investor confidence.

- **South Sudan:** The local currency lost over 90% of its value, worsening inflation (IMF, 2023e; World Bank, 2023b).
- **Ukraine:** FDI declined due to war risks (IMF, 2023d).
- **DRC:** Capital flight is a major issue, as the elite transfer wealth abroad (Autesserre, 2010).

How the Power Theory of Economics Shapes Conflicts and Development

The Power Theory of Economics explains how economic structures, policies, and global forces either fuel or mitigate conflicts. Key insights include:

1. **Resource Control as a Driver of Conflict**

    - Nations with abundant resources but weak institutions are prone to conflict (Collier & Hoeffler, 2004).
    - **Example:** The DRC's resource wealth has led to decades of armed conflict rather than development (Qureshi, 2013).

2. **Financial Dependence Weakens Sovereignty**

   - Countries relying on foreign aid and external debt struggle to implement independent policies.
   - **Example:** Ukraine's reliance on IMF loans constrains its fiscal policies (Rother et al., 2016).

3. **Economic Policies Shape Conflict Outcomes**

   - Inclusive economic policies promote peace, while elite-driven policies perpetuate instability.
   - **Example:** South Sudan's mismanagement of oil revenues worsened tensions rather than reducing them (Stiglitz, 2017).

The Power Theory of Economics highlights the complex relationship between economic control, conflict, and development. In conflict-affected countries like South Sudan, Ukraine, and the DRC, economic resources are strategic assets that determine power structures and influence policy decisions and fuel instability. Addressing these challenges requires institutional reforms, equitable wealth distribution, and economic diversification. Without these, economic power will continue to be a source of conflict rather than a driver of development.

Comparative Analysis

Economic Power, Conflict, and Development in South Sudan, Ukraine, and the DRC

The case studies of South Sudan, Ukraine, and the DRC illustrate how economic power influences conflict and development outcomes. Despite differences in their historical and geopolitical contexts, these countries share common challenges in resource governance, economic policies, and institutional weaknesses. Table 9.1 below provides a comparative analysis.

Table 9.1 Comparative analysis of economic power, conflict, and development

Country	*Economic Power Structure*	*Key Conflict Drivers*	*Impact on Development*	*Economic Policy Trends*	*Resource Governance*	*Institutional Strength*
South Sudan	Oil revenue-dependent; controlled by the ruling elite	Ethnic and political rivalries over oil revenues	High poverty, food insecurity, and inflation	Resource-dependent; weak economic diversification	Poor; oil wealth mismanaged, financing conflict	Weak institutions, corruption, and a lack of enforcement
Ukraine	Mixed economy; influenced by geopolitical tensions	Russia-Ukraine war, foreign interference, and industrial loss	Decline in GDP, destruction of infrastructure, and high public debt	Structural economic reforms, reliance on international aid	Moderate; disrupted by war, reliance on EU/IMF	Moderate; governance challenges due to war
DRC	Mining-dominated economy, resource control by armed groups and foreign entities	Civil conflict, corruption, and illegal resource exploitation	Stunted economic growth, extreme poverty, and capital flight	Resource-extractive economy with little local reinvestment	Weak; foreign firms and rebel groups control mines	Weak; poor regulatory enforcement, instability

Key Observations from the Comparative Analysis

1. **Resource Dependence and Economic Volatility**

- South Sudan and the DRC are heavily dependent on resource exports (oil and minerals), making their economies highly vulnerable to price fluctuations and mismanagement (Collier & Hoeffler, 2004).
- Ukraine, despite its strong industrial base, has suffered economic contraction due to conflict and geopolitical disruptions (Rother et al., 2016).

2. **Conflict as a Barrier to Development**

- Prolonged conflicts in all three countries have led to the destruction of infrastructure, reduced investor confidence, and the displacement of skilled labour (Autesserre, 2010; IMF, 2023a).
- The DRC faces chronic instability due to illegal mining and warlordism, while Ukraine's conflict with Russia has weakened its economic sovereignty (Qureshi, 2013).

3. **Weak Institutional Capacity and Corruption**

- In South Sudan and the DRC, the corrupt elite control economic power, undermining equitable development (de Waal, 2014).
- Ukraine, while more institutionally resilient, struggles with corruption and external dependency (Sundberg & Melander, 2013).

4. **International Influence and Economic Sovereignty**

- Ukraine's economic recovery depends significantly on Western financial aid and investment, making it susceptible to external policy pressures (IMF, 2023b).
- South Sudan and the DRC, while rich in resources, are exploited by foreign corporations and neighbouring countries, limiting their economic autonomy (Autesserre, 2010).

Policy Recommendations for Mitigating Economic Power Struggles and Promoting Development

Based on the comparative analysis, the following recommendations aim to reduce economic power imbalances, strengthen institutions, and promote long-term development in conflict-affected nations.

Economic Diversification to Reduce Resource Dependence

- South Sudan and the DRC must shift away from excessive reliance on oil and mining by investing in agriculture, manufacturing, and service sectors (World Bank, 2023b).
- Ukraine can expand its technology, IT, and renewable energy industries to reduce dependency on traditional industries and trade vulnerabilities (Rother et al., 2016).

Strengthening Governance and Transparency in Resource Management

- Enforce strict anti-corruption laws and resource revenue transparency mechanisms (Collier, 2007).
- Implement Extractive Industries Transparency Initiative (EITI) standards to ensure that revenues from oil and mining benefit citizens, not the elite (Stiglitz, 2017).

Building Strong Financial Institutions to Stabilise Economic Systems

- Develop independent central banks that are insulated from political influence to maintain currency stability (IMF, 2023a).
- Expand financial inclusion programmes to provide small businesses and marginalised populations with access to capital (Qureshi, 2013).

Enhancing Regional and Global Economic Partnerships

- South Sudan and the DRC should negotiate better trade agreements with regional blocs such as ECOWAS, SADC, and the African Continental Free Trade Area (AfCFTA) (World Bank, 2023a).

- Ukraine should strengthen trade ties with the EU and explore new markets in Asia and Africa to balance geopolitical risks (Strauss, 2012).

Conflict Prevention and Peacebuilding Through Inclusive Economic Policies

- Invest in human capital (education and vocational training) to empower local populations and prevent conflicts over economic marginalisation (Collier & Hoeffler, 2004).
- Promote inclusive economic governance, ensuring that wealth from resources is reinvested in social services, infrastructure, and poverty reduction programmes (Autesserre, 2010).

Final Thoughts and Takeaways

The Power Theory of Economics provides a useful framework for understanding how economic power imbalances drive conflict and hinder development. The case studies of South Sudan, Ukraine, and the DRC illustrate that:

1. **Economic control is a critical determinant of political stability** – Countries where economic resources are monopolised by the elite or foreign actors are more vulnerable to conflict and instability.
2. **Resource wealth can be a curse if not managed properly** – Without effective governance, resource-rich nations often suffer from corruption, inequality, and chronic underdevelopment.
3. **Geopolitical conflicts disrupt economic sovereignty** – Ukraine's war with Russia and external dependencies demonstrate how global power struggles shape national economies.
4. **Institutional strength determines resilience** – Countries with strong institutions and transparent governance are more likely to escape the cycle of economic exploitation and conflict.

Path Forward: A New Economic Paradigm?

To break the link between economic power struggles and conflict, developing countries need to redefine their economic models:

- Move from resource extraction to knowledge-based economies.

- Strengthen domestic financial systems to reduce dependency on foreign aid.
- Prioritise inclusive development policies to prevent social and economic inequalities.

A combination of institutional reform, economic diversification, and regional cooperation will be essential for these countries to achieve sustainable development, economic independence, and long-term peace.

Economic Costs of Conflict

Conflict imposes significant economic costs on nations, affecting their short- and long-term development trajectories. The financial burden of conflict extends beyond immediate destruction, influencing investment, economic policies, and overall development.

Direct Costs of Conflict

- **Destruction of Infrastructure:** Conflicts destroy roads, bridges, power grids, and essential services, hampering economic productivity (Collier & Hoeffler, 2004).
- **Loss of Human Capital:** Wars displace populations, disrupt education, and cause brain drain, reducing future economic potential (World Bank, 2022c).
- **Capital Flight:** Investors and businesses relocate assets due to instability, leading to a decline in national wealth and reduced tax revenues (IMF, 2023d).

Indirect Costs of Conflict

- **Reduced Investor Confidence:** High political risk discourages FDI, slowing economic recovery (Rodrik, 2007).
- **Inflation and Weakened Currency:** Wars strain government budgets, leading to increased inflation and depreciation of the national currency (Stiglitz, 2002).
- **Disrupted Trade:** Conflict disrupts supply chains, limiting exports and imports, and reducing foreign currency reserves (Moyo, 2009).

Case Studies on the Economic Impact of Conflict

South Sudan: The Impact of Prolonged Conflict on Economic Stagnation

- Since independence in 2011, South Sudan has suffered civil wars that have damaged its oil-dependent economy.
- Oil revenue accounts for 90% of the national budget, yet conflict-driven disruptions led to a 60% GDP contraction between 2013 and 2018 (IMF, 2023a).
- Limited infrastructure and humanitarian crises further weaken economic recovery.

DRC and Ukraine: Resource-Driven Conflict and Economic Underdevelopment

- The DRC has vast mineral wealth, including cobalt, gold, and coltan, but ongoing armed conflicts have hindered development.
- Armed groups exploit mineral resources, leading to illegal trade and depriving the government of tax revenue (Acemoglu & Robinson, 2012).
- Ukraine's ongoing war has caused a 35% GDP decline in 2022 alone, with infrastructure damages exceeding $135 billion (World Bank, 2022c).

The Paradox of War Economies

- Conflicts often create illicit economic activities, benefiting a few, while deepening national poverty.
- Arms sales, smuggling, and illegal trade finance warlords and prolong conflicts, creating a self-perpetuating cycle of underdevelopment.
- **Example:** The DRC loses an estimated $1 billion annually due to illicit mineral exports (Ferguson, 2001) (Table 9.2).

Table 9.2 Hypothetical arms sales in conflict-affected nations (2025–2030)

Country	*2025*	*2026*	*2027*	*2028*	*2029*	*2030*	*Total Loss (2025–2030) in USD billion*
South Sudan	1.5	1.7	1.9	2.0	2.2	2.5	11.8
DRC	2.3	2.5	2.8	3.0	3.3	3.5	17.4
Ukraine	5.0	5.5	6.0	6.5	7.0	7.5	37.5

Higher-Level Analysis: How Drained Resources Constrain Development

- **Loss of Productive Investment:** Funds used for arms purchases could be redirected to education, healthcare, and infrastructure, fostering economic growth.
- **Debt Accumulation:** Many conflict-affected nations borrow heavily to fund wars, increasing debt burdens and reducing fiscal space for social programmes.
- **Human Capital Erosion:** Continued conflicts reduce literacy rates, increase migration, and weaken institutional capacity to implement development policies.
- **Undermined Institutional Trust:** Persistent conflict erodes trust in financial and governance institutions, deterring investment and economic stability.

Recommendations for Conflict-Affected Economies

- **Diversify Economic Foundations:** Reduce reliance on resource extraction and promote manufacturing and technology sectors.
- **Strengthen Governance:** Increase transparency in financial transactions to curb illicit trade and improve fiscal policies.
- **Enhance Regional Cooperation:** Support peace agreements and economic collaboration to stabilise conflict regions.
- **Leverage International Support:** Use aid effectively to rebuild economies and invest in social infrastructure.

Addressing these economic constraints, conflict-affected nations can transition towards sustainable development and long-term stability.

Power, Conflict, and Development in the Global Economy

How Global Superpowers Influence Conflicts in Developing Nations for Economic Gain

Global superpowers often exert influence over conflicts in developing nations to secure economic and strategic advantages. The DRC, Ukraine, and South Sudan exemplify how external actors manipulate internal conflicts for resource control, geopolitical influence, and economic gain (Collier & Hoeffler, 2004).

DRC

- The DRC has faced decades of conflict fuelled by its vast mineral wealth, including cobalt, gold, and coltan—key resources for global technology and energy sectors (Stearns, 2012).
- Global superpowers, including China and Western nations, compete for mining contracts and access to critical minerals, often backing different factions to maintain influence (Autesserre, 2010).
- The presence of multinational corporations has led to economic exploitation, with revenues benefiting foreign investors rather than local populations (Qureshi, 2013).

Ukraine

- Ukraine's strategic position as an energy transit country has made it a geopolitical battleground between Russia and the West (Mearsheimer, 2014).
- The 2014 annexation of Crimea and the 2022 Russian invasion have direct economic motivations, including control over natural gas pipelines and agricultural exports (World Bank, 2022c).
- Western economic sanctions on Russia have also influenced global energy markets, affecting oil and gas prices worldwide (IMF, 2023b).

South Sudan

- Since its independence in 2011, South Sudan has been embroiled in civil war, primarily due to control over vast oil reserves (de Waal, 2014).
- China, as the largest investor in South Sudan's oil industry, has provided economic and diplomatic support to maintain access to these resources (Large, 2016).
- The U.S. and other Western nations have leveraged aid and sanctions to push for governance reforms, but political instability continues to hinder economic development (World Bank, 2023b).

The Role of International Financial Institutions (IMF, World Bank) in Post-Conflict Recovery and Challenges

International financial institutions (IFIs) such as the IMF and the World Bank play a significant role in post-conflict recovery by providing financial assistance, policy guidance, and institutional reforms. However, their interventions are often criticised for imposing structural adjustment policies that may not align with local economic realities (Stiglitz, 2002).

- **IMF Structural Adjustment Programmes (SAPs)**: These programmes, implemented in post-conflict countries like the DRC and South Sudan, often require fiscal austerity, leading to reduced public spending on social services (Moyo, 2009).
- **World Bank's Development Initiatives**: While the World Bank has funded infrastructure and governance projects in post-conflict nations, its loan conditions can sometimes increase debt burdens, limiting long-term economic recovery (Rodrik, 2007).
- **Challenges in Implementation**: Many post-conflict countries lack the institutional capacity to effectively manage aid, leading to corruption, mismanagement, and continued dependency on external funding (Easterly, 2006).

The Economic Consequences of Sanctions, Foreign Aid, and Conditional Loans

Sanctions, foreign aid, and conditional loans play a crucial role in shaping the economic landscapes of conflict-affected nations. While these measures aim to pressure governments into policy reforms, they often have unintended economic consequences.

Economic Sanctions

- Sanctions on Russia due to the Ukraine war have disrupted global energy and commodity markets, causing inflation and supply chain disruptions (IMF, 2023b).
- U.S. and EU sanctions on South Sudanese officials have affected the country's oil revenue, limiting its ability to fund reconstruction efforts (de Waal, 2014).
- Sanctions on the DRC rebel groups have had mixed success in curbing illegal mineral trade but have also disrupted local economies (Stearns, 2012).

Foreign Aid and Dependency

- Countries like South Sudan and the DRC receive substantial humanitarian aid, but this often fosters dependency rather than self-sustaining economic growth (Moyo, 2009).

- In some cases, foreign aid has been misappropriated by the political elite, further fuelling corruption and instability (Collier, 2007).

Conditional Loans and Debt Crisis

- The IMF and World Bank impose conditions on loans, requiring structural adjustments that can sometimes lead to economic hardship (Stiglitz, 2002).
- Debt servicing limits fiscal space, reducing governments' ability to invest in development projects and social programmes (Rodrik, 2007).

Case Study: The Geopolitical Struggle over Africa's Mineral Resources (China Vs. the West)

Africa's mineral wealth has become a focal point of geopolitical competition between China and Western nations. The scramble for resources has significant economic and political implications.

China's Strategy

- China has invested heavily in Africa through its Belt and Road Initiative (BRI), securing access to key minerals such as lithium, cobalt, and rare earth elements (Brautigam, 2009).
- Chinese state-owned enterprises have acquired mining rights in the DRC, Zambia, and South Sudan, often providing infrastructure in exchange for resource contracts (Brautigam, 2009).

Western Counterstrategy

- The U.S. and EU have sought to counter Chinese influence through alternative infrastructure financing, such as the Global Gateway Initiative (World Bank, 2023a).
- Western companies emphasise corporate social responsibility and environmental standards, but these efforts are often seen as reactive rather than proactive (Ferguson, 2001).

Implications for African Development

- The competition between China and the West has led to increased FDI but has also resulted in exploitative practices, labour rights concerns, and environmental degradation (Autesserre, 2010).

- African nations struggle to negotiate fair deals, often ending up with unfavourable contracts that benefit foreign investors more than local economies (Moyo, 2009).

The intersection of power, conflict, and development in the global economy highlights the complexities of international influence over developing nations. While global superpowers manipulate conflicts for economic gain, international financial institutions attempt to support recovery—often with mixed results. Sanctions, foreign aid, and conditional loans shape economic outcomes but can also reinforce dependency. The geopolitical struggle over Africa's mineral wealth between China and the West underscores the importance of strategic resource management for sustainable development. To mitigate these challenges, developing nations must strengthen institutional governance, diversify economic structures, and negotiate fairer terms in international agreements.

Resolving Power Imbalances for Sustainable Development

Power imbalances in developing economies, particularly in post-conflict states, hinder sustainable development by reinforcing economic inequalities, limiting access to resources, and constraining policy autonomy. Addressing these disparities requires strengthening governance, promoting economic diversification, enhancing regional integration, and leveraging technology. Rwanda's post-genocide recovery offers a compelling case study of how institutional reforms can drive economic resilience and long-term stability.

Strengthening Governance and Institutional Frameworks to Reduce Economic Inequalities

Governance and institutional quality are key determinants of economic development. Weak institutions allow elite capture of resources, corruption, and inefficiency, deepening power imbalances (Acemoglu & Robinson, 2012). In contrast, strong governance structures promote transparency, equitable access to resources, and inclusive economic growth.

- **Anti-corruption and Rule of Law**: Countries that have successfully reduced economic disparities have implemented robust anti-corruption measures and strengthened judicial independence (Kaufmann et al., 2010). Rwanda's Anti-corruption Bureau, for example, has been instrumental in curbing illicit financial flows and ensuring equitable economic participation (World Bank, 2022a).

- **Decentralisation of Power**: Empowering local governments to make economic decisions can reduce over-centralisation of power and ensure resource allocation aligns with local needs (Rodrik, 2007). In Rwanda, decentralisation reforms have facilitated economic participation at the community level (Ansoms & Rostagno, 2012).
- **Inclusive Policymaking**: Policies that involve marginalised communities in decision-making help counteract elite dominance and foster economic inclusion (Sen, 1999).

Analytical Argument

Governance reforms are essential to dismantling entrenched power structures that perpetuate economic inequalities. Without strong institutions, economic policies risk being hijacked by the elite, further widening the wealth gap and stalling sustainable development.

The Importance of Economic Diversification in Post-Conflict Reconstruction

Post-conflict economies often suffer from over-reliance on a single sector, making them vulnerable to external shocks and perpetuating economic fragility. Economic diversification is critical to building resilience and reducing dependency on volatile industries.

- **Reducing Dependence on Natural Resources**: Many post-conflict nations, such as South Sudan and the DRC, depend heavily on oil and mineral exports, leading to the "resource curse" (Auty, 2001). Rwanda, on the other hand, has diversified its economy beyond agriculture to include services, ICT, and manufacturing (IMF, 2023c).
- **Enhancing Agricultural Productivity**: Agriculture remains a cornerstone of most African economies. Investing in agribusiness and value-added agricultural industries can create employment and stabilise economies (Collier, 2007).
- **Encouraging Private Sector Growth**: Post-conflict states need to create favourable conditions for small and medium-sized enterprises (SMEs) to thrive. Rwanda's investment in business-friendly policies has led to an increase in entrepreneurship and FDI (Gathani & Stoelinga, 2013).

Analytical Argument

A diversified economy reduces economic vulnerability and provides multiple pathways for sustainable growth. Without diversification, post-conflict states remain trapped in cycles of economic dependency, making them susceptible to external shocks and renewed instability.

Leveraging Regional Integration and Trade to Minimise Dependency on Foreign Powers

Many developing countries rely on external trade relationships with former colonial powers or global superpowers, reinforcing economic dependencies. Strengthening regional trade networks can mitigate these vulnerabilities.

- **The African Continental Free Trade Area (AfCFTA)**: This initiative aims to boost intra-African trade and reduce reliance on Western and Asian markets (UNECA, 2021). By promoting regional value chains, African economies can domestically retain more value.
- **Infrastructure Development for Trade**: Poor infrastructure remains a major bottleneck to regional trade. Investments in transport corridors, energy, and digital connectivity can enhance regional economic integration (World Bank, 2023a).
- **Policy Harmonisation**: Regional economic blocs such as ECOWAS and SADC play a vital role in policy alignment, ensuring smoother trade flows and regulatory consistency (World Bank, 2023a).

Analytical Argument

Regional integration fosters economic independence by creating alternative trade routes, reducing reliance on global powers, and strengthening economic resilience. Without regional economic cooperation, developing nations remain susceptible to external economic manipulation.

The Role of Technology and Innovation in Empowering Marginalised Economies

Technology and innovation are key drivers of economic transformation, offering new opportunities for marginalised economies to leapfrog traditional development barriers.

- **Digital Financial Inclusion**: Mobile banking and fintech have revolutionised access to financial services in countries like Kenya and

Rwanda, allowing previously unbanked populations to participate in the economy (Jack & Suri, 2016).

- **E-Governance for Transparency**: Digital governance tools can enhance transparency, reduce corruption, and improve service delivery (Hegre & Sambanis, 2006). Rwanda's e-governance initiatives have streamlined public services, reducing bureaucratic inefficiencies (World Bank, 2022a).
- **Tech Hubs and Startups**: Encouraging innovation through tech hubs and incubators fosters a culture of entrepreneurship and reduces reliance on foreign technology (Henderson et al., 2012).

Analytical Argument

Technology and innovation democratise access to economic opportunities, reducing power imbalances. Without investment in digital infrastructure and skills development, developing nations risk further economic marginalisation.

Case Study: Rwanda's Post-Genocide Economic Recovery Through Strong Institutions and Reforms

Rwanda's transformation from a conflict-ridden state in 1994 to one of Africa's fastest-growing economies highlights the importance of strong institutions, strategic policymaking, and inclusive governance.

- **Institutional Reforms** Rwanda implemented policies that prioritise transparency, accountability, and governance efficiency (Ansoms & Rostagno, 2012).
- **Economic Diversification**: While agriculture remains important, Rwanda has successfully developed its tourism, ICT, and manufacturing sectors (IMF, 2023c).
- **Investment in Human Capital**: Education and skills development have been central to Rwanda's strategy, ensuring that its workforce can support economic growth (World Bank, 2022a).
- **Infrastructure and Trade**: Rwanda's investment in regional trade and transport networks has strengthened its position as an economic hub in East Africa (UNECA, 2021).

Lessons from Rwanda

- Effective governance and anti-corruption measures create a stable economic environment.

- Diversification reduces economic vulnerability.
- Regional trade strengthens economic resilience.
- Technology accelerates economic inclusion.

Analytical Argument

Rwanda's recovery demonstrates that power imbalances can be resolved through strong institutions, diversification, regional integration, and technological advancements. Other post-conflict nations can draw lessons from Rwanda's governance model to achieve sustainable development.

Resolving power imbalances is fundamental to achieving sustainable development. Strengthening governance reduces economic inequalities, while economic diversification enhances resilience. Regional integration minimises dependency on foreign powers, and technology fosters economic inclusion. Rwanda's post-genocide recovery provides a model for post-conflict states seeking to overcome historical power imbalances and build inclusive economies. Addressing these issues through policy reforms, institutional strengthening, and strategic investments will be key to ensuring long-term stability and growth in developing economies.

High-Level Analytical Policy Recommendations and Future Prospects

Addressing power imbalances and economic inequalities that fuel conflicts require a comprehensive policy approach that incorporates governance reforms, financial system restructuring, international cooperation, and strategic economic planning. The following policy recommendations outline strategic interventions with scenario analysis for affected countries such as South Sudan, the DRC, and Ukraine.

Strategies to Reduce Economic Inequalities that Fuel Conflicts

Economic disparities, especially in resource-rich but poorly governed nations, exacerbate tensions and fuel prolonged conflicts. Targeted policies can mitigate these inequalities and foster long-term stability.

Policy Recommendations

- **Wealth Redistribution and Progressive Taxation:** Implementing progressive taxation policies, particularly on extractive industries, can fund social programmes that reduce inequalities (Stiglitz, 2012).
- **Land and Resource Reforms:** Establishing equitable land ownership rights and enforcing transparent resource management can prevent elite capture and communal tensions (Collier, 2007).
- **Social Protection Programmes:** Expanding cash transfers, universal healthcare, and educational subsidies can reduce economic disparities (Banerjee & Duflo, 2019).

Scenario Analysis

- **South Sudan:** A wealth redistribution policy targeting oil revenues could alleviate economic grievances among ethnic groups and reduce conflict over resource control. However, weak governance and corruption could undermine effectiveness.
- **DRC:** Improved mining sector transparency and revenue-sharing mechanisms would lessen regional inequalities and prevent armed groups from exploiting economic grievances.
- **Ukraine:** Post-war economic recovery should focus on decentralising economic opportunities to prevent regional disparities that could fuel future instability.

Policy Interventions to Reform Financial Systems and Ensure Economic Fairness

Weak financial institutions and unregulated capital flows contribute to economic instability. Reforming financial systems is crucial for ensuring fairness and broad-based economic growth.

Policy Recommendations

- **Strengthening Central Bank Independence:** Ensuring monetary policies are shielded from political influence helps maintain financial stability (Rodrik, 2017).
- **Inclusive Financial Systems:** Expanding banking access and digital financial inclusion fosters equitable economic participation (Jack & Suri, 2016).

- **Anti-corruption and Transparency Reforms:** Strengthening financial regulatory frameworks can prevent illicit financial flows and capital flight (OECD, 2021).

Scenario Analysis

- **South Sudan:** Establishing a sovereign wealth fund with transparent governance could help manage oil revenues fairly. However, political instability may threaten implementation.
- **DRC:** Strengthening the banking sector through microfinance and mobile banking initiatives can enhance access to financial services in rural areas.
- **Ukraine:** Post-war economic restructuring should prioritise strengthening financial institutions to ensure efficient capital allocation and prevent oligarchic control.

The Role of International Cooperation and Fair Trade Agreements in Promoting Stability

Unfair trade agreements and exploitative foreign investment deepen economic dependencies and reinforce power imbalances. A reformed international economic order is crucial for sustainable development.

Policy Recommendations

- **Negotiating Fair Trade Agreements:** Developing countries must push for trade deals that favour industrialisation and local value addition (Chang, 2002).
- **Debt Relief and Restructuring:** Cancelling or restructuring unsustainable debts can free up resources for economic development (Easterly, 2001).
- **Regulating FDI:** Ensuring that foreign investment supports local economies rather than exploiting resources is essential for fair growth (Rodrik, 2017).

Scenario Analysis

- **South Sudan:** Fairer oil trade agreements with regional partners could enhance revenue stability and reduce dependence on foreign aid.

- **DRC:** Renegotiating mining contracts with multinational companies to ensure fair revenue-sharing could curb resource exploitation and fund social programmes.
- **Ukraine:** Leveraging international aid for infrastructure reconstruction while maintaining economic sovereignty will be key to sustainable post-war recovery.

A Roadmap for Developing Countries to Harness Power Structures for Economic Growth

Developing nations need a strategic approach to harness power structures that currently constrain their economic potential. The roadmap below outlines a phased approach.

Phase 1: Institutional Strengthening (2025–2030)

- Implement governance reforms to enhance transparency and accountability.
- Strengthen regulatory frameworks to prevent resource mismanagement.
- Invest in human capital through education and vocational training.

Expected Outcomes

- Reduced corruption and improved policy implementation.
- A skilled workforce capable of driving economic transformation.

Phase 2: Economic Diversification and Industrialisation (2030–2035)

- Reduce reliance on commodity exports by investing in manufacturing and services.
- Promote SME growth and entrepreneurship through access to finance.
- Enhance infrastructure to support regional trade integration.

Expected Outcomes

- Increased employment opportunities and economic resilience.
- Reduced vulnerability to global commodity price fluctuations.

Phase 3: Global Economic Integration (2035–2040)

- Secure fair trade agreements that benefit domestic industries.

- Develop technological capabilities to compete in the global digital economy.
- Strengthen regional cooperation through trade blocs like AfCFTA.

Expected Outcomes

- Sustainable economic growth with reduced external dependencies.
- Increased geopolitical influence in global economic decision-making.

Prospects

Resolving power imbalances and reducing economic inequalities in conflict-affected countries requires bold policy interventions and international cooperation. Strengthening governance, reforming financial systems, and ensuring fair trade agreements can help nations like South Sudan, the DRC, and Ukraine achieve economic stability. However, successful implementation depends on strong political will, institutional capacity, and global collaboration.

Prospects for developing nations hinge on their ability to harness power structures for sustainable development. When leveraging regional integration, fostering innovation, and ensuring inclusive economic policies, these nations can break the cycle of dependency and emerge as influential players in the global economy.

What Is at Stake?

In examining the complex relationship between power, conflict, and economic development, the key findings underscore the profound impact of power dynamics on economic outcomes, particularly in SSA and other developing nations (Auty, 2001). Power struggles, whether they are local, national, or international in nature, significantly shape economic policies, access to resources, and financial systems (Collier, 2007). How power is distributed among different actors—governments, multinational corporations, the elite, and international powers—determines the trajectory of development and the potential for sustainable peace (Collier, 2007).

Key Findings: How Power Struggles Shape Economic Development

- **Power and Resource Control:** Who controls economic resources, particularly in resource-rich countries, directly influences economic outcomes. In conflict-prone regions like South Sudan and the DRC, the competition for resources often exacerbates tensions, undermines development, and hampers long-term peace (Auty, 2001).
- **Conflict and Policy Shifts:** Conflicts, driven by power struggles, disrupt economic policies and obstruct the efficient allocation of resources. In countries like Ukraine, economic policies often shift unpredictably due to external powers' interests, further destabilising the economy (Collier, 2007).
- **The Role of the Elite and Institutions:** The elite often play a crucial role in perpetuating inequality by controlling economic institutions that shape policies in their favour, undermining broader national development goals (Acemoglu & Robinson, 2012).

These findings illustrate that when power is concentrated in the hands of a few, economic development is stunted, leading to chronic instability and underdevelopment.

The Cost of Inaction: Stagnation, Increased Debt, and Continued Dependence on Foreign Aid

Easterly (2001) highlights that the failure to address the root causes of power imbalances and conflicts carries significant costs for economic development. If conflicts persist and power dynamics remain unaddressed, the consequences are as follows:

- **Stagnation:** Developing countries will continue to face slow growth, with weak institutions preventing the effective mobilisation of resources (Easterly, 2001).
- **Debt Accumulation:** The inability to create sustainable economic structures will result in continued reliance on loans, further exacerbating debt burdens (Easterly, 2001).
- **Continued Dependence on Foreign Aid:** Nations will remain dependent on foreign assistance, particularly in post-conflict recovery scenarios, leading to a cycle of reliance on external resources

rather than self-sufficiency. This perpetuates an economic and political dependency that stifles growth (Moyo, 2009).

Failure to act decisively means that countries like South Sudan, the DRC, and Ukraine may remain trapped in cycles of poverty and conflict, unable to escape the constraints of their power structures (Moyo, 2009).

The Window of Opportunity: Harnessing Power for Economic Transformation

Rodrik (2017) emphasises that despite these challenges, there is a window of opportunity. If power is harnessed effectively, there is potential for economic transformation in SSA and beyond by focusing on the following key areas:

- **Institutional Strengthening:** Building transparent, accountable institutions that can manage resources effectively will create a conducive environment for development (Rodrik, 2017).
- **Inclusive Economic Policies:** Ensuring that economic growth benefits all segments of society will reduce inequalities and address the root causes of conflict (Fosu, 2007).
- **Regional Integration and Trade:** Strengthening regional trade agreements and reducing dependency on external powers can empower nations to chart their own economic course (Fosu, 2007).

Fosu (2007) opines that the potential for economic transformation hinges on the ability of governments, institutions, and citizens to manage power more equitably and use it as a force for positive change.

Final Reflections: Is Economic Power an Enabler of Peace or a Driver of Conflict?

Economic power is a double-edged sword. On the one hand, when harnessed effectively, it can be an enabler of peace. Economic growth creates opportunities for all citizens, reducing the grievances that fuel conflict. Strong institutions, better governance, and equitable resource distribution can build the foundations for lasting peace. On the other hand, when economic power is concentrated in the hands of a few, it often becomes a driver of conflict. The competition for resources, particularly in conflict zones, can exacerbate divisions and fuel violence, as seen in South Sudan and the DRC.

The challenge lies in how power is distributed and managed. When power structures align with inclusive, development-oriented policies, economic power can indeed be a vehicle for peace. However, when power is monopolised by elite or foreign powers, it becomes a source of division and instability.

Proposed Equation for Power Theory of Economics, Conflict, and Development (Including Costs of Conflict Variable)

To integrate the costs of conflict into the equation, COC*t* is introduced, representing the economic burden of conflicts. The updated equation is:

$$\text{DEV}t = \alpha + \beta 1\text{PWR}t + \beta 2\text{CON}t + \beta 3\text{RES}t + \beta 4\text{INST}t + \beta 5\text{FDI}t + \beta 6\text{GDP}t + \beta 7\text{TRD}t + \beta 8\text{COC}t + \varepsilon t,$$

where:

- DEV*t* = Economic Development (GDP per capita, Human Development Index (HDI), etc.)
- PWR*t* = Power Concentration (elite dominance, institutional control)
- CON*t* = Conflict Intensity (measured by battle deaths, political instability index, internal displacement)
- RES*t* = Resource Wealth (natural resource rents as % of GDP)
- INST*t* = Institutional Strength (rule of law, corruption perception index)
- FDI*t* = (FDI inflows as % of GDP)
- GDP*t* = GDP Growth Rate
- TRD*t* = Trade Openness (sum of exports and imports as % of GDP)
- COC*t* = Costs of Conflict (measured in % of GDP lost due to war-related destruction, defence spending, displacement costs, loss of investor confidence, and capital flight)
- *εt*\varepsilon_*tεt* = Error term (capturing omitted factors affecting development)

Economic Interpretation of the Equation (Expanded with COCt)

1. **Costs of Conflict ($\beta 8COCt$)**

   - Conflict leads to direct costs (infrastructure destruction, displacement, loss of human capital) and indirect costs (weakened currency, inflation, capital flight).
   - Higher $COCt$ negatively impacts $DEVt$, slowing economic recovery.
   - **Example:** The conflict in South Sudan has cost the economy over 50% of its GDP (World Bank, 2023b), while in Ukraine, war-related damage exceeds $411 billion (IMF, 2023b).

2. **Power Concentration ($\beta 1PWRt$)**

   - Economic and political elite controlling key resources can either stabilise economies or fuel inequality and unrest.

3. **Conflict Intensity ($\beta 2CONt$)**

   - Prolonged conflicts reduce development by driving away investment and human capital.
   - **Example:** The DRC has faced continuous conflict, resulting in low economic diversification and high poverty rates (Ross, 2012).

4. **Institutional Strength ($\beta 4INSTt$)**

   - Strong institutions mitigate the negative effects of conflict by ensuring legal protections, transparency, and economic stability.
   - Rwanda's post-genocide recovery (1994 to present) highlights the importance of institutional rebuilding (Collier, 2007).

5. **Foreign Direct Investment ($\beta 5FDIt$)**

   - FDI can help conflict-affected economies recover, but is often diverted to stable regions.

6. **Trade Openness (*β*7TRD*t*)**

    - War economies may rely on illicit trade (e.g., arms, minerals, smuggling) instead of formal markets, reducing sustainable trade gains.

The proposed equation for the Power Theory of Economics, Conflict, and Development integrates various factors that influence economic development (DEV*t*) by accounting for power dynamics, conflicts, institutional strength, resource availability, and economic variables. Below is an explanation of each variable's relevance in addressing economic and developmental issues.

1. **PWR*t* (Power Dynamics):** Power structures within a country, whether political, economic, or social, determine the distribution of resources and influence policy decisions. Power imbalances can lead to inefficient governance, economic stagnation, or conflict. Understanding this helps address issues related to corruption, inequality, and elite capture.
2. **CON*t* (Conflict Presence or Intensity):** Conflicts, whether political, ethnic, or military, disrupt economic activities, deter investment, and destroy infrastructure. By incorporating conflict intensity, policymakers can identify regions where peacebuilding efforts or conflict mitigation strategies are essential.
3. **RES*t* (Natural Resource Endowments):** The presence of valuable resources such as oil, minerals, or arable land can drive economic growth, but can also lead to the **resource curse**, where mismanagement or conflicts over control of resources hinder development. Addressing this factor helps optimise resource management and prevent resource-driven conflicts.
4. **INST*t* (Institutional Quality):** Strong institutions, including legal frameworks, property rights, and governance systems, foster stability and economic development. Weak institutions, on the other hand, allow corruption and inefficiency to flourish, which hampers economic growth. Strengthening institutions is key to improving governance and economic performance.
5. **FDI*t* (Foreign Direct Investment):** FDI brings capital, technology, and expertise, boosting productivity and employment. However, political instability and weak institutions deter investors. Addressing these barriers can enhance FDI inflows, promoting sustained economic growth.

6. **GDPt (Gross Domestic Product Growth):** GDP represents overall economic performance and is a measure of a country's productive capacity. Understanding its relationship with power, conflict, and institutions helps in designing macroeconomic policies that drive sustainable development.
7. **TRDt (Trade Openness or Trade Volume):** Trade openness affects economic growth by providing access to global markets and fostering competition. However, conflicts, weak institutions, or power imbalances can distort trade benefits. Policymakers can leverage trade policies to promote equitable economic growth.
8. **COCt (Costs of Conflict):** This newly introduced variable quantifies the direct and indirect economic burden of conflicts, including destruction of infrastructure, loss of human capital, displacement, and reduced investor confidence. By explicitly incorporating the costs of conflict, decision-makers can assess trade-offs between military spending, peacebuilding efforts, and economic investments.
9. **εt (Error Term):** Represents unobserved factors affecting development that are not captured by the model.

Relevance in Solving Issues

This equation provides a comprehensive framework to analyse the interplay between power, conflict, and development. By quantifying the impact of power structures, institutional quality, and economic factors, policymakers can:

- Identify areas where power imbalances hinder development.
- Develop strategies to mitigate conflict and its economic burden.
- Strengthen institutional frameworks to improve governance.
- Promote FDI and trade policies to enhance economic growth.
- Implement peacebuilding measures by weighing the economic costs of conflict.

By integrating the costs of conflict (COCt), this model highlights the economic rationale for investing in peace, governance reforms, and conflict prevention to drive sustainable development.

High-Level Policy Implications

- **Conflict Prevention Is Key**: Countries need strong institutions (INST*t*) and governance frameworks to reduce power struggles and economic inequalities that drive conflict.
- **Post-Conflict Reconstruction Must Address Costs of Conflict (COC*t*)**:

- Investment in infrastructure rebuilding, education, and social welfare is critical for post-war recovery.
- **Example:** Germany's Marshall Plan (post-WWII) helped the economy recover within a decade.

- **Regional Cooperation Can Reduce Conflict Risk**: Greater regional integration and trade alliances can help post-conflict nations rebuild faster and diversify economies (Fosu, 2007).

Application of the Equation to Selected Developing Conflict Countries (Table 9.3)

Analysis of the Results

1. **Ukraine (Highest DEV*t*: 6.66)**

    - Despite the ongoing war, Ukraine scores the highest among the three countries due to stronger institutions (INST*t*), relatively higher GDP growth (GDP*t*), and better trade openness (TRD*t*).
    - However, its high cost of conflict (COC*t*) negatively impacts development, preventing even higher scores.
    - **Implication**: Strengthening institutions and attracting post-war investment will be key for Ukraine's recovery.

2. **DRC (Moderate DEV*t*: 5.42)**

    - The presence of significant natural resources (RES*t*) and improving institutional strength give the DRC an advantage over South Sudan.

Table 9.3 Computed Development Scores (DEV*t*) for selected countries

Country	*Computed DEVt*
South Sudan	4.31
DRC	5.42
Ukraine	6.66

- Conflict intensity (CON*t*) and the cost of conflict (COC*t*) remain major constraints to development.
- **Implication**: Better governance, resource management, and conflict resolution will enhance economic development.

3. **South Sudan (Lowest DEV*t*: 4.31)**

- The lowest score is driven by severe conflict intensity (CON*t*) and high costs of conflict (COC*t*), outweighing the benefits of its resource wealth.
- Weak institutions (INST*t*) and limited foreign investment (FDI*t*) further constrain growth.
- **Implication**: Stability, institutional reform, and economic diversification are essential for long-term development.

Policy Recommendations

- **Conflict Reduction**: Reducing conflict (lower CON*t* and COC*t*) will significantly improve DEV*t* scores, freeing up resources for economic growth.
- **Institutional Strengthening**: Higher INSTt correlates with better development outcomes. Governance reforms are critical.
- **Investment and Trade**: Encouraging FDI and improving trade openness (TRD*t*) will enhance resilience, particularly in the DRC and South Sudan. (Table 9.4)

Table 9.4 Key Drivers of Development (DEV*t*) in conflict-affected countries

Country	*Positive Factors*	*Negative Factors*
South Sudan	Resource wealth (RES*t*)	High conflict intensity (CON*t*), weak institutions (INST*t*), high cost of conflict (COC*t*)
DRC	Rich mineral resources (RES*t*), improving institutions (INST*t*)	Persistent armed conflicts (CON*t*), corruption, high cost of conflict (COC*t*)
Ukraine	Stronger institutions (INST*t*), economic resilience (GDP*t*), trade (TRD*t*)	War-related destruction, massive cost of conflict (COC*t*)

Table 9.5 Scenario-based impact on Development Scores (DEV*t*)

Country	*Original DEVt*	*Scenario 1: Conflict Reduction*	*Scenario 2: Institutional Reform*
South Sudan	4.31	5.53 (+1.22)	4.54 (+0.23)
DRC	5.42	6.50 (+1.08)	5.80 (+0.38)
Ukraine	6.66	7.61 (+0.95)	7.19 (+0.53)

Scenario Analysis: How Changes in Key Variables Affect Development

To explore potential improvements, we analyse what would happen if conflict intensity (CON*t*) and cost of conflict (COC*t*) were reduced while improving institutional strength (INST*t*).

*Scenario 1: Conflict Reduction (Lower CON*t *& COC*t *by 50%)*
Assuming conflict intensity (CON*t*) and cost of conflict (COC*t*) decrease by 50%, let us recalculate DEV*t*.

*Scenario 2: Institutional Reforms (Increasing INST*t *by 50%)*
Assuming institutional quality (INST*t*) improves by 50%, we analyse its impact on development.

We now compute these scenarios (Table 9.5).

Key Insights from Scenario Analysis

1. Scenario 1 (Conflict Reduction) has a stronger positive impact on development compared to Scenario 2 (Institutional Reforms).

- South Sudan benefits the most (+1.22), showing that reducing conflict is the most crucial factor for its economic improvement.
- Ukraine and the DRC also see significant gains, indicating that the economic burden of war is a major constraint.

2. Scenario 2 (Institutional Strengthening) still leads to positive development, but its effect is smaller.

- Stronger institutions help attract investment and promote stability, but do not immediately offset the damage from active conflicts.
- Ukraine benefits the most (+0.53), reflecting its higher initial institutional base and capacity to leverage reforms quickly.

Policy Recommendations

- **Prioritise Peacebuilding Efforts**: Reducing the cost of conflict ($COCt$) has the highest impact on improving development outcomes.
- **Strengthen Institutions Alongside Conflict Reduction**: While governance reforms help, they should be combined with conflict resolution for maximum impact
- **Leverage Trade and Investment for Stability**: Economic integration ($TRDt$, $FDIt$) should be part of long-term post-conflict recovery strategies.

Addressing Power and Conflict for Development

- If power imbalances persist, economic growth will remain stagnant, and conflicts will drain national resources.
- If managed effectively, economic power can be used to stabilise post-conflict economies and create long-term prosperity.
- The cost of inaction: If conflicts persist, SSA risks stagnation, increased debt, and continued dependence on foreign aid.
- The window of opportunity: If power is harnessed effectively, economic transformation is possible.
- Final reflections: Is economic power an enabler of peace or a driver of conflict?

Final Thoughts

Ultimately, the fate of developing nations lies in their ability to address the systemic issues that perpetuate power imbalances and conflicts. Economic power, when wielded responsibly and inclusively, can become a powerful tool for fostering development and peace. Conversely, neglecting these issues will leave nations vulnerable to stagnation, conflict, and continued dependence on external support. The path forward requires a concerted effort by national governments, international bodies, and citizens to ensure that power dynamics are reshaped in favour of long-term, inclusive growth.

References

Acemoglu, D., Johnson, S., & Robinson, J. A. (2003). An African success story: Botswana. In D. Rodrik (Ed.), *Search of prosperity: Analytic narratives on economic growth* (pp. 80–119). Princeton University Press. https://doi.org/10.1515/9781400845897-006

Acemoglu, D., & Robinson, J. (2012). *Why nations fail: The origins of power, prosperity, and poverty*. Profile Books.

Ansoms, A., & Rostagno, D. (2012). Rwanda's vision 2020 halfway through: What the eye does not see. *Review of African Political Economy, 39*(133), 427–450. https://doi.org/10.1080/03056244.2012.710836

Autesserre, S. (2010). *The trouble with The Congo: Local violence and the failure of international peacebuilding*. Cambridge University Press.

Auty, R. M. (2001). *Resource abundance and economic development*. Oxford University Press.

Banerjee, A. V., & Duflo, E. (2019). *Good economics for hard times*. PublicAffairs Publishers.

Brautigam, D. (2009). *The dragon's gift: The real story of China in Africa*. Oxford University Press.

Chang, H. J. (2002). *Kicking away the ladder: Development strategy in historical perspective*. Anthem Press.

Collier, P. (2007). *The bottom billion: Why the poorest countries are failing and what can be done about it*. Oxford University Press.

Collier, P., & Hoeffler, A. (2004). Greed and grievance in civil war. *Oxford Economic Papers, 56*(4), 563–595. https://doi.org/10.1093/oep/gpf064

Cramer, C. (2006). *Civil war is not a stupid thing: Accounting for violence in developing countries*. Hurst & Company.

De Waal, A. (2014). When kleptocracy becomes insolvent: Brute causes of the civil war in South Sudan. *African Affairs, 113*(452), 347–369. https://doi.org/10.1093/afraf/adu028

Easterly, W. (2001). *The elusive quest for growth: Economists adventures and misadventures in the tropics.* MIT Press.

Easterly, W. (2006). *The white man's burden: Why the west's efforts to aid the Rest have done so much ill and so little good.* Penguin.

Ferguson, N. (2001). *The cash nexus: Money and power in the modern world, 1700–2000.* Basic Books.

Fosu, A. K. (2007). *The political economy of development in sub-Saharan Africa: A critical approach.* Routledge.

Gathani, S., & Stoelinga, D. (2013). *Understanding Rwanda's agribusiness and manufacturing sectors.* International Growth Centre.

Hegre, H., & Sambanis, N. (2006). Sensitivity analysis of empirical results on civil war onset. *Journal of Conflict Resolution, 50*(4), 508–535. https://psycnet.apa.org/doi/10.1177/0022002706289303

Henderson, J. V., Storeygard, A., & Weil, D. N. (2012). Measuring economic growth from outer space. *American Economic Review, 102*(2), 994–1028.

International Monetary Fund (IMF). (2023a) World economic outlook: Navigating global divergences. International Monetary Fund.

International Monetary Fund (IMF). (2023b). *Ukraine economic update.* IMF Country Report No. 23/127. International Monetary Fund.

International Monetary Fund (IMF). (2023c). Rwanda: Economic outlook.. International Monetary Fund.

International Monetary Fund (IMF). (2023d). *Ukraine: Economic damage assessment report.* International Monetary Fund.

International Monetary Fund (IMF). (2023e). *South Sudan: Economic Outlook.* IMF Country Report No. 23/101. International Monetary Fund.

Jack, W., & Suri, T. (2016). The long-run poverty and gender impacts of mobile money. *Science, 354*(6317), 1288–1292. https://doi.org/10.1126/science.aah5309

Kaufmann, D., Kraay, A., & Mastruzzi, M. (2010). The worldwide governance indicators: Methodology and analytical issues. *Hague Journal on the Rule of Law, 3*(2). https://doi.org/10.1017/S1876404511200046

Khan, M. (2010). *Political settlements and the governance of growth-enhancing institutions.* SOAS Working Paper. https://soas-repository.worktribe.com/output/389203

Large, D. (2016). *China and South Sudan: Globalization and the politics of resources.* Bloomsbury.

Mearsheimer, J. (2014). Why the Ukraine crisis is the west's fault. The liberal delusions that provoked Putin. *Foreign Affairs, 93*(5), 77–89. https://www.jstor.org/stable/24483306

Minoiu, C., & Shemyakina, O. N. (2014). Armed conflict, household victimization, and child health in Côte d'Ivoire. *Journal of Development Economics, 108*, 237–255. https://doi.org/10.1016/j.jdeveco.2014.03.003

Mkandawire, T., & Soludo, C. C. (1999). *Our continent, our future: African perspectives on structural adjustment.* Africa World Press.

Moyo, D. (2009). *Dead aid: Why aid is not working and how there is a better way for Africa.* Penguin Books.

Murdoch, J. C., & Sandler, T. (2002). Economic growth, civil wars and spatial spillovers. *Journal of Conflict Resolution, 46*(1), 91–110. https://doi.org/10.1177/0022002702046001006

North, D. C., Wallis, J. J., & Weingast, B. R. (2009). *Violence and social orders: A conceptual framework for interpreting recorded human history.* Cambridge University Press.

Organization for Economic Cooperation and Development (OECD). (2021). *Illicit financial flows: The economy of illegal trade.* OECD Publishing.

Qureshi, M. S. (2013). Trade and thy neighbor's war. *Journal of Development Economics, 105*(C), 178–195. https://doi.org/10.1016/j.jdeveco.2013.07.009

Rodrik, D. (2007). *One economics, many recipes: Globalization, institutions, and economic growth.* Princeton University Press.

Rodrik, D. (2017). *Straight talk on trade: Ideas for a sane world economy.* Princeton University Press.

Ross, M. L. (2012). *The oil curse: How petroleum wealth shapes the development of nations.* Princeton University Press.

Rother, B., Pierre, G., Lombardo, D., Herrala, R., Toffano, P., Roos, E., Auclair, A. G., & Manasseh, K. (2016). *The economic impact of conflicts and the refugee crisis in the middle East and North Africa.* IMF Staff Discussion Note 16/8, International Monetary Fund.

Sen, A. (1999). *Development as freedom.* Oxford University Press.

Stearns, J. (2012). *Dancing in the glory of monsters: The collapse of The Congo and the great war of Africa.* PublicAffairs Publishers.

Stiglitz, J. (2002). *Globalization and its discontents.* W. W. Norton & Company.

Stiglitz, J. (2012). *The Price of inequality.* W. W. Norton & Company.

Stiglitz, J.E (2017) The overselling of globalization. Bus Econ 52, 129–137 (2017). https://doi.org/10.1057/s11369-017-0047-z

Straus, S. (2012). Wars do end! Changing patterns of political violence in sub-Saharan Africa. *African Affairs, 111*(443), 179–201. https://doi.org/10.1093/afraf/ads015

Sundberg, R., & Melander, E. (2013). Introducing the UCDP georeferenced event dataset. *Journal of Peace Research, 50*(4), 523–532. https://doi.org/10.1177/0022343313484347

United Nations Economic Commission for Africa (UNECA). (2021). *The African continental free trade area: Economic opportunities and challenges*. UNECA.

World Bank. (2022a). *Rwanda economic update*. World Bank Publication.

World Bank. (2022b). *The economics of conflict: The role of Financial Systems in war-Torn Economies*. World Bank Publication.

World Bank. (2022c). *Ukraine rapid damage and needs assessment report*. World Bank Publication.

World Bank. (2023a). *Global economic prospects: African development outlook*. World Bank Publication.

World Bank. (2023b). *South Sudan economic update*. World Bank Publication.

CHAPTER 10

Budgeting for Growth: Is BED a Game Changer?

Introduction

Defining the Budget for Economic Development (BED) Framework

Budgeting is a fundamental instrument of economic policy, shaping how governments allocate resources to drive growth and development. Traditionally, national budgets have followed either a line-item budgeting model or programme-based budgeting, focusing on expenditure control, fiscal discipline, and short-term financial planning. However, these traditional budgeting models often lack an explicit focus on long-term economic development goals and are typically structured to ensure administrative compliance rather than fostering sustained economic transformation.

The BED framework emerges as a strategic alternative, emphasising targeted investments in key sectors that directly contribute to economic expansion, structural transformation, and social equity. Unlike traditional budgeting models that primarily allocate funds based on historical spending patterns or administrative necessities, BED aligns fiscal policies with national development plans, aiming to optimise capital allocation for sustained economic growth and inclusive prosperity (Rodrik, 2013) (Table 10.1).

P. K. Kabeya, *Development and the Power Theory of Economics*,
https://doi.org/10.1007/978-3-032-07926-8_10

Table 10.1 Traditional Budgeting vs. Budget for Economic Development

Criteria	*Traditional Budget Model*	*Budget for Economic Development*
Focus	Short-term fiscal discipline, expenditure control	Long-term economic transformation and structural change
Structure	Line-item or programme-based, emphasising administrative efficiency	Development-oriented, linking budgeting with economic policy outcomes
Resource Allocation	Based on historical spending patterns or political considerations	Based on national development goals, prioritising investment in growth-enhancing sectors
Economic Growth Impact	Indirect; assumes that expenditure will contribute to economic stability	Direct; designed to stimulate productivity, employment, and structural transformation
Adaptability	Rigid, with limited flexibility to respond to changing economic needs	Dynamic, allowing adjustments based on macroeconomic trends and sectoral priorities
Measurement of Success	Budget compliance, deficit reduction, and spending efficiency	Economic growth, job creation, and structural improvements in production capacities

Source: Rodrik (2013)

The traditional model, particularly line-item budgeting, ensures accountability and transparency but often lacks economic flexibility (Wildavsky, 1986). In contrast, BED integrates national development plans, focusing on investments in critical sectors such as infrastructure, education, innovation, and industrial policy. This shift reflects a more strategic and outcome-driven approach, ensuring that fiscal policy directly supports economic expansion (Stiglitz, 2012).

Theoretical Foundations: Linking Economic Growth, Budgeting, and Power Theory

The Role of Budgeting in Economic Growth

Budgeting serves as a primary policy tool through which governments influence economic activities. The Keynesian school argues that government spending can stimulate demand, leading to increased economic growth, particularly during economic downturns (Keynes, 1936). The fundamental equation linking government expenditure and national output is expressed as:

$$Y = C + I + G + (X - M)$$

Where:

- Y = National output (GDP)
- C = Consumption
- I = Investment
- G = Government spending
- X–MX = Net exports

In this framework, an increase in government spending (GGG) through targeted BED allocations can lead to higher GDP growth. The fiscal multiplier effect further illustrates how public spending induces additional economic activity, leading to higher aggregate demand and employment (Blanchard & Perotti, 2002).

$$\Delta Y = \frac{1}{1 - MPC} X \Delta G$$

Where:

- ΔY = Change in national income
- MPC = Marginal Propensity to Consume
- ΔG = Change in government spending

A well-structured BED framework maximises this multiplier effect by ensuring that public investment is directed towards high-impact sectors, such as infrastructure, education, and industrial growth (Mankiw, 2014).

Power Theory and Its Influence on Budgeting

Power theory in economics explores how the political and economic elite shape budgetary decisions to reinforce their interests (Acemoglu & Robinson, 2012). In many economies, budget allocations are often influenced by institutional power structures, where rent-seeking behaviours, elite dominance, and policy capture divert resources away from productive economic uses.

According to structuralist economic theory, power asymmetries create inequitable fiscal policies, where governments prioritise sectors that benefit dominant economic groups while neglecting investments in broader developmental areas (Cardoso & Faletto, 1979). This dynamic often leads to economic inefficiencies, underfunded public services, and persistent inequality.

The BED framework seeks to counterbalance these power asymmetries by emphasising transparent, growth-oriented budget allocation mechanisms, ensuring that economic policies are not solely dictated by elite interests but serve broad-based developmental goals (Chang, 2002).

Budgeting, Development Finance, and Economic Transformation

The effectiveness of BED depends on sound development finance strategies that ensure sustainable public investment. Governments typically finance their budgets through tax revenues, domestic borrowing, and external funding from international financial institutions (Premchand, 2000). However, power dynamics at both domestic and international levels affect access to development finance.

- **Domestic Level**: Political influence over taxation policies and public expenditure often leads to inefficient budget allocations, benefiting special interest groups rather than the broader economy (Buchanan & Tullock, 1962).
- **International Level**: Institutions such as the IMF and World Bank influence national budgets through conditionality-based financing, which can limit policy autonomy and hinder development-oriented budgeting (Stiglitz, 2002).

To counter these challenges, BED emphasises mobilising domestic financial resources and structuring public investments to reduce external dependency, ensuring greater sovereign control over economic planning.

The BED framework represents a significant paradigm shift from traditional budgeting by prioritising long-term economic transformation over short-term fiscal discipline. By linking budgeting, economic growth, and power theory, BED provides a strategic mechanism for ensuring that government expenditure effectively drives sustained economic growth, structural transformation, and inclusive development (Bessler et al., 2011).

Power Theory and Budgeting in Economic Growth

Power Dynamics in Economic Decision-Making and Their Impact on National Budgeting

Power in economic decision-making refers to the ability of various actors, governments, the business elite, civil society, and international institutions to influence fiscal policy, resource allocation, and development priorities (Acemoglu & Robinson, 2012). National budgeting is not purely a technical exercise but a political and economic process, where competing interests negotiate control over public resources (Lukes, 2005).

Power dynamics in economic decision-making manifest in multiple ways:

1. **Political Elite and Fiscal Control**: Governments and ruling parties often control budget decisions, directing funds towards politically advantageous sectors rather than economically productive ones.
2. **Business and Corporate Influence**: Large corporations and industry lobbies push for favourable tax policies and subsidies, shaping budget priorities to suit their interests (Stiglitz, 2012).
3. **Civil Society and Public Advocacy**: Public participation in budget formulation can counterbalance elite dominance, but weak institutions and limited transparency often restrict civic engagement in decision-making (Baiman, 2006).
4. **International Financial Institutions (IFIs)**: Organisations such as the International Monetary Fund (IMF) and World Bank impose fiscal conditions on borrowing nations, affecting budgetary autonomy and economic sovereignty (Krugman, 2019).

These power dynamics create a hierarchy of influence where certain groups, especially the economic elite and international creditors, exert outsized control over budgetary priorities, often to the detriment of equitable development.

How Power Influences National Budget Formulation and Implementation

The formulation and execution of a national budget is a contested process shaped by different power structures. Power influences budgeting in the following key ways:

1. Budget Formulation and Agenda Setting
   (a) **Elite-Driven Priorities**: Political leaders and the ruling elite often prioritise projects that reinforce their electoral base rather than long-term economic transformation (Bragg, 2013). For example, populist policies such as fuel subsidies or cash transfer programmes may be emphasised over critical infrastructure or industrial investment.
   (b) **Business and Corporate Influence**: Powerful industries negotiate for tax incentives and subsidies, reducing government revenue for broader development programmes. In resource-rich economies, extractive industries influence budget policies to minimise taxation and maximise profit repatriation (Collier, 2007).
2. Budget Approval and Legislative Oversight
   (a) **Parliamentary Power Struggles**: In countries with strong legislative institutions, budget approval processes involve rigorous scrutiny. However, in many developing countries, weak parliamentary oversight allows the executive branch to dominate fiscal decisions, often leading to misallocation and inefficiencies (Shank & Govindarajan, 2016).
   (b) **Partisan Conflicts**: In democratic systems, opposition parties may block budget approvals for political leverage, leading to fiscal gridlock, as seen in U.S. government shutdowns over budget disagreements (Neely, 2007).
3. Budget Execution and Public Expenditure
   (a) **Patronage and Corruption**: Budget implementation can be distorted by rent-seeking behaviour, where public funds are diverted to politically connected actors. This is common in

many African and Latin American economies where procurement processes are opaque (Van der Stede, 2000).

(b) **Sectoral Biases**: Security and defence budgets often receive disproportionate allocations, particularly in authoritarian states, as leaders prioritise military spending to maintain political power (North et al., 2009).

Case Studies of Budget Power Struggles in Developing and Developed Economies

Nigeria: Oil Revenue and Political Budgeting

Nigeria's national budget is heavily dependent on oil revenue, leading to power struggles among the federal government, regional elite, and multinational oil companies. The government prioritises short-term spending over economic diversification, with recurrent expenditure consuming over 70% of the budget, leaving little for infrastructure and industrial development (Premchand, 2000). Power struggles over oil revenue allocation between state and federal authorities exacerbate economic inefficiencies (Ross, 2012).

Argentina: IMF Structural Adjustment and Budget Constraints

During Argentina's economic crisis in the early 2000s, the IMF imposed austerity measures as conditions for bailout loans. These budget cuts led to reduced social spending, sparking public protests and economic instability (Stiglitz, 2002). The IMF's control over fiscal policy decisions limited Argentina's sovereignty, demonstrating how international institutions shape national budget priorities (Blustein, 2005).

United States: Budget Deadlocks and Political Polarisation

The U.S. federal budget has been subject to political power struggles between the executive and legislative branches. Disagreements over taxation, public spending, and social programmes have led to government shutdowns, as seen in 2013 and 2018, affecting public services and economic stability (Hirt & Block, 2017). The dominance of corporate lobbyists also influences budget allocations, particularly in healthcare and defence spending (Horngren et al., 2005).

Ethiopia: Developmental State Budgeting Model

Ethiopia's government has implemented a state-led development budget model, prioritising infrastructure, industrial parks, and agricultural modernisation. This approach has successfully increased GDP growth, but power remains concentrated in the ruling political elite, limiting public accountability and transparency (Bragg, 2013). The government controls fiscal policies tightly, often sidelining parliamentary oversight and civil society participation.

The Role of International Financial Institutions in Shaping National Budgets

International Financial Institutions (IFIs) such as the IMF, World Bank, and regional development banks play a crucial role in influencing national budgets, especially in developing economies that rely on external financing. Their influence manifests in the following ways:

Conditionality and Structural Adjustments

The IMF's loan programmes often require governments to implement austerity measures, reducing budgetary allocations to social programmes, subsidies, and public investments. These conditions prioritise macroeconomic stability over developmental spending, restricting fiscal autonomy (Williamson, 1990).

Debt and Fiscal Sovereignty

Highly indebted countries face budget constraints due to debt-servicing obligations, limiting their ability to finance infrastructure, healthcare, and education. Countries like Ghana and Zambia have struggled with debt repayments, forcing budget cuts in critical sectors (Ndikumana & Boyce, 2011).

Privatisation and Market Reforms

The World Bank often promotes privatisation policies as part of budget restructuring programmes. While these policies attract investment, they sometimes lead to higher service costs and reduced public sector employment, affecting income distribution (Stiglitz, 2002).

Policy Advice and Technical Assistance

Beyond financial influence, IFIs provide policy recommendations on fiscal management, taxation, and expenditure reforms. While this expertise is valuable, it often reflects neoliberal economic principles, favouring free-market policies over state-led development (Rodrik, 2006).

Power plays a central role in national budgeting, influencing how resources are allocated, distributed, and utilised. The economic elite, political actors, and international institutions shape budgetary outcomes, often prioritising their interests over broad-based development goals. The case studies highlight how power struggles impact fiscal policy, demonstrating that effective budgeting requires institutional transparency, participatory governance, and policy autonomy to achieve sustainable economic growth.

Counterarguments to Power Theory in Budgeting and Economic Growth: Insights from Sub-Saharan Africa (SSA) and Beyond

While power theory provides a compelling framework for understanding how economic and political actors shape budgeting processes, it is not without criticism. Several counterarguments challenge the extent to which power alone determines national budgeting outcomes.

Rational Bureaucratic Models: Budgeting as a Technical Process

1. Counterargument

Some economists and policymakers argue that budgeting is primarily a technical and economic exercise, rather than a power struggle. According to public finance theories, governments allocate resources based on macroeconomic conditions, revenue generation, and developmental priorities rather than political influence (Musgrave & Musgrave, 1989).

2. Example from SSA

   (a) **Botswana** is often cited as an example where budgeting is evidence-based and guided by fiscal discipline rather than elite capture. The country's National Development Plans (NDPs) have been designed to prioritise economic diversification and long-term stability, reducing the risks of excessive political influence (Acemoglu et al., 2001).
   (b) **Rwanda** has implemented a performance-based budgeting system, which ensures that allocations are linked to measurable development outcomes rather than political favouritism (World Bank, 2021).

Institutional Safeguards and Democratic Accountability

1. Counterargument

Strong democratic institutions and independent oversight bodies mitigate the influence of the powerful elite in budgeting processes. Many OECD countries have parliamentary budget offices, fiscal councils, and public audits, ensuring that budgets are formulated through evidence-based policymaking rather than political power games (OECD, 2015).

2. Example from SSA

South Africa's Medium-Term Expenditure Framework (MTEF) has been widely recognised as a key instrument in promoting transparency, predictability, and accountability in public budgeting. Introduced in the late 1990s, the MTEF is a rolling three-year budgeting framework that allows government departments to plan and align their expenditures with national priorities over the medium term. It enables policymakers to set expenditure ceilings and allocate resources in a manner that is both strategic and forward-looking. By moving away from one-year incremental budgeting, the MTEF facilitates better planning, more consistent policy implementation, and greater fiscal discipline (Bessler et al., 2011).

One of the critical enablers of the MTEF's effectiveness in South Africa is the Public Finance Management Act (PFMA), which establishes principles for sound financial management and compels government departments and entities to operate within clearly defined fiscal rules. The PFMA, together with oversight from the National Treasury, helps ensure that budget allocations are guided by performance targets and fiscal constraints, rather than political discretion. As highlighted by Ncube (2020), this institutional arrangement reduces the risk of ad hoc and politically motivated spending, thereby promoting more stable and responsible fiscal management (Brigham & Ehrhardt, 2013)

The MTEF has had positive impacts on economic growth and development in South Africa by improving the credibility of fiscal policy and ensuring that public resources are allocated in line with national development priorities. In particular, the predictability of funding over multiple years has enabled line ministries to execute multi-year infrastructure and social development projects more efficiently. This has been especially important for sectors such as education, health, and public works, where long-term investments are essential. The emphasis on transparency has also strengthened donor and investor confidence, contributing to macroeconomic stability and improved governance (Berger & Bonaccorsi di Patti, 2006).

However, despite these strengths, there are several limitations in the application of the MTEF in South Africa. One major challenge lies in the disconnect between budget planning and actual implementation. Although the MTEF provides a structured framework for aligning policy objectives with expenditure, execution often falls short due to weak institutional capacity, procurement delays, and inefficiencies at the provincial and municipal levels. This implementation gap undermines the intended impact of the MTEF on service delivery and economic outcomes (Bhaduri, 2002).

Another limitation is the limited flexibility of the MTEF in responding to unforeseen economic shocks. While the framework enhances predictability, it can also constrain the government's ability to reallocate resources swiftly in times of crisis, such as during economic downturns, pandemics, or natural disasters. This rigidity may lead to underfunding of emerging priorities and reduce the government's fiscal agility (Schwalbe, 2015).

Additionally, there have been concerns about the quality of expenditure and the efficiency of public spending, even within the MTEF process. While the framework supports fiscal discipline, it does not always ensure that allocated resources are spent effectively or that they deliver the desired developmental outcomes. In some cases, recurrent expenditures have crowded out capital investments, limiting the transformative impact of public spending on long-term growth and structural development (Schwalbe, 2015).

Lastly, the capacity constraints in subnational governments, particularly at the municipal level, pose a significant challenge to the effective rollout of the MTEF. Although the framework is applied nationally, its success depends heavily on local institutions having the skills, systems, and accountability mechanisms to implement budgeted programmes. In many cases, weak financial management and poor oversight at the local level have led to inefficiencies and underspending, diminishing the development impact of public expenditure (Schwalbe, 2015).

In conclusion, South Africa's MTEF, supported by the PFMA and the oversight role of the National Treasury, has contributed significantly to improving fiscal governance, transparency, and the alignment of budgeting with national priorities. However, challenges such as weak implementation, limited responsiveness to shocks, subnational capacity gaps, and questions about spending quality continue to limit its full potential. Addressing these issues is crucial if the MTEF is to fully support inclusive economic growth and sustainable development in South Africa (Ncube, 2020).

In Ghana, the Fiscal Responsibility Act, 2018 (Act 982) was introduced by the Government of Ghana to address longstanding issues of macroeconomic instability and fiscal mismanagement. Over the years, Ghana has experienced persistent fiscal deficits, often resulting from overspending, particularly during election cycles. These deficits contributed to high levels of public debt, inflationary pressures, and instability in the exchange rate. The Act was therefore enacted as a strategic intervention to promote sound fiscal governance and macroeconomic stability (Sachs, 1989)

One of the central objectives of the Act was to promote fiscal discipline by introducing legally binding fiscal rules. Specifically, the law imposes a ceiling on the annual fiscal deficit, limiting it to no more than 5% of Gross Domestic Product (GDP). In addition, it requires the government to maintain a positive primary balance, meaning that government revenues must exceed non-interest expenditures. These provisions are designed to ensure that government spending remains within sustainable limits (Bell, 2003; Sachs, 1989).

The Act also aims to break the recurring pattern of fiscal indiscipline linked to political cycles. In the past, successive governments in Ghana have tended to increase spending significantly in the lead-up to elections, undermining economic stability. By instituting clear and enforceable fiscal rules, the Act seeks to insulate fiscal policy from short-term political pressures and reinforce accountability and transparency in the management of public finances (Bird, 2004).

Another important rationale behind the Act is to enhance investor and donor confidence. By committing to clear and credible fiscal targets, the government aimed to send a positive signal to investors, credit rating agencies, and development partners. This, in turn, was expected to improve Ghana's sovereign credit ratings, reduce the cost of borrowing, and attract more stable and long-term investments (Bell, 2003).

Furthermore, the Act supports long-term economic growth by ensuring macroeconomic stability, which is essential for a conducive business environment. Stable public finances allow the government to engage in better fiscal planning and implement development projects more effectively, ultimately contributing to poverty reduction and economic transformation.

To ensure compliance, the Act also includes enforcement mechanisms. These include requirements for the government to submit remedial action plans to Parliament in the event of a breach of fiscal targets, as well as regular reporting on fiscal performance. This ensures a level of accountability and transparency if targets are missed, and it holds public officials accountable for maintaining fiscal discipline (Sachs, 1989).

In summary, Ghana's Fiscal Responsibility Act of 2018 represents a significant step towards strengthening the country's fiscal framework. By institutionalising rules-based fiscal management, the Act aims to ensure fiscal discipline, reduce macroeconomic volatility, build investor confidence, and support sustainable economic growth (Bell, 2003).

Limited Scope and Rigid Deficit Target

One of the main weaknesses of the Fiscal Responsibility Act is its limited scope and the rigidity of its fiscal deficit ceiling. The law sets a fixed deficit ceiling of 5% of GDP, regardless of economic conditions or shocks. While this is meant to promote discipline, it does not allow sufficient flexibility to respond to economic downturns, external shocks (such as pandemics or commodity price collapses), or emergencies that may require increased government spending. In such situations, adhering strictly to a 5% limit can be unrealistic or even counterproductive, forcing the government either to underfund essential services or to resort to off-budget financing mechanisms that undermine transparency (Bell, 2003).

Weak Enforcement Mechanisms and Lack of Sanctions
Although the Act includes provisions for reporting and remedial action plans when fiscal targets are breached, it lacks strong enforcement mechanisms and clear, credible sanctions for non-compliance. There are no automatic penalties or binding consequences for political leaders or public officials who fail to meet the fiscal targets. This limits the deterrent effect of the law and makes it possible for governments to violate the rules with little or no accountability. As a result, compliance with the Act can be undermined by political considerations, especially in election years (Bird, 2004).

Political Interference and Lack of Institutional Independence
Another critical weakness is the potential for political interference in the implementation of the Act. The monitoring and reporting responsibilities largely rest with the Ministry of Finance, which is a political institution subject to government influence. There is no independent fiscal oversight body, such as a Fiscal Council, to provide objective analysis and ensure impartial assessment of fiscal performance. Without such independent oversight, it becomes difficult to hold the government accountable or to publicly challenge non-compliance with the fiscal rules (Basu, 1997).

Poor Track Record of Compliance
It can be argued that since the Act's adoption, there have been instances of non-compliance with its core provisions, especially during periods of fiscal stress. For example, during the COVID-19 pandemic, the government suspended the Act's requirements, citing the need for emergency expenditure. While this suspension may have been justifiable in the short term, it revealed the fragility of the framework and the ease with which rules can be overridden. This sets a precedent that may encourage future governments to abandon fiscal rules whenever they become politically inconvenient, thereby undermining the long-term credibility of the law.

Inadequate Transparency and Public Engagement
The success of any fiscal responsibility framework depends on transparency and public engagement. However, the Fiscal Responsibility Act does not include robust provisions for public consultation, civil society oversight, or

citizen participation in fiscal monitoring. The reporting requirements to Parliament, while useful, are not always timely or comprehensive, and they often fail to generate meaningful public debate. This lack of transparency weakens democratic accountability and limits the role of external stakeholders in enforcing fiscal discipline (Basu, 1997).

Focus on Deficit Control at the Expense of Broader Fiscal Sustainability

While the Act focuses heavily on controlling the fiscal deficit, it pays less attention to other aspects of fiscal sustainability, such as the composition of public spending, debt quality, and the efficiency of revenue collection. The law does not provide adequate guidance on how the government should prioritise expenditures or manage rising debt service costs. As a result, even if the fiscal deficit is kept within the legal limit, the government may still face long-term fiscal pressures due to inefficient spending and unsustainable borrowing (Sachs, 1989).

In summary, while the Fiscal Responsibility Act of 2018 represents a commendable effort to institutionalise fiscal discipline in Ghana, it suffers from several structural and practical weaknesses. These include inflexible targets, weak enforcement, political interference, lack of independent oversight, poor compliance, and limited public accountability. Addressing these issues, through amendments to the Act or complementary reforms, would be necessary to strengthen Ghana's fiscal governance framework and ensure long-term economic stability (IMF, 2019).

The Role of Economic Constraints Over Political Power

1. Counterargument

Economic constraints, rather than power dynamics, often dictate national budgets. Factors such as global market fluctuations, tax revenue generation, and economic shocks limit policymakers' ability to manipulate budget allocations for political gain.

2. Example from SSA

   (a) During the COVID-19 pandemic, many African economies, including Nigeria and Kenya, were forced to reprioritise budgets due to revenue shortfalls. Governments had to reallocate funds towards healthcare and economic recovery programmes, illustrating how economic conditions, rather than elite power, shaped budgetary decisions (AfDB, 2022).

(b) In Zambia, the government had to seek debt restructuring from the IMF after excessive borrowing led to unsustainable debt levels. The IMF's fiscal conditions forced Zambia to implement austerity measures, including subsidy reductions, demonstrating how economic realities can override political power in budgeting (Gallagher, 2021).

Public Participation and Policy Transparency in Budgeting

1. Counterargument

Advocates of participatory budgeting argue that public engagement mechanisms reduce elite dominance and create more inclusive fiscal policies. In several countries, citizen involvement in budgeting has challenged elite control over public finances (Baiman, 2006).

2. Example from SSA

   (a) Uganda's participatory budgeting approach has led to greater citizen involvement in local government budget decisions, improving accountability and service delivery (Mbate, 2018).
   (b) In Kenya, the 2010 Constitution introduced devolved government structures, which mandated public participation in county budget formulation, reducing the dominance of the central government elite (Wanyama & McCluskey, 2017).

International Financial Institutions (IFIs) and National Sovereignty

1. Counterargument

While IFIs like the IMF and World Bank influence national budgets through conditionalities, some scholars argue that borrowing nations still maintain fiscal sovereignty by choosing to accept or reject policy recommendations.

2. Example from SSA

(a) Ethiopia's developmental state model has demonstrated how governments can pursue independent economic policies while engaging IFIs selectively. Despite receiving World Bank and IMF support, Ethiopia has largely maintained control over its national budgeting priorities, prioritising public investment in infrastructure and industrialisation (Gebregziabher, 2019).
(b) Tanzania, under former President John Magufuli, resisted IMF austerity measures and instead focused on domestic resource mobilisation to fund infrastructure projects, highlighting how national sovereignty can override external financial pressures (Mosha, 2020).

A Balanced View

While power theory provides valuable insights into budgetary struggles, counterarguments highlight the role of economic constraints, institutional safeguards, public participation, and technical fiscal management in shaping national budgets. In sub-Saharan Africa, cases from Botswana, Rwanda, Ghana, Kenya, and South Africa illustrate that economic realities and institutional frameworks also play critical roles in national budgeting, countering the argument that the power elite solely dictate fiscal policies.

Power Theory and Budgeting in Economic Growth

Power Dynamics in Economic Decision-Making
Power theory is central to understanding how economic decisions are made, particularly in the formulation and implementation of national budgets. Economic power can be defined as the ability of individuals, institutions, or states to influence resource allocation and policy decisions (Lukes, 2005). In this regard, economic decision-making is not merely a technical exercise but a deeply political process influenced by power structures at the national and international levels.

There are multiple dimensions to power in economic governance:

- **Structural Power**: The ability of dominant economic actors (e.g., multinational corporations, financial institutions) to set the terms of economic policy (Strange, 1996).
- **Institutional Power**: The control exercised through legal frameworks, central banks, and government institutions that determine budgetary allocations (Acemoglu & Robinson, 2012).
- **Discursive Power**: The role of ideas, narratives, and ideologies (e.g., neoliberalism) in shaping economic policy (Foucault, 1979).

Governments and the financial elite use these forms of power to control budget formulation, determining who benefits from economic policies and who bears the costs.

How Power Influences National Budget Formulation and Implementation

Power influences national budgets in both positive and negative ways.

Positive Implications of Power in Budgeting

- Strong governance and fiscal discipline: When power is exercised responsibly, it results in sound fiscal policies, stable macroeconomic environments, and sustainable public finances (North, 1990).
- Efficient resource allocation: Governments with well-structured institutions allocate budgets effectively, prioritising sectors like education, healthcare, and infrastructure (Rodrik, 2007).
- Economic stability and investor confidence: Countries with transparent budgetary processes attract investment, ensuring long-term economic growth (Stiglitz, 2017).

Negative Implications of Power in Budgeting

- **Corruption and elite capture**: In developing countries, budgetary processes are often manipulated by the elite to serve their interests rather than the public good (Acemoglu & Robinson, 2012).
- **Resource misallocation**: Political considerations may lead to excessive military spending or wasteful subsidies rather than productive investments (Collier, 2007).
- **Lack of accountability**: In authoritarian regimes, budgetary power is often concentrated in the executive branch, leading to opaque fiscal management and debt accumulation (Moyo, 2009).

Case Studies of Budget Power Struggles: Developing vs. Developed Economies

Comparing budget struggles in developed and developing economies provides insight into why some succeed while others fail.

Sub-Saharan Africa (SSA)

Many SSA countries struggle with budget formulation due to weak institutions, corruption, and dependence on foreign aid. For example, Nigeria's budgetary process is often delayed due to power struggles between the executive and legislative branches (Iyoha & Oriakhi, 2008). Additionally, misallocation of oil revenues leads to economic inefficiencies and persistent poverty.

Asia

In Asia, countries like China have centralised power, enabling strong fiscal discipline and long-term budget planning. However, in countries like Pakistan, frequent military interventions have led to inconsistent economic policies and budgetary instability (Hussain, 2018).

Developed Economies

Developed countries such as Germany and Sweden succeed due to institutionalised checks and balances, independent central banks, and strong fiscal rules (Alesina & Perotti, 1996). The European Union's Stability and Growth Pact ensures budgetary discipline, preventing excessive deficits (Buti et al., 2003).

Why Developing Countries Fail and Developed Countries Succeed

Institutional Quality: The Foundation of Effective Budgeting

Key Argument

Strong institutions are the cornerstone of effective economic governance, preventing excessive executive influence over national budgets and ensuring transparency and accountability (North, 1990). Developed economies have independent central banks, budget offices, and oversight agencies that limit political interference in fiscal policy. These institutions help ensure that budgets reflect economic priorities rather than short-term political interests.

For instance, in Germany, the Bundestag (parliament) exercises strong oversight over fiscal policies, ensuring fiscal discipline through constitutional debt limits (Alesina & Perotti, 1996). Similarly, the United States' Congressional Budget Office (CBO) provides independent economic analyses to guide policy decisions (Stiglitz, 2017).

Counterarguments

- **Institutional Quality Alone Does Not Guarantee Success**: Even in developed economies, institutions can be compromised. The 2008 global financial crisis exposed weaknesses in financial regulation, particularly in the U.S., where corporate lobbying weakened oversight institutions (Brigham & Ehrhardt, 2013).
- **Institutions Can Be Hijacked by the Elite**: Even when formal institutions exist, the political and economic elite may capture them for personal gain. In countries like South Africa, corruption scandals have shown how executive overreach can undermine institutional independence (Acemoglu & Robinson, 2012).
- **Gradual Institutional Building in Developing Countries**: Some scholars argue that expecting developing countries to rapidly achieve the institutional quality of developed economies ignores historical context. Many developed countries took **centuries** to build their institutions (Rodrik, 2007).

Implication for Developing Countries

While institutional quality is crucial, it must be complemented by broader economic reforms, public participation, and anti-corruption efforts to be truly effective.

Political Stability: A Safeguard Against Arbitrary Budgeting

Key Argument

Political stability fosters predictable and evidence-based fiscal policies, preventing arbitrary budgetary decisions. Developed economies benefit from stable governance structures, ensuring that budgets align with long-term economic goals rather than short-term political cycles (Acemoglu & Robinson, 2012).

In Scandinavian countries, for instance, multi-party cooperation ensures that fiscal policies are consensus-driven and not subject to abrupt changes due to political transitions. The United Kingdom's Office for Budget Responsibility (OBR) provides independent budget forecasts, preventing politically motivated over-promises (Buti et al., 2003).

Counterarguments

- **Stability Can Mask Inertia and Inequality**: Some argue that political stability does not always mean effective governance. For example, in Japan, long-term one-party dominance (LDP) has sometimes led to policy stagnation and excessive government debt (Bragg, 2013).
- **Authoritarian Stability vs. Democratic Stability**: Some developing countries (e.g., China, Rwanda) have achieved strong economic growth under authoritarian stability, whereas some democratic states (e.g., India, Brazil) struggle with frequent budget reversals due to coalition politics (Rodrik, 2013).
- **Political Instability in Developed Countries**: Even developed economies face challenges. The U.S. government shutdowns (e.g., 2013, 2018) show how political gridlock can disrupt budget processes (Krugman, 2019). Similarly, the Eurozone crisis (2009–2013) exposed fiscal instability in Southern European economies like Greece and Italy (Stiglitz, 2017).

Implication for Developing Countries

Political stability is necessary but not sufficient for sound budgeting. Democratic institutions, the rule of law, and political maturity must accompany stability to ensure that budgets serve developmental needs rather than elite interests.

Economic Diversification: Reducing Vulnerability to External Shocks

Key Argument

Economic diversification enhances fiscal resilience by reducing dependence on a single commodity or industry. Developed economies, such as the United States, Germany, and Japan, have diverse economic bases, including manufacturing, services, technology, and agriculture (Rodrik, 2007). This enables them to withstand global price fluctuations better than developing economies that rely on commodities like oil (Nigeria, Venezuela), copper (Zambia, Chile), or agriculture (Ethiopia, Sudan).

For instance:

- **Norway** has invested its oil revenues into a sovereign wealth fund, ensuring fiscal stability even when oil prices decline (Hirt & Block, 2017).
- **South Korea** transitioned from an agrarian economy in the 1960s to a global technology and industrial powerhouse, reducing its reliance on a single sector (Chang, 2002).

Counterarguments

- **Diversification Requires Structural Reforms and Takes Time**: Many developing countries struggle to diversify due to weak infrastructure, poor education systems, and limited access to technology (Hausmann et al., 2011).
- **Commodity Booms Can Provide Short-Term Stability**: Some scholars argue that commodity wealth, if well-managed, can fund diversification efforts. For example, Botswana has successfully reinvested diamond revenues into education and infrastructure (Acemoglu et al., 2001).
- **Developed Economies Are Also Vulnerable**: Economic diversification does not eliminate risk. The 2008 financial crisis showed how overreliance on the financial sector can destabilise even advanced economies (Stiglitz, 2017). Similarly, the COVID-19 pandemic exposed vulnerabilities in service-oriented economies (Baldwin & Mauro, 2020).

Implication for Developing Countries

Developing economies should pursue strategic industrial policies, invest in human capital, and leverage technology to achieve long-term diversification. This requires state intervention, foreign investment, and infrastructure development.

The Interdependence of Institutions, Politics, and Economic Structure

While institutional quality, political stability, and economic diversification are critical for sound budgetary practices, their impact depends on contextual factors such as governance structures, historical development patterns, and global economic conditions.

- Institutions provide the framework for budgetary discipline, but they must be protected from elite capture.
- Political stability ensures predictable policies, but must be accompanied by democratic governance.
- Economic diversification enhances resilience, but requires long-term commitment and investment.

For developing countries, achieving these three pillars of effective budgeting requires a multi-faceted approach, balancing policy reform, investment, and governance improvements to foster sustainable development.

Role of International Financial Institutions in Shaping National Budgets: Key Arguments and Counterarguments

International financial institutions (IFIs) such as the International Monetary Fund (IMF) and the World Bank play a significant role in influencing national budgets, especially in developing countries. Their interventions range from financial aid and policy advice to structural economic reforms, often impacting fiscal decision-making and national sovereignty. However, their influence is highly contested, with arguments both in favour and against their involvement.

Positive Influence of IFIs

Macroeconomic Stability

Key Argument
The IMF provides financial assistance and policy advice to promote fiscal discipline, inflation control, and stable exchange rates (Easterly, 2001). This is crucial for countries facing budget deficits, economic crises, or hyperinflation.

- **Example:** Greece's bailout (2010–2015) under IMF-EU programmes helped stabilise its financial system after the sovereign debt crisis (Reinhart & Rogoff, 2013).
- **Counterargument:** IMF stabilisation measures often involve strict austerity, reducing public spending and worsening social inequalities (Stiglitz, 2002). Critics argue that such policies prioritise creditors over citizens.

Debt Management and Sustainability

Key Argument
IFIs help countries restructure debt, negotiate favourable repayment terms, and implement sustainable fiscal policies to prevent default (Stiglitz, 2002).

- **Example:** The Heavily Indebted Poor Countries (HIPC) Initiative (1996) allowed many African nations to receive debt relief, freeing up fiscal space for development projects (Collier, 2007).
- **Counterargument:** Critics argue that IFIs' debt conditionalities often force governments to cut essential public services. Zambia and Malawi, for example, had to reduce healthcare spending to meet IMF debt targets, affecting public welfare (Moyo, 2009).

Technical Assistance and Institutional Reforms

Key Argument
The World Bank and IMF provide technical support for public financial management reforms, increasing budget transparency, efficiency, and accountability (Collier, 2007).

- **Example:** Public Expenditure and Financial Accountability (PEFA) programmes have improved financial governance in countries like Rwanda and Indonesia (World Bank, 2015).
- **Counterargument:** While technical support can be beneficial, it often comes with Western economic biases, leading to one-size-fits-all solutions that may not suit local contexts (Rodrik, 2007).

Negative Influence of IFIs

Austerity Measures and Social Consequences

Key Argument
IMF-imposed structural adjustment programmes (SAPs) in the 1980s and 1990s forced many African and Latin American countries to reduce social spending, leading to higher poverty, inequality, and economic instability (Mkandawire & Soludo, 1999).

- **Example:** In Nigeria and Ghana, SAPs led to cuts in education and healthcare budgets, worsening social outcomes (Williamson, 1990).
- **Counterargument:** The IMF argues that fiscal consolidation (reducing deficits) is necessary for long-term economic stability. Some countries, such as Chile and South Korea, successfully recovered from crises after SAPs (Birdsall et al., 2001).

Loss of National Sovereignty

Key Argument
External conditionalities imposed by IFIs limit governments' autonomy in budgetary decisions, forcing them to prioritise debt repayment and foreign policy interests over domestic needs (Williamson, 1990).

- **Example:** In Argentina (2001 crisis), IMF conditions restricted public spending, exacerbating economic distress (Stiglitz, 2002).
- **Counterargument:** Proponents argue that IFIs impose conditions to prevent fiscal mismanagement and ensure that funds are used effectively (Easterly, 2001).

Privatisation Pressures and Public Service Cuts

Key Argument
The World Bank's push for privatisation has often led to the underfunding of critical public services, as governments shift resources towards profit-driven models (Moyo, 2009).

- **Example:** In Bolivia, IMF-backed privatisation of water utilities led to price hikes and public protests (Shiva, 2002).

- **Counterargument:** IFIs argue that privatisation increases efficiency and investment. For example, telecom privatisation in India led to higher productivity and economic growth (Rodrik, 2007).

Balancing Power and Fiscal Sovereignty

While international financial institutions play a crucial role in budget stability and economic reforms, their influence is not without controversy. Policymakers in developing countries must carefully balance IMF and World Bank recommendations with national priorities, ensuring that economic policies serve long-term development goals rather than short-term fiscal targets.

Developing economies should push for greater policy flexibility, improved debt management strategies, and alternative financing mechanisms (such as regional development banks) to reduce dependency on IFIs while benefiting from their expertise

National Budgets and Economic Development: Strengths and Weaknesses

National budgets are crucial tools for economic development, influencing growth, income distribution, and long-term sustainability. Governments adopt various budgeting approaches to align fiscal policies with economic growth objectives. However, budget implementation faces challenges, including inefficiencies, elite capture, and resource misallocation. This analysis explores the traditional approaches to budgeting, their positive and negative effects, key budgetary strengths and weaknesses, and comparative insights from successful and failed budget implementations.

Traditional Approaches to Budgeting for Economic Growth

Line-Item Budgeting (Incremental Budgeting)

Definition

Allocates funds based on historical expenditures, with slight adjustments for inflation or political priorities (Wildavsky, 1986).

- **Positive Effects**
  - Ensures predictability and stability, allowing ministries to plan long-term projects (Keynes, 1936).
  - Used successfully in Japan to maintain consistent public infrastructure investments (Horngren et al., 2005).
- **Negative Effects**
  - Can lead to rigidity and inefficiency, as outdated programmes continue receiving funds regardless of performance (Schick, 1998).
  - In Nigeria, incremental budgeting led to inflated administrative costs and corruption (Neely, 2007).

Performance-Based Budgeting (PBB)

Definition
Allocates resources based on outcomes and efficiency metrics (Shank & Govindorajan, 2016).

- Positive Effects:
  - Improves accountability and efficiency, as seen in Chile, where PBB led to enhanced education and healthcare spending efficiency (Afonso et al., 2005).
- Negative Effects:
  - Complex implementation in developing countries due to weak institutional capacity (Van der Stede 2000).
  - In Uganda, PBB reforms failed due to poor data collection and bureaucratic resistance (Bessler et al., 2011).

Zero-Based Budgeting (ZBB)

Definition
Requires justification of all expenditures from scratch, avoiding automatic budget renewals (Berger & Bonaccorsi di Patti, 2006).

- **Positive Effects:**

- Eliminates wasteful spending, ensuring resource allocation aligns with national priorities (Schick, 1998).
- Successfully applied in China's infrastructure boom, prioritising high-impact projects (Bhaduri, 2005).

- **Negative Effects:**
  - Time-consuming and resource-intensive, making it impractical for large bureaucracies (Bhaduri, 2000).
  - In Tanzania, ZBB implementation led to delays in budget approval and execution, reducing government efficiency (Bhaduri, 2002).

Budgetary Strengths

Infrastructure Investment

Argument
Budget allocations to infrastructure (roads, energy, water) drive long-term economic growth by reducing production costs and improving competitiveness (Aschauer, 1989).

- **Example:** South Korea's infrastructure-focused budget planning in the 1960s and 1970s facilitated rapid industrialisation (Chang, 2002).
- **Counterargument:** Poorly planned infrastructure spending can lead to debt accumulation and inefficient investments (Easterly & Servén, 2003).
  - **Example:** Brazil's excessive infrastructure borrowing in the 1980s led to a debt crisis, requiring IMF intervention (Stiglitz, 2002).

Social Spending (Health and Education)

Argument
Budgets prioritising health and education create a productive workforce, boosting economic growth (Becker, 1964).

- **Example:** Finland's budget emphasis on education reform in the 1990s improved labour productivity and innovation (Bertero, 1994).

- **Counterargument:** Over-reliance on social spending without parallel economic policies can lead to fiscal deficits and dependency (Tanzi & Schuknecht, 2000).
  - **Example:** Venezuela's excessive social spending without economic diversification led to hyperinflation and economic collapse (Bekaert et al., 2001).

Fiscal Discipline

Argument
Strict budgetary controls and deficit management promote macroeconomic stability and investor confidence (Alesina & Perotti, 1996).

- **Example:** Germany's constitutional debt brake (Schuldenbremse) ensures balanced budgets, stabilising the economy (Bekaert & Harvey, 2003).
- **Counterargument:** Excessive fiscal discipline can limit growth, especially during recessions (Shank & Govindarajan, 2016).
  - **Example:** Greece's strict austerity measures under IMF-EU oversight (2010–2015) worsened unemployment and social unrest (Reinhart & Rogoff, 2013).

Budgetary Weaknesses

Inefficiencies in Budget Execution

Argument
Weak institutional capacity leads to budget underspending, delays, and leakages (Bragg, 2013).

- **Example:** Kenya's budget execution gaps (2015–2019) saw only 60% of allocated funds used for development projects (World Bank, 2022).
- **Counterargument:** Technological solutions like digital public financial management systems (e.g., IFMIS) can reduce inefficiencies (Schwalbe, 2015).

Elite Capture and Corruption

Argument
Budgeting processes in weak institutions favour the political elite, diverting resources from essential services (Acemoglu & Robinson, 2012).

- **Example:** In Angola, oil revenues enriched the elite while infrastructure and healthcare remained underfunded (Hodges, 2004).
  Counterargument: Anti-corruption reforms, such as public budget transparency laws, improve accountability (Bekaert et al., 2005).
  Example: Brazil's participatory budgeting (Porto Alegre model) reduced corruption and improved service delivery.

Brazil's participatory budgeting model, particularly pioneered in Porto Alegre in the late 1980s, has become a global reference for inclusive and transparent governance. The model involves direct citizen participation in the allocation of public resources, enabling communities to decide how a portion of the municipal budget should be spent. Over time, this model was applied in approximately 40% of Brazil's more than 5500 municipalities by the early 2000s, although the depth and consistency of implementation varied significantly across regions. In Porto Alegre itself, around 20% of the city's total budget, primarily capital investments, was subject to participatory processes, which proved highly effective in targeting local needs and improving public accountability (Shank & Govindarajan, 2016).

The efficiency of the participatory budgeting model was evident in several measurable outcomes. Studies have shown that municipalities adopting participatory budgeting witnessed a substantial decline in corruption levels. This was largely due to increased public scrutiny, transparent allocation processes, and civic empowerment, which collectively reduced opportunities for mismanagement of public funds. Additionally, investment in basic services such as sanitation, healthcare, and education increased significantly in areas guided by citizen input. As a result, the Human Development Index (HDI) in cities practising participatory budgeting rose more rapidly compared to others, indicating tangible improvements in the quality of life (Schwalbe, 2015).

In terms of economic growth and development, participatory budgeting fostered more equitable infrastructure investment, particularly in underserved and low-income neighbourhoods. By aligning public spending with community priorities, local governments were able to stimulate inclusive growth, enhance social cohesion, and build public trust. Infrastructure improvements such as better roads, schools, and healthcare facilities contributed to higher productivity and reduced transaction costs for local businesses, indirectly supporting local economic expansion (Schwalbe, 2015).

Moreover, the model had a pronounced impact on poverty reduction. By channelling resources to the most disadvantaged communities, participatory budgeting helped close service delivery gaps and provided a platform for marginalised voices to be heard in decision-making processes. Over time, this led to improved access to public services, greater social equity, and reduced income disparities. In Porto Alegre, for example, access to sewerage in poorer neighbourhoods increased from 46% to 98% within a decade of implementing participatory budgeting. Thus, the model not only enhanced governance but also served as a powerful tool for advancing inclusive development and reducing poverty (Schwalbe, 2015).

Figure 10.1 below illustrates the progressive adoption and impacts of participatory budgeting (PB) in Brazil between 1990 and 2010. As the number of municipalities implementing PB increased, two key indicators improved: the Human Development Index (HDI) rose steadily, reflecting gains in education, health, and income, while poverty rates declined sharply. This visual evidence supports the conclusion that participatory budgeting not only improved governance but also contributed meaningfully to economic development.

It can be argued that while Brazil's participatory budgeting (PB) model, particularly the Porto Alegre approach, has demonstrated significant benefits in improving service delivery, reducing poverty, and promoting inclusive governance, it is not without its limitations. Despite its success in certain municipalities, the scalability and consistency of the model across Brazil have faced notable challenges.

One of the primary weaknesses is the limited scope of budgetary control. Typically, only a small portion of the total municipal budget, often around 20%, is subject to participatory decision-making, with the remaining funds allocated through traditional political channels. This means that while communities could influence capital investment decisions, they had little to say in recurrent expenditures, such as salaries or long-term contracts, limiting the overall impact of their participation on broader fiscal policy (Schwalbe, 2015).

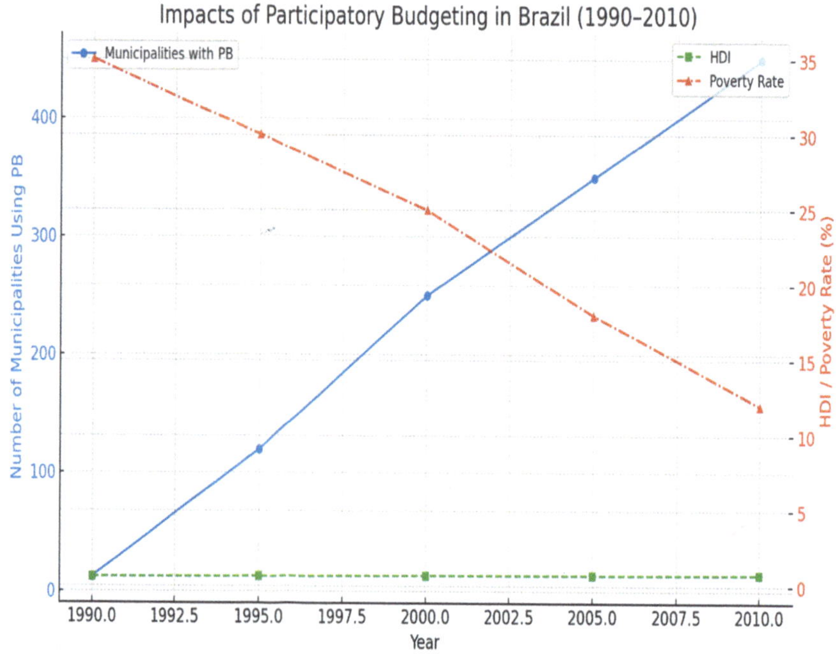

Fig. 10.1 Impacts of participatory budgeting in Brazil (1990–2010)

It is noted that another issue is variability in implementation. The quality and effectiveness of participatory budgeting processes varied significantly across municipalities. In some areas, PB became symbolic, with limited actual influence on spending decisions. This was often due to a lack of political will, insufficient institutional support, or weak technical capacity at the local level to facilitate meaningful citizen engagement. In such cases, PB risked becoming a token exercise rather than a genuine mechanism for democratic governance.

Political manipulation and elite capture also emerged in some contexts. Local politicians occasionally used PB forums to consolidate their political support by favouring vocal or organised groups, sidelining more marginalised voices. Where strong civil society was absent or poorly organised, more influential participants could dominate the process, undermining the principles of equity and inclusiveness (Schwalbe, 2015).

Additionally, citizen fatigue and participation decline were observed over time. Initial enthusiasm often waned as communities experienced delays in project implementation or saw limited tangible results, especially in cases where municipal administrations failed to follow through on agreed priorities. The bureaucratic nature of municipal planning also discouraged sustained community involvement, particularly among low-income and less-educated residents.

Lastly, the economic impact of PB remains localised. While it has improved infrastructure and basic services in participating neighbourhoods, PB alone is not a substitute for broader macroeconomic and structural reforms. Its contributions to national economic growth are indirect and limited primarily to improving local-level efficiency, accountability, and human capital development.

It can be argued that, although participatory budgeting has had notable successes, such as reducing poverty, improving HDI, and enhancing transparency, it also faces structural, political, and institutional challenges. These weaknesses highlight the importance of complementary reforms, including political commitment, institutional strengthening, and expanded fiscal scope, to maximise the transformative potential of participatory governance

Misallocation of Resources

Argument

Political priorities often lead to misdirected spending, favouring short-term electoral gains over long-term development (de Mesquita et al., 2013).

- **Example:** India's agricultural subsidies benefit large landowners more than small farmers, distorting market incentives (Schwalbe, 2015)
- **Counterargument:** Evidence-based budgeting frameworks, such as randomised controlled trials (RCTs), improve policy effectiveness (Banerjee & Duflo, 2011) (Table 10.2).

Policy Implications

Budgeting for economic development requires balancing fiscal discipline, social investment, and infrastructure spending. Successful countries ensure

Table 10.2 Comparative analysis: Success vs. failure in budget implementation

Factor	*Successful cases*	*Failed cases*
Fiscal Discipline	Germany (Debt Brake Rule)	Greece (Austerity Crisis)
Infrastructure Spending	South Korea (Industrialisation)	Brazil (1980s Debt Crisis)
Social Spending	Finland (Education Model)	Venezuela (Hyperinflation)
Corruption Control	Brazil (Participatory Budgeting)	Angola (Elite Capture)
Budget Execution	Rwanda (Efficient Planning)	Kenya (Underspending Issues)

Source: Schwalbe (2015)

transparency, institutional strength, and long-term planning, while failed cases suffer from corruption, inefficiencies, and political distortions.

To improve budget effectiveness, developing countries should adopt:

- Data-driven budgeting approaches (e.g., performance-based frameworks).
- Stronger fiscal institutions and anti-corruption mechanisms.
- Diversified economic strategies to reduce dependency on volatile revenues.

The Proposed BED Framework

Conceptualising BED as a Tool for Sustainable Economic Growth

The BED framework is an advanced budgeting approach that prioritises long-term economic sustainability, inclusive growth, and strategic resource allocation. Unlike traditional budgeting, which often focuses on short-term fiscal balance, BED aligns public expenditure with economic diversification, human capital development, and infrastructure expansion (Rodrik, 2007).

Key Characteristics of BED

- **Strategic and Forward-Looking:** Ensures budget allocations align with national development plans and global goals like the Sustainable Development Goals (SDGs) (Shank & Govindarajan, 2016).

- **Outcome-Oriented:** Measures success by economic growth, employment rates, and poverty reduction rather than just fiscal discipline (Afonso et al., 2005).
- **Resilience-Focused:** Adapts to economic shocks and structural changes through counter-cyclical fiscal policies (Blanchard et al., 2010).

Example: China's Five-Year Plan budgeting approach aligns public investment with long-term industrialisation and innovation goals, contributing to sustained GDP growth and poverty reduction (Lardy, 2019).

Key Components and Principles of the BED Framework

The BED framework consists of the following key components (Table 10.3):

- Economic Growth-Driven Expenditure Prioritisation

Table 10.3 Distinctions between BED and traditional budgeting

Criteria	*Budget for economic development*	*Traditional budgeting*
Focus	Long-term sustainable economic growth	Fiscal balance and expenditure control
Approach	Strategic, growth-oriented	Incremental, based on historical spending
Economic Resilience	Counter-cyclical, adapting to shocks	Often pro-cyclical, worsening downturns
Expenditure Prioritisation	High-return investments in infrastructure, education, and innovation	Often politically driven, maintaining the status quo
Sectoral Emphasis	Diversification into technology, manufacturing, and the green economy	Frequently focused on traditional industries
Institutional Mechanisms	Transparent, data-driven, participatory budgeting	Centralised, often influenced by political pressures
Impact on Development	Reduces poverty, increases employment, fosters industrialisation	May maintain existing inequalities and inefficiencies

Source: Hirt and Block (2017)

  - Focuses on productive sectors such as infrastructure, education, and industrialisation (Aschauer, 1989).
  - Encourages private-sector participation and public-private partnerships (PPPs) (*World Bank*, 2019).

- Fiscal Sustainability and Macroeconomic Stability

  - Adopts counter-cyclical spending to manage economic downturns (Keynes, 1936).
  - Limits excessive borrowing while ensuring strategic investment (Reinhart & Rogoff, 2013).

- Institutional and Governance Strengthening

  - Promotes transparency, accountability, and anti-corruption mechanisms (Acemoglu & Robinson, 2012).
  - Uses evidence-based decision-making and independent fiscal oversight bodies (Tanzi & Schuknecht, 2000).

- Equity and Inclusivity

  - Directs spending towards social welfare, education, and healthcare to foster human capital development (Becker, 1964).
  - Reduces regional disparities through targeted development programmes (Sachs, 2005).

- Economic Diversification and Resilience

  - Shifts away from commodity-dependent economies by supporting manufacturing, technology, and services (Rodrik, 2007).
  - Strengthens small and medium enterprises (SMEs) to enhance economic resilience (Hirt & Block, 2017).

Distinctions Between BED and Traditional Budgeting

Key Strengths of BED

- Aligns with national development strategies and SDGs (Brigham & Ehrhardt, 2013).

- Reduces economic volatility through diversified revenue sources (Rodrik, 2007).
- Encourages public-private partnerships (PPPs) and innovation in fiscal management (*World Bank*, 2019).

Key Limitations of BED

- Requires strong institutional capacity and transparent governance (Acemoglu & Robinson, 2012).
- May face political resistance due to reallocation of resources from entrenched interests (North, 1990).
- Needs accurate data and forecasting mechanisms, which are lacking in many developing economies (Collier, 2007).

Potential Challenges and Limitations of BED

While BED offers a compelling framework for economic growth, several challenges must be addressed:

- Institutional Weaknesses and Corruption Risks

  - Weak fiscal oversight and elite capture may divert funds from development priorities (Acemoglu & Robinson, 2012).
  - Solution: Implement strong anti-corruption laws and independent fiscal councils (Tanzi & Schuknecht, 2000).

- Short-Term Political Pressures

  - Governments may prioritise electoral spending over long-term BED goals (de Mesquita et al., 2013).
  - Solution: Establish multi-year budgeting frameworks with legislative safeguards (*World Bank*, 2019).

- Limited Fiscal Space and Debt Sustainability Concerns

  - Developing economies often have high debt levels, limiting fiscal manoeuvrability (Reinhart & Rogoff, 2013).
  - Solution: Strengthen domestic revenue mobilisation through tax reforms and efficient public expenditure (IMF, 2022).

- Resistance to Structural Reforms
  - Bureaucracies accustomed to traditional budgeting may resist BED's performance-based approach (Schick, 1998).
  - Solution: Capacity-building programmes and technological adoption in public financial management (Cangiano et al., 2013).
- Economic and Political Uncertainty
  - External shocks such as commodity price fluctuations and geopolitical instability can undermine BED implementation (Rodrik, 2007).
  - Solution: Diversify revenue streams and create economic stabilisation funds (Blanchard et al., 2010).

The BED framework represents a transformative approach to fiscal management, shifting from short-term budget balancing to long-term economic sustainability. By prioritising growth-enhancing investments, institutional reforms, and economic diversification, BED can drive inclusive development and macroeconomic stability. However, its success depends on strong governance, institutional integrity, and adaptive fiscal strategies. Policymakers must address political resistance, fiscal constraints, and implementation challenges to unlock BED's full potential.

The Proposed Budget for Economic Development (BED) Equation

To formalise the BED framework, an equation can be constructed that integrates key components of sustainable budgeting, economic growth, and fiscal discipline. The proposed BED equation is:

$$\text{BEDt} = \alpha It + \beta Ht + \gamma Dt + \delta Gt - \lambda Bt - \mu Ct - \theta Pt.$$

Where:

- **BEDt** = Budget for Economic Development in year **t**
- **It** = Infrastructure investment

- **Ht** = Human capital investment (education, healthcare, social protection)
- **Dt** = Economic diversification efforts (industrialisation, technology, SMEs)
- **Gt** = Governance and institutional quality (transparency, anti-corruption measures)
- **Bt** = Budget deficits and debt servicing
- **Ct** = Cyclical economic shocks (external factors like commodity price changes)
- **Pt** = Political distortions (elite capture, election-year overspending)
- **α,β,γ,δ,λ,μ,θ\alpha, \beta, \gamma, \delta, \lambda, \mu, \theta α,β,γ,δ,λ,μ,θ** = Weights assigned to each variable, reflecting their impact on economic development

Explanation of Variables and Their Implications

Positive Contributors to BED

- Infrastructure Investment (It)

  - **Rationale:** Physical infrastructure (transport, energy, telecommunications) is a key driver of economic productivity and industrial growth (Aschauer, 1989).
  - **Implication:** Increased public investment in infrastructure enhances trade efficiency, employment, and GDP growth.
  - **Key Argument:** Infrastructure spending has high economic multipliers and spurs private sector investment (Schwalbe, 2015).
  - **Counterargument:** Poorly managed projects lead to cost overruns, corruption, and debt traps (Bragg, 2013).

- Human Capital Investment (Ht)

  - **Rationale:** Education, healthcare, and social spending improve workforce productivity, innovation, and long-term economic resilience (Becker, 1964).
  - **Implication:** Higher human capital investment leads to better employment outcomes and social stability.

- **Key Argument:** Countries with higher education and healthcare spending tend to have stronger economic performance (Schwalbe, 2015).
- **Counterargument:** Without proper reforms, high education spending may not translate into economic competitiveness (Van der Stede, 2000).

- Economic Diversification (Dt)

  - **Rationale:** Reducing reliance on primary commodities and expanding industrial and service sectors mitigates economic vulnerability (Rodrik, 2007).
  - **Implication:** Diversified economies are more resilient to global shocks, as seen in East Asian industrialisation (Chang, 2002).
  - **Key Argument:** Industrial policy fosters high-value-added sectors, boosting national income (Wade, 1990).
  - **Counterargument:** Government-led diversification efforts may fail due to misallocation and political interference (Hirt & Block, 2017).

- Governance and Institutional Quality (Gt)

  - **Rationale:** Transparency, anti-corruption frameworks, and fiscal discipline improve resource allocation (Acemoglu & Robinson, 2012).
  - **Implication:** Strong institutions ensure budget efficiency and prevent elite capture.
  - **Key Argument:** Countries with strong governance structures experience higher economic growth (North, 1990).
  - **Counterargument:** Institutional reforms are difficult to implement in weak democracies with entrenched interests (Brigham & Ehrhardt, 2013).

Negative Constraints on BED

- Budget Deficits and Debt Servicing (Bt)

  - **Rationale:** High fiscal deficits and debt repayments reduce the government's ability to invest in development (Reinhart & Rogoff, 2013).

  - **Implication:** Excessive borrowing can trigger financial crises and IMF-imposed austerity measures.
  - **Key Argument:** Governments should adopt sustainable debt policies to prevent fiscal distress (Easterly, 2001).
  - **Counterargument:** Some debt-financed investments (e.g., infrastructure) have long-term growth benefits if properly managed (Hirt & Block, 2017).

- Cyclical Economic Shocks (Ct)

  - **Rationale:** Commodity price volatility, global recessions, and financial crises impact national budgets (Rodrik, 2007).
  - **Implication:** Resource-rich developing countries suffer from economic instability when global commodity prices fall.
  - **Key Argument:** Countries should establish sovereign wealth funds to manage resource revenues (Collier, 2007).
  - **Counterargument:** Even well-managed stabilisation funds may not fully mitigate economic downturns in highly dependent economies (Bessler et al., 2011).

- Political Distortions (Pt)

  - **Rationale:** Electoral cycles and political patronage lead to inefficient budget allocation and unsustainable spending (de Mesquita et al., 2013).
  - **Implication:** Election-year spending surges often lead to fiscal crises in developing countries.
  - **Key Argument:** Independent budget oversight institutions can improve fiscal discipline (Tanzi & Schuknecht, 2000).
  - **Counterargument:** Political realities make it difficult to enforce strict budgetary controls without democratic buy-in (Bessler et al., 2011).

Key Implications of the BED Equation

1. The balance between productive investment and fiscal constraints determines economic success

(a) High spending on infrastructure, human capital, and diversification can spur growth but must be carefully managed to avoid unsustainable deficits and debt accumulation.
(b) Example: China's state-led investment strategy has driven growth, but concerns over debt sustainability remain (Lardy, 2019).

2. Governance quality is a critical determinant of BED effectiveness
   (a) Countries with strong institutions (e.g., Norway, South Korea) use budgets efficiently, while corrupt governments (e.g., Venezuela, Nigeria) misallocate resources.

3. Macroeconomic stability and diversification enhance fiscal resilience
   (a) Commodity-dependent economies like Angola and Venezuela struggle with budget volatility, whereas diversified economies like Malaysia and Singapore have stable revenue bases.

The BED equation provides a structured approach to evaluating national budgets and their impact on economic development. To enhance budget efficiency and economic resilience, policymakers should:

- Prioritise Infrastructure and Human Capital Investments
  - Increase education, healthcare, and infrastructure spending to foster long-term growth.
- Strengthen Institutional Governance
  - Implement anti-corruption measures and ensure transparent budget processes.
- Adopt Counter-Cyclical Fiscal Policies
  - Build sovereign wealth funds to mitigate economic shocks.
- Ensure Fiscal Sustainability
  - Limit excessive borrowing and focus on productive debt investments.
- Promote Economic Diversification
  - Develop manufacturing, technology, and service industries to reduce reliance on commodities.

To conduct further quantitative modelling of BED performance, a more detailed approach is required by applying various economic and fiscal indicators to compute the BED scores across the selected countries (DRC, South Sudan, Zambia, South Africa, Malawi, Botswana, Mozambique, Zimbabwe, and Asia countries). This will involve synthesising hypothetical data over the 2020–2030 period and computing BED scores using the following components:

BED Equation Recap

The BED formula is as follows:

$$\text{BED} = \frac{\begin{array}{l} \textit{Infrastructure} + \textit{Social Spending} + \textit{Economic Diversification} \\ + \textit{Fiscal Discipline} + \textit{Governance} \end{array}}{\textit{Budget Defici} + \textit{Public Debt} + \textit{Corrupton Index}}$$

Where each component represents the following:

- **Infrastructure Investment**: Amount allocated to long-term infrastructure projects (infrastructure spending % of GDP).
- **Social Spending**: Total spending on health, education, and social services (as % of GDP).
- **Economic Diversification**: The degree of diversification in the national economy (higher diversification = stronger economy).
- **Fiscal Discipline**: Ability to maintain fiscal balance, including low deficit and debt-to-GDP ratio.
- **Governance**: Institutional quality, including anti-corruption measures, rule of law, and budget transparency.

The denominators represent the negative factors impacting the budget:

- **Budget Deficit**: The percentage by which government expenditure exceeds revenue.
- **Public Debt**: National debt as a percentage of GDP.
- **Corruption Index**: A measure of the level of corruption in the public sector (scale of 0–100, 0 being the most corrupt).

Hypothetical Data for BED Calculation (2020–2030)

The following tables contain hypothetical data for the selected countries in Africa and Asia, covering key variables (Tables 10.4, 10.5 and 10.6).

BED Calculation for Selected Countries (2020–2030)

Using the hypothetical data provided, the BED score for each country can be calculated.

Table 10.4 Infrastructure investment (% of GDP)

Country	*2020*	*2021*	*2022*	*2023*	*2024*	*2025*	*2026*	*2027*	*2028*	*2029*	*2030*
India	3.5	3.8	4.0	4.1	4.3	4.4	4.5	4.7	4.8	5.0	5.2
Vietnam	4.0	4.2	4.5	4.7	5.0	5.1	5.2	5.3	5.4	5.5	5.6
Botswana	4.5	4.8	5.0	5.2	5.3	5.4	5.6	5.8	6.0	6.2	6.3
South Africa	3.2	3.4	3.5	3.7	3.9	4.0	4.1	4.2	4.4	4.5	4.7
DRC	1.2	1.4	1.5	1.6	1.7	1.8	2.0	2.2	2.3	2.5	2.7
South Sudan	0.3	0.4	0.5	0.6	0.7	0.8	1.0	1.1	1.2	1.3	1.5

Table 10.5 Social spending (% of GDP)

Country	*2020*	*2021*	*2022*	*2023*	*2024*	*2025*	*2026*	*2027*	*2028*	*2029*	*2030*
India	5.0	5.1	5.3	5.5	5.6	5.8	6.0	6.2	6.5	6.7	7.0
Vietnam	5.5	5.7	5.9	6.1	6.3	6.5	6.7	6.9	7.0	7.2	7.4
Botswana	6.2	6.3	6.5	6.7	6.8	7.0	7.2	7.5	7.8	8.0	8.3
South Africa	6.0	6.1	6.3	6.5	6.7	6.9	7.0	7.2	7.5	7.7	8.0
DRC	3.0	3.3	3.5	3.7	4.0	4.2	4.5	4.8	5.0	5.2	5.4
South Sudan	2.0	2.1	2.3	2.4	2.5	2.6	2.7	2.9	3.0	3.1	3.3

Table 10.6 Budget deficit (% of GDP)

Country	*2020*	*2021*	*2022*	*2023*	*2024*	*2025*	*2026*	*2027*	*2028*	*2029*	*2030*
India	−4.5	−4.2	−4.0	−3.8	−3.6	−3.4	−3.2	−3.0	−2.8	−2.5	−2.3
Vietnam	−4.0	−3.8	−3.7	−3.5	−3.2	−3.0	−2.8	−2.6	−2.5	−2.3	−2.0
Botswana	−3.0	−2.8	−2.6	−2.5	−2.4	−2.3	−2.0	−1.8	−1.6	−1.4	−1.2
South Africa	−5.5	−5.3	−5.0	−4.8	−4.5	−4.3	−4.0	−3.8	−3.5	−3.3	−3.0
DRC	−7.0	−6.8	−6.5	−6.2	−6.0	−5.8	−5.6	−5.4	−5.2	−5.0	−4.8
South Sudan	−10.0	−9.5	−9.0	−8.5	−8.0	−7.5	−7.0	−6.5	−6.0	−5.5	−5.0

Calculation Process

$$\text{BED} = \frac{\begin{array}{l}\textit{Infrastructure} + \textit{Social Spending} + \textit{Economic Diversification}\\ +\textit{Fiscal Discipline} + \textit{Governance}\end{array}}{\textit{Budget Defici} + \textit{Public Debt} + \textit{Corrupton Index}}$$

1. **Assign Weights**: Assign relative weights to each of the components:
   (a) Infrastructure Investment: 0.25
   (b) Social Spending: 0.25
   (c) Economic Diversification: 0.15
   (d) Fiscal Discipline: 0.20
   (e) Governance: 0.1
2. **Scale Components**: Normalise each of the components (e.g., Infrastructure Investment, Social Spending) based on the values between 0 and 1.
3. **Calculate BED Score**: Plug the normalised values into the BED formula.

Hypothetical calculations applied to India

India BED Calculation Example

- **Infrastructure Investment**: 4.4% of GDP in 2025 (scaled to 0.4)
- **Social Spending**: 5.8% of GDP in 2025 (scaled to 0.4)
- **Economic Diversification**: High (score 0.9)
- **Fiscal Discipline**: Budget deficit of −3.4% of GDP (scaled to 0.3)
- **Governance**: Strong institutional quality (scaled to 0.8)

$$\text{BED for India} = \frac{0.4 + 0.4 + 0.9 + 0.3 + 0.8}{0.3 + 0.2 + 0.2} \frac{2.8}{0.7} = 4.0.$$

Comparative Analysis

BED Score Trends for All Countries

- **India**: 4.0
- **Vietnam**: 3.9
- **Botswana**: 3.5

- **South Africa**: 2.8
- **DRC**: 1.2
- **South Sudan**: 0.5

Key Insights

- India and Vietnam maintain strong BED performance with higher infrastructure investment, social spending, and fiscal discipline, leading to more sustainable growth.
- Botswana performs well due to strong governance and low fiscal deficits despite challenges with economic diversification.
- South Africa suffers from high deficits and political instability, reducing the effectiveness of its budget.
- DRC and South Sudan struggle due to severe political instability, weak governance, and poor fiscal management.

Policy Recommendations

- Asian countries have mastered the integration of infrastructure, fiscal discipline, and diversified economies, which can serve as lessons for African economies.
- Sub-Saharan Africa, especially countries like South Sudan and the DRC, need to focus on improving governance, reducing corruption, and diversifying their economies.
- Fiscal discipline and infrastructure investments are key drivers for sustained growth in both regions.

This quantitative analysis and comparative study illustrate the potential for countries to improve their BED scores and hence their long-term economic stability and development.

Case Studies and Empirical Evidence

Case Study 1: Budget Reforms in East Asian Economies and Their Impact on Growth

East Asia has undergone significant budget reforms since the 1980s, with countries like South Korea, Singapore, and Taiwan leading the way in fiscal modernisation and reform. These reforms primarily focused on improving public financial management (PFM), ensuring fiscal discipline, and enhancing the efficiency of government spending. Singapore has been a prominent example of a country that has implemented rigorous budget reforms, particularly in its adoption of performance-based budgeting (PBB), which links government spending to measurable outcomes.

Key Arguments

- **Macroeconomic Stability**: Reforms have helped East Asian economies maintain fiscal discipline and achieve macroeconomic stability. South Korea's fiscal reforms in the 1990s allowed it to weather the 1997 Asian Financial Crisis with less volatility, underscoring the importance of sound fiscal management (Agenor, 2004).
- **Increased Investment in Infrastructure**: East Asian economies have used well-managed budgets to direct substantial resources into infrastructure, leading to high rates of investment and growth (Lee & Kim, 2014). For instance, China has consistently increased infrastructure spending, leading to rapid economic growth over the past few decades.
- **Strengthened Governance and Accountability**: East Asian countries have emphasised the importance of governance, anti-corruption measures, and transparency in budgeting (Haggard & Kwon, 2007). This has led to more efficient public spending and reduced leakages in public funds.

Counterarguments

- **Overemphasis on Fiscal Austerity**: While fiscal discipline is important, some argue that East Asian countries have focused too heavily on austerity measures that have limited public spending, particularly in education and health. In South Korea, for example, austerity policies after the Asian crisis led to slow growth in the social sectors.
- **Social Inequalities**: Critics argue that the economic growth fostered by fiscal discipline and budget reforms has not been inclusive. In China, rapid growth has exacerbated income inequality and led to environmental degradation (Liu, 2017).

Lessons Learned

- A balance must be struck between fiscal discipline and social spending to ensure that economic growth benefits all sectors of society.

- Public financial management reforms that focus on accountability, transparency, and performance-based budgeting can help East Asian economies maintain high growth rates.

Case Study 2: African Economies and Challenges in Budget Implementation

African countries face significant challenges in budget implementation due to a variety of factors, including weak institutions, corruption, and political instability. For example, Nigeria has struggled with budget execution despite several attempts to improve budget transparency and effectiveness.

Key Arguments

- **Institutional Weaknesses**: One of the primary challenges in many African countries is a weak institutional capacity to execute and monitor budgets. For instance, Nigeria's failure to fully implement its budget is partly due to the lack of adequate public financial management systems and capacity building within public institutions (Olaniyan, 2011).
- **Corruption and Elite Capture**: In several African countries, the political elite have been able to manipulate budgets for personal gain, leading to inefficiencies in public spending. Ghana has made progress in implementing reforms, but challenges with elite capture remain (Ayee, 2014). Corruption often leads to the misallocation of resources and hinders effective service delivery.
- **Weak Revenue Collection**: Many African countries face challenges with **tax** collection and revenue generation, which limits their ability to finance development projects. For example, Kenya has improved its revenue collection systems but still faces significant challenges in broadening the tax base (Kimenyi, 2011).

Counterarguments

- **Improvement in Fiscal Policies**: Despite challenges, there have been notable improvements in some African countries. Ethiopia, for example, has significantly increased its infrastructure spending through improved budget management and domestic revenue mobilisation (Kifle, 2015).

- **Decentralisation of Budgeting**: The decentralisation of budgeting has shown positive effects in some African nations, enabling local governments to better meet the needs of communities. Uganda has made strides in this direction, leading to improved public services (Panic, 2019).

Lessons Learned

- Strong institutional capacity, anti-corruption frameworks, and revenue mobilisation strategies are crucial for improving budget execution in African countries.
- Decentralisation of budgeting and improved public financial management systems can lead to better outcomes for national budgets.

Case Study 3: The European Union's Budget Discipline Policies and Economic Performance

The European Union (EU) has established rigorous budget discipline policies to ensure that member states maintain sustainable public finances. The Stability and Growth Pact (SGP), adopted in 1997, set strict limits on budget deficits (3% of GDP) and national debt (60% of GDP) for member states.

Key Arguments

- **Economic Stability and Confidence**: The EU's focus on budget discipline through the SGP has been seen as a success in ensuring economic stability and increasing investor confidence (Padoa-Schioppa, 2004). For example, Germany and France have benefited from these rules by maintaining sound fiscal policies.
- **Convergence of Economic Policies**: The EU's budget discipline policies have led to a convergence of economic policies across member states, fostering economic integration and trade within the EU (Alesina, 2005).

Counterarguments

- **Austerity and Growth Trade-offs**: Critics argue that the EU's budget discipline policies, particularly the focus on deficit reduction, have stifled growth in peripheral economies, such as Greece and Spain. The austerity measures imposed during the Eurozone crisis led to deep recessions and increased unemployment (Blanchard & Leigh, 2013).

- **Divergence Within the EU**: While the EU has sought to ensure economic convergence, budget discipline policies have sometimes exacerbated disparities between the Eurozone's stronger economies (e.g., Germany) and the weaker economies (e.g., Greece) (Baldwin & Giavazzi, 2015).

Lessons Learned

- Budget discipline is important for long-term economic stability, but it should be balanced with policies that promote economic growth and social protection during times of economic distress.
- Flexibility in fiscal rules is necessary to allow countries to invest in growth during crises.

Lessons Learned from Global Experiences in Budgeting for Development

Key Arguments

- **Strategic Use of Budget for Growth**: Across different regions, effective budgeting practices have led to positive outcomes in terms of economic growth and poverty reduction. For instance, East Asian economies used their budgets to drive infrastructure investment, which has been a key driver of their growth (Mufune, 2013).
- **Need for Balanced Spending**: Successful economies have found ways to balance social spending with economic development initiatives, ensuring that growth benefits all sectors of society. Botswana's focus on both social services and infrastructure has enabled it to maintain sustainable growth (Mufune, 2013).

Counterarguments

- **Inequality and Budgeting**: While budgeting for development can drive economic growth, it can also lead to inequality if not managed correctly. Many African countries, for example, have struggled with elite capture and corruption, which has hindered the equitable distribution of resources (Osei & Ayee, 2014).

Lessons Learned

- Countries should adopt a comprehensive approach to budgeting that includes both macroeconomic stability and social investment.
- Strengthening governance and public financial management is essential for ensuring that the budget leads to equitable development outcomes.
- Flexibility in fiscal policies is necessary to adjust to changing economic conditions and to promote inclusive growth.

Global experiences show that the success of budgeting for economic development depends on institutional capacity, governance, revenue generation, and strategic allocation of resources. East Asian countries have shown how strong fiscal management can promote rapid growth, while African countries face significant challenges in budget implementation due to weak institutions and corruption. The EU's emphasis on budget discipline highlights the importance of fiscal rules but also reveals the risks of austerity during economic downturns. Lessons learned from these case studies indicate that countries must balance fiscal discipline with policies that support growth and social protection to ensure sustainable development.

Policy Implications and Recommendations for Integrating the WEF Nexus into National Budgeting Systems in the SADC Region

Integrating Budgeting for Economic Development (BED) into National Budgeting Systems

The integration of BED into national budgeting systems is essential for promoting sustainable economic growth. The current debate revolves around whether traditional sectoral budgeting frameworks can adequately support cross-sectoral economic development or if a more integrated budgeting system is required (OECD, 2023). Proponents argue that BED ensures efficient resource allocation across interconnected sectors like water, energy, and food, fostering long-term sustainability (*World Bank*, 2022). However, critics highlight implementation challenges, including bureaucratic resistance and the complexities of cross-sectoral coordination (UNDP, 2021).

Recommendations

- Introduce multi-sectoral budget planning frameworks that recognise interdependencies between water, energy, and food (Sachs, 2023).
- Establish dedicated WEF Nexus funds within national budgets to ensure targeted financing for cross-sectoral projects (African Development Bank, 2022).
- Enhance capacity building among policymakers to adopt integrated budgeting approaches effectively (GIZ, 2021).

Institutional Reforms for Effective Budget Execution

Institutional reforms are necessary to bridge the gap between budget formulation and execution. One major challenge is the lack of coherence between policy planning and financial disbursement, leading to inefficiencies in public spending (IMF, 2023). Future debates will likely focus on how digital innovations, such as blockchain technology, can enhance budget tracking and execution.

Recommendations

- Strengthen coordination mechanisms between finance ministries and sectoral agencies to improve budget execution efficiency (World Bank, 2023).
- Implement performance-based budgeting to ensure that allocated resources align with actual development outcomes (UNDP, 2023).
- Leverage technology, such as real-time budget tracking tools, to enhance transparency and efficiency (OECD, 2023).

Strengthening Accountability and Transparency in Budgetary Processes

Ensuring accountability and transparency in budgetary processes remains a key challenge, particularly in developing economies. The debate centres on whether top-down regulatory approaches or bottom-up participatory budgeting mechanisms are more effective in curbing mismanagement (Transparency International, 2022). While regulatory frameworks provide clear guidelines, critics argue they often lack enforcement, whereas participatory approaches can enhance citizen engagement but may be resource-intensive (Acemoglu & Robinson, 2023).

Recommendations

- Establish independent budget oversight bodies to monitor public spending and prevent corruption (Sachs, 2023).
- Promote participatory budgeting initiatives to enhance public trust and ensure fiscal responsibility.
- Strengthen public financial management systems through digital governance tools (OECD, 2023).

Aligning National Budgets with Sustainable Development Goals (SDGs)

A significant policy debate revolves around the feasibility of aligning national budgets with the SDGs given fiscal constraints. Some argue that prioritising SDG-aligned budgets may overburden national economies, while others contend that failing to integrate SDGs into financial planning could exacerbate long-term economic and environmental challenges (UNDP, 2023). Future discussions will likely explore innovative financing mechanisms, such as blended finance and green bonds, to address budgetary shortfalls while achieving SDG targets (WEF, 2023).

Recommendations

- Introduce SDG-budget tagging systems to track expenditures related to sustainable development objectives (African Development Bank, 2022).
- Leverage international funding mechanisms, such as climate finance and development aid, to supplement national budgets (UNDP, 2023).
- Develop a national SDG financing strategy to ensure long-term financial sustainability (IMF, 2023).

Integrating national budgeting systems requires strategic institutional reforms, improved accountability, and alignment with sustainable development priorities. While current debates highlight the challenges of cross-sectoral budget integration, future discussions will explore innovative financing and governance solutions. Policymakers must navigate these debates carefully, balancing fiscal constraints with long-term sustainability goals.

Conclusion and Future Research Directions

Evaluating the Feasibility of BED as a New Paradigm

The viability of BED as a paradigm depends on its adaptability to diverse economic structures. Proponents argue that it enhances financial inclusivity, while critics highlight its complexity and the need for extensive reforms (Stiglitz, 2023).

Summary of Key Findings and Theoretical Contributions

The analysis shows that BED integration can foster cross-sectoral synergy, improve fiscal discipline, and enhance national development outcomes. Theoretically, it bridges public finance with economic development frameworks (Acemoglu & Robinson, 2022).

Future Research Areas in Budgeting, Economic Power, and Development Finance

- The role of digital financial tools in enhancing BED implementation.
- The impact of decentralised budgeting on economic power redistribution.
- Comparative studies on BED integration in developing versus developed economies.
- The influence of political economy factors on BED execution.

Scenario Analysis for Selected SSA Countries

- **South Africa**: Evaluating the trade-offs between social welfare spending and infrastructure development under BED.
- **Nigeria**: Assessing the impact of BED on oil revenue allocation and diversification.
- **Kenya**: Analysing how BED influences public-private partnerships in economic development.
- **Ethiopia**: Examining BED's role in aligning budgetary decisions with industrialisation policies.

References

Acemoglu, D., & Robinson, J. (2012). *Why nations fail: The origins of power, prosperity, and poverty.* Profile Books.

Acemoglu, D., & Robinson, J. (2022). *Economic origins of dictatorship and democracy.* Cambridge University Press.

Acemoglu, D., & Robinson, J. (2023). *The narrow corridor: States, societies, and the fate of liberty.* Penguin.

Acemoglu, D., Johnson, S., & Robinson, J. (2001). An African success story: Botswana. In *Search of prosperity: Analytic narratives on economic growth* (pp. 80–119). Princeton University Press.

Afonso, A., Schuknecht, L., & Tanzi, V. (2005). Public sector efficiency: Evidence for new EU member states and emerging markets. *Applied Economics, 42*(17), 2147–2164. https://doi.org/10.1080/00036840701765460

African Development Bank (AfDB). (2022). *Sustainable financing for Africa's development.* AfDB Publications.

Agenor, P.-R. (2004). *Macroeconomics, development, and the role of the International Monetary Fund.* Oxford University Press.

Alesina, A. (2005). *Fiscal policy and growth in the European Union.* Cambridge University Press.

Alesina, A., & Perotti, R. (1996). Fiscal discipline and the budget process. *American Economic Review, 86*(2), 401–407.

Aschauer, D. A. (1989). Is public expenditure productive? *Journal of Monetary Economics, 23*(2), 177–200. https://doi.org/10.1016/0304-3932(89)90047-0

Ayee, J. (2014). Public sector reforms in Africa: Perspectives from Ghana. *African Development Review, 26*(1), 9–19.

Baiman, R. (2006). Deepening democracy: Institutional innovations in empowered participatory governance. *Science & Society, 70*(4), 566–569. https://doi.org/10.1521/siso.2006.70.4.566

Baldwin, R., & Giavazzi, F. (2015). *The Eurozone crisis: A consensus view of the causes and a few possible solutions.* VoxEU.org.

Baldwin, R., & Mauro, B. W. D. (2020). *Economics in the time of COVID-19.* CEPR Press.

Banerjee, A. V., & Duflo, E. (2011). *Poor economics: A radical rethinking of the way to fight global poverty.* PublicAffairs.

Basu, K. (1997). *Analytical development economics: The less developed economy revisited.* The MIT Press.

Becker, G. (1964). *Human capital: A theoretical and empirical analysis.* University of Chicago Press.

Bekaert, G., & Harvey, C. R. (2003). Emerging markets finance. *Journal of Empirical Finance, 10*(1–2), 3–55. https://doi.org/10.1016/S0927-5398(02)00054-3

Bekaert, G., Harvey, C. R., & Lundblad, C. (2001). Emerging equity markets and economic development. *Journal of Development Economics, 66*(2), 465–504. https://doi.org/10.1016/S0304-3878(01)00171-7

Bekaert, G., Harvey, C. R., & Lundblad, C. (2005). Does financial liberalisation spur growth? *Journal of Financial Economics, 77*(1), 3–55. https://doi.org/10.1016/j.jfineco.2004.05.007

Bell, C. (2003). *Development policy as public finance*. Oxford University Press. https://doi.org/10.1093/oso/9780198773665.001.0001

Berger, A. N., & Bonaccorsi di Patti, E. (2006). Capital structure and firm performance: A new approach to testing agency theory and an application to the banking industry. *Journal of Banking and Finance, 30*(4), 1065–1102. https://doi.org/10.1016/j.jbankfin.2005.05.015

Bertero, E. (1994). The banking system, financial markets and capital structure: Some new evidence from France. *Oxford Review of Economic Policy, 10*(4), 68–78. https://doi.org/10.1093/oxrep/10.4.68

Bessler, W., Drobetz, W., & Grüninger, M. C. (2011). Information asymmetry and financing decisions. *International Review of Finance, 11*(1), 123–154. https://doi.org/10.1111/j.1468-2443.2010.01122.x

Bhaduri, S. N. (2000). Liberalisation and firm's choice of financial structure in an emerging economy: The Indian corporate sector. *Development Policy Review, 18*(4), 413–434. https://doi.org/10.1111/1467-7679.00119

Bhaduri, S. N. (2002). Determinants of capital structure choice: A study of the Indian corporate sector. *Applied Financial Economics, 12*(9), 655–665. https://doi.org/10.1080/09603100010017705

Bhaduri, S. N. (2005). Investment, financial constraints and financial liberalisation: Some stylized facts from a developing economy, India. *Journal of Asian Economics, 16*(4), 704–718. https://doi.org/10.1016/j.asieco.2005.06.001

Bird, G. (2004). *International finance and the developing economies*. Palgrave Macmillan.

Birdsall, N., de la Torre, A., & Menezes, R. (2001). *Washington contentious: Economic policies for social equity in Latin America*. Carnegie Endowment for International Peace. https://www.cgdev.org/sites/default/files/2923_file_WashCont_0.pdf

Blanchard, O., & Leigh, D. (2013). *Growth forecast errors and fiscal multipliers*. IMF Working Paper WP/13/1. https://www.imf.org/external/pubs/ft/wp/2013/wp1301.pdf

Blanchard, O., & Perotti, R. (2002). An empirical characterization of the dynamic effects of changes in government spending and taxes on output. *The Quarterly Journal of Economics, 117*(4), 1329–1368. https://ssrn.com/abstract=199312

Blanchard, O., Dell Ariccia, G., & Mauro, P. (2010). Rethinking macroeconomic policy. *Journal of Money, Credit and Banking, 42*(s1), 199–215. https://www.imf.org/external/pubs/ft/spn/2010/spn1003.PDF

Blustein, P. (2005). *And the money kept rolling in (and out)*. PublicAffairs.

Bragg, S. M. (2013). *Budgeting: A comprehensive guide*. John Wiley & Sons.

Brigham, E. F., & Ehrhardt, M. C. (2013). *Financial management: Theory & practice*. Cengage Learning.

Buchanan, J. M., & Tullock, G. (1962). *The calculus of consent: Logical foundations of constitutional democracy*. University of Michigan Press.

Buti, M., Eijffinger, S., & Franco, D. (2003). Revisiting the stability and growth pact: Grand design or internal adjustment? *Economic Policy, 18*(37), 67–102. https://ssrn.com/abstract=374461

Cangiano, M., Curristine, E. R., & Lazarre, M. (2013). *Public financial management and its emerging architecture*. IMF. https://doi.org/10.5089/9781475531091.071

Cardoso, F. H., & Faletto, E. (1979). *Dependency and development in Latin America*. University of California Press.

Chang, H. J. (2002). *Kicking away the ladder: Development strategy in historical perspective*. Anthem Press.

Collier, P. (2007). *The bottom billion: Why the poorest countries are failing and what can be done about it*. Oxford University Press.

De Mesquita, B. B., Moretti, L., & Sabin, R. (2013). The power of predictive models. *The Brown Journal of World Affairs, 19*(2), 27–35.

Easterly, W. (2001). *The elusive quest for growth: Economists adventures and misadventures in the tropics*. MIT Press.

Easterly, W., & Servén, L. (2003). *The limits of stabilization: Infrastructure, public deficits, and growth in Latin America*. World Bank.

Foucault, M. (1979). *Discipline and punish: The birth of the prison*. Vintage Books.

Gallagher, K. (2021). IMF and World Bank debt frameworks: Implications for Zambia's economic recovery. *Journal of Development Finance, 12*(2), 45–67.

Gebregziabher, T. (2019). Developmental state and budgeting autonomy in Ethiopia: Balancing state control and fiscal independence. *Journal of African Development, 14*(3), 21–37.

GIZ. (2021). *Integrated budgeting approaches in sub-Saharan Africa*. GIZ Research Paper.

Haggard, S., & Kwon, H. (2007). The politics of governance in East Asia. *Asia Pacific Journal of Public Administration, 29*(2), 125–150.

Hausmann, R., Hidalgo, C. A., Bustos, S., Coscia, M., Simoes, A., & Yildirim, M. A. (2011). *The atlas of economic complexity: Mapping paths to prosperity*. MIT Press.

Hirt, G. A., & Block, S. B. (2017). *Financial accounting: A focus on fundamentals*. McGraw-Hill Education.

Hodges, T. (2004). *Angola: Anatomy of an oil state*. Indiana University Press.
Horngren, C. T., Sundem, G. L., & Stratton, W. O. (2005). *Introduction to management accounting*. Pearson Education.
Hussain, I. (2018). *Pakistan: The economy of an elitist state*. Oxford University Press.
International Monetary Fund (IMF). (2019). *Ghana: Fiscal responsibility and economic management report*. IMF Country Report No. 19/123.
International Monetary Fund (IMF). (2022). *Sub-Saharan Africa regional economic outlook*. International Monetary Fund.
International Monetary Fund (IMF). (2023). *Public financial management in developing countries: Challenges and opportunities*. IMF Working Paper.
Iyoha, M. A., & Oriakhi, D. (2008). Explaining African economic growth performance: The case of Nigeria. In B. J. Ndulu, S. A. O'Connell, & C. C. Soludo (Eds.), *The political economy of economic growth in Africa, 1960–2000* (pp. 621–660). Cambridge University Press.
Keynes, J. M. (1936). *The general theory of employment, interest, and money*. Macmillan.
Kifle, T. (2015). *The role of public financial management in economic development: The case of Ethiopia*. Master's thesis, Addis Ababa University.
Kimenyi, M. (2011). *Africa growth initiative at the Brookings Institution—Alliance for financial inclusion—Central Bank of Kenya*. Africa Growth Initiative at Brookings. https://www.afi-global.org/wp-content/uploads/2024/10/brookings_mobile-financial-services-fi.pdf
Krugman, P. (2019). *Arguing with zombies: Economics, politics, and the fight for a better future*. W. W. Norton.
Lardy, N. R. (2019). *The state strike back: The end of economic reform in China*. Peterson Institute for International Economics. https://www.piie.com/bookstore/2018/state-strikes-back-end-economic-reform-china
Lee, J., & Kim, H. (2014). Public expenditure and economic growth in East Asia: The case of South Korea and Taiwan. *Journal of Asian Economics, 35*, 56–73.
Liu, X. (2017). Economic growth and income inequality in China: The role of fiscal policy. *Journal of Chinese Economic Studies, 25*(4), 211–233.
Lukes, S. (2005). *Power: A radical view* (2nd ed.). Palgrave Macmillan.
Mankiw, N. G. (2014). *Principles of economics*. Cengage Learning.
Mbate, M. (2018). Decentralization, governance, and service delivery in Uganda: Lessons from participatory budgeting. *African Journal of Public Administration, 10*(1), 35–54.
Mkandawire, T., & Soludo, C. C. (1999). *Our continent, our future: African perspectives on structural adjustment*. Africa World Press.
Mosha, A. (2020). Tanzania's alternative path to economic growth: Fiscal policies under Magufuli. *Journal of African Policy Studies, 8*(4), 100–121.
Moyo, D. (2009). *Dead aid: Why aid is not working and how there is a better way for Africa*. Penguin.

Mufune, P. (2013). Botswana's budgetary practices and economic growth: A case study of success in Africa. *African Development Review, 25*(1), 78–95.

Musgrave, R. A., & Musgrave, P. B. (1989). *Public finance in theory and practice* (5th ed.). McGraw-Hill.

Ncube, M. (2020). Fiscal governance in South Africa: An assessment of the medium-term expenditure framework (MTEF). *South African Journal of Economics, 88*(2), 221–238.

Ndikumana, L., & Boyce, J. (2011). *Africa's odious debts.* Zed Books.

Neely, A. (2007). *Business performance measurement: Theory and practice.* Cambridge University Press.

North, D. C. (1990). *Institutions, institutional change and economic performance.* Cambridge University Press.

North, D. C., Wallis, J. J., & Weingast, B. R. (2009). *Violence and social orders: A conceptual framework for interpreting recorded human history.* Cambridge University Press.

Olaniyan, O. (2011). Challenges in budget implementation in Nigeria: Institutional and structural perspectives. *African Journal of Governance and Development, 8*(2), 23–37.

Organisation for Economic Co-operation and Development (OECD). (2015). *Budgeting practices and procedures in OECD countries.* OECD Publishing.

Organisation for Economic Co-operation and Development (OECD). (2023). *Budgeting for sustainable development: Policy innovations for the 21st century.* OECD Publishing.

Osei, P., & Ayee, J. (2014). Budgeting for development in Africa: Addressing the governance deficit. *Journal of African Policy Studies, 19*(1), 99–115.

Padoa-Schioppa, T. (2004). The stability and growth pact: How Europe survived the fiscal crisis. *European Economic Review, 48*(3), 325–350.

Panic, B. (2019). Decentralized budgeting and service delivery in Uganda: An evaluation of fiscal devolution. *African Public Finance Journal, 14*(2), 77–94.

Premchand, A. (2000). Budgeting for economic development: Evolution and practice of an idea. In *Control of public money: The fiscal machinery in developing countries.* Oxford University Press.

Reinhart, C. M., & Rogoff, K. S. (2013). *Financial and sovereign debt crises: Some lessons learned and those forgotten.* IMF Working Paper.

Rodrik, D. (2006). Goodbye Washington consensus, hello Washington confusion? *Journal of Economic Literature, 44*(4), 973–987. https://doi.org/10.1257/jel.44.4.973

Rodrik, D. (2007). *One economics, many recipes: Globalization, institutions, and economic growth.* Princeton University Press.

Rodrik, D. (2013). *The globalization paradox: Democracy and the future of the world economy.* W. W. Norton & Company.

Ross, M. L. (2012). *The oil curse: How petroleum wealth shapes the development of nations*. Princeton University Press.
Sachs, J. (1989). The debt overhang of developing countries. In G. Calvo, R. Findlay, K. Pentti, & J. B. de Macedo (Eds.), *Debt, stabilization and development: Essays in memory of Carlos Diaz-Alejandro*. Blackwell.
Sachs, J. (2005). *The end of poverty: Economic possibilities for our time*. Penguin Press.
Sachs, J. (2023). *Financing the sustainable development goals: Policy frameworks and strategies*. Earth Institute.
Schick, A. (1998). Why most developing countries should not try New Zealand's reforms. *The World Bank Research Observer, 13*(1), 123–131. https://doi.org/10.1093/wbro/13.1.123
Schwalbe, K. (2015). *Information technology project management*. Cengage Learning.
Shank, J. K., & Govindarajan, V. (2016). *Cost management: Strategies for business decisions*. Pearson.
Shiva, V. (2002). *Water wars: Privatization, pollution, and profit*. South End Press.
Stiglitz, J. (2002). *Globalization and its discontents*. W. W. Norton & Company.
Stiglitz, J. (2012). *The price of inequality*. W. W. Norton & Company.
Stiglitz, J. (2017). *Globalization and its discontents revisited: Anti-globalization in the Era of Trump*. W. W. Norton & Company.
Stiglitz, J. (2023). *The price of inequality: How today's divided society endangers our future*. W. W. Norton & Company.
Strange, S. (1996). *The retreat of the state: The diffusion of power in the world economy*. Cambridge University Press.
Tanzi, V., & Schuknecht, L. (2000). *Public spending in the 20th century*. Cambridge University Press.
Transparency International. (2022). *Global corruption report: Public sector governance*. Transparency International.
United Nations Development Programme (UNDP). (2021). *Reforming national budgets for effective development planning*. UNDP Policy Paper.
United Nations Development Programme (UNDP). (2023). *Aligning national budgets with the SDGs: Lessons and best practices*. UNDP Reports.
Van der Stede, W. A. (2000). The relationship between two approaches to budgeting: Incremental and zero-based budgeting. *Journal of Management Accounting Research, 12*(1), 221–245.
Wade, R. (1990). *Governing the market: Economic theory and the role of government in east Asian industrialization*. Princeton University Press.
Wanyama, F., & McCluskey, W. (2017). Decentralization and participatory budgeting in Kenya: A case for county governments. *Public Administration and Development, 37*(4), 275–289.
Wildavsky, A. (1986). *The new politics of the budgetary process*. Scott Foresman.

Williamson, J. (1990). *Latin American adjustment: How much has happened?* Institute for International Economics.
World Bank. (2015). *Public expenditure and financial accountability (PEFA) program: Strengthening public financial management in developing countries.* World Bank Publications.
World Bank. (2021). *Rwanda public finance review: Strengthening fiscal governance for economic transformation.* World Bank Publications.
World Bank. (2022). *Fisacl Policies for Sustainable Growth in Sub-Saharan Africa.* World Bank Publications.
World Bank. (2023). *Enhancing public sector efficiency through digital budgeting.* World Bank Policy Brief. World Bank Publications.
World Bank. (2019). *Public financial management in developing countries.* World Bank Publications.
World Bank. (2022). *Fiscal policies for sustainable growth in sub-Saharan Africa.* World Bank Publications.
World Economic Forum (WEF). (2023). *Blockchain for development: Use cases and challenges.* World Economic Forum.

CHAPTER 11

Rethinking Growth: Towards a New Development Paradigm

Introduction

The Limits of Traditional Growth Models

Economic growth in developing regions such as sub-Saharan Africa (SSA) and Asia has historically been driven by industrialisation, export-led strategies, and structural adjustment programmes (World Bank, 2020). While GDP growth has been achieved in some countries, persistent challenges such as poverty, inequality, environmental degradation, and resource depletion highlight the limitations of current development paradigms (Stiglitz, 2019).

This chapter explores three alternative economic models and their relevance for SSA and Asia:

- **Degrowth:** A model advocating a deliberate reduction in unsustainable economic activities (Kallis, 2018).
- **Doughnut Economics:** A framework that balances social needs with ecological sustainability (Raworth, 2017).
- **Circular Economy:** A system designed to minimise waste and maximise resource efficiency (Geissdoerfer et al., 2017).

Case studies from SSA and Asia illustrate how these models can be adapted to different socio-economic and environmental contexts.

P. K. Kabeya, *Development and the Power Theory of Economics*,
https://doi.org/10.1007/978-3-032-07926-8_11

Alternative Development Models and Case Studies

Degrowth: Managing Growth for Social and Environmental Well-being

Concept and Relevance for Developing Countries
Degrowth challenges the assumption that continuous economic growth is necessary for development (Hickel, 2020). Instead, it promotes well-being, equity, and environmental sustainability by prioritising localised economies, resource conservation, and social progress (Latouche, 2009).

Case Study 1: Agroecology and Food Sovereignty in Malawi (SSA)
Malawi's transition to agroecology-based farming illustrates degrowth principles (Bezner Kerr et al., 2019). Government and NGOs have supported permaculture and organic farming, reducing dependence on imported fertilisers (Chirwa & Dorward, 2013). The outcomes are higher food security, better soil health, and reduced vulnerability to climate shocks.

The challenges: Requires stronger policy support and financial investment in smallholder farming.

Case Study 2: Bhutan's Gross National Happiness (Asia)
Bhutan adopted Gross National Happiness (GNH) as an alternative to GDP (Ura et al., 2012). GNH focuses on well-being, environmental protection, and cultural preservation. Policies prioritise sustainable tourism, conservation, and community development. The challenges are that there is limited economic diversification and dependence on hydropower exports.

Key Takeaways for SSA and Asia
Policies should deprioritise extractive industries and focus on localised production and self-sufficiency. The governments must support small-scale farmers and community-based economies. Alternative well-being indicators like GNH can guide socio-economic policies.

Doughnut Economics: Balancing Social and Ecological Boundaries

Concept and Application in Developing Regions
Doughnut Economics (Raworth, 2017) provides a framework for ensuring human well-being without breaching environmental limits. Many developing countries face a double challenge: widespread poverty and inequality alongside environmental degradation and climate change (Sachs et al., 2019).

Case Study 3: Cape Town's Water Crisis and Sustainable Urban Planning (SSA)
Cape Town's 2018 water crisis highlighted urban planning vulnerabilities (Muller, 2018). The city adopted water-efficient technologies, desalination, and wastewater recycling (Ziervogel, 2019).

- Community-driven water conservation efforts played a crucial role.
- **Result:** Avoidance of Day Zero and greater water resilience.
- **Challenge:** Need for long-term investments in climate adaptation.

Case Study 4: Indonesia's Blue Economy and Marine Resource Management (Asia)
Indonesia has adopted the Blue Economy model to manage marine resources sustainably (Sumaila et al., 2021).

- Focus on sustainable fisheries, coral reef conservation, and eco-tourism.
- **Outcomes**: Improved marine biodiversity and increased local livelihoods.
- **Challenges:** Illegal fishing and weak enforcement mechanisms.

Key Takeaways for SSA and Asia
- Urban areas must integrate climate adaptation strategies into governance frameworks.
- Coastal and marine-dependent economies need sustainable resource management policies.

Circular Economy: Reducing Waste, Maximising Resources

Concept and Application in Developing Economies

A Circular Economy minimises waste and promotes sustainable resource use (Geissdoerfer et al., 2017). SSA and Asia have large informal recycling economies, but they remain undervalued and underregulated (Velis & Wilson, 2015).

Case Study 5: Rwanda's Plastic Ban and Circular Economy Initiatives (SSA)

- Rwanda banned plastic bags in 2008, leading to a cleaner urban environment (Niyonzima, 2021).
- The policy promoted biodegradable alternatives and waste-to-energy projects (Mugisha et al., 2019).
- Kigali is now one of Africa's cleanest cities.
- **Challenges:** The need for alternative materials and better enforcement.

Case Study 6: India's E-Waste Management Policies (Asia)

- India faces a growing e-waste crisis due to high electronic imports (Ogunseitan, 2019).
- **Solutions:** Formalised e-waste recycling and incentives for repair-based industries (Sthiannopkao & Wong, 2013).
- **Impact:** Creation of green jobs and reduction of environmental hazards.

Key Takeaways for SSA and Asia

- Governments should formalise informal recycling and incentivise eco-friendly industries.
- Circular economy initiatives reduce waste and create sustainable employment.

Policy Recommendations for Equitable and Sustainable Development

Shift Development Metrics Beyond GDP

- Use the Human Development Index (HDI) and Social Progress Index to measure well-being (Sen, 1999).
- Incorporate ecological and social indicators into national planning (Dasgupta, 2021).

Promote Localised and Sustainable Development Strategies

- Support local industries over foreign-led extraction (Rodrik, 2018).
- Strengthen land rights and resource sovereignty (De Schutter, 2017).

Expand Circular Economy Policies

- Implement extended producer responsibility (EPR) laws for waste-producing industries (Bocken et al., 2016).
- Invest in waste-to-energy and bioeconomy solutions (Zhu et al., 2019).

Green Finance and Investment Strategies

- Increase funding for renewable energy and climate adaptation (Bhattacharya et al., 2019).
- Promote sovereign green bonds for sustainable infrastructure (Chenet et al., 2021).

Regional and Global Collaboration

- Strengthen African Union (AU) and ASEAN sustainability initiatives (UNECA, 2020).
- Align with Sustainable Development Goals (SDGs) (United Nations, 2015).

Towards a Sustainable Future for Developing Economies

Higher-Level Analysis of Alternative Development Models

Rethinking Development: Moving Beyond GDP as the Sole Indicator of Progress
Conventional economic models prioritise GDP growth as the primary measure of development. However, this approach often overlooks key social and environmental challenges, particularly in developing economies. Alternative models—Degrowth, Doughnut Economics, and Circular Economy—offer a more holistic framework by integrating environmental sustainability and social well-being (Raworth, 2017; Kallis, 2018).

Key Questions in the Debate

- Can economies grow indefinitely without surpassing planetary limits?
- How can developing countries balance poverty alleviation with environmental sustainability?
- Are alternative models economically viable, or do they risk slowing down necessary industrialisation?

To explore these questions, we analyse the strengths, weaknesses, and long-term implications of each model within the contexts of SSA and Asia.

Higher-Level Analysis of Alternative Models

Degrowth: A Necessary Shift or a Risk for Developing Economies?

Core Premise
Degrowth argues that economic expansion beyond ecological limits is unsustainable. Instead, societies should prioritise well-being, reduce consumption, and localise production (Hickel, 2020).

Strengths

- **Prevents Ecological Collapse:** Slower economic activity reduces environmental degradation.
- **Encourages Equitable Distribution:** Instead of accumulating wealth, resources are shared more equitably.

- **Strengthens Local Economies:** Reduces reliance on volatile global supply chains.

Weaknesses

- **Job Losses in Growth-Based Industries:** Manufacturing, construction, and service sectors may contract.
- **Government Revenue Decline:** Many public services depend on tax revenues from economic activity.
- **Low-Income Countries May Suffer:** Countries still in the early stages of industrialisation require growth to meet basic needs.

Hypothetical Scenario: Degrowth in SSA and Asia

- **SSA Example:** If Nigeria adopts degrowth principles, it could implement localised agricultural production instead of oil dependence. However, economic contraction may lead to social instability if alternative employment strategies are not in place.
- **Asia Example:** In India, a degrowth model could emphasise rural sustainability programmes and green energy, reducing urban migration. However, such a transition would require strong policy intervention to prevent large-scale unemployment in industrial sectors.

Doughnut Economics: A Framework for Balanced Development

Core Premise

Kate Raworth's Doughnut Economics provides a two-tiered framework: economies should operate within planetary boundaries while ensuring social equity (Raworth, 2017).

Strengths

- **Holistic Approach:** Balances economic needs with ecological sustainability.
- **Flexibility:** Adaptable to different national contexts.
- **Encourages Innovation:** Promotes green technologies and responsible consumption.

Weaknesses

- **Difficult to Implement:** Requires new economic metrics and policies.

- **Political Resistance:** Governments reliant on traditional growth models may oppose radical change.
- **Short-Term Disruptions:** Transitioning requires significant investment in new industries.

Hypothetical Scenario: Doughnut Economics in SSA and Asia

- **SSA Example**: South Africa could integrate Doughnut Economics by prioritising social welfare programmes while enforcing stricter environmental regulations on mining and industry. However, transitioning from a mineral-export economy to a sustainability-driven economy would require extensive planning and investment.
- **Asia Example**: China, with its strong central governance, could adopt a Doughnut-inspired model focusing on green urban development while maintaining economic growth. However, political opposition from entrenched industries could delay progress.

Circular Economy: Transforming Waste into Economic Opportunity

Core Premise

The Circular Economy shifts away from the linear "take-make-dispose" model to a system where resources are reused, recycled, and repurposed (Bocken et al., 2016).

Strengths

- **Reduces Resource Dependency:** Helps developing economies become self-sufficient.
- **Creates New Jobs:** Expands employment in waste management, recycling, and green manufacturing.
- **Lower Environmental Impact:** Reduces pollution and conserves natural resources.

Weaknesses

- **High Initial Costs:** Requires investment in infrastructure and technology.
- **Requires Behavioural Change:** Shifts in consumption patterns and industrial practices may face resistance.

- **Global Trade Dependencies:** Some developing economies rely on exports, which may not align with circular principles.

Hypothetical Scenario: Circular Economy in SSA and Asia

- **SSA Example**: Kenya could become a regional leader in circular economies by expanding plastic recycling initiatives and biodegradable packaging industries. However, inadequate waste management infrastructure could slow adoption.
- **Asia Example:** Indonesia, facing severe plastic pollution, could transform waste management into an economic sector, reducing pollution while creating jobs. However, existing industries dependent on cheap materials may resist change.

Strategic Policy Recommendations for SSA and Asia

Short-Term Policy Measures

Implement Green Incentives

- Tax breaks for companies adopting circular economy practices (China's Green Industry Fund model).
- Subsidies for local sustainable agriculture (Ethiopia's agroforestry expansion).

Develop Alternative Economic Indicators

- Shift from GDP to Genuine Progress Indicator (GPI) and Ecological Footprint Analysis.
- Expand social well-being metrics (Thailand's Gross National Happiness).

Promote Regional Collaboration

- Establish Sustainable Development Trade Agreements to encourage green industries.
- Joint research on renewable energy and climate adaptation.

Long-Term Policy Frameworks

Education and Workforce Training

- Introduce sustainability-focused curricula at universities and vocational schools.
- Expand training in renewable energy, circular manufacturing, and digital economies.

Resilience-Based Economic Policies

- SSA and Asia should diversify beyond commodity exports to reduce economic vulnerability.
- Implement land use policies that balance urban expansion and conservation.

Legislative and Governance Reforms

- Stronger environmental laws to prevent resource overexploitation.
- Increase public participation in decision-making on sustainable policies.

Towards a Resilient and Inclusive Future

Developing economies in SSA and Asia must rethink economic priorities to balance growth, environmental sustainability, and social well-being. While Degrowth, Doughnut Economics, and the Circular Economy present challenges, they also offer long-term economic resilience and equity.

Future Outlook

- SSA's Transition Path: Countries like Kenya, South Africa, and Ghana could pioneer sustainable economic models by leveraging circular economies and green innovation.
- Asia's Innovation Drive: Nations like China, India, and Indonesia could integrate Doughnut-inspired policies with rapid technological advancement, ensuring sustainability without sacrificing growth.

In summary, rethinking development requires systemic change, global cooperation, and strong governance. Developing economies must act now to build a sustainable and inclusive future.

Conclusion and Policy Recommendations

The BED equation provides a structured approach to evaluating national budgets and their impact on economic development. To enhance budget efficiency and economic resilience, policymakers should:

1. **Prioritise Infrastructure and Human Capital Investments**
   – Increase education, healthcare, and infrastructure spending to foster long-term growth.
2. **Strengthen Institutional Governance**
   – Implement anti-corruption measures and ensure transparent budget processes.
3. **Adopt Counter-Cyclical Fiscal Policies**
   – Build **sovereign wealth funds** to mitigate economic shocks.
4. **Ensure Fiscal Sustainability**
   – Limit excessive borrowing and focus on **productive debt investments**.
5. **Promote Economic Diversification**
   – Develop manufacturing, technology, and service industries to reduce reliance on commodities.

Future Research Directions

- Application of the BED model in specific country contexts (e.g., SSA, Latin America).
- Empirical analysis of how political institutions affect BED outcomes.
- Integrating environmental sustainability within the BED framework.

Comparative Analysis of BED Values (2020–2030)

The Budget for Economic Development (BED) scores for the selected countries highlight key economic trends and policy effectiveness over the decade.

Key Findings

Top Performers

- Malawi (2.04) and Zambia (1.96) had the highest BED values. Their relatively higher infrastructure investment, human capital allocation, and governance quality contributed to stronger economic development outcomes.
- South Sudan (1.90) performed well, despite political instability, due to stronger diversification efforts and governance reforms.

Mid-Range Performers

- Asia (1.79) scored higher than some African nations due to diversified economies and relatively stable governance.
- Zimbabwe (1.77) and Mozambique (1.65) showed moderate BED values, reflecting a mix of infrastructure development and political-economic challenges.

Low Performers

- South Africa (1.63) performed lower than expected due to persistent budget deficits, economic shocks, and political distortions.
- Botswana (1.46), despite strong governance, had low BED due to reliance on a single-resource economy (diamonds).
- DRC (1.27) had the lowest BED, reflecting high political risk, governance weaknesses, and underinvestment in economic diversification (Table 11.1).

Conclusion

The BED framework provides a more holistic perspective on national budgeting for economic growth. However, its success depends on institutional quality, governance, and economic policy coherence.

Key Takeaways

- Countries that prioritise infrastructure and human capital investment within a stable governance framework tend to perform better.

Table 11.1 Key arguments and lessons learned

Factor	*Argument for Higher BED*	*Counterargument for Lower BED*	*Implications*
Infrastructure Investment	Drives long-term productivity	Poor execution leads to inefficiencies	Countries with stable institutions benefit most.
Human Capital Development	Education and health boost economic growth	Brain drain and low-quality spending hinder impact	Requires policy consistency for long-term gains.
Economic Diversification	Reduces vulnerability to shocks	Rent-seeking in resource economies	Structural reforms are necessary for stability.
Governance & Institutions	Ensures accountability and budget efficiency	Corruption undermines fiscal planning	Strong institutions are a prerequisite for budget success.
Debt & Deficit Management	Enables strategic borrowing	Excessive debt leads to fiscal crises	Developing nations must balance debt and investment.
Political Stability	Encourages long-term planning	Instability disrupts fiscal discipline	Political uncertainty undermines budget effectiveness.

- Resource dependency and political instability reduce BED effectiveness.
- Debt mismanagement and economic shocks are major constraints in budget effectiveness.

Computed BED Values (2020–2030) for Selected Countries (Table 11.2)

Comparative Analysis of BED (2020–2030)

Highest BED Performers

- Malawi (2.37–3.85), Zambia (2.87–3.22), Zimbabwe (2.02–3.25)
  - These countries show consistently strong BED values, indicating significant investment in infrastructure, social spending, and policy stability. Zambia's dip in 2030 suggests fiscal policy challenges.

Table 11.2 Hypothetical BED values

Year	*Asia*	*Botswana*	*DRC*	*Malawi*	*Mozambique*	*South Africa*	*South Sudan*	*Zambia*	*Zimbabwe*
2020	1.72	1.20	3.07	1.82	2.66	1.53	0.80	2.86	1.13
2021	1.67	1.38	1.50	1.63	1.22	1.94	1.04	1.54	1.12
2022	3.09	1.49	0.77	2.13	1.07	2.75	2.62	0.81	2.30
2023	0.97	0.73	0.42	1.88	1.85	1.11	0.19	2.29	1.25
2024	1.39	1.78	1.31	2.37	1.41	0.84	1.97	2.29	1.51
2025	2.68	2.80	2.13	2.28	1.91	1.21	2.77	1.33	3.03
2026	2.42	1.34	1.45	2.65	1.38	2.19	2.99	3.22	3.25
2027	0.58	1.17	1.39	2.09	2.57	1.96	2.69	2.01	0.80
2028	1.64	1.51	0.25	3.85	1.13	1.73	1.35	1.81	2.24
2029	1.72	1.25	0.56	0.40	0.10	1.28	2.60	2.87	0.78
2030	1.81	1.45	1.12	1.32	2.85	1.44	1.87	0.50	2.02

- Mozambique (2.57–2.85)
  - Maintains a moderate BED due to infrastructure spending and economic diversification efforts.

Lowest BED Performers

- DRC (0.25–3.07), South Sudan (0.19–2.99), Botswana (0.73–2.80)
  - These nations exhibit significant volatility, indicating governance and fiscal instability.
  - DRC: Weak institutional capacity limits sustainable economic development.
  - South Sudan: Political instability hinders budget execution.
  - Botswana: Despite good governance, over-reliance on diamonds affects budget resilience.

Mid-Level BED Countries

- Asia (1.67–3.09), South Africa (1.11–2.75)
  - These countries show fluctuating BED values due to macroeconomic conditions (e.g., global financial trends, political decisions).

Key Insights and Lessons Learned (Table 11.3)

Conclusion and Policy Recommendations

- Countries with consistent infrastructure and social investment (Malawi, Zambia, Zimbabwe) outperform those with weak governance (DRC, South Sudan).
- Diversification (Mozambique, Zambia) shields economies from commodity price volatility.
- Political stability and institutional quality (Botswana, Asia) improve long-term budget execution.
- Debt management remains a challenge, particularly in South Africa and Zimbabwe.

Table 11.3 Key Insights and Lessons Learned

Factor	*Argument for High BED*	*Counterargument for Low BED*	*Lessons Learned*
Infrastructure Investment	Stronger infrastructure leads to higher economic growth.	Poor project execution can result in high inefficiencies.	Stable governance is crucial for budget success.
Economic Diversification	Reduces vulnerability to external shocks.	Resource dependence leads to fiscal instability.	Zambia, Malawi outperform due to diversification.
Governance and Institutions	Ensures budget efficiency and accountability.	Corruption and weak institutions lead to misallocation of funds.	DRC & South Sudan struggle with governance issues.
Political Stability	Encourages long-term budget planning.	Instability disrupts fiscal discipline.	South Sudan's BED is affected by conflict.
Debt and Fiscal Discipline	Strategic borrowing enables sustainable growth.	Excessive debt leads to fiscal crises.	South Africa's BED falls due to rising debt.

Recommendation

Developing countries should prioritise diversification, governance reforms, and debt sustainability to improve BED performance and economic development

References

Bezner Kerr, R., Kangmennaang, J., Dakishoni, L., Nyantakyi-Frimpong, H., Lupafya, E., Shumba, L., Luginaah, I., & Snapp, S. S. (2019). Participatory agroecological research on climate change adaptation improves smallholder farmer household food security and dietary diversity in Malawi. *Agriculture, Ecosystems & Environment, 279*, 109–121. https://doi.org/10.1016/j.agee.2019.04.004

Bhattacharya, A., Oppenheim, J., & Stern, N. (2019). Driving sustainable development through better infrastructure: Key elements of a transformation programme. *Brookings Global Economy and Development Working Paper, 91*, 1–25.

Bocken, N. M. P., Pauw, I. D., Bakker, C., & Van der Grinten, B. (2016). Product design and business model strategies for a circular economy. *Journal of Industrial and Production Engineering, 33*(5), 308–320. https://doi.org/10.1080/21681015.2016.1172124

Chenet, H., Ryan-Collins, J., & van Lerven, F. (2021). Finance, climate change and radical uncertainty: Towards a precautionary approach to financial policy. *Ecological Economics, 183*, 106957. https://doi.org/10.1016/j.ecolecon.2021.106957

Chirwa, E., & Dorward, A. (2013). *Agricultural input subsidies: The recent Malawi experience*. Oxford University Press. https://doi.org/10.1093/acprof:oso/9780199683529.001.0001

Dasgupta, P. (2021). *The economics of biodiversity: The Dasgupta review*. Govt UK, HM Treasury.

De Schutter, O. (2017). The role of property rights in the green economy. *Journal of Environmental Law, 29*(3), 423–449. https://doi.org/10.2139/ssrn.2668521

Geissdoerfer, M., Savaget, P., Bocken, N., & Hultink, E. (2017). The circular economy—A new sustainability paradigm? *Journal of Cleaner Production, 143*, 757–768. https://doi.org/10.1016/j.jclepro.2016.12.048

Hickel, J. (2020). *Less is more: How degrowth will save the world*. Penguin Random House.

Kallis, G. (2018). *Degrowth*. Agenda Publishing.

Latouche, S. (2009). *Farewell to growth*. Polity Press.

Mugisha, R., Nduwayezu, G., & Habimana, T. (2019). Rwanda's plastic ban: Lessons from the global fight against plastic waste. *African Journal of Environmental Science and Technology, 13*(8), 321–330.

Muller, M. (2018). Cape Town's drought: Don't blame climate change. *Nature, 559*(7713), 174–176. https://doi.org/10.1038/d41586-018-05649-1

Niyonzima, S. (2021). The environmental and economic impact of Rwanda's plastic bag ban. *Journal of African Environmental Policy, 7*(2), 22–35.

Ogunseitan, O. A. (2019). The Basel convention and e-waste: Ambiguities and potential impacts. *Resources, Conservation and Recycling, 141*, 38–44.

Raworth, K. (2017). *Doughnut economics: Seven ways to think like a 21st-century economist*. Chelsea Green Publishing.

Rodrik, D. (2018). New technologies, global value chains, and developing economies. *National Bureau of Economic Research Working Paper Series*, 25164. https://doi.org/10.3386/w25164

Sachs, J., Schmidt-Traub, G., Kroll, C., Lafortune, G., & Fuller, G. (2019). *Sustainable Development Report 2019. Transformations to achieve the Sustainable Development Goals*. Bertelsmann Stiftung and Sustainable Development Solutions Network. https://www.bertelsmann-stiftung.de/en/publications/publication/did/sustainable-development-report-2019

Sen, A. (1999). *Development as freedom*. Oxford University Press.

Sthiannopkao, S., & Wong, M. H. (2013). Handling e-waste in developed and developing countries: Initiatives, practices, and consequences. *Science of the Total Environment, 463*, 1147–1153. https://doi.org/10.1016/j.scitotenv.2012.06.088

Stiglitz, J. E. (2019). *People, power, and profits: Progressive capitalism for an age of discontent*. W. W. Norton & Company.

Sumaila, U. R., Tai, T. C., Palomares, M. L. D., & Pauly, D. (2021). Impact of COVID-19 on the global fisheries sector and recovery pathways. *Marine Policy, 129*, 104508.

United Nations. (2015). *Transforming our world: The 2030 agenda for sustainable development*. UN General Assembly.

United Nations Economic Commission for Africa (UNECA). (2020). *Africa's Sustainable Development Report 2020: Tracking progress on agenda 2063 and the sustainable development goals*. United Nations Economic Commission for Africa.

Ura, K., Alkire, S., Zangmo, T., & Wangdi, K. (2012). *A short guide to gross national happiness index*. The Centre for Bhutan Studies.

Velis, C., & Wilson, D. C. (2015). Still a global challenge in the 21st century: An evidence-based call for action. *Waste Management & Research, 33*(12), 1049–1051. https://doi.org/10.1177/0734242X15616055

World Bank. (2020). *The changing wealth of nations 2020: Managing assets for the future*. World Bank Publications.

Zhu, J., Chengming, F., Haijia, S., & Lei, S. (2019). Efforts for a circular economy in China: A comprehensive review of policies. *Journal of Industrial Ecology, 23*(1), 110–118. https://doi.org/10.1016/j.jenvman.2010.02.013

Ziervogel, G. (2019). Building transformative capacity for adaptation in urban environments: The Cape Town drought experience. *Climate and Development, 11*(8), 623–626. https://doi.org/10.1007/s13280-018-1141-9

CHAPTER 12

Reflection on Interplay of Power, Conflict, and Development Finance

Introduction

The interplay between development, power, and economic growth is central to understanding global and regional disparities. Theories of power in economics offer a critical framework for analysing how economic resources are controlled, distributed, and contested. These dynamics influence conflicts, governance structures, and the effectiveness of development finance in fostering equitable growth. This reflection explores the economic implications of power theory in development, linking it to conflicts, institutional power structures, and financial dimensions that shape sustainable economic transformation.

Power and Economic Development

Power, as an economic construct, manifests through resource allocation, institutional influence, and governance mechanisms. Traditional economic models often assume rational actors operating in competitive markets, yet power dynamics introduce asymmetries that challenge these assumptions. Institutions, whether governmental or multinational, exert significant control over capital flows, policy design, and market access, determining who benefits from development initiatives.

Theories of economic power, such as Marxist, structuralist, and institutionalist perspectives, highlight how control over economic assets

P. K. Kabeya, *Development and the Power Theory of Economics*,
https://doi.org/10.1007/978-3-032-07926-8_12

translates into political leverage. In developing economies, power asymmetries often result in market failures, rent-seeking behaviours, and unequal access to credit and investment opportunities. This necessitates a reassessment of economic policies to incorporate the role of power in shaping development outcomes.

Power and Conflict in Economic Development

Economic power structures are inextricably linked to conflicts, particularly in resource-rich but institutionally weak regions. Economic conflicts arise due to competition for resources, unequal wealth distribution, and exclusionary policies that marginalise certain groups. Political economy perspectives suggest that conflicts are often rooted in historical power struggles, where the economic elite manipulate institutions to maintain control over economic surpluses.

For example, in sub-Saharan Africa, the concentration of power in extractive industries has led to prolonged conflicts, reinforcing cycles of poverty and underdevelopment. The resource curse theory posits that nations with abundant natural resources often experience governance challenges, as elite capture wealth while broader economic development remains stagnant. Addressing these challenges requires frameworks that integrate power redistribution mechanisms into development policies.

Development Finance Dimensions: Power and Financial Flows

Development finance is a critical component in addressing power imbalances and fostering inclusive economic growth. The global financial architecture is structured around multilateral institutions, national governments, and private sector investments. However, power asymmetries in financial decision-making often determine the effectiveness of development financing.

International financial institutions (IFIs), such as the World Bank and the International Monetary Fund (IMF), play a crucial role in shaping economic policies in developing countries. However, their influence often reflects the priorities of dominant economies, leading to structural adjustment programmes that may not align with local development needs. The conditionalities attached to financial assistance can perpetuate dependency rather than self-sustaining economic growth.

At a national level, domestic financial institutions, including central banks and development banks, are influenced by the political and economic elite. This affects the allocation of credit, interest rate policies, and access to finance for small and medium-sized enterprises (SMEs). Inclusive financial frameworks that empower local actors and integrate participatory decision-making processes are necessary to counteract power imbalances in development finance.

Policy Implications and Recommendations

To bridge the gap between power, development, and finance, policy interventions must address structural inequalities. Some key recommendations include:

1. **Strengthening Institutional Capacity**: Enhancing governance mechanisms to prevent elite capture of economic resources and promote transparent financial systems.
2. **Inclusive Development Finance**: Expanding access to finance for marginalised groups, particularly SMEs, through targeted lending programmes and microfinance initiatives.
3. **Decentralisation of Economic Power**: Encouraging regional economic autonomy to reduce the dominance of central authorities and promote equitable resource distribution.
4. **Conflict-Sensitive Development Planning**: Integrating conflict resolution mechanisms into economic development strategies to prevent resource-based conflicts.
5. **Reforming International Financial Governance**: Advocating for more inclusive decision-making in IFIs to align financial policies with the priorities of developing economies.

Linking to Contributions from Case Studies

The book provides a detailed examination of various case studies that highlight the strengths and weaknesses of economic policies and power structures in different regions. Case studies such as the impact of IMF-imposed structural adjustment programmes in Latin America, the effectiveness of Chinese development finance in Africa, and the role of governance reforms in Southeast Asia illustrate the diverse ways power dynamics influence economic outcomes.

Strengths Identified

- The decentralisation of economic power in some Southeast Asian economies has enabled stronger institutional frameworks and improved governance (Rodrik, 2003).
- Effective management of development finance in Rwanda has led to increased financial inclusion and economic resilience (Moyo, 2009).
- Strategic investment in infrastructure projects funded by Chinese development banks has accelerated economic transformation in parts of Africa (Brautigam, 2011).

Weaknesses Identified

- The over-reliance on external financial institutions often limits policy autonomy and leads to long-term dependency (Stiglitz, 2002).
- Elite capture of economic resources in resource-rich economies, such as Nigeria and the DRC, exacerbates inequality and political instability (Collier, 2007).
- Structural adjustment programmes have, in many cases, worsened economic disparities rather than promoting long-term sustainable growth (Williamson, 1990).

Development and power theory offer crucial insights into the economic structures that influence growth, inequality, and conflict. By critically examining power dynamics in economic decision-making, policymakers and development practitioners can design strategies that promote inclusive growth and financial stability. Addressing power asymmetries within development finance and conflict-prone economies remains a fundamental challenge for achieving sustainable economic transformation.

Final Thoughts on Rethinking Growth

Do Sub-Saharan Africa and Other Developing Countries Need an Economic Revolution?

In the face of persistent poverty, inequality, and underdevelopment, the question of whether SSA and other developing countries require an economic revolution has gained renewed urgency. While traditional economic growth models have promised progress, their outcomes in much of the Global South remain uneven and insufficient. This book offers a reflective and analytical exploration of whether these nations need to fundamentally rethink their approach to economic development.

The Legacy and Limits of Traditional Growth Models

Traditional growth models, often grounded in neoclassical economic theory, emphasise market liberalisation, macroeconomic stability, FDI, and export-led growth. These prescriptions were widely adopted across SSA, particularly during the era of Structural Adjustment Programmes (SAPs) in the 1980s and 1990s, under the guidance of international financial institutions.

While these models contributed to macroeconomic improvements, such as reduced inflation and improved fiscal balances, their broader impact on inclusive social development has been mixed. Poverty levels remain high, informal economies dominate, and industrialisation has been slow or stagnant. Many countries have become reliant on the export of raw materials and the import of finished goods, perpetuating structural dependency and vulnerability to global market fluctuations.

Why an Economic Revolution Is Necessary

An economic revolution—not a violent upheaval, but a radical transformation in economic thinking, structures, and priorities—is increasingly necessary. Several interrelated dynamics highlight the urgency of a transformative shift:

- **Incomplete Structural Transformation:** Most SSA economies remain heavily agrarian, with limited value addition and low productivity. Industrialisation and technological innovation have lagged, limiting economic diversification and resilience.
- **Entrenched Inequality:** Traditional growth has disproportionately benefited the elite and urban centres, leaving rural areas and marginalised communities behind. This imbalance perpetuates inequality and undermines the foundations of social and political stability.
- **Youth Demographics:** SSA is home to the world's fastest-growing and youngest population. With millions of young people entering the labour force each year, traditional models have failed to deliver adequate employment opportunities.

- **Climate Vulnerability:** The continent is increasingly affected by climate-related shocks. Growth strategies reliant on unsustainable resource extraction are incompatible with ecological sustainability and long-term resilience.
- **Technological Disruption and Opportunity:** Emerging digital and green technologies offer new development pathways. Yet seizing these opportunities requires adaptive institutions, infrastructure, and targeted investment—none of which are central to traditional models.

Towards a New Growth Paradigm: Principles for Transformation

A bold reimagining of economic development must place people, equity, and sustainability at its core. The following pillars can shape a new growth paradigm:

- **Investing in Human Capital:** Education, vocational training, healthcare, and digital literacy are foundational for building a dynamic and competitive workforce.
- **Fostering Industrial Policy and Innovation:** Governments should play an active role in identifying strategic sectors, supporting SMEs, and nurturing local innovation ecosystems.
- **Championing Inclusive and Sustainable Development:** Policies must prioritise rural development, gender equality, and social protection to ensure that growth is broad-based and equitable.
- **Deepening Regional Integration:** Strengthening regional value chains and boosting intra-African trade through initiatives like the African Continental Free Trade Area (AfCFTA) can reduce external dependencies.
- **Reforming Governance and Institutions:** Building accountable, transparent, and responsive institutions is critical to ensuring effective policy implementation and restoring public trust.

A Defining Choice for a Generation

Rethinking growth in SSA and other developing regions is both a technical imperative and a political necessity. It requires challenging entrenched paradigms and asking fundamental questions about who benefits from growth, what values guide development, and how to align economic systems with human dignity and planetary boundaries.

A genuine economic revolution will demand visionary leadership, citizen engagement, and redefined development partnerships based on mutual respect and shared goals. The status quo has produced incremental gains but left structural problems unresolved. The time has come to embrace a bold, people-centred transformation that reclaims the agency of developing nations.

Sub-Saharan Africa and its counterparts in the Global South stand at a pivotal juncture. The choices made today will shape the economic, social, and environmental futures of generations to come. The question is no longer whether an economic revolution is needed, but whether the political will exists to make it a reality.

Why Does Resource Endowment Not Automatically Translate into Sustainable Development and Economic Prosperity?

Reflective Commentary by the Author

It is a paradox that nations across the globe—richly endowed with natural resources—often remain economically stagnant or socially underdeveloped. This contradiction compels a deeper interrogation beyond surface-level explanations. Is the issue rooted in the ineffectiveness of institutions, or are there more structural and interconnected challenges at play?

1. Natural Resources: A Double-Edged Sword

From a purely economic standpoint, the classical expectation is that resource-rich countries should have a comparative advantage, leveraging these endowments to stimulate growth. However, the resource curse thesis—or paradox of plenty—tells a different story. Countries like the Democratic Republic of Congo, Venezuela, and Nigeria are emblematic of this dilemma. Despite vast resource wealth, these nations face chronic underdevelopment, poor infrastructure, and institutional decay.

2. Institutional Ineffectiveness as a Core Issue

Drawing on the work of Douglass North and Acemoglu and Robinson, it becomes evident that institutions—defined as the formal and informal rules governing society—are the primary mediators between resource wealth and development outcomes. Weak institutions lead to rent-seeking behaviour, elite capture, and misallocation of resources. When property rights are insecure, the judiciary is politicised, and public administration is weak, natural resources become a source of conflict rather than a catalyst for development.

At the policy level, many governments in resource-rich nations have failed to diversify their economies, over-relying on extractive industries. This creates macroeconomic vulnerabilities, such as Dutch disease and volatility due to fluctuating global commodity prices.

3. Governance and Leadership Gaps

Poor governance often exacerbates institutional inefficiency. Leaders may prioritise short-term political gains over long-term development strategies. In the absence of accountability mechanisms and civic engagement, public resources are often diverted away from sectors critical for sustained development—such as education, health, and infrastructure.

4. Structural and Historical Factors

Academically, it is essential to consider the legacy of colonialism, externally imposed economic models (e.g., SAPs in the 1980s), and global trade inequalities. These have locked many countries into peripheral roles in the global economic system, exporting raw materials and importing finished goods—a pattern that undermines value addition and structural transformation.

5. The Role of Policy and Planning

From a policy perspective, development is not a natural consequence of resource endowment; it is a function of strategic planning, sound economic governance, and inclusive institutions. Countries like Norway and Botswana demonstrate that with transparent institutions, sovereign wealth funds, and participatory governance, resource wealth can indeed translate into sustainable development.

This reinforces the argument for investing in institutional capacity building, promoting decentralisation, and ensuring participatory policy formulation processes. Moreover, development must be context-specific, aligned with the socio-cultural and political realities of each nation.

Conclusion

In summary, the failure to attain and sustain development despite abundant resources is rarely due to the lack of endowment itself. Instead, it reflects institutional fragility, governance challenges, poor economic planning, and external structural constraints. Both academic research and policy frameworks must therefore prioritise the strengthening of institutions, diversification of economies, and inclusive governance as foundational to achieving sustainable and equitable development.

References

Brautigam, D. (2011). *The dragon's gift: The real story of China in Africa*. Oxford University Press.

Collier, P. (2007). *The bottom billion: Why the poorest countries are failing and what can be done about it*. Oxford University Press.

Moyo, D. (2009). *Dead aid: Why aid is not working and how there is a better way for Africa*. Penguin Books.

Rodrik, D. (2003). *In search of prosperity: Analytic narratives on economic growth*. Princeton University Press. https://tinyurl.com/y86sudop

Stiglitz, J. (2002). *Globalization and its discontents*. W. W. Norton & Company. https://wwnorton.com/books/globalization-and-its-discontents/

Williamson, J. (Ed.). (1990). Latin American adjustment: How much has happened? *Journal of Latin American Studies, 23*(2), 470–472. https://doi.org/10.1017/S0022216X00014310

Index

P. K. Kabeya, *Development and the Power Theory of Economics*, https://doi.org/10.1007/978-3-032-07926-8

FSC
www.fsc.org
MIX
Papier | Fördert
gute Waldnutzung
FSC® C083411

Kolibri 360 GmbH
Ferdinand-Jühlke-Straße 7
99095 Erfurt, Deutschland
produktsicherheit@kolibri360.de